The Internet All-in-One Desk Reference For Dummies
2nd Edition

SO-CAT-743

E-Mail Abbreviations and Emoticons

Abbreviation	What It Means		Emoticon	What It Means
AFAIK	As far as I know		:) or :-)	Smile
AFK	Away from keyboard		:(or :-(	Frown
BAK	Back at keyboard		;) or ;-)	Wink
BFN	Bye for now		:D or :-D	Big smile (or laugh)
BRB	Be right back		:'(	Crying
BTW	By the way		8-) or B-)	Sunglasses
CYA	See ya!		:-@	Screaming
FWIW	For what it's worth		:-o	Uh-oh!
GMTA	Great minds think alike		:-#	Lips are sealed
IMHO	In my humble opinion		>:-(	Mad
L8R	Later		:-P	Sticking tongue out
LOL	Laughing out loud		o:-)	Angel
OIC	Oh, I see		:-\	Undecided
OTOH	On the other hand		\o/	Praise the Lord!
ROFL	Rolling on floor, laughing		{}	Hug
SO	Significant other		:-*	Kiss
TIA	Thanks in advance		{*}	Hug and a kiss
TTFN	Ta-ta for now		@-}————-	Rose
WB	Welcome back		<g> or <grin>	Same as :-)
WTG	Way to go!		<sigh>	Sigh

E-Mail Etiquette

- **Proofread, proofread, proofread.** Misspellings (or bad grammar) create an impression of you that may not be the one you want to convey.

- **Don't type everything in ALL CAPS.** Using caps makes your text LOOK LIKE YOU'RE SHOUTING. Use sparingly for emphasis only.

- **Make your subject line specific, but not too lengthy.** "Tonight's baseball game canceled" is much better than "Important announcement."

- **Use shorthand and emoticons like LOL and :) to help convey meaning.** You should avoid these in most business messages, however.

- **Double-check your humor — irony and sarcasm are easy to miss.** Sometimes, it helps to add a smiley to let your reader in on the joke. :-)

- **When in doubt, save your message overnight.** Read and edit it again in the morning before you send it. *Never send e-mail when you are upset.*

For Dummies: Bestselling Book Series for Beginners

The Internet All-in-One Desk Reference For Dummies, 2nd Edition

Cheat Sheet

Search Engines and Directories

If you can't find the Internet site you're looking for, try these helpful search engines and directories:

AltaVista

www.altavista.com

Sophisticated Internet searching

Dogpile

www.dogpile.com

Simultaneous multi-engine searching

Excite

www.excite.com

News, directories, searching, reviews

EZ-Find

info.theriver.com/TheRiver/ezfind.htm

Several search engines on one page

Go.com

infoseek.go.com

Internet, Usenet, and e-mail searching

Google

www.google.com

Simple design, lightning-fast search results

HotBot

www.hotbot.com

State-of-the-cool Net searching

LookSmart

www.looksmart.com

Internet directory with a useful design

Lycos

www.lycos.com

Magazine-style Web directory

Northern Light

www.northernlight.com

Comprehensive, accurate search results

ProFusion

www.profusion.com

Flexible and fast multi-engine searching

Starting Point

www.stpt.com

Small, compact Net directory

WebCrawler

webcrawler.com

Veteran search engine with new directory

Yahoo!

www.yahoo.com

The granddaddy of Internet directories

Yahooligans!

www.yahooligans.com

Kid-safe Internet directory

Hungry Minds, the Hungry Minds logo, For Dummies, the For Dummies Bestselling Book Series logo, and all related trade dress are trademarks or registered trademarks of Hungry Minds, Inc. All other trademarks are the property of their respective owners.

Hungry Minds™

Copyright © 2002 Hungry Minds, Inc.
All rights reserved.

Cheat Sheet $2.95 value. Item 1659-0.

For more information about Hungry Minds,
call 1-800-762-2974.

For Dummies: Bestselling Book Series for Beginners

2002 50¢

™

References for the Rest of Us!®

BESTSELLING BOOK SERIES

Are you intimidated and confused by computers? Do you find that traditional manuals are overloaded with technical details you'll never use? Do your friends and family always call you to fix simple problems on their PCs? Then the For Dummies® computer book series from Hungry Minds, Inc. is for you.

For Dummies books are written for those frustrated computer users who know they aren't really dumb but find that PC hardware, software, and indeed the unique vocabulary of computing make them feel helpless. For Dummies books use a lighthearted approach, a down-to-earth style, and even cartoons and humorous icons to dispel computer novices' fears and build their confidence. Lighthearted but not lightweight, these books are a perfect survival guide for anyone forced to use a computer.

"I like my copy so much I told friends; now they bought copies."
— Irene C., Orwell, Ohio

"Quick, concise, nontechnical, and humorous."
— Jay A., Elburn, Illinois

"Thanks, I needed this book. Now I can sleep at night."
— Robin F., British Columbia, Canada

Already, millions of satisfied readers agree. They have made For Dummies books the #1 introductory level computer book series and have written asking for more. So, if you're looking for the most fun and easy way to learn about computers, look to For Dummies books to give you a helping hand.

Hungry Minds™

1/01

The Internet

ALL-IN-ONE DESK REFERENCE

FOR

DUMMIES®

2ND EDITION

The Internet
ALL-IN-ONE DESK REFERENCE
FOR
DUMMIES®
2ND EDITION

by Kelly Ewing, John Levine, Arnold Reinhold,
Margaret Levine Young, Doug Lowe,
Greg Harvey, Viraf Mohta, Jennifer Kaufeld,
John Kaufeld, Peter Weverka, Brad Hill,
and Lee Musick

Hungry Minds™

Best-Selling Books • Digital Downloads • e-Books • Answer Networks • e-Newsletters • Branded Web Sites • e-Learning

New York, NY ◆ Cleveland, OH ◆ Indianapolis, IN

The Internet All-in-One Desk Reference For Dummies® 2nd Edition

Published by
Hungry Minds, Inc.
909 Third Avenue
New York, NY 10022
www.hungryminds.com
www.dummies.com

Copyright © 2002 Hungry Minds, Inc. All rights reserved. No part of this book, including interior design, cover design, and icons, may be reproduced or transmitted in any form, by any means (electronic, photocopying, recording, or otherwise) without the prior written permission of the publisher.

Library of Congress Control Number: 2002102419

ISBN: 0-7645-1659-0

Printed in the United States of America

10 9 8 7 6 5 4 3 2 1

2B/QR/QV/QS/IN

Distributed in the United States by Hungry Minds, Inc.

Distributed by CDG Books Canada Inc. for Canada; by Transworld Publishers Limited in the United Kingdom; by IDG Norge Books for Norway; by IDG Sweden Books for Sweden; by IDG Books Australia Publishing Corporation Pty. Ltd. for Australia and New Zealand; by TransQuest Publishers Pte Ltd. for Singapore, Malaysia, Thailand, Indonesia, and Hong Kong; by Gotop Information Inc. for Taiwan; by ICG Muse, Inc. for Japan; by Intersoft for South Africa; by Eyrolles for France; by International Thomson Publishing for Germany, Austria and Switzerland; by Distribuidora Cuspide for Argentina; by LR International for Brazil; by Galileo Libros for Chile; by Ediciones ZETA S.C.R. Ltda. for Peru; by WS Computer Publishing Corporation, Inc., for the Philippines; by Contemporanea de Ediciones for Venezuela; by Express Computer Distributors for the Caribbean and West Indies; by Micronesia Media Distributor, Inc. for Micronesia; by Chips Computadoras S.A. de C.V. for Mexico; by Editorial Norma de Panama S.A. for Panama; by American Bookshops for Finland.

For general information on Hungry Minds' products and services please contact our Customer Care Department within the U.S. at 800-762-2974, outside the U.S. at 317-572-3993 or fax 317-572-4002.

For sales inquiries and reseller information, including discounts, premium and bulk quantity sales, and foreign-language translations, please contact our Customer Care Department at 800-434-3422, fax 317-572-4002, or write to Hungry Minds, Inc., Attn: Customer Care Department, 10475 Crosspoint Boulevard, Indianapolis, IN 46256.

For information on licensing foreign or domestic rights, please contact our Sub-Rights Customer Care Department at 212-884-5000.

For information on using Hungry Minds' products and services in the classroom or for ordering examination copies, please contact our Educational Sales Department at 800-434-2086 or fax 317-572-4005.

For press review copies, author interviews, or other publicity information, please contact our Public Relations Department at 317-572-3168 or fax 317-572-4168.

For authorization to photocopy items for corporate, personal, or educational use, please contact Copyright Clearance Center, 222 Rosewood Drive, Danvers, MA 01923, or fax 978-750-4470.

LIMIT OF LIABILITY/DISCLAIMER OF WARRANTY: THE PUBLISHER AND AUTHOR HAVE USED THEIR BEST EFFORTS IN PREPARING THIS BOOK. THE PUBLISHER AND AUTHOR MAKE NO REPRESENTATIONS OR WARRANTIES WITH RESPECT TO THE ACCURACY OR COMPLETENESS OF THE CONTENTS OF THIS BOOK AND SPECIFICALLY DISCLAIM ANY IMPLIED WARRANTIES OF MERCHANTABILITY OR FITNESS FOR A PARTICULAR PURPOSE. THERE ARE NO WARRANTIES THAT EXTEND BEYOND THE DESCRIPTIONS CONTAINED IN THIS PARAGRAPH. NO WARRANTY MAY BE CREATED OR EXTENDED BY SALES REPRESENTATIVES OR WRITTEN SALES MATERIALS. THE ACCURACY AND COMPLETENESS OF THE INFORMATION PROVIDED HEREIN AND THE OPINIONS STATED HEREIN ARE NOT GUARANTEED OR WARRANTED TO PRODUCE ANY PARTICULAR RESULTS, AND THE ADVICE AND STRATEGIES CONTAINED HEREIN MAY NOT BE SUITABLE FOR EVERY INDIVIDUAL. NEITHER THE PUBLISHER NOR AUTHOR SHALL BE LIABLE FOR ANY LOSS OF PROFIT OR ANY OTHER COMMERCIAL DAMAGES, INCLUDING BUT NOT LIMITED TO SPECIAL, INCIDENTAL, CONSEQUENTIAL, OR OTHER DAMAGES.

Trademarks: For Dummies, Dummies Man, A Reference for the Rest of Us!, The Dummies Way, Dummies Daily, and related trade dress are registered trademarks or trademarks of Hungry Minds, Inc. in the United States and other countries, and may not be used without written permission. All other trademarks are the property of their respective owners. Hungry Minds, Inc. is not associated with any product or vendor mentioned in this book.

Hungry Minds™ is a trademark of Hungry Minds, Inc.

Hungry Minds gratefully acknowledges the contributions of these authors and contributing writers: Kelly Ewing, John Levine, Arnold Reinhold, Margaret Levine Young, Doug Lowe, Greg Harvey, Viraf Mohta, Jennifer Kaufeld, John Kaufeld, Peter Weverka, Brad Hill, and Lee Musick. Joyce J. Nielsen's editorial expertise also served to help make this book an invaluable resource.

Publisher's Acknowledgments

We're proud of this book; please send us your comments through our Hungry Minds Online Registration Form located at www.dummies.com.

Some of the people who helped bring this book to market include the following:

Acquisitions, Editorial, and Media Development

Project Editor: Kelly Ewing
   (Previous Edition: Jodi Jensen)

Acquisitions Editor: Steven H. Hayes

Copy Editors: Rebecca Huehls, Jean Rogers
   (Previous Edition: Gwenette Gaddis, Jeremy Zucker)

Technical Editor: Shannon Ryan

Editorial Manager: Constance Carlisle

Editorial Assistant: Amanda Foxworth

Project Coordinator: Jennifer Bingham

Layout and Graphics: Mary J. Virgin, Jacque Schneider, Betty Schulte, Jeremey Unger, Erin Zeltner

Proofreaders: Laura Albert, David Faust Arielle Carole Mennelle, Susan Moritz

Indexer: Sherry Massey

General and Administrative

Hungry Minds Technology Publishing Group: Richard Swadley, Vice President and Executive Group Publisher; Bob Ipsen, Vice President and Executive Publisher; Joseph Wikert, Vice President and Publisher; Barry Pruett, Vice President and Publisher; Mary Bednarek, Editorial Director; Mary C. Corder, Editorial Director; Andy Cummings, Editorial Director

Hungry Minds Manufacturing: Ivor Parker, Vice President, Manufacturing

Hungry Minds Marketing: John Helmus, Assistant Vice President, Director of Marketing

Hungry Minds Production for Branded Press: Debbie Stailey, Production Director

Hungry Minds Sales: Michael Violano, Vice President, International Sales and Sub Rights

Contents at a Glance

Cartoons at a Glance

"This afternoon, I want everyone to go online and find out all you can about Native American culture, history of the old west, and discount airfares to Hawaii for the two weeks I'll be on vacation."

page 115

By Rich Tennant

"...so if you have a message for someone, you write it on a piece of paper and put it on their refrigerator with those magnets. It's just until we get our e-mail system fixed."

page 387

"He found a dog site over an hour ago and has been in a staring contest ever since."

page 227

"Would it ruin the online concert experience if I vacuumed the mosh pit between songs?"

page 41

page 273

"The doctor wants to know if he can perform your endoscopy with a Web Cam for the hospital Web site."

page 611

page 7

"For 30 years, I've put a hat and coat on to make sales calls, and I'm not changing now just because I'm doing it on the Web from my living room."

page 493

"It's a free starter disk for AOL."

page 185

Cartoon Information:
Fax: 978-546-7747

E-Mail: richtennant@the5thwave.com
World Wide Web: www.the5thwave.com

"Honey—remember that pool party last summer where you showed everyone how to do the limbo in just a sombrero and a dish towel? Well, look at what the MSN Daily Video Download is."

page 557

Table of Contents

Introduction

The Internet has become so popular that it's now difficult to get through an entire day without hearing it mentioned on TV, reading about it in the newspapers, or going online yourself. The number of people connecting to the Internet continues to grow at a startling rate. A recent survey estimates the number of Internet users in the United States and Canada at 136 million people, with more than 275 million users worldwide (NUA Internet Surveys, February 2000). Unfortunately, there is no "Internet Users Manual." *The Internet All-in-One Desk Reference For Dummies* can fill that void, however, by providing one-stop, quick guidance for the tasks and tools you'll need to experience the best of the Internet.

The Internet is an active medium. You can't just sit and watch it like television; you have to try things, poke around, and find the sites, information, and people that you're interested in. Figuring out how to jump on board and navigate the Internet effectively can be a daunting task. Fortunately, *The Internet All-in-One Desk Reference For Dummies* can get you started and help you along on your journey. We show you how to use online services that offer Internet access, including America Online. We also cover the latest and greatest versions of the two most widely used Web browsers: Netscape Navigator 6.2 and Microsoft Internet Explorer 6.0. You receive simple and helpful information about using e-mail, reading newsgroups, chatting, browsing the Web, and creating Web pages.

After you're comfortable with the programs and tasks that you need to know to thrive on the Internet, you'll want to check out the Internet Activities portion of this book. Here, you get expert advice on how to shop online, plan your next vacation, use the Internet to help you become a better investor, and delve into your family tree. The Internet Directory (flip to the yellow pages at the back of the book) provides an excellent resource to tried and true sites on the Web that deliver great content and services. We've also provided a glossary of Internet terms for your perusal.

About This Book

The Internet All-in-One Desk Reference For Dummies is intended to be a reference for all the great things (and maybe a few not-so-great things) that you may need to know when you're browsing the Internet, writing e-mail, using newsgroups, creating your own Web pages, and so on. Of course, you could go out and buy a book on each of these Internet-related topics, but why would you want to when they're all conveniently packaged for you in this handy reference? *The Internet All-in-One Desk Reference For Dummies* doesn't pretend to be a comprehensive reference for every detail of these topics. Instead, this book shows you how to get up and running fast so that you have more time to do the things that you really want to do. Designed using the easy-to-follow *For Dummies* format, this book helps you get the information you need without laboring to find it.

The Internet All-in-One Desk Reference For Dummies is a big book made up of several smaller books — *minibooks*, so to speak. Whenever one big thing is made up of several smaller things, confusion is always a possibility, right? That's why *The Internet All-in-One Desk Reference For Dummies* is designed to have multiple access points (should we call them MAPs?) to help you find what you want. Each minibook begins with a parts page that includes a contents at a glance that tells you what chapters are included in that minibook. Useful *running heads* (the text you can find at the very top of a page) point out the current topic being discussed on that page. And who can overlook those handy thumb tabs that run down the side of the page and display the minibook number and chapter title and number? Finally, a small index is located at the end of each minibook, in addition to the regular full-length index at the end of the entire book.

How to Use This Book

This book acts like a reference so that you can locate what you want to know, get in, and get something done as quickly as possible. In this book, you can find concise descriptions introducing important concepts, task-oriented topics to help you realize what you need to do, and step-by-step instructions, where necessary, to show you the way.

At times, this book presents you with specific ways of performing certain actions. For example, when you must use a menu command, you see a command sequence that looks like this:

File➪Print

This simply means that you use the mouse to click open the File menu and then click the Print command. If you look closely, you can see some underlined letters. Those letters are the keyboard hot keys for the command in case you prefer to use the keyboard instead of the mouse. To use a keyboard hot key, first press the Alt key and release it, and then press the underlined letter. In the case of the File➪Print example, you press Alt, release it, press the F key, and the File menu opens. Then you press the P key to activate the Print command from the File menu, and the Print dialog box opens. Easy, huh? In this book, we include hot keys for menu command sequences whenever they're available.

Sometimes, we tell you about keyboard shortcuts. These shortcuts are key combinations such as

Ctrl+C

When you see this shortcut, it means to press and hold down the Ctrl key as you press the C key. Then release both keys together. (Don't attempt to type the plus sign!)

Throughout the book, information that you need to type appears in **boldface**. If what you're being asked to type appears within a step that's already bold, however, it appears in regular (nonbold) type.

Names of dialog boxes, menu commands, and options are spelled with the first letter of each main word capitalized, even though those letters may not be capitalized on your screen. This format makes sentences filled with long option names easier for you to read. (Haven't we thought of *everything?*)

When you're asked to click or double-click something, this book assumes that your mouse settings have not been changed from the default. In this case, when you're told to click, use the left mouse button. When you need to use the right mouse button (to display a shortcut menu, for example), you'll be specifically told to *right-click*. So be sure to make the mental adjustments to these instructions if, for example, you're left-handed and have reversed your mouse buttons.

How This Book Is Organized

Each of the minibooks contained in *The Internet All-in-One Desk Reference For Dummies* can stand alone — each has its own contents and index. The first minibook covers the Internet basics that you should know to help you understand the rest of the stuff in this book. Of course, if you've been surfing the Net for a while now, you can probably skip Book I and surf on over to the minibook that truly interests you. The remaining minibooks cover a variety of Internet topics and software that you would normally find in multiple books. Here is a brief description of what you'll find in each minibook.

Book 1: Internet Basics

This minibook covers the basics for getting started with the Internet, including whether you should buy a new computer for Internet access or consider upgrading your existing computer. You find out about the software that you need to go online and how to select an Internet Service Provider. We also cover issues relating to Internet safety, security, and troubleshooting here.

Book II: E-Mail

Book II demystifies the basics of e-mail and describes the many popular mail programs, including Eudora, Netscape Mail, and Outlook Express. This minibook also includes a list of common abbreviations and some e-mail etiquette tips. You also discover how to use e-mail mailing lists to communicate effectively with a group of people who share a common interest with you.

Book III: Web Browsing with Internet Explorer 6

This minibook begins with a Web primer, of sorts, for those of you who are new to Web browsing. After you've mastered the basics, you'll be ready to explore the Web with Internet Explorer 6, keep track of favorite Web pages, print and save Web information, and customize Internet Explorer 6 to fit your personal browsing style.

Book IV: Web Browsing with Netscape Navigator

Turn here to read about Netscape's latest browser and discover how to go about surfing the Web with it. Other topics presented here include printing, saving, bookmarking, reloading, stopping, searching, browsing Web pages offline, customizing Navigator, and more!

Book V: Newsgroups, Chats, and Other Internet Communication

Here, we introduce you to *Usenet,* a worldwide information system in which you can read messages about thousands of different topics every day, and Google Groups (groups.google.com), a Web site that helps you sort out Usenet. This minibook also explains how to find and join chat groups, make free phone calls via the Internet, and use FTP to transfer files over the Internet.

Book VI: Creating Web Pages

Book VI teaches you the basics of designing and building your own Web pages by using common Web-authoring tools such as FrontPage 2002 and Netscape Composer. You can choose between using automated wizards that set up your Web pages for you or learning the basics of HTML so that you can do it yourself. We also tell you how to publish your site and then announce it to the world!

Book VII: America Online

If you're an America Online subscriber (or think you might want to be), this minibook explains the ins and outs of this popular online service — signing on, using keywords, navigating through the system, communicating with others, creating and using Buddy Lists, reading newsgroups, and cruising the Internet.

Book VIII: Internet Activities

This minibook contains valuable information that can help you make the most of your online Internet activities. You discover the best places to go shopping online and how to use "bots" (robots) to comparison-shop for items that you're searching for. We also tell you how to use the Internet to plan your next vacation and find cheap flights, start investing and become a better investor, and find information about your ancestors.

Book IX: Internet Directory

Look here for a directory of some of the best sites that the Web has to offer. The sites listed here are organized by categories such as Internet and computer help, search engines and directories, news and information, research and education, sports and leisure, arts and entertainment, and fun and free stuff.

Appendix

We don't count this as one of the nine minibooks, so you can consider it a bonus. The Appendix is a glossary of the most common Internet terms that you'll come across in this book, as well as in your Internet travels.

Icon Alert!

As you flip through this book, funny-looking pictures, called *icons*, in the margins draw your attention to important information. You'll find the following icons in this book.

This icon points out tidbits of information that may come in handy as you're performing a task.

Watch out! This icon warns you of things that can go wrong, such as data loss or unexpected events.

Just a reminder . . . this information may be worth keeping in mind.

This icon appears beside Internet guru-type stuff that you may want to skip over or read later.

This icon highlights a feature or procedure that may not work as you would expect.

You'll see this icon when we reference another book or a chapter within this book that provides additional details on the topic at hand.

Book I

Internet Basics

The 5th Wave   By Rich Tennant

@RICHTENNANT

"The doctor wants to know if he can perform your endoscopy with a Web Cam for the hospital Web site."

Contents at a Glance

Chapter 1: Getting to Know the Internet

*B*ig as it is, the Internet is still in its early stages. Destined to become a primary means of communication and commerce in the twenty-first century, the Net now resembles a new city, filled with magnificent architecture and empty facades, broad boulevards and dirt roads, sumptuous plazas and muddy lots. Swarms of people are already working there, some in carefully planned facilities and others in makeshift shacks. Tycoons and bankers keep looking for the next great investment, while politicians and bureaucrats keep trying to establish control. Reporters comb the back alleys for stories about its dark side. Even though the Net is only half built and the architects are continually revising the plans, its diverse neighborhoods are throbbing with energy.

What Is the Internet?

The *Internet* is a system that lets computers all over the world talk to each other. That's all you really need to know. If you have access to a computer, you can probably use "the Net."

The U.S. Department of Defense Advanced Research Projects Agency originally sponsored Internet development because it wanted a military communications system that could survive a nuclear war. Later, the National Science Foundation funded the Internet as a research support system. That's all ancient history now, though, because support for the Internet comes almost entirely from commercial sources.

Today, an Internet Society tries to make policy, and an Internet Engineering Task Force sets standards with considerable aplomb. The White House is trying to establish an international Internet organization, although at the moment no one is in charge. The Internet is anarchy at its best and worst.

The term Internet is often used interchangeably with the *Web*, although this isn't really accurate. The *World Wide Web* (or just the *Web*) is actually one special area of the Internet (other areas include newsgroups, mailing lists, FTP, and chat). The Web is based on *links*, which enable Web surfers to travel quickly from one Web server to another. The Web allows pages with fancy graphic and multimedia elements to be constructed, while other areas of the Internet do not.

What's So Great about the Internet?

What makes the Internet great is that it brings together the best qualities of the communications systems that preceded it while improving on their worst features:

✦ **Postal mail (known as *snail mail* on the Net):** Takes at least a day — often a week — to get to its destination, and you must have envelopes and stamps, and find a mailbox. If you are away from home, your mail piles up unanswered. E-mail is quicker to compose, arrives faster, and doesn't require a stamp.

✦ **The telephone:** The other person must be available to talk, and usually no record exists of what was said. You can read e-mail when you feel like it, and it doesn't interrupt you during dinner.

✦ **The fax machine:** It's a chore to incorporate a fax into another document or to pass it on to someone else. Faxes of faxes of faxes become illegible. E-mail stays readable no matter how many times it's forwarded.

✦ **The public library:** You have to go to the library to find information, and half the time the book you want is checked out or missing. By the time information gets into the library, it's often out of date. The Internet is open 24 hours a day, 7 days a week, and you don't have to get in your car to go there. (On the other hand, even if the books in the library aren't always current, you do have a better idea of where the information came from — and what the writer's "expertise" really is.)

✦ **The newspaper:** Most newspapers come out only once a day, and they decide what news you get to see and what spin to put on it. On the World Wide Web, news is updated continuously. (On the other hand, it's hard to line a litter box with a Web page.)

Here are some other qualities that make the Internet compelling to "surf":

✦ Its democratic nature

✦ Its capability to let people communicate, even if they are never at their computers at the same time

✦ Its basis in text, getting people to communicate in writing again

✦ Its relatively low cost to use

✦ Its lack of geographic boundaries

✦ Its capacity to bring together people with similar interests

✦ Its offer of instant gratification

The Internet is also full of contradictions:

✦ It is amazingly fast, yet it often feels agonizingly slow.

✦ It is held together by chewing gum and baling wire, yet it survives man-made and natural disasters when other communications systems fail. (Remember why it was invented?)

✦ It is scandalously vulnerable to hackers, yet it hosts an encryption system, PGP, that is almost the only truly secure means of communication available to the general public.

✦ Its content is often sophomoric, yet powerful corporations and governments fear it and seek to rein it in.

✦ Its day-to-day operation depends on the cooperation of thousands of computers and their human administrators, yet it lacks any central control, operating almost entirely by consensus and social pressure.

No one really knows what the Net will be like in ten years, although one thing is for sure: We won't think of it as a single "thing." Different parts of the Net have already developed their own characteristics. No one knows all its intricacies, any more than anyone can know all the regions of a large country or all the neighborhoods of a great city.

What Services Does the Internet Provide?

The Internet provides these basic services:

✦ Electronic mail, or *e-mail*

✦ Access to the World Wide Web, or just the Web — the information system of the twenty-first century

✦ Newsgroups

✦ Mailing lists

✦ File transfers from other computers

✦ The capability to log on to other computers

✦ Discussions with other people using chat

Advanced services include multimedia broadcasts, Internet radio, secure transactions, and video conferencing. Even wireless communication is available.

You can do an almost endless list of things with the Internet, from finding a job to finding a mate, from searching the online catalogs of the greatest libraries in the world to ordering a pizza. Most important, the Internet is the place to learn more about the Internet. In Chapter 2 of this minibook, we tell you how to get on the Internet. Have fun!

Will the Internet Take a Bunch of Your Time?

Not necessarily. Reading your e-mail and catching up on a favorite mailing list can take just 15 minutes per day. But beware: The Internet can be addictive! You don't have enough hours in a day to keep up with all of it.

People who spend too much time surfing the Net are often told, "Get a life!" On the other hand, a recent survey shows that the average American spends, on a weekly basis, 2.6 hours a day watching television and videos. Watching the tube ranks third only to sleeping (7.2 hours) and working (3.1 hours). Other surveys show that, when people start using the Net, they spend less time watching TV.

So, you couch potatoes out there: Turn off the TV and log on! It's happening big time on the Internet.

Chapter 2: Getting Started with the Internet

In This Chapter

✔ Buying a computer for Internet access

✔ Upgrading your current computer

✔ Selecting a modem

✔ Knowing what software you need to use the Internet

✔ Deciding how to get connected: Online service or ISP?

Getting on the Internet is much easier than it used to be, but the process still can be daunting to new users. We try to help you as you figure out the world of modems, Internet Service Providers, and communications software that you need to connect to the Net. It used to be that either your computer had a direct connection to the Internet at school or work, or you bought a modem and dialed in over an ordinary phone line. Today, you have many more choices, including cable and specialized telephone services, such as DSL and ISDN.

Buying a Computer for Internet Access

Almost any new computer you can buy today is ready for Internet use. Of course, computer salespeople will try to sell you the most expensive model possible. This section tells you what you really need to know when you purchase an Internet-ready computer.

For a lot more information about what to look for when you're getting ready to buy a computer, check out a copy of *Upgrading and Fixing PCs For Dummies*, 5th Edition, by Andy Rathbone (published by Hungry Minds, Inc.).

What should you do with your old computer? Give it to a charitable institution and take a tax deduction. Call your local school district, library, church, synagogue, mosque, or other charity and offer the computer as a donation, or visit `www.microweb.com/pepsite/Recycle/recycle_index.html`, which lists computer recyclers by state and country. Be sure to get a written receipt that details everything you donated, including software. Tax laws are changing, so get up-to-date advice about how much you can deduct.

Macintosh versus Windows

Should you buy a Mac or a Windows-based PC? Apple fanatics tout the clean design and ease of use of Macintosh software. Microsoft users point out that they're in the majority and claim that Windows 98 or Windows XP makes a PC almost as good as a Mac. Both work fine.

The iMac and iBook

Apple's Internet-ready iMac and iBook (the notebook model) come in spiffy packages with a built-in color display screen and are very easy to set up. You need to know the following things about the iMac and iBook:

✦ Both have built-in modems and Ethernet ports, so they're ready for cable and DSL modems.

✦ Neither has a floppy disk, although you can buy one as an option or just use the Internet to transfer files.

✦ The new iMac DV connects directly to digital camcorders and lets you edit your home movies and put your work on the Internet in QuickTime format.

Set-top boxes

One new option for connection to the Internet is the set-top box. As its name implies, it's a box the size of a small VCR that sits on top of your television set. (The best-known brand is called WebTV, from Microsoft.) You hook it up to your TV in much the same way that you hook up a VCR, and you also plug the set-top box into a telephone jack. *Voilà!* You're connected to the Internet — without a computer. These units are available for as little as $100 plus $21.95 per month for Internet service. Although set-top boxes do work, they have some drawbacks:

✦ Because televisions can display only a half-dozen or so lines of text at a time, you have to press Page Down repeatedly to read even a modest-size Internet page, which can become tedious.

✦ You're usually limited to one Internet Service Provider. The monthly rate is about the same as for regular Internet service.

✦ You cannot use set-top boxes for much more than looking at World Wide Web pages, text chat, and e-mail.

Desktop versus laptop

Although laptops are really cool, they cost much more for the same performance. Get a desktop model unless you plan to travel frequently with your computer.

Is Linux for you?

Linux is a free version of the Unix operating system. It supports a full range of tools for Internet access and has a loyal following. Indeed, many ISPs use Linux on their servers. Although Linux is powerful, it is still complex to install and use; beginners may want to stick to Macs and Windows.

"Free" computers

You may have seen the ads lately. Some companies are offering computers for under $400, and others are even free. There's a catch, however: You're required to sign up for several years of pricey Internet service. If you aren't happy with the service, if prices drop, or if you decide a year from now to switch to cable or DSL, too bad. However, if you're in need of a computer now and you don't have the cash or other means of purchasing a computer, this may be a good option for you. Just be sure to read all the small print on the contract and understand what you're agreeing to.

Make sure that your computer is cable or DSL ready

Make sure that any computer you buy can be used with a cable or DSL modem — some new lower-priced PCs cannot. To be cable ready, your computer must have either an *Ethernet port* or an available slot into which you can plug an Ethernet card. The slot may be called a PCI, ISA, NuBus, or PCcard slot — just make sure that any computer you buy has one. In some cases, you can run a cable modem through a USB port by using an adapter. (Check with your cable company to see whether this is an option for you.)

Memory, hard drive, monitor, and printer

An adequate amount of memory (RAM) does more for your computer's performance than processor speed. These days, 64 megabytes (MB) of RAM is the minimum. Get 128MB or more if you can afford it. Most new desktop machines come with at least 10 gigabytes (GB) of hard drive (sometimes called *hard disk*) space. A gigabyte is about 1,000MB.

The basic monitor that comes with most computers these days will do for Internet use. Step up one level if you feel rich. Anything beyond that level is overkill for the Net.

Most modern printers can print graphics. Any printer will do. You can even live without a printer while you're getting started, although having one is handy.

Prepare to back up

Hard drives are much more reliable these days, although they still crash sometimes. And they're just too big to back up to floppy disks. A removable cartridge tape or disk drive is cheap insurance against data loss. Remember to back up regularly, or you'll be sorry that you didn't.

Some companies can back up your computer automatically over the Internet — for a fee, of course. You can find a list of such companies at Yahoo! (www.yahoo.com): Click Business and Economy➪Business to Business➪Computers➪Services➪Backup.

Upgrading Your Old Computer

If you already have a computer, you may be in luck: You might be able to use it as is to access the Internet. If not, a few simple improvements might be all it takes to make your computer ready for the Internet. The following sections show you how to determine what upgrades, if any, your computer needs in order to access the Internet.

To upgrade or not to upgrade

With the price of new Internet-ready computers at or below $1,000, your old computer might not be worth upgrading. In fact, you can easily spend more money upgrading an old computer than you would spend on a new computer. Here are some signs that you should buy a new computer rather than waste time and money upgrading an old computer:

✦ The computer is more than a few years old.

✦ The computer runs Windows 3.1.

✦ The computer has vacuum tubes inside.

✦ The computer is only a year or two old, but you've read through the rest of this section and found out that you need to upgrade everything.

The bare minimum

To access the Internet and enjoy it, your Windows computer should at least have the following components:

✦ **A Pentium-class processor:** The faster the better, but any Pentium computer can do the job.

✦ **At least 64MB of RAM:** More is better, of course, but 64MB is adequate. (Technically, you can get by with as little as 16MB, but performance is slow.)

✦ **At least 1GB of free drive space:** In most cases, this means that your hard drive should have a total capacity of 2GB or more. If your computer doesn't have enough free drive space, you see You have run out of space on Drive C messages instead of the Web sites that you want to visit.

✦ **A modem:** Yep, you need one of those things. (For more information, see "Choosing a Modem," later in this chapter.)

Do it yourself?

If you're a bit of a techno-geek and enjoy opening up a computer and fiddling with its innards, you can perform hardware upgrades, such as adding more memory, installing a hard drive, or upgrading your sound or video card yourself. You can purchase any of these components at your local computer store or at one of the large office supply chain stores. You can find step-by-step installation instructions inside the box.

If you prefer, you can have the service department of your local computer store install the upgrade for you. You pay a fee, of course, but you don't have to spend the time performing the upgrade yourself, and you know that they'll do it right.

Upgrading the processor

The processor is the heart of your computer. Unfortunately, heart transplants are among the most difficult of all surgeries. If your computer doesn't have an adequate processor, you're almost certainly better off purchasing a new computer, rather than trying to upgrade your old one.

To find out what type of processor your computer has, choose Start↪Settings↪Control Panel. When the Control Panel folder opens, double-click the System icon. The System Properties dialog box appears. You'll find a description of your computer's processor near the bottom of this dialog box, as shown in Figure 2-1.

The processor doesn't have to be an actual Intel Pentium processor — a Pentium-class processor made by AMD or Cyrix works just as well.

Note that the System Properties dialog box tells you what type of processor your computer has, but it doesn't tell you how fast the processor is. If you want to find out how fast your Pentium processor is, watch the messages that appear on your computer's screen when you first turn it on. One of those messages indicates the speed at which your computer's processor runs.

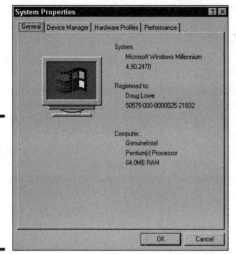

Figure 2-1:
The System
Properties
dialog box
lists your
computer's
processor
type.

A faster processor means better performance for games as well as Internet features, such as online video. But even the slowest Pentium processors (100 MHz or less) can give you acceptable performance, assuming that the computer has sufficient memory and free drive space.

Adding more memory

Next to the processor, the amount of memory on your computer is the most important factor in determining your system's overall performance. For Internet features, such as video and multimedia, your computer can't have too much memory: The more memory you add, the better your system performs. At the minimum, your computer needs 64MB of memory. For better performance, upgrade to 128MB. For the best multimedia and video performance, upgrade to 256MB.

To find out how much memory your computer has, open the System Properties dialog box by choosing Start⇨Settings⇨Control Panel and then double-clicking the System icon. The amount of memory is listed near the bottom of this dialog box.

Fortunately, adding more memory to your computer is not a difficult task. Most Pentium-class computers use one of two types of packages:

✦ **SIMM** memory is used on older Pentium computers and comes in sizes of 8MB, 16MB, 32MB, and 64MB.

✦ **DIMM** memory is used on newer Pentium computers and comes in 16MB, 32MB, 64MB, and 128MB sizes.

And now two new types of memory are available:

✦ **Double data rate (DDR)** memory is like SDRAM (synchronous DRAM), but it transfers twice as fast. (SDRAM transfers data at up to 100 MHz.) DDR modules use DIMM-like SDRAMs. It uses less power, so it's ideal for notebook computers.

✦ **Rambus memory (RDRAM)** uses RIMM (Rambus inline memory modules). It transfers less information than SDRAM, but sends it more frequently. RDRAM transfers data at up to 800 MHz.

To find out what type of memory your computer requires, you have to check the manual that came with your computer.

When you add memory to a Pentium computer that uses SIMM memory, you must always add two identical SIMM modules at a time. For example, to upgrade a 32MB computer to 64MB, you would add two identical 16MB SIMM modules, not a single 32MB module. For computers that use DIMM memory, you can add memory one module at a time. You have to add memory in this way because SIMMs are *Single Inline Memory Modules* and DIMMs are *Dual Inline Memory Modules*; therefore, DIMMs are already in a pair.

Adding more drive space

If your computer has a smallish hard drive and you're nearly out of drive space, a new hard drive is the ticket to better Internet performance.

The first step is finding out how large your computer's drive is and how much free space it has. To find out this information, double-click the My Computer icon on your desktop, right-click the icon representing your hard drive, and choose Properties. The capacity and amount of free space appear on the General tab of the Properties dialog box, as shown in Figure 2-2. In this example, Drive C is a 1.46GB hard drive with 1.14GB of free drive space.

Installing a new hard drive is harder than making a grilled cheese sandwich, but it isn't rocket science. The following paragraphs describe a few things you need to know before you begin.

Two types of hard drives are commonly used in PCs today: EIDE drives (also known as IDE/AT) and SCSI drives. The vast majority of PCs use EIDE drives. SCSI drives, which cost more but are faster, are used mostly in network file servers or in high-performance workstations. When you buy a new drive, make sure that you get the correct type for your computer: EIDE or SCSI.

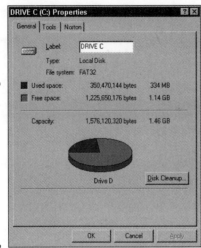

Figure 2-2:
Use My
computer
and the
Properties
dialog box
to view your
hard drive's
size and
free space.

If you aren't sure whether your computer has an EIDE or SCSI drive, choose
Start⇨Settings⇨Control Panel. Then double-click the System icon and click
the Device Manager tab at the top of the System Properties dialog box.
Click the Plus sign located next to Disk Drives to reveal a list of hard drives
attached to your system.

If you decide to add a hard drive to your computer, buy the largest drive you
can afford. Sometimes for just a few dollars more, you can buy a substantially
larger drive.

If your computer is more than a year old, you might find that it has trouble
supporting hard drives larger than 8.4GB. Fortunately, there are two easy
ways to solve this little problem. The first is to use the software that comes
with your new drive to work around the computer's 8.4GB limitation. The
second is to purchase an inexpensive (under $50) disk controller card that
can support larger drives.

Other goodies you should have

Besides an adequate Pentium or better processor, RAM, and drive storage,
your Internet computer needs the following:

✦ **Video card capable of displaying at least 800 x 600 resolution with
24-bit color:** Higher resolutions are nice, but most Web pages are
designed to be viewed at 800 x 600. To find out if your video card is up
to snuff, right-click on a blank spot of your desktop, choose Properties,
and click the Settings tab. Then see whether you can set the Desktop
Area or Screen Area control to 800 x 600 pixels. If you can't, you need to

purchase and install a better video card. (To view Internet graphics and video at their best, make sure that you can set the Color control to True Color while the resolution is set to 800 x 600 pixels.)

✦ **Monitor large enough to prevent squinting when viewing an 800 x 600 screen:** If you have a small (13-inch or 14-inch) monitor, you might want to upgrade to a larger 19-inch monitor or invest in stronger glasses.

✦ **CD-ROM drive:** Although a CD-ROM drive is not an absolute necessity for accessing the Internet, most software is distributed via CD-ROM these days. So if you plan on purchasing and using any Internet software, you need a CD-ROM drive.

✦ **Sound card and speakers:** You don't have to worry too much about how good your sound card and speakers are unless you are an audiophile. Just about any sound card is capable of playing most of the sounds you listen to over the Internet; but if you aren't happy with the quality of what you hear, you can upgrade to a better sound card and speakers.

✦ **Microphone:** An inexpensive microphone plugged into your sound card enables you to send your voice over the Internet.

✦ **Camera:** Better yet, an inexpensive ($50 or so) Web cam lets you send video images over the Internet.

✦ **Scanner:** This enables you to scan your family photographs and attach them to e-mail messages or post them on Web pages that you create. You can purchase a decent scanner for as little as $100.

Choosing a Modem

A *modem* is a device that enables your computer to connect to the Internet via a telephone line, also known as a *dial-up connection*. (An alternative to using a modem is a high-speed connection, such as DSL — see "High-Speed Connections," later in this chapter.)

You can find out if your computer has a modem installed by choosing Start⇨ Settings⇨Control Panel and double-clicking the Modems icon to open the Modems Properties dialog box. This dialog box lists any modems installed on your computer.

There are two basic types of modems: *internal*, which are cards placed in a slot within your computer's case, and *external*, which are small boxes that live outside your computer and connect to your computer through a cable. Either type works. Internal modems are a bit cheaper than external modems, but an internal modem requires that you take your computer apart to install the modem card. External modems are a bit more expensive but easier to install.

Modems are rated by their speed, using a measurement called *bps* (which stands for *bits per second*). Although you can connect to the Internet with a 28,800 bps (28.8K) modem, your Internet experience is much more satisfying if you use a faster modem, such as 33.6K or 56K. You can purchase a 56K modem for well under $100. (Unfortunately, your phone line might not be able to handle connections faster than 28.8K. Even if you upgrade to the fastest modem available, your Internet speed may be limited by your phone connection.)

To connect to the Internet, the modem requires a telephone line. You don't need a special computer-type telephone line; your standard telephone line that you hold conversations on can work. However, be warned that whenever you connect your computer to the Internet, you can't use that telephone line for anything else. If you try calling home and the phone is busy for hours, don't automatically assume that it's your teenager talking — it could be your spouse using the Internet. (For this reason, many people add a second phone line just for Internet access.)

High-Speed Connections

If you use the Internet a lot and aren't satisfied with the slow speeds of dial-up connections via a modem, consider one of the following high-speed alternatives:

✦ **Cable modem:** This type of connection lets you connect to the Internet via your cable television provider. Cable modem connections are lightning fast — from 500 Kbps to 10 Mbps — and cost about $50 per month. Call your local cable company to find out whether cable modem service is available in your area.

✦ **Digital Subscriber Line (DSL):** A high-speed digital phone line provided by your local telephone company, DSL offers speeds similar to cable modems, but uses your existing phone line rather than your TV cable. DSL can even share its high-speed Internet connection with your telephone, so you can talk to your mother-in-law and access the Internet at the same time by using the same phone line. The bad news is that DSL is more expensive than cable. You can expect to pay $100 per month for good DSL service. (In some areas, you can get DSL for as little as $50 per month, but at that price, the DSL connection is usually limited to speeds that are only about twice that of regular phone connections.) Contact your local phone company to find out whether DSL service is available in your area.

Both cable modems and DSL modems connect to your computer via an Ethernet network card, which you must purchase and install in your computer if it doesn't have a card already. An inexpensive Ethernet card will set you back about $30. Alternatively, you may be able to connect your cable or DSL modem to your computer via your computer's USB port. Ask your cable company or DSL provider for more information.

Besides the speed, the biggest advantage of cable and DSL connections is that you are always connected to the Internet, 24 hours a day. As a result, you can access the Internet instantly, without waiting for your modem to dial and establish a connection.

An alternative to high-speed cable and DSL connections is DirecPC, a satellite connection that lets you access the Internet as much as eight times faster than with a standard phone connection. The main advantage of DirecPC over cable and DSL connections is that DirecPC is available almost anywhere (well, at least in the U.S.). However, DirecPC is considerably more expensive than cable or DSL. Recent prices from www.direcpc.com indicate that you can obtain a family connection for around $50 a month for 100 online hours. On the surface, that looks like about the same price as a cable connection. Keep in mind, however, that you are limited to only 100 hours of online time for that price, and you still have to buy the equipment.

An older digital telephone service, known as ISDN, lets you connect to the Internet at twice the speed of a standard dial-up connection and share the connection with a voice phone. As DSL becomes more popular, ISDN will soon fade into memory.

Gathering the Software You Need

Before you can access the Internet, you need to build a small collection of software. Fortunately, most of the software you need is inexpensive or — believe it or not — free. The following sections describe the software you need.

You can get most of the software you need by installing one of the two leading Web browser suites: Microsoft's Internet Explorer or Netscape 6.2. Both suites include tools for browsing the World Wide Web, accessing e-mail and Internet newsgroups, creating Web pages, and much more.

Internet Explorer 6

If you have a computer with Windows 95 (or later), you already have Microsoft's Internet Explorer. However, you may not have the latest version. If not, you can download a free copy from www.microsoft.com/ie, or you can order Internet Explorer 6 on CD for a mere $10 (the CD is free, but you're paying for shipping and handling) by calling 1-800-Microsoft (800-642-7676). (See Book III for lots more on Web browsing with Internet Explorer 6.)

Netscape 6.2

Netscape is a complete package of Internet access tools from Netscape and includes the following components:

✦ **Navigator:** For Web browsing

✦ **Netscape Mail:** For e-mail and newsgroups

✦ **Netscape Instant Messenger:** For sending instant messages to other Internet users

✦ **Netscape Calendar:** For scheduling meetings

✦ **Composer:** For creating Web pages

✦ **Net2Phone:** For PC-to-phone calls anywhere in United States, which are free for the first five minutes and then cost two cents per minute.

You can download Netscape 6.2 from `home.netscape.com/computing/ download/index.html`, or you can order it on CD for $6.95 from `cd.netscape.com`. (See Book IV to find out more about Web browsing with Navigator.)

Other software you might need

Both Microsoft Internet Explorer and Netscape 6.2 contain most of the software you need to access the Internet. The following list describes other software you might also need.

✦ **Instant messenger software:** Messenger software lets you chat one-on-one with other Internet users. You get Microsoft Messenger Service as a part of Internet Explorer, or you can download it from `messenger.msn.com`. Likewise, you get AOL Instant Messenger with Netscape Navigator, or you can download it from `www.aim.com`. Besides these two, another popular instant messaging program is ICQ, which you can download from `www.icq.com`.

✦ **Filtering software:** This type of software protects your family from offensive Web sites. Some good ones are CyberPatrol (`www. cyberpatrol.com`), Net Nanny (`www.netnanny.com`), Pearl Software's Cyber Snoop (`www.pearlsw.com`), and Norton Internet Security 2002 (`www.symantec.com`).

✦ **Adobe Acrobat Reader:** Many Web sites let you download documents that require you to have the Adobe Acrobat Reader in order to read them. Sooner or later, you'll need to download and install this free software from `www.adobe.com`.

✦ **Macromedia Shockwave:** Many Web pages display complicated multimedia graphics using a program called Shockwave. You can download it free of charge from `sdc.shockwave.com/shockwave`.

✦ **Apple QuickTime Player:** QuickTime is a video format popular on Macintosh computers. If you have a Windows computer and want to view QuickTime movies, you can download a free Windows QuickTime player from `www.apple.com/quicktime`. (If you own a Macintosh, you already have QuickTime. However, you still need to check `www.apple.com/quicktime` to see whether a newer version is available.)

✦ **RealPlayer:** RealOne Player (formerly known as RealAudio) is a must if you want to listen to real-time audio or watch real-time video over the Internet. You can get RealOne Player from `www.real.com`.

✦ **Windows Media Player:** Microsoft's media player is the standard program for playing sound and video files under Windows. If you have Windows 2000, you probably already have this program. If not, you can download Windows Media Player at `www.microsoft.com/windows/windowsmedia.default.asp`.

✦ **Compression software:** Many files that you can download from the Internet are stored in a compressed format. To access these files, you need compression software. For Windows, get WinZip from `www.winzip.com`. If you have a Mac, get Stuffit Lite from `www.aladdinsys.com`.

Getting Connected

Perhaps the most important — and confusing — decision you have to make to get on the Internet is figuring out how you want to connect. As this section shows, you can choose to connect to the Internet through an online service, which offers you some additional features besides just Internet access, or you can choose from a couple of other options, including contracting with a standard *Internet Service Provider (ISP)*. Read on to discover your available options.

Online services

An *online service* is a company that provides information online, separate from what is available on the Internet. The term *value-added* has been attached to these online services because they offer their members additional information above and beyond the basic Internet access provided by standard ISPs.

America Online (AOL) is by far the largest of these value-added online services, and many consider it the best service for beginners. AOL acquired CompuServe and promotes that service for business and professional users. Microsoft Network is still trying to become a player, while Prodigy has faded. All these online services also provide access to the Internet itself, including sending and receiving Internet e-mail and viewing Web pages.

If you call any of the major online services, they can send you a free starter kit with the software you need and usually some promotional offer.

Online Service	Phone Number(s)
America Online (AOL)	800-827-6364; Callers outside the U.S. (toll call) +1 703-264-1184
CompuServe	800-848-8990; 614-457-8600
Microsoft Network (MSN)	800-Free-MSN

Reasons for picking an online service include a user-friendly interface, special features unique to that provider, and lots of user support.

Although the online services support users well, when something new comes along, months (or even years) may pass before they can offer it. And most of the unique features that online services have typically provided — such as stock quotes, airline reservations, and news magazines — are now available directly on the Internet.

Internet Service Providers (ISPs)

Standard ISPs just connect you to the Internet. They can be big corporations, such as AT&T or Sprint, or they can be run from someone's garage. Bigger is not necessarily better. The most important feature to check about an ISP is that it has an access number that is a local call for you. Otherwise, your phone bill goes through the roof. Here are other reasons to go with an ISP over an online service:

+ Lower cost

+ Higher speeds

+ A choice of access tools (Netscape Navigator, Internet Explorer, or Eudora, for example)

+ The capability to use the latest Internet services as soon as they hit the Net

+ Less censorship

+ Inclusion in your cable or DSL service package

To find an ISP, ask around, check the business pages in your local newspaper, or peruse the Yellow Pages. If someone you know has access to the World Wide Web, see whether she'll let you get online long enough to check out `thelist.internet.com`, which provides a huge list of providers sorted by state or area code. Consider the following issues when you're picking an ISP:

+ Flat fee versus hourly charge

+ System availability during peak periods

+ Good support, particularly when you're first getting connected and after normal business hours

+ Space provided for building your own Web pages

+ Modem speeds and support for 56 Kbps technology

+ Arrangements to let you dial in from other locations

+ For Macintosh users, assurance that your ISP offers wholehearted support for Macintosh Internet applications

It's not unreasonable to try several ISPs before picking the one you like best. Remember, however, that after you start giving out your e-mail address, it's harder to switch ISPs.

PPP accounts

Most dial-up ISPs offer *PPP accounts* — accounts that let your computer connect directly to the Internet. You can use all kinds of cool Windows and Mac software, such as Netscape Navigator, Internet Explorer, and Eudora. In case you're curious, PPP stands for *Point-to-Point Protocol.*

Shell accounts

If you have a very old computer or have special access needs, you may prefer a *shell account,* an account that connects your computer to the ISP's computer, which is usually a Unix machine. From there, you can hop on the Internet. With a shell account, you generally can see only text, not graphics, on Web pages, so you miss out on some of the glitz and excitement that the Internet has to offer. The Pine e-mail program, which is a text-only program, is popular with shell account users (see Book II, Chapter 4).

See *UNIX For Dummies,* 4th Edition, by John Levine and Margaret Levine Young (published by Hungry Minds, Inc.) for more information about how to use Unix shell accounts.

Free e-mail and Internet access services

Several companies offer free Internet access in return for showing you ads. (See Book II, Chapter 4, for additional details.) Although these free services are perfect for nonprofit organizations or anyone with a tight budget, don't expect much support:

✦ **Juno:** Juno provides a free e-mail account for Windows users. You see advertisements when you check your mail. You can download the Juno software from `www.juno.com` or get a copy from a friend who has Juno.

✦ **NetZero:** NetZero offers free, advertising-supported Internet and e-mail access for Windows 95/98/NT users. Go to `www.netzero.com` for information or phone 800-333-3633 to request a CD-ROM containing the necessary software. You pay a small charge for shipping and handling.

For information on other companies that provide free e-mail or Internet access, start at Yahoo! (`www.yahoo.com`) and then click Business and Economy➪Business to Business➪Communications and Networking➪ Internet and World Wide Web➪Network Service Providers➪Internet Service Providers (ISPs)➪National (U.S.).

Many free services analyze what you do online so that they can target the ads they display to your interests.

Libraries and cybercafés

You don't have to spend any money to use the Internet. Many local libraries now have public Internet-access machines. With free e-mail services, you can have your own, private Internet address.

You can also visit a *cybercafé* — a coffee bar that rents time on online computers. You may meet some people there who can help you with whatever problems you encounter.

Chapter 3: Internet Safety, Security, and Troubleshooting

In This Chapter

✔ Considering privacy, security, and cookies

✔ Understanding encryption and Internet security

✔ Monitoring kids, porn, and the Web

✔ Troubleshooting problems and error messages

*S*urfing the Web from your home may feel totally safe and anonymous. It isn't. Computer vandals and criminals can intercept the messages you send, such as completed forms, as the messages pass through the network. This chapter gives you the basics on privacy on the Net and tells you how to encrypt your messages for added security.

In addition, this chapter provides suggestions and lists programs useful for controlling your kids' access to the Internet. You also read about some of the most frequently encountered problems on the Web, along with solutions or explanations.

Privacy, Security, and Cookies

The messages your browser sends to get information from the Web are often recorded. Web sites can also ask your browser to save (or set up) a small lump of information, called a *cookie*, that the site can request the next time you visit. Cookies are commonly used to

✦ Track how often you visit a site.

✦ Save your logon name and site password so that you don't have to go through a logon procedure every time you visit.

✦ Store your billing address and credit card number.

✦ Save a user profile so that the site can present information customized to your needs.

Your browser enforces these rules to prevent cookie abuse:

✦ Cookies are limited in size (4K).

✦ Only the site that set the cookies can access them.

✦ They must have an expiration date.

You can ask your browser to tell you when a Web site wants to set a cookie:

✦ **Netscape Navigator:** Choose Edit⇨Preferences, click Advanced on the Category list, and then click the Warn Me Before Accepting a Cookie option in the Cookies box. (Or is it cookie jar?)

✦ **Internet Explorer:** Choose Tools⇨Internet Options, click the Privacy tab, and then scroll higher or lower to the setting desired.

Web sites can track visitors in ways other than the use of cookies. If the lack of Web privacy makes you nervous, visit `www.anonymizer.com` before you go surfing. It blocks the common ways that sites use to track you. This Web site also provides details on what information is collected about your computer and connection when you visit a Web site.

Encryption and Internet Security

As your e-mail message or filled-out credit card form travels through the Internet, it passes through many different computers. Someone with the proper skills and equipment can intercept and read your message anywhere along the way without much trouble. You can prevent anyone from reading your messages by *encrypting* them in a secret code. Many sites offer encrypted transactions for form submittals and credit card purchases. Unfortunately, the United States and other governments have attempted to hobble the use of this technology so that they can read messages that they believe pose a threat to their interests. This section describes methods people have developed for improving Internet and e-mail security.

If you obtained your browser via a free download without answering questions about your citizenship, the browser probably uses one of the weaker international security levels. Your browser's About box tells you which you have. Try to get the U.S. or 128-bit version, if you can. International users can upgrade Netscape to U.S. security standards by using tools available from `www.fortify.net`.

Cryptography

A solution to the Internet's security problem is a process called *cryptography* — the use of special computer programs to scramble data.

Others can't read the scrambled data unless they have the correct electronic key. *Keys* are short files of unique bits needed to unscramble messages. A file or message that has been deliberately scrambled by using cryptography is *encrypted*.

Public-key cryptography

Public-key cryptography, invented in the mid-1970s, simplifies encrypted communication by making it much easier to exchange keys. Public-key cryptography gives you two keys: one you keep secret (your *private key*) and another you can give to everyone (your *public key*). No one ever needs to give anyone else a private key, yet everyone can communicate confidentially.

Internet Explorer and Netscape Navigator

Internet Explorer and Netscape Navigator use public-key cryptography to let you send and receive encrypted information from special sites called *secure servers*. They use a version of public-key cryptography called *SSL (Secure Sockets Layer)*. This feature is particularly useful when you want to send your credit card number over the Net. These programs also allow you to encrypt e-mail.

Netscape Navigator and Internet Explorer 6 show a closed lock icon in the status bar if the connection is secure. If the lock is missing or is depicted as open, the connection is not secure.

Malicious individuals can hijack your connection and send you to their own, nonsecure site, just when a legitimate site is about to ask for your credit card number. Always look for the closed-lock icon in your browser window before giving out sensitive information!

Outlook Express and Netscape Mail

Both Outlook Express, which comes with Windows XP and Mac OS X Version 10.1, and Netscape Messenger, which comes with Netscape 6.2, enable you to send encrypted e-mail using public-key cryptography.

✦ To encrypt a message with Outlook Express, click the envelope-with-a-lock icon in the New Message window.

✦ To encrypt a message with Netscape Messenger, click the Security button on the toolbar of the Message Composition window.

Pretty Good Privacy

PGP, which stands for Pretty Good Privacy, is a freeware encryption program with a strong following on the Internet. Although other software manufacturers talk about e-mail security, PGP has been providing it for years.

The latest version of PGP is available as a plug-in that adds encryption and electronic signatures to the menus of popular e-mail programs, including Eudora, Microsoft Exchange, Microsoft Outlook, and Claris Emailer.

Getting your own copy of PGP is an adventure in itself. The free version of PGP is distributed in the United States and Canada via the Massachusetts Institute of Technology PGP site: web.mit.edu/network/pgp.html. You can purchase PGP from the PGP Division of Network Associates, at www.pgp.com.

 For more information about PGP and related issues, visit Francis Litterio's Cryptography, PGP, and Your Privacy page at world.std.com/~franl/ crypto.html. You may also want to follow the Usenet newsgroups alt. security.pgp and comp.security.pgp.discuss.

HushMail

An alternative to PGP is a Web site named HushMail at www.hushmail.com. HushMail is similar to other Web-based, advertising-supported, free e-mail sites, such as Hotmail or Yahoo!, but with one very big difference: HushMail offers strong encryption.

HushMail uses public key encryption but keeps your secret key on its server in encrypted form. This feature means that you can use HushMail from anywhere. Because HushMail utilizes the latest Java technology, you need a fairly recent browser to access its site.

The designers of HushMail seem committed to doing things the right way. They have published the source code for the Java applet that performs encryption on your computer.

Passwords and pass phrases

A first line of defense against someone stealing your private key is to use software, such as PGP, that encrypts your private key before storing it. You choose a password or phrase that is used as the key for this encryption. If you pick a pass phrase that is too easy to guess (a single word will never do), the encryption can be broken. For advice about picking a secure pass phrase, see the Diceware page, at www.diceware.com.

Kids, Porn, and the Web

The World Wide Web abounds in great resources for kids. Many kids have their own home pages, and cyberspace is filled with scanned artwork of the kind that once adorned refrigerator doors.

Though pornography and other dangerous material on the Internet have been overhyped, more than enough of it is available to fill anyone's hard drive. If you have underage children, you need to control their access to the Internet. You can exercise this control in three primary ways: Watch over your kid's shoulder, use filtering (censoring) software, and sign up with an Internet provider that filters out unwanted stuff.

Supervising kids' access

Using this method, you simply don't let your kid on the Net unless you or an adult you trust is present. You may choose to have your kids save pages that they find and look at them later — offline. Although this method takes a great deal of your time and limits your kids' spontaneity online, it can be very effective and also encourages quality family time.

Buying filtering software

Several companies sell software that filters out Web pages that are inappropriate for kids. After you load the software on your computer, your kids are blocked from seeing inappropriate stuff without restricting your access. Here are some popular vendors:

+ **CyberPatrol:** www.cyberpatrol.com

+ **Net Nanny:** www.netnanny.com

+ **SafeSurf:** www.safesurf.com

+ **SurfWatch:** www.surfwatch.com

+ **Cybersitter:** www.solidoak.com

Using an online service with built-in filtering

Both America Online and CompuServe help parents limit their kids' access. Although the filtering programs described in the preceding section work adequately if you install and use them properly, your kids probably know more about them than you do. Software that runs at the service-provider level may be more foolproof.

+ **On AOL:** Click in the keyword box (in the middle of the row of buttons just below the toolbar), type **parental control**, and press Enter.

+ **On CompuServe:** Type **controls** in the address box on the toolbar and then click Go.

You must set some rules for your kids. Here are a few, based on the America Online guidelines:

+ Never agree to meet someone in person or call someone on the phone without asking a parent first.

✦ Never give out your last name, address, phone number, Social Security number, or the name of your school without asking a parent first.

✦ Never share your logon password, even with your best friend.

✦ If someone tells you not to tell your parents about him or her, tell your parents right away!

✦ If you see anything that makes you feel scared or uncomfortable, or if you just aren't sure, ask a parent or teacher.

Ask your kids to give *you* a tour of the Internet. You can find out a great deal by seeing it through their eyes.

Problems and Error Messages

Because the Web is so new and is growing so fast, much of the software that makes it work is full of bugs and is often downright user-hostile. This section describes some of the most frequently encountered problems that exasperate new and old Web users and offers some solutions (or at least explanations).

Displaying a page takes too long

The Web can be slow for a number of reasons. If you feel like your pages are loading too slowly, Table 3-1 helps you figure out the more common problems and solutions.

Table 3-1	Troubleshooting Slow Activity
Problem	*Solution*
Too many graphics are on the page.	You can turn off the display of graphics to speed the loading process. Unfortunately, many pages have links that you can see only when the graphics are turned on.
The modem is too slow.	Upgrade to a faster modem or get cable or DSL access.
You hear noise on the telephone line when you're dialing in.	Modems slow down automatically when line quality is poor. Disconnect and redial. If the problem persists, pester your phone company to fix your line.
You get a busy signal when you're dialing in.	Try surfing at a less popular time or shop for an ISP that's equipped to handle peak loads.
The site you're visiting is overloaded.	Try connecting to the site at a later time.

Your browser keeps crashing

This problem is a common one, unfortunately, as software vendors rush to get the latest version of their browsers to market. Make sure that your computer has enough memory — 64MB is the minimum, and 128MB is recommended. Also, make sure that you have the latest release (not beta) versions of all the required software.

You get the error message "The server does not have a DNS entry"

DNS stands for *domain name server*, a computer that helps other computers figure out the numerical address of a domain from its name. (A *domain* is the last part of a computer's Internet host name, such as dummies.com or whitehouse.gov.) Your service provider keeps a list of common names but asks remote DNS computers for help with names it can't find. Here are some solutions:

✦ If you typed the URL from a printed source, for example, make sure that you didn't make a typing error.

✦ Be aware that printed sources sometimes transcribe URLs incorrectly. They may, for example, add a hyphen or space at the end of a line, fail to include a tilde (~) character, or spell out the word *dot*: dummies-dot-com rather than dummies.com.

✦ If you clicked a hypertext link or you're sure that you typed the URL correctly, wait a few seconds and try again. Because browsers often don't leave enough time for the name-lookup message to get to the DNS and return, a second try to the same URL often works.

✦ Try typing the URL that you want in an Internet search engine, perhaps with additional keywords.

You get the error message "www.bigsite.com has refused your connection" or "Broken pipe"

The Web found the page you were looking for but didn't get back the data in time. It usually means that the site's computer server is down or overloaded or that the Web itself is congested. Try again later.

You get the error message "404 File Not Found"

The good news is that the DNS found the computer associated with the URL you selected. The bad news is that the data file specified in your URL — the stuff after the first single slash — doesn't match what is now on that computer. If you typed the URL from a printed source, make sure that you typed it exactly as it was printed, including capitalization and the funny tilde (~) character; watch out for the hyphen at the end of a printed line, though. That hyphen may or may not be part of the URL.

If you've clicked a hypertext link or you're sure that you typed the URL correctly, the data on the site may have been reorganized. Try "walking up" the URL by deleting the portion to the right of the last slash character, and then the next-to-last slash character, and so on. For example, instead of `www.madlibs.org/cgi-bin/madlib?rigby.ml2`, you can try to find what you want from the main page by going to `www.madlibs.org`. You can also use a search engine. In the query box, type the filename or topic you are seeking (such as **rigby.ml2** or **mad libs rigby**) and the domain name (such as **www.madlibs.org**).

Some Web sites offer information on pages with temporary URLs. If you add those pages to your browser's bookmark or favorites list, the pages may not be there when you go back to them. If that happens, go to the site's main page and look for your information again. For example, if you search for the movie *Star Wars* in the Internet Movie Database (at `www.imdb.com`) and save its page as a bookmark, the URL may be stored as `us.imdb.com/cache/title-exact/108972` at the time you create it. Unfortunately, if you visit the IMDB later, that URL may not work. Because many Web sites create Web pages from information in databases, the information and the pages are different every time you visit the site.

Index

Book II

E-Mail

"Would it ruin the online concert experience if I vacuumed the mosh pit between songs?"

Contents at a Glance

Chapter 1: E-Mail Basics

In This Chapter

✓ Getting up to speed on e-mail basics: acronyms, emoticons, and etiquette

✓ Understanding e-mail addresses

✓ Attaching files to e-mail messages

*E*lectronic mail, or *e-mail*, is without a doubt the most widely used Internet service. Internet mail is connected to most other e-mail systems, such as those within corporations. That means that after you master Internet e-mail, you can send messages to folks with accounts at most big organizations and educational institutions as well as to folks with accounts at Internet providers and online services. This chapter covers the e-mail basics you need to know, such as how to interpret acronyms and emoticons, how to figure out what your e-mail address is, and how to practice proper e-mail etiquette.

The ABCs of E-Mail

This section covers a few things that you need to know to survive in the world of e-mail, such as abbreviations, emoticons, and electronic etiquette.

Abbreviations and acronyms

EUOA! (E-mail users often abbreviate.) People frequently use abbreviations in e-mail messages and chat rooms to help communicate. The abbreviations or acronyms in Table 1-1 can get you started.

Table 1-1	E-Mail Abbreviations and Acronyms
Abbreviation	*What It Means*
AFAIK	As far as I know
AFK	Away from keyboard
BAK	Back at keyboard
BFN	Bye for now
BRB	Be right back
BTW	By the way

(continued)

Table 1-1 *(continued)*

Abbreviation	What It Means
CYA	See ya!
FWIW	For what it's worth
GMTA	Great minds think alike
IMHO	In my humble opinion
IMNSHO	In my not-so-humble opinion
L8R	Later
LOL	Laughing out loud
NRN	No response necessary
OIC	Oh, I see
OTOH	On the other hand
ROFL	Rolling on floor, laughing
RSN	Real soon now (not!)
SO	Significant other
TIA	Thanks in advance
TTFN	Ta-ta for now
WB	Welcome back
WRT	With respect to
WTG	Way to go!

Emoticons

Emoticons (sometimes called *smileys*) substitute for the inflection of voice that is missing in e-mail messages. Most emoticons are supposed to look like faces when you turn your head sideways. Other emoticons (such as <g> or <grin>) are not pictorial; they're hints about the writer's feelings or actions. Because emoticons are still the e-mail equivalent of slang, you probably shouldn't use them in a formal message at work. Table 1-2 shows some common emoticons.

Table 1-2	**Emoticons**
Emoticon	What It Means
:) or :-)	Smile
:(or :-(	Frown
;) or ;-)	Wink
:D or :-D	Big smile (or laugh)
:'(	Crying
8-) or B-)	Sunglasses

Emoticon	What It Means
:-@	Screaming
:-o	Uh-oh!
:-#	Lips are sealed
>:-(	Mad
:-P	Sticking tongue out
o:-)	Angel
:-\	Undecided
\o/	Praise the Lord!
{}	Hug
{{()}}	Hugs
:-*	Kiss
{*}	Hug and a kiss
@-}——	Rose
<g> or <grin>	Same as :-)
<sigh>	Sigh!
::	Action markers, as in ::picks up hammer and smashes monitor::

Electronic etiquette

E-mail uses an etiquette all its own, and it differs from the etiquette of normal spoken or written language. Because e-mail messages are entirely text and usually are short, paying attention to e-mail manners helps avoid misunderstandings. Follow these suggestions:

✦ **Proofread, proofread, proofread.** The recipient sees only words on a page; if those words are horribly misspelled, they create an impression of you — who you are and what's important to you — that may not be the one you want to convey.

✦ **Don't type everything in ALL CAPS.** Using caps makes your text LOOK LIKE YOU'RE SHOUTING. It's okay to use all capitals for emphasis some-times but use them sparingly.

✦ **In your subject line, tell the recipient as much as possible about your message, but don't make it too long.** "Tonight's softball game canceled" is much better than "Important announcement." Don't try to put your entire message on the subject line, though.

✦ **Denizens of the Internet use shorthand and emoticons like LOL and ;) to help convey meaning.** Although these devices are quite acceptable for informal e-mail, avoid them in business messages (unless you're writing to Internet denizens).

✦ **Double-check your humor — irony and sarcasm are easy to miss.** Sometimes, it helps to add a smiley to let your reader in on the joke (see the section, "Emoticons," earlier in this chapter).

✦ **Let the other person have the last word.** If you get involved in a vitriolic exchange of messages, known on the Net as a *flame war,* let the discussion die down by letting the party on the other end have the final word.

✦ **When in doubt, save your message overnight.** Read and edit it again in the morning before you send it. *Never send e-mail when you're upset!*

E-mail caveats

Here are additional caveats to keep in mind as you read and send e-mail:

✦ Forging e-mail return addresses is not very hard, so if you get a totally off-the-wall message that seems out of character coming from that person, somebody else may have forged the message as a prank.

✦ Many people on the Internet adopt fictional personas. The lonely flight attendant you're chatting up may be a 15-year-old boy. "On the Internet, no one knows you're a dog," says a cartoon in *The New Yorker.*

✦ E-mail is not very private. As your mail passes from site to site, it can be read not only by hackers but also by your system administrator. Your employer may even have a legal right to read your e-mail at work. If you really need privacy, refer to Book I, Chapter 3.

✦ Use the Bcc (blind carbon copy) field when you're sending mail to a long list of addresses. That way, each recipient doesn't have to wade through the entire list to read the message (e-mail addresses listed in the Bcc field aren't sent with the message).

✦ Don't pass on chain letters like the one about the dying boy who wants greeting cards (he doesn't), the modem-tax rumor (a proposal squelched in 1987), the Good News or Good Times virus warning (a hoax), Bill Gates paying you for sending e-mail (not a chance), or any letter that offers you a way to make money fast by putting your name at the bottom of the list and sending it to ten friends. (These moneymaking schemes are illegal, are guaranteed to annoy your friends, and don't work.)

If you're not sure whether the information you're receiving is true, check out Hoaxbusters at `hoaxbusters.ciac.org` or vmyths at `www.vmyths.com` for the scoop on the latest hoaxes.

✦ Mass distribution of unsolicited e-mail, known as *spam,* is becoming more and more of a problem. Because most spammers use phony return addresses, replying with a complaint is usually a waste of time. In fact, your reply proves that your address is good and may result in your receiving even more spam.

✦ Not every mail address has an actual person behind it. Some are mailing lists (see Book II, Chapter 5), and some are *robots,* or *mailbots.* Mail robots have become popular as a way to query databases and retrieve files.

✦ Unless you're using versions of Outlook Express and Windows 98 or XP without the latest security updates, your computer cannot get a virus by reading a text e-mail message. However, you can infect your computer by opening files attached to e-mail. Don't *ever* open *any* file attached to messages from strangers or people you don't trust — or even from people you *do* know if you're not expecting a file from them. Some viruses distribute themselves by sending messages to everyone in the unsuspecting victim's e-mail address book, so the messages appear to be from a friend.

Headers

Headers are the lines of text that appear at the beginning of every Internet mail message. Use Table 1-3 as a guide to what these lines mean.

Table 1-3	E-Mail Headers
Header	*Description*
Subject	Describes message (recommended; sometimes required)
To	Lists recipients of the message (at least one required)
Cc	Lists carbon copy recipients (optional)
Bcc	Lists blind carbon copy recipients; recipients' names not listed with the message (optional)
From	Address of message author (required; provided automatically)
Organization	Where the sender works, or whatever
X-Sender	Used with mailing lists to show who sent the message originally
Reply-To	Address to send replies to if it's different from the From line (optional)
Date	Time and date message was sent (provided automatically)
Expires	Date after which message expires (optional)
Message-ID	Unique, machine-generated identifier for message (provided automatically)
Lines	Number of text lines in message (optional; provided automatically)

Rejected mail (bounces)

Every Internet host that can send or receive mail has a special mail address called postmaster that is supposed to be guaranteed to get a message to the person responsible for that host. If you send mail to someone and receive strange failure messages in return, you may try sending a polite message to the postmaster.

For example, if mail sent to king@bluesuede.org returns with an error, you may send e-mail to postmaster@bluesuede.org asking, "Does Elvis the King have a mailbox on this system? TIA, Ed Sullivan."

E-Mail Addresses

To send e-mail to someone, you need his address. Roughly speaking, mail addresses consist of these elements:

+ **Mailbox name:** Usually, the username of the person's account.

+ **@:** The *at* sign.

+ **Host name:** The name of the host's computer. (See "Host names and domain names," later in this chapter.)

For example, elvis@gurus.com is a typical address, where elvis is the mailbox name and gurus.com is the host name.

Internet mailbox names should *not* contain commas, spaces, or parentheses. Mailbox names can contain letters; numerals; and some punctuation characters, such as periods, hyphens, and underscores. Capitalization normally doesn't matter in e-mail addresses.

The most common situation in which these restrictions cause problems is in numeric CompuServe addresses, which consist of two numbers separated by a comma. When you're converting a CompuServe address to an Internet address, change the comma to a period. For example, the address 71053,2615 becomes 71053.2615@compuserve.com as an e-mail address. Similarly, some AOL users put spaces in their screen names. You just drop the spaces when you're sending the e-mail. If, for some reason, you must send mail to an address that does include commas, spaces, or parentheses, enclose the address in double quotes.

What's my address?

If you're accessing the Internet through a service provider, your address is most likely

your_login_name@your_provider's_host_name

If you're connected through work or school, your e-mail address is typically

your_login_name@your_computer's_host_name

A host name, however, is sometimes just a department or company name rather than your computer's name. If your login name is `elvis` and your computer is `shamu.strat.gurus.com`, your mail address may look like one of these examples:

```
elvis@shamu.strat.gurus.com
elvis@strat.gurus.com
elvis@gurus.com
```

or even this one:

```
elvis.presley@gurus.com
```

Host names and domain names

Hosts are computers that are directly attached to the Internet. Host names have several parts strung together with periods, like this:

```
ivan.iecc.com
```

You decode a host name from right to left:

- ✦ The rightmost part of a name is its *top-level domain,* or *TLD* (in the preceding example, `com`). See "Top-level domains," later in this chapter.
- ✦ To the TLD's left (`iecc`) is the name of the company, school, or organization.
- ✦ The part to the left of the organization name (`ivan`) identifies the particular computer within the organization.

**Book II
Chapter 1**

E-Mail Basics

In large organizations, host names can be further subdivided by site or department. The last two parts of a host name are known as a *domain.* For example, `ivan` is in the `iecc.com` domain, and `iecc.com` is a *domain name.*

For a list of organizations that can register a domain name for you, go to the following URL:

```
www.icann.org/registrars/accredited-list.html
```

Internet Service Providers often charge substantial additional fees for setting up and supporting a new domain. Shop around.

IP addresses and the DNS

Network software uses the IP address, which is sort of like a phone number, to identify the host. IP addresses are written in four chunks separated by periods, such as

```
208.31.42.77
```

A system called the *domain name system (DNS)* keeps track of which IP address (or addresses, for popular Internet hosts) goes with which Internet host name. Usually, one computer has one IP address and one Internet host name, although this isn't always true. For example, the Web site at www. yahoo.com is so heavily used that a group of computers, each with its own IP address, accept requests for Web pages from that name.

The most important IP addresses to know are the IP addresses of the computers at the Internet provider you use. You may need them in order to set up the software on your computer; if things get fouled up, the IP addresses help the guru who fixes your problem.

Top-level domains

The *top-level domain (TLD),* sometimes called a *zone,* is the last piece of the host name on the Internet (for example, the zone of gurus.com is com). TLDs come in two main flavors:

✦ Organizational

✦ Geographical

If the TLD is three or more letters long, it's an *organizational name.* Table 1-4 describes the organizational names that have been in use for years.

Table 1-4	Organizational TLDs
TLD	*Description*
com	Commercial organization
edu	Educational institution, usually a college or university
gov	U.S. government body or department
int	International organization (mostly NATO, at the moment)
mil	U.S. military site (can be located anywhere)
net	Networking organization
org	Anything that doesn't fit elsewhere, usually a not-for-profit group

It used to be that most systems using organizational names were in the United States. The com domain has now become a hot property; large corporations and organizations worldwide consider it a prestige Internet address. Address "haves" and "have-nots" are contesting a plan to add additional top-level domain names to those already in use.

If the TLD is two letters long, it's a *geographical name.* The two-letter code specifies a country, such as us for the United States, uk for the United

Kingdom, au for Australia, and jp for Japan. The stuff in front of the TLD is specific to that country. Often, the letter group just before the country code mimics the style for U.S. organizational names: com or co for commercial, edu or ac for academic institutions, and gov or go for government, for example.

The us domain — used by schools, cities, and small organizations in the United States — is set up strictly geographically. The two letters just before us specify the state. Other common codes are ci for city, co for county, cc for community colleges, and k12 for schools. The Internet site for the city of Cambridge, Massachusetts, for example, is www.ci.cambridge.ma.us.

Port numbers

Internet host computers can run many programs at one time, and they can have simultaneous network connections to lots of other computers. *Port numbers,* which identify particular programs on a computer, keep the different connections straight. For example:

✦ File transfer (FTP) uses port 21.

✦ E-mail uses port 25.

✦ The Web uses port 80.

Typically, your file transfer, e-mail, or newsgroup program automatically selects the correct port to use, so you don't need to know these port numbers. Now and then, you see a port number as part of an Internet address (URL).

URLs versus e-mail addresses

URLs (Uniform Resource Locators) contain the information that your browser software uses to find Web pages on the World Wide Web. URLs look somewhat like e-mail addresses in that both contain a domain name. E-mail addresses almost always contain an @, however, and URLs never do.

URLs that appear in newspapers and magazines sometimes have an extra hyphen added at the end of a line when the URL continues on the next line. If the URL doesn't work as written, try deleting that hyphen. (See Book III, Chapter 1, for more details on URLs.)

E-mail addresses usually are not case-sensitive — capitalization doesn't matter — but parts of URLs *are* case-sensitive. Always type URLs *exactly* as written, including capitalization.

Attachments

To send a file by e-mail, you *attach* it to an e-mail message. Compose and address the message as usual, using your e-mail program (see Book II, Chapters 2 through 4). Then use the program's toolbar buttons or menu commands to attach the file to the message. You can attach more than one file to a message, but don't send files that are too large — your recipient's mail system may choke on large files. To send a file larger than 100K, use a compression program such as WinZip (www.winzip.com) or ZipMagic (www.zipmagic.com) to make the file smaller. Before you send someone an attached file, make sure that he wants it. Ask for permission to send the file, and ask whether the recipient has the necessary program to open the file that you're sending. For example, if you're sending a Microsoft Word document, the recipient of the file needs a program that can open a Word document.

E-mail programs use one of three methods to encode an attached file so that it can travel through the e-mail system: MIME, uuencoding, and BinHex. MIME is the most widely used encoding system.

Chapter 2: Composing E-Mail with Outlook Express

In This Chapter

- ✔ Mastering the Address Book
- ✔ Jazzing up your messages
- ✔ Sending e-mail — now or later
- ✔ Getting organized
- ✔ Printing and saving e-mail messages

*I*f you're using Internet Explorer 6, you have Outlook Express — Microsoft's friendly e-mail program. If you're not sure how to do something in Outlook Express, don't despair. This chapter tells you what you need to know to get up and running quickly and efficiently with this program.

This chapter shows you all the tricks of the trade, such as how to store e-mail addresses for your favorite pals in your handy-dandy Address Book, how to master the basics of composing and sending e-mail, how to get fancy by using color and images in your e-mail, and how to use folders to organize your e-mail messages.

Adding Entries to Your Address Book

One of the first things you'll want to do is add the names of all the people with whom you regularly correspond to your Outlook Express Address Book. That way, you'll avoid retyping e-mail addresses each time you want to send a message. Instead, you can simply type the name of your intended recipient.

Good news! If you're switching from some other e-mail program, like the one that comes with Netscape Navigator, and you've already created an address book, you can import all those addresses into the Address Book in Outlook Express. So no retyping required!

Creating a new address

You'll want to add all your frequent e-mailees to your Address Book. To add a new recipient, follow these steps:

1. In Internet Explorer 6, click the Mail button on the toolbar and then choose New Message from the drop-down list.

The New Message window appears.

2. Choose Tools➪Address Book to open the Address Book.

You can combine Steps 1 and 2 by choosing File➪New➪Contact from the Internet Explorer menu bar.

3. Click the New Contact button.

The Properties dialog box appears, as shown in Figure 2-1.

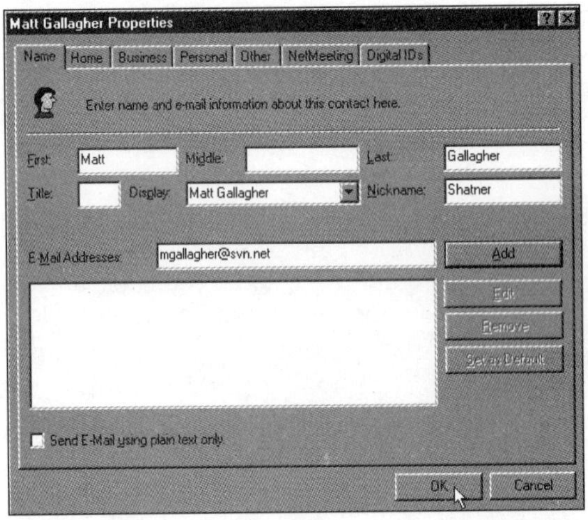

Figure 2-1: The Properties dialog box.

4. Fill out the Name section with information about the new contact. Then, in the E-Mail Addresses text box, type the recipient's e-mail address and click the Add button.

When you click the Add button, Outlook Express adds the address to the list box and designates it as the default e-mail address for the individual you named.

If the person you're adding to the Address Book has more than one e-mail address (for example, if he maintains an e-mail account with one address at home and an e-mail account with another address at work), you can add the additional e-mail address by repeating this step.

5. **(Optional) Repeat Step 4 to add an additional e-mail address for the same recipient.**

   If you want to make the second e-mail address the default one (that is, the one that Outlook Express automatically uses when you compose a new message to this person), you need to select it in the list box and then click the Set As Default button.

6. **Click OK to close the Properties dialog box and return to the Address Book.**

   Your new contact's Display name appears in the Address Book, followed by the default e-mail address.

7. **Click OK to close the Address Book.**

**Book II
Chapter 2**

**Composing
E-Mail with
Outlook Express**

Importing addresses from somewhere else

To import into the Address Book addresses from an address book created with Eudora, Microsoft Exchange, Microsoft Internet Mail for Windows, Netscape Navigator, or stored in a comma-separated text file, follow these steps:

1. **Choose File⇨Import⇨Other Address Book on the Address Book menu bar.**

   The Address Book Import Tool dialog box appears, as shown in Figure 2-2.

Figure 2-2:
The
Address
Book Import
Tool dialog
box.

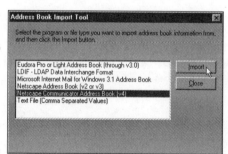

2. **Click the type of address book that you want to import from the list box of the Address Book Import Tool dialog box; then click the Import button.**

   Outlook Express now imports the names and e-mail addresses of all the contacts in the existing address book.

3. **Click Close after all the information is imported.**

   The Address Book Import Tool dialog box closes, and you return to the Address Book dialog box, where the imported contacts now appear.

4. **(Optional) To sort the contacts in the Address Book by their last names, click the Name column head above the first entry. To sort the contacts by their e-mail addresses, click the E-Mail Address column head.**

5. **Click OK to close the Address Book.**

Outlook Express automatically adds the e-mail address of anyone who sends you an e-mail message to which you reply.

Finding a recipient's e-mail address

Sometimes, you may know that a person you want to correspond with has an e-mail address, but you don't remember it. Conversely, you know a person's e-mail address but need to look up her telephone number or, heaven forbid, her regular (snail) mail address.

In those situations, you can use the Find People feature in Outlook Express to search a number of different online address directories. You can also use this feature to search for someone you've entered in the Address Book, in the rare instance that the number of contacts in the Address Book is so large that doing this kind of search is significantly faster than scrolling to the person's name.

To look up someone's e-mail address with the Find People feature, follow these steps:

1. **In the Outlook Express window, click the Find button and choose People from the drop-down list.**

   The Find People dialog box appears, as shown in Figure 2-3.

Figure 2-3:
The Find
People
dialog box.

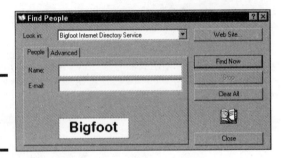

2. **Click the name of the directory that you want to use from the Look In drop-down list.**

3. **Type the name of the person whose e-mail address you want to look up in the Name field; then click the Find Now button.**

   When you click Find Now, Outlook Express searches the directory that you selected for all the people whose names closely or identically match the name you entered. (Of course, you need to be online for this search to occur.) The results of the search then appear in the list box in the lower part of the Find People dialog box, shown in Figure 2-4.

**Book II
Chapter 2**

**Composing
E-Mail with
Outlook Express**

Figure 2-4:
The results
of your
search.

4. **Scroll through the list to see whether the person is listed with his or her e-mail address.**

5. **If you find the person you are searching for in the list, click his listing to select it; then click the Add To Address Book button to add the person to your Address Book.**

6. **When you finish searching the various directories, click the X in the upper-right corner of the dialog box to return to the Select Recipients dialog box.**

7. **(Optional) To add the new contact (assuming that your search was successful, which it often won't be) as a recipient in your new e-mail message, click the To:->, Cc:->, or Bcc:-> button before you click OK.**

Checking for New Mail

After you start sending messages and giving out your e-mail address, your Inbox will fill up with new mail in no time at all. You need to know not only how to access all the latest tidbits headed your way, but also how to reply to these messages.

Setting Outlook Express to check for mail

Normally, when you launch Outlook Express, the program doesn't automatically tell you when you have new e-mail except when you click the Send/Recv button on the toolbar. If you want, you can have Outlook Express automatically inform you of new e-mail anytime you open the program.

If your computer is not connected to the Internet, Outlook Express dials out, connects, and retrieves your mail at this set interval.

To set this up, follow these steps:

1. **Launch Outlook Express either by clicking the Launch Outlook Express button on the Windows taskbar or by clicking the Mail button on the Internet Explorer toolbar and choosing Read Mail from the pop-up menu.**

   You need to launch Outlook Express in this manner because you can't change any of the program's settings from a New Message window.

2. **Choose Tools⇨Options on the Outlook Express menu bar to open the Options dialog box with the General tab selected.**

3. **Select the Check for New Messages Every 30 Minute(s) check box and then, in the associated text box, replace 30 with the new number of minutes you desire, or use the spinner buttons to select this interval value.**

   When you enable the Check for New Messages Every "So Many" Minutes check box, Outlook Express automatically checks your mail server for new messages whenever you launch the program and then continues to check at the specified interval as you work in the program.

4. **(Optional) To have Outlook Express play a chime whenever new e-mail messages are downloaded while you're working in the program, select the Play Sound When New Messages Arrive check box.**

5. **Click Apply.**

6. **Click OK.**

   The Options dialog box closes, you return to Outlook Express, and the automatic e-mail checking goes into effect.

After the automatic e-mail checking goes into effect, Outlook Express informs you of the delivery of new e-mail by placing an envelope icon on the Outlook Express status bar (and "dinging" if you enabled the Play Sound When New Messages Arrive check box).

This is very nice for those times when you're spending a great deal of time working in Outlook Express. However, don't expect to get this kind of indicator when browsing the Web with Internet Explorer 6. The only way to know whether you have any new e-mail when working in this program is by clicking the Mail button on the Internet Explorer toolbar and then choosing the Read Mail command.

Reading e-mail

When you use Outlook Express as your e-mail program, you read the messages that you receive in an area known as the Inbox. To open the Inbox in Outlook Express and read your e-mail messages from Internet Explorer 6, follow these steps:

1. **With the Internet Explorer 6 window active, click the Mail button in the toolbar and then choose Read Mail on the pop-up menu that appears.**

   After you choose the Read Mail command, Outlook Express opens the Inbox — that is, as long as Outlook Express is configured as your e-mail program.

2. **Click the Send/Recv button on the Outlook Express toolbar to download any new messages.**

   As soon as you click the Send/Recv button, Outlook Express opens a connection to your mail server where it checks for any new messages to download for all e-mail accounts on the computer. New messages are then downloaded to your computer and placed in the Outlook Express Inbox. To create automatic rules that move your messages into another folder see "Organizing your e-mail with the Rule Editor" later in this chapter.)

   Descriptions of any new messages appear in bold in the upper pane of the Inbox, which is divided into six columns: Priority (indicated by the red exclamation point); Attachments (indicated by the paper clip); Flag Status (indicated by the flag); From; Subject; and Received (showing both the date and time that the e-mail message was downloaded to your computer).

   Note that mail messages you haven't yet read are indicated not only by bold type, but also by the presence of a sealed envelope icon in the From column. Mail messages that you've read are indicated by the presence of an opened envelope icon.

3. **To read one of your new messages, click the message in the upper pane of the Inbox.**

   It doesn't matter if your mouse pointer is located in the From, Subject, or Received column when you click the message.

   The message opens and the text appears in the lower pane of the Inbox. The From and Subject information appears on the bar dividing the upper pane from the lower pane.

   If you want the message to open in its own window, rather than in the lower pane of the Inbox, double-click the message.

4. **When you're finished reading your e-mail, click the Close box in the upper-right corner of the Outlook Express Inbox window.**

Replying to a message

Often, you want to reply to a message right away — especially if the e-mail message uses the High Priority (!) icon. Follow these steps:

1. **To reply to the author of the message, click the Reply button. To reply to the author and send copies of the reply to everyone copied on the original message, click the Reply All button instead.**

2. **In the message window, type the text of your reply above the text of the original message and then send the reply by clicking the Send button.**

Forwarding a message

Sometimes, in addition to or instead of replying to the original message, you need to send a copy of it to someone who was not listed in the Cc: field. To do so, you forward a copy of the original message to new recipients of your choosing. When you forward a message, Outlook Express copies the Subject: field and contents of the original message to a new message, which you then address and send.

To forward the e-mail message to another e-mail address, click the Forward button on the Outlook Express toolbar and then fill in the recipient information in the To:, and, if applicable, Cc: and Bcc: fields. Add any additional text of your own above that of the original message; then click the Send button to send the forwarded message on its way.

Composing E-Mail Messages

Outlook Express makes it easy to compose and send e-mail messages to anyone in the world who has an e-mail address.

Drafting a message

You can follow these steps to create a new e-mail message:

1. From the Internet Explorer toolbar, click the Mail button and then choose New Message on the pop-up menu that appears.

Internet Explorer responds by opening an Outlook Express New Message window. (Note that you can also start a new message from within Outlook Express by clicking the Create Mail button on its toolbar.)

2. Type the recipient's e-mail address in the text box of the To: field and click OK.

If the recipient is already listed in your Address Book, click the word To: to open the Select Recipients dialog box. Then in the Name list box, click the name of the recipient and click the To:-> button. If you don't want to send the message to anyone else, click OK.

3. (Optional) Click somewhere in the Cc: field, type the e-mail addresses of everyone you want to add to the list, separated by semicolons (;), and then click OK.

**Book II
Chapter 2**

**Composing
E-Mail with
Outlook Express**

When composing a new message, you can send copies of it to as many other recipients (within reason) as you want. To send copies of the message to other recipients, type their e-mail addresses in the Cc: field (if you don't care that they'll see all the other people copied on the message) or in the Bcc: field (if you don't want them to see any of the other people copied on the message). To access the Bcc: field, click the To: or Cc: button and indicate Bcc: in the Select Recipients dialog box.

4. Click somewhere in the Subject: field and type a brief description of the contents or purpose of the e-mail message.

When your message is delivered, the descriptive text that you entered in the Subject: field appears in the Subject column of each recipient's Inbox.

In Outlook Express, you can change the priority of the e-mail message from normal to either high or low by using the Priority button. When you make a message either high or low priority, Outlook Express attaches a priority icon to the message that indicates its relative importance. (Keep in mind that whether the recipient sees this icon depends on the e-mail program he's using.) The high-priority icon places an exclamation mark in front of the envelope; the low-priority icon adds a downward-pointing arrow.

5. (Optional) To boost the priority of the message, click the drop-down list next to the Priority button and choose High Priority, Normal Priority, or Low Priority.

6. **Click the cursor in the body of the message and type the text of the message as you would in any text editor or word processor, ending paragraphs and short lines by pressing Enter.**

   When composing the text of the message, keep in mind that you can insert text directly into the body of the message from other documents via the Clipboard (using the old Cut, Copy, and Paste commands) or, in the case of text or HTML documents, by choosing Insert⇨Text From File and selecting the name of the file in the Insert Text File dialog box.

7. **(Optional) To spell-check the message, click the cursor at the beginning of the message text and click the Spelling button.**

   When spell-checking the message, Outlook Express flags each word that it can't find in its dictionary and tries its best to suggest an alternative word.

   - To replace the unknown word in the text with the word suggested in the Change To text box of the Spelling window, click the Change button or, if it's a word that occurs frequently in the rest of the text, click Change All.

   - To ignore the unknown word and have the spell checker continue to scan the rest of the text for possible misspellings, click Ignore or, if it's a word that occurs frequently in the rest of the text, click Ignore All.

8. **To send the e-mail message to the recipient(s), click the Send button on the Outlook Express toolbar.**

Attaching a file to an e-mail message

In Outlook Express, you can attach files to your e-mail messages to transmit information that you don't want to appear in the body of the message. For example, you may need to send an Excel worksheet to a client in another office.

To attach a file to an e-mail message in Outlook Express, follow these steps:

1. **From the Internet Explorer 6 toolbar, click the Mail button and then choose New Message on the pop-up menu that appears.**

   Internet Explorer responds by opening a new message in Outlook Express.

2. **Add the recipient(s) of the e-mail message in the To: or Cc: field(s), the subject of the message in the Subject: field, and any message text explaining the attached files in the body of the message.**

3. **Click the Attach button on the toolbar to open the Insert Attachment dialog box.**

4. **In the Look In drop-down list box, choose the folder that contains the file you want to attach. Then click the filename in the main list box before you click the Attach button.**

   Outlook Express adds an Attach field under the Subject: field displaying the icon(s), filename(s), and size of the file(s) attached to the message.

5. **Click the Send button on the Outlook Express toolbar to send the message to the recipient(s).**

   After sending your message, the Outlook Express window closes, and you return to the Internet Explorer 6 window.

Adding an image to your message

If you want to spice up your message even more, consider adding a graphic.

To insert a graphic in the message that appears in front of your stationery, choose Insert⇨Picture. Use the Browse button in the Picture dialog box to select the graphics file you want to use and then click OK.

Formatting Your Messages

Want to send your friends and colleagues a message they'll remember — or at least that they'll find attractive? Then consider experimenting with the Formatting toolbar. This toolbar, which separates the header section of the message from the body window, becomes active as soon as you click the cursor in the body of the message. You can then use its buttons to format the text of your message.

If you don't see this toolbar when you click the message body area, this means that someone has changed the Mail sending format from its default of HTML to Plain Text. (See the next section, "Rich Text (HTML) messages versus Plain Text messages," to see how to change it back.)

Rich Text (HTML) messages versus Plain Text messages

Outlook Express can use one of two file formats for the e-mail messages that you compose. The Rich Text (HTML) format can display all the formatting you see on Web pages on the Internet (including graphics). The Plain Text format can display only text characters (similar to a file opened in the Windows Notepad text-editing utility).

When you first install Outlook Express, it uses the Rich Text (HTML) format for any new e-mail messages that you compose. This setting is fine as long as the e-mail program used by the recipient(s) of the message can deal with HTML formatting. (Many older e-mail programs, especially ones running under the Unix operating system, cannot.)

If you send a message using the Rich Text (HTML) format to someone whose e-mail program can't accept anything but plain text, the message comes to the recipient as plain text with an HTML document attached. That way, she can view all the HTML formatting bells and whistles that you added to the original e-mail message by opening the attached document in her Web browser.

To make Plain Text the new default format for Outlook Express, follow these steps:

1. **Launch Outlook Express.**

2. **Choose Tools➪Options to open the Options dialog box.**

3. **Click the Send tab and then select the Plain Text Settings button in the Mail Sending Format area.**

   If you don't want Outlook Express to put a greater-than symbol (>) in front of each line of the original message when forwarding it to another recipient, click the Plain Text Settings button to open the Plain Text Settings dialog box. Then click the check box labeled Indent the Original Text With to remove the check mark.

   If you want to change the greater-than symbol (>) to a vertical bar (|) or colon (:), choose the new symbol from the drop-down list to the right.

4. **After making your changes, click OK or press Enter to close the Plain Text Settings dialog box.**

5. **Click OK to close the Options dialog box and put your new settings into effect.**

Adding bold, italics, underline, and color to your text

The Formatting toolbar in the Outlook Express New Message window makes it easy to add basic HTML formatting to your e-mail message. For example, you can highlight the text that you want to change and then use the Bold, Italics, and Underline buttons to change the way it looks.

In addition to doing basic formatting, you can make your message a little fancier by changing the color of the text. To do so, simply select the text by dragging through it with the mouse pointer and then click the Font Color button on the Formatting toolbar. On the pop-up menu that appears, choose the color that you want the text to be.

Changing the font type and font size

If you really want to make your point, try changing your font type or enlarging its size. To do so, highlight the text you'd like to change and then choose the type and size you'd like from the two drop-down lists on the left side of the Formatting toolbar.

Sending an E-Mail Message

When you're online (or are about to go online), you can send an e-mail message as soon as you finish writing (and, hopefully, spell-checking). Simply click the Send button in the New Message window (or press Ctrl+Enter or Alt+S) and away it goes, winging its way through cyberspace.

This method doesn't work at all, however, when you're composing an e-mail message while traveling on a plane or train where you may not be able to connect your modem.

For those times when you can't send the message right away, you need to choose File⇨Send Later on the New Message menu bar. When you choose this command, Outlook Express displays an alert box indicating that the message will be placed in your Outbox folder ready to be sent the next time you choose the Send and Receive command. When you click OK, the e-mail message you just composed goes into your Outbox folder. Then the next time you connect to the Internet, you can send all the e-mail messages waiting in the Outbox to their recipients by clicking the Send/Recv button.

Organizing Your Messages with Folders

Getting e-mail is great, but it doesn't take long for you to end up with a disorganized mess. If you don't watch it, your Outlook Express Inbox can end up with hundreds of messages, some of which are still unread and all of which are lumped together in one extensive list.

Outlook Express offers a number of methods for organizing your mail, including a handy little feature known as the Inbox Assistant, which can automatically sort incoming mail according to rules that you set.

Don't forget that the most basic way to organize your e-mail is to sort the messages in the Inbox. To sort all the messages in the Inbox (or any of the other Outlook Express folders, for that matter), click a column heading. For example, if you want to sort the e-mail in your Inbox by subject, click the Subject column heading at the top of the list. And if you want to sort the messages by the date and time received (from most recent to oldest), click the Received column heading at the top of that column.

Clicking the Received column heading once sorts the messages in ascending or descending order according to date. If you click the column heading again, the messages appear in the opposite order.

Creating a new folder

Creating a new folder is easy. Just right-click in the Folders list and choose New Folder from the pop-up menu that appears. Type a name for the folder in the Folder Name text box and click OK. Then click the Inbox icon before clicking the name of the newly created subfolder.

Moving e-mail into a folder

Outlook Express makes easy work of arranging your e-mail messages in folders. To send a bunch of related e-mail messages into a new or existing folder, follow these steps:

1. **Open the Inbox in Outlook Express either by clicking the Mail button in Internet Explorer 6 and then choosing Read Mail on the pop-up menu or, if you already have Outlook Express running, by clicking the Inbox icon in the Folders pane.**

2. **Select all the messages that you want to put in the same folder.**

    To select a single message, click it. To select a continuous series of messages, click the first one and hold down the Shift key as you click the last one. To click multiple messages that aren't in a series, hold down Ctrl as you click the description of each one.

3. **After you finish selecting the messages to be moved, choose Edit⇨Move to Folder on the Outlook Express menu bar.**

4. **Click the plus sign next to the Local Folders icon; then click the name of the subfolder into which you want to move the selected messages.**

5. **Click the OK button in the Move dialog box to move the messages into the selected folder.**

To verify that the items are in the correct folder, click the big Inbox button with the downward-pointing arrow on the bar at the top of the pane with the messages and then select the subfolder on the pop-up outline.

Organizing your e-mail with the Rule Editor

The Rule Editor can automate the organization of your e-mail by using rules that you create in its Rule Editor dialog box. Outlook Express uses the rules that you create to forward e-mail from particular correspondents to particular folders that you've set up.

To create a new rule for systematizing your e-mail, follow these steps:

1. **Launch Outlook Express.**

2. **On the menu bar, choose Tools⇨Message Rules⇨Mail.**

3. **If you have previously set up mail rules in your copy of Outlook Express, the Message Rules dialog box opens on your screen; click the New button to open the New Mail Rule dialog box.**

If this is the first time you've opened the Rule Editor to create a mail rule, the New Mail Rule dialog box opens automatically at this point.

4. **In section 1 of the New Mail Rule dialog box, click to select a check box or boxes for the conditions that must be met by the incoming e-mail.**

5. **In section 2, select a check box or boxes for the action or actions that you want to occur when a message meets the condition(s) you selected in section 1.**

6. **In section 3, click each underlined hyperlink until you have provided all the necessary information that the rule requires.**

The subsequent dialog boxes that open and the information you are prompted for depend on the options you selected in the New Mail Rule dialog box.

As an example, assume that you select Where the From Line Contains People in section 1 and Copy It to the Specified Folder in section 2. So in section 3, you click the underlined hyperlink in the Where the From Line Contains People option to open the Select People dialog box. Here, you specify the sender for whom you are establishing the rule. After you type the sender's name, you click the Add button and then OK. The Select People dialog box closes, and you return to the New Mail Rule dialog box. At this point, you click the hyperlink in the Move It to the Specified Folder option in section 3, which opens the Move dialog box. After choosing a folder or clicking the New Folder button to create a new folder, you click OK to exit the Move dialog box. You return to the New Mail Rule dialog box.

7. **(Optional) Type a descriptive name in the Name of The Rule text box to replace the generic name and click OK.**

The New Mail Rule dialog box closes, and you return to the Message Rules dialog box.

8. **Click the Apply Now button to open the Apply Mail Rules Now dialog box where you choose the folder (most often the Inbox) to which the new rule should be applied.**

9. **Click Close to exit the Apply Rules Now dialog box; then click OK to close the Message Rules dialog box.**

Book II
Chapter 2

Composing
E-Mail with
Outlook Express

You can set up multiple rules to apply to e-mail messages in the Inbox folder. Just be aware that Outlook Express applies the rules in the order in which they appear on the Mail Rules tab in the Message Rules dialog box. You can use the Move Up and Move Down buttons to rearrange their order.

Deleting and compacting your e-mail

As you get more and more e-mail in your Inbox, you may want to use the File⇨Folder⇨Compact command to compress the messages, thus freeing up valuable disk space. When you have e-mail in all sorts of different folders, you can compact all the messages by choosing File⇨Folder⇨Compact All Folders instead.

To remove messages from the Inbox without permanently deleting them, select the messages and then press the Delete key. The messages instantly disappear from the Inbox window. However, if you ever need any of these messages again, you can display them by clicking the Deleted Items icon in the pane on the left side of the Outlook Express window.

When you have messages (especially those from blocked senders) that you no longer need to store on your computer's hard disk, you can remove them from the Deleted Items folder permanently by selecting them and then choosing Edit⇨Delete. Click Yes in the alert dialog box that tells you that you are about to delete the selected messages forever. (Alternatively, you can simply press the Delete key.)

Normally, Outlook Express deletes all messages from your mail server as soon as they are downloaded to your computer. To keep the original messages on the mail server, giving you not only a backup, but also the means to retrieve the mail from somebody else's computer, follow these steps:

1. **Launch Outlook Express.**

2. **Choose Tools⇨Accounts; then click the "friendly" name for your mail account and click the Properties button.**

3. **Click the Advanced tab; then, in the Delivery section, click the Leave a Copy of the Messages on Server check box.**

   The next time you download messages, these copies will be downloaded to your computer again. Their filenames will be appended with a number to differentiate them from the original copy if it still exists in the same folder.

4. **(Optional) To have the mail left for a set period of time, click the Remove from Server After *xx* Day(s) check box and enter the number of days in the associated text box or use the spinner buttons to select this time period.**

5. **(Optional) To have the mail deleted from the server when you permanently (Ctrl+D) delete them, click the Remove from Server When Deleted from the Deleted Items check box.**

6. **Click OK to close the Properties dialog box; and then click Close to make the Internet Accounts dialog box go away.**

Deleting and renaming folders

If you decide that a folder is no longer useful in your organization scheme, deleting the folder is no problem. Simply highlight the folder, press the Delete key, and the folder is gone. Or you may opt to rename the folder, using a more useful moniker. Click the folder to highlight it, wait a second, and then click again. A rectangular box appears around the folder. Position your cursor inside the box and type your folder's new and improved name.

Printing a Message

Sometimes, you may need to get a hard copy of a message to share with other less fortunate workers in the office who don't have e-mail. To print the contents of an e-mail message, choose File⇨Print and then click OK in the Print dialog box. Now you have your hard copy!

Saving a Message to Your Hard Drive

Occasionally, an e-mail message contains some information that you want to be able to reuse in other documents without having to retype the information. Rather than opening the message in the Outlook Express Inbox and then copying its contents to a new document via the Clipboard, you can save the message as either a mail document that can be opened in Outlook Express or as a text file that can be opened with a text editor, such as Notepad, or a word processor, such as Word 2002.

To save the contents of an e-mail message as a mail document or text file:

1. **Choose File⇨Save As to open the Save Message As dialog box.**

2. **Choose the folder in which to save the message in the Save In drop-down list and then select the file type (Mail or Text Files) in the Save As Type drop-down list.**

3. **Click Save.**

Chapter 3: Composing E-Mail with Netscape Mail

In This Chapter

✔ Discovering the Address Book

✔ Composing, sending, receiving, and replying to e-mail

✔ Managing your folders

✔ Printing and saving messages

*N*etscape Mail is the e-mail component in Communicator. Yes, you can use Mail to send and receive e-mail, but Mail also offers many other cool features that make the program stand out, including an Address Book, rich text capability, and e-mail processing options.

Adding Entries to the Address Book

The Mail Address Book is more than just a storehouse for e-mail addresses. The Address Book is also a really neat way of maintaining addresses because it saves you a lot of typing. For example, when you receive e-mail, you can add the sender's e-mail address to the Address Book without typing it.

Creating a new address

If you send a lot of e-mail to one address, consider adding that address to your Address Book. If you need to send only a few e-mails to an address, you can just type the address directly into the To field on the message form.

To type an address into the Address Book, follow these steps:

1. **Click the Address Book icon on the Component bar or choose Tasks⇨Address Book.**

   The Address Book dialog box appears, as shown in Figure 3-1.

2. **Click New Contact.**

   The New Contact dialog box appears, as shown in Figure 3-2.

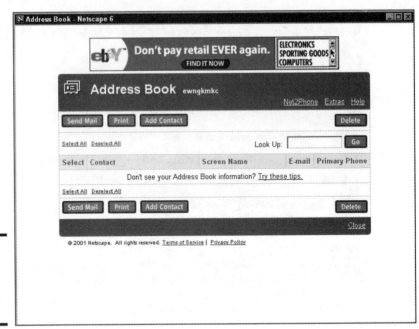

Figure 3-1:
The
Address
Book
dialog box.

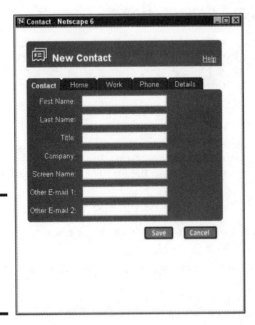

Figure 3-2:
Ready
to add
someone
to your
Address
Book?

3. **In the New Contact dialog box, fill in the relevant information about the individual.**

   You can use a nickname in the To field of a message in place of the lengthy e-mail address that it may represent. You can just type the nickname, which is always easier to remember, and let Mail convert the nickname into an e-mail address.

   You're also able to fill out additional information about the person by clicking the other tabs.

4. **Click Save.**

   A dialog box appears asking whether you'd like to remember the values you entered in the Address Book.

5. **Click Yes.**

   You now have a new entry in your Address Book.

If you hate typing e-mail addresses, then you're in luck. With Mail, all you have to do is wait until someone sends you an e-mail, and then you can shuffle the address straight into your Address Book without typing so much as one letter. Simply click the person's e-mail address and supply the requested information in the New Contact dialog box that appears, as described in Steps 2 and 3.

Importing addresses from somewhere else

To import the addresses in an address book created elsewhere, follow these steps:

1. **Choose T̲asks➪T̲ools➪Import Uti̲lity.**

   The Mail Import Wizard appears, as shown in Figure 3-3.

**Book II
Chapter 3**

Composing
E-Mail with
Netscape Mail

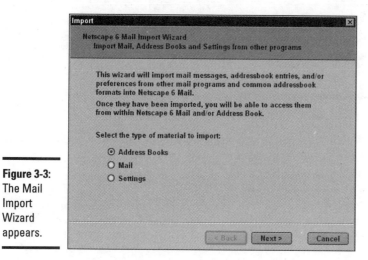

Figure 3-3:
The Mail
Import
Wizard
appears.

2. **Follow the wizard's on-screen instructions to import your Address Book.**

Finding a recipient's e-mail address

Here's how you use directory information from within Mail to look up a long lost pal's e-mail address:

1. **Choose Search➪People Finder.**

   The White Pages window opens, as shown in Figure 3-4.

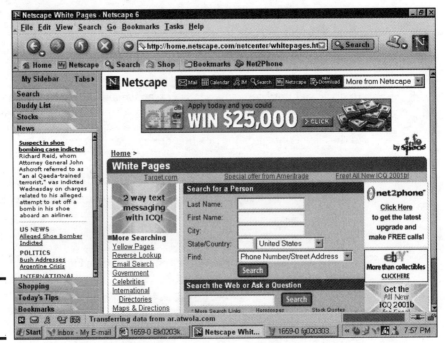

Figure 3-4: Looking for someone?

2. **Type your friend's name in the Last Name and First Name text boxes.**

3. **If you know your friend's city, state, and country, type them as well.**

   If you don't know where your friend lives, you have the option of locating his or her phone number and address in the Find box.

4. **From the Find drop-down list, choose Email Address.**

5. **Click Search.**

   If any matches appear, they'll be listed. Otherwise, you'll see a screen that tells you no one was found that matches the parameters you specified.

Responding to Incoming E-Mail

To check for e-mail, click Get Mail on the Mail toolbar.

To read your e-mail, follow these steps:

1. **Click the Get Mail button on the toolbar to begin downloading your new mail from the mail server to your Inbox.**

   A status window shows the progress of the download and tells you when the download has been completed.

   You see all the messages within the Inbox folder. New messages appear in bold type, with the New Message icon next to the folder names.

2. **Select the message that you want to read by clicking the subject text.**

   The message opens in a new window, begging you to read its text.

3. **To read the next unread message in the Inbox, click the Next button on the Mail toolbar.**

To reply to an e-mail message, follow these steps:

1. **Click the message to which you want to reply by clicking it once on the subject line.**

   The message opens.

2. **Click Reply to send your reply only to the sender of the message.**

   Click Reply All to send your reply to all recipients of that message. In other words, everybody who was on the To and Cc fields of the original message gets copies of your reply if you click Reply All.

3. **Type the text of your message in the text area of the Type Your Message Here window.**

4. **Click Send.**

If the message you received is so interesting that you want to share it with others, you can forward it to them. To forward a message, follow these steps:

1. **Open the message that you want to forward by clicking the subject text.**

2. **Click Forward to send the message to the person of your choice.**

3. **In the To field, type the e-mail address of the person to whom you want to forward the message.**

4. **Type any text that you'd like to include above the forwarded message.**

5. **Click Send.**

Composing E-Mail Messages

When you feel like you have information that you want to share with someone, take a few moments to think about what you want to say and then follow these steps to write and send your message:

1. **Click the Write Mail button on the Mail toolbar.**

   The Compose a Message window appears, as shown in Figure 3-5.

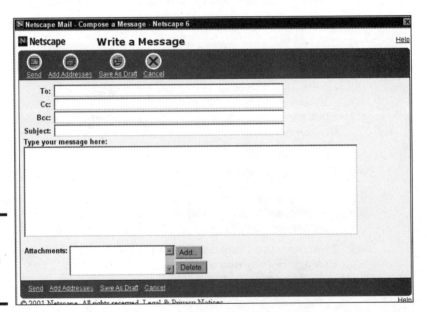

Figure 3-5:
The
Compose a
Message
window.

2. **Type the e-mail address of the person you're sending the message to in the To field.**

   When the time comes to address your e-mail, save time by using the addresses and mailing list groupings in your Address Book or by typing the nickname.

3. **Type a brief description of the message in the Subject field to give your reader some indication of what your message is about (and, consequently, whether he or she wants to read the message).**

4. Type the text of the message in the message composition area.

5. Click Send.

Drafting a message

At times, you may sit down to compose a message, get halfway through it, and get interrupted to attend to something else. Rather than send an incomplete message or close the message and start all over again later, you can save the message as a draft. You can then edit the draft at any time. Here's how you create a draft:

1. **Click the Write Mail button in the Mail toolbar to begin creating a message.**

2. **Begin writing your message.**

3. **Click Save As Draft.**

The message is saved in the Drafts folder.

4. **Click OK.**

**Book II
Chapter 3**

Composing
E-Mail with
Netscape Mail

Okay, so you got halfway through a message, saved it as a draft, and now want to continue where you left off. Here's how you do that:

1. **Click the Draft tab.**

All the messages in the Draft folder appear.

2. **Double-click the message on which you want to work.**

The message opens in the Composition window. You can now continue where you left off. When you're ready to send the message, just click Send.

Attaching a file to an e-mail message

Sending plain text e-mail messages can get boring after a while. Thank goodness Mail enables you to liven things up by sending pictures, word-processing files, Web pages, and other files attached to your messages. You can even attach more than one file to a message.

Some e-mail services and e-mail software have limitations on the size of the attachments that you can send. Check with the recipient about such limitations before sending a file. If possible, use compression software (such as PKZip or WinZip) to compress files and package several files into a single file prior to sending them. Compressing files makes them smaller and, thereby, faster to send.

To attach a file to a message, follow these steps:

1. **Click the Write Mail button on the Mail toolbar to begin composing a message.**

2. **Fill in the relevant information, such as the address of the person you're sending the message to and the text of the message.**

3. **Next to the Attachments area, click the Add button.**

   The Attach a File dialog box appears, as shown in Figure 3-6.

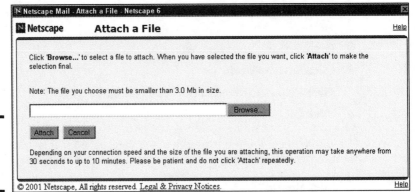

Figure 3-6:
The Attach
a File
dialog box.

4. **Click Browse to find the file you want to attach and then click Open to return to the Attach a File dialog box.**

5. **Click Attach and wait patiently.**

   How long you have to wait depends on the size of the file that you're attaching.

Telling Mail What to Do When Someone Can't Receive HTML Messages

By default, Mail is set up for handling HTML messages, which are also called rich text messages. Everything should be working fine — unless someone can't receive this type of message. If you want to change your settings just in case, follow these steps to instruct Mail what to do:

1. **Choose Edit⇨Preferences.**

   The Preferences dialog box appears, as shown in Figure 3-7.

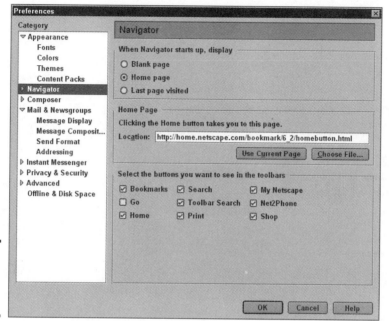

Book II
Chapter 3

Composing
E-Mail with
Netscape Mail

Figure 3-7:
The
Preferences
dialog box.

2. **In the Category pane on the left side of the window, expand the Mail & Newsgroups heading by double-clicking it or clicking once on the arrow to the left of it.**

3. **Select the Send Format subheading within the Mail & Newsgroups heading.**

   The Send Format window appears.

4. **Select the option that tells Mail what it should do when your intended recipient can't receive messages in HTML format.**

5. **Click OK.**

Organizing Your Messages with Folders

A folder within Mail is much like a regular folder in your file cabinet in which you store bills, recipes, documents, and so on — except, in Mail, you store e-mail messages within folders. You can have a folder in which you store only messages related to your job and another for storing only messages from friends. You can have as many folders as you like. You can even create subfolders within your folders if you're the truly organized type.

Creating a new folder

To create a new folder, follow these steps:

1. In Mail, click the Folder tab.

A list of all your folders appears.

2. Click the New Folder button.

The Prompt dialog box appears, as shown in Figure 3-8.

Figure 3-8:
Ready to
create a
new folder?

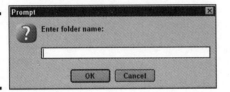

3. Enter the name of your folder and click OK.

Your new folder appears in the list.

Moving e-mail into a folder

To move e-mail into a folder, place a checkmark next to the message that you want to move and then find the folder in the Move Message To drop-down list. Your message moves to that folder.

Deleting and compacting your e-mail

After you decide that a message is no longer useful, you need to delete it. Place a checkmark next to the message and click the Delete button. The message disappears from your Inbox and reappears in your Trash folder. To permanently remove the message from your hard drive, simply click the Trash tab, click next to the message to add a checkmark next to it, and then click Empty Trash.

Deleting and renaming folders

Deleting a folder is easy if you follow these steps:

1. In Mail, click the Folders tab.

A list of all your folders appears.

2. Select the folder that you want to delete.

Remember that you can't delete the default folders.

3. **Click the Delete button.**

   You see a message asking you to confirm the deletion.

4. **Click OK.**

You can't delete the Inbox, Drafts, and Trash folders.

Renaming a folder takes all of 30 seconds; just follow these steps:

1. **In Mail, click the Folders tab.**

   A list of all your folders appears.

2. **Select the folder that you want to rename.**

3. **Click the Rename button.**

   The Prompt box asks you to `Enter a new name for the folder 'foldername'`.

4. **In the text box, type a new name for the folder; then click OK.**

   The folder appears in the folder list with its new name.

Printing a Message

To print an e-mail message, follow these steps:

1. **Double-click the message to open it.**

   Alternatively, you can print a message without opening it. You simply click to select it in the list of messages and then proceed to Step 2.

2. **Choose File⇨Print or click the Print button on the toolbar.**

   The Print dialog box opens.

3. **Specify any preferences that you want to use for this printing job, such as printing only specific pages or changing the number of copies that you want to print.**

4. **Click OK.**

Saving a Message to Your Hard Drive

At times, you may receive a message that you want to file away for future reference. To prevent accidentally deleting this message from your Mail folder, consider making a copy of it on your hard drive.

To save messages to your hard drive, follow these steps:

1. **Select the message from the message list by clicking it once.**
2. **Choose File⇨Save As.**
3. **Choose the location where you'd like to save the file.**
4. **Rename the file if necessary.**
5. **Click Save.**

   Your message is now saved on your computer.

Chapter 4: Other E-Mail Readers

In This Chapter

✔ **Using Eudora to manage e-mail**

✔ **Reading mail with Pine**

✔ **Using free e-mail from Juno**

✔ **Getting free e-mail through Hotmail**

✔ **Taking advantage of Yahoo! Mail**

*B*esides the two most common e-mail readers — Outlook Express and Netscape Mail (see Book II, Chapters 2 and 3, for more information on those programs) — several other e-mail readers are available to you. You may discover that one of them fits your needs better than either Outlook Express or Netscape Mail.

In this chapter, you find out how to use Eudora (for Windows and Mac users) and Pine (for Unix and Linux users), as well as how to subscribe to free e-mail readers, such as Juno, Hotmail, and Yahoo! Mail.

Using Eudora

Eudora is a popular e-mail program developed by Qualcomm, Inc. that you can use with any SLIP or PPP Internet account. It runs on Windows 95 or later or Windows NT 4.0 or greater and the Mac and is available at www.eudora. com. Eudora 5.1 can operate in three different modes — Sponsored, Light, and Paid:

✦ **Sponsored mode:** When you download the free version of Eudora 5.1, the program automatically installs in Sponsored mode. This is a full-featured version of Eudora that includes advertising.

✦ **Light mode:** After you install Eudora, you can switch to Light mode if you are upgrading from a previous version of Eudora Light. This mode includes no advertising, but offers fewer features than the Sponsored and Paid modes.

✦ **Paid mode:** This mode provides all the features available in Sponsored mode, without the advertising. The suggested retail price for this version is $49.95, less a $10 rebate offer for residents of the U.S. and Canada. Paid mode is free if you are upgrading from Eudora 4.*x*.

If you live in the United States or Canada and you want to protect your e-mail in Eudora from prying eyes, download the PGP encryption plug-in from www.pgp.com. (See Book I, Chapter 3, for more information about encryption.)

Configuring Eudora

After you install Eudora and restart your computer, double-click the Eudora icon to start the program. The first time you do so, the New Account Wizard displays and guides you through the process of setting up your e-mail account. (Click the Help button at any time if you need more information.)

If you already have another e-mail reader on your machine, the New Account Wizard may not open automatically. Instead, Eudora may ask whether you want to import settings from that e-mail program.

After you complete the wizard, you have to tell the program how to send your mail. Ask your Internet Service Provider (ISP) for the name of your SMTP server (for outgoing mail).

To configure Eudora, follow these steps:

1. **Choose Tools➪Options.**

   You see the Options dialog box, with a column of category icons or names down the left side.

2. **Click the Sending Mail icon.**

3. **In the SMTP Server text box, type the host name of your ISP's mail server.**

   Call your ISP if you don't know this information.

4. **Click OK to save your configuration settings.**

Getting incoming mail

To manually retrieve your incoming mail, follow these steps:

1. **Choose File➪Check Mail or click the Check Mail button.**

   If requested, enter your password and click OK.

   Eudora dials up your account (if you're not already connected) and downloads new mail to your computer.

2. **If you have mail, Eudora displays a message and alerts you with a sound; click OK to make the message go away.**

To set up Eudora to automatically check for and transfer incoming mail at set intervals, follow these steps:

1. **Choose Tools⇨Options.**

The Options dialog box displays.

2. **Click the Checking Mail icon.**

3. **In the Check for Mail Every X Minutes text box, type the interval at which you want Eudora to check for new mail.**

If the field is set to 0, you must manually retrieve your mail (according to the preceding steps).

4. **Click OK.**

**Book II
Chapter 4**

**Other E-Mail
Readers**

Eudora can create filters that automatically check incoming messages against a list of senders and subjects and file them in appropriate mailboxes. Choose Tools⇨Filters, click the New button, and fill in the requested information. Press F1 if you need help.

Reading incoming mail

To read your incoming mail, follow these steps:

1. **Start Eudora; any new mail is displayed in the In folder.**

If you don't see a list of mail, choose Mailbox⇨In or press Ctrl+1.

2. **To read a message, double-click it in the list.**

The message opens in a window.

3. **(Optional) To add this person's address to your Eudora address book, choose S Address Book Entry.**

4. **When you finish reading the message, close its window.**

Sending new mail

When you want to send an e-mail, follow these steps:

1. **Choose Message⇨New Message or click the New Message button.**

Eudora opens a new message window.

2. **Type the recipient's e-mail address on the To line.**

3. **Press Tab to move to the Subject line; then type the subject.**

4. **Press Tab a few more times to skip the Cc and Bcc lines or fill in these lines with the addresses of people who should get courtesy copies or blind copies of the message.**

5. In the large text area, type your message.

6. To send the message, click the button in the upper-right corner of the message window which, depending on how Eudora is configured, is marked Send or Queue.

   If you click Send, Eudora sends the message immediately. If you click Queue, your message is stashed in your Outbox folder for transmission later, when you connect to your Internet provider.

Replying to messages

To reply to an e-mail that you received, follow these steps:

1. After reading a message, choose Message⇨Reply or click the Reply button.

   Eudora opens a message window with the recipient's address filled in and the recipient's message displayed.

   To reply to all persons listed in the original message header, choose Message⇨Reply to All or click the Reply All button.

2. Type your reply.

   Be sure to edit the original message so that only the important parts remain.

3. To send the message, click the button in the upper-right corner of the window labeled Send or Queue.

Forwarding messages

To forward an e-mail message to another person, follow these steps:

1. After reading a message, choose Message⇨Forward or click the Forward button.

   Eudora opens a message window with the current message displayed. Each line is preceded with a gray bar.

2. Type the recipient's e-mail address.

3. Edit the original message or type more text, if you want.

4. To send the message, click the button in the upper-right corner of the window labeled Send or Queue.

Saving messages

To save a message into a specified mailbox, follow these steps:

1. **Select the message by bringing its window to the front or by clicking its line in the In window.**

2. **Choose Transfer; then choose a mailbox from the menu.**

You can create additional mailboxes by choosing Transfer⇨New.

Reading saved messages

To read a message that you saved in a mailbox, follow these steps:

1. **Choose Mailbox; then select the mailbox that you want.**

2. **Double-click the message in the mailbox window that appears.**

Attaching a file

To attach a file to an e-mail message, follow these steps:

1. **Compose the message as usual.**

   You can compose a new message by clicking the New Message button, or you can reply to or forward a message by clicking the appropriate button.

2. **Choose Message⇨Attach File.**

3. **In the Attach File dialog box, choose the directory and filename of the file you want to attach and click Open.**

   In the message window's toolbar, the third box from the left shows which kind of encoding Eudora plans to use. The box usually displays MIME, indicating that the file will be sent as a MIME attachment.

4. **(Optional) To change the type of encoding, click the drop-down arrow in the Encoding box and choose a different type (BinHex or Uuencode).**

5. **Send the message as usual.**

The contents of the attached file don't appear as part of the message. The file is "stapled" to the message but remains separate. If you change your mind about attaching the document, click the filename in the message header and press the Delete key to delete it.

Incoming attachments are automatically saved to files, and the name and location of each saved file are shown at the end of the message. Eudora also shows the file as an icon that you can double-click to open.

Using Pine

Pine is (in our humble opinion) the best mail reader for Unix systems. Versions of Pine are also available for GNU/Linux and MS-DOS operating systems. Like most Unix programs, Pine uses commands that are single keystrokes — no mouse, no muss, no fuss.

Running Pine

To run (and then quit) Pine, follow these steps:

1. **To run Pine, type** pine.

   You see the Pine main menu. Type **?** for help.

2. **When you're done with Pine, press** q **to quit.**

   Pine asks whether you really, really want to quit.

3. **Press** y **to leave.**

   If you left messages in your inbox that you have read but not deleted, Pine asks whether you want to move the messages to your read-messages folder — press **y** or **n**. If you deleted messages, Pine asks whether you really want to delete them. Again, press **y** or **n**.

Reading incoming mail

To read incoming mail in Pine, follow these steps:

1. **Press** i **to see the messages in the current folder, which is usually the Incoming folder.**

2. **To read a message, move the highlight to it and press** v **(for view) or Enter.**

3. **To delete the current message, press** d**. To go to the next message without deleting this one, press** n**.**

4. **When you finish reading messages, press** m **to return to the main menu.**

Sending new mail

To send a new e-mail message, follow these steps:

1. **Press** c **to compose a message.**

   You see a blank message.

2. **Enter the addresses and the subject line.**

3. **If you want to attach a file to a message, type the filename on the Attchmnt: (attachment) line.**

   Or, if you don't feel like typing, move the cursor to the Attchmnt: line, press ^t, find the file on your computer, and attach it.

4. **Type the text of the message.**

5. **When you want to send the message, press Ctrl+X.**

   Pine asks whether you really want to send the message.

6. **Press y.**

7. **Press s to send the message. Press n if you don't want to send it.**

   Pine sends the message and displays the main menu again.

   If you've reconsidered sending the message, you can press Ctrl+C to delete the message.

   Depending on your version of Pine, you may not have to do Step 7. In Version 4.21, for example, when you press **y** in Step 6, the message is sent and you return to the last screen you were viewing before you opted to write a message.

Book II
Chapter 4

Other E-Mail
Readers

Replying to messages

To reply to a message, follow these steps:

1. **Display the message onscreen.**

2. **Press r.**

   You see the same screen that you see when you're composing a new message, with the address and subject filled in.

3. **Edit the message and send the reply the same way as you send a new message.**

   (See the preceding section, "Sending new mail.")

Forwarding messages

To forward a message to someone else, follow these steps:

1. **Display the message onscreen.**

2. **Press f to forward the message.**

   You see the same screen that you see when you're composing a new message, with the subject and text of the message filled in.

3. **Edit and send the message the same way that you send a new message.**

   (See "Sending new mail," earlier in this section.)

Saving messages to a file

To save an e-mail message, follow these steps:

1. **Display the message onscreen.**

2. **Press e (for export).**

   Pine asks for the filename in which to save the message (it puts the file in your home directory).

3. **Type the filename and press Enter.**

Free E-Mail with Juno

Juno is a service that lets you send and receive e-mail from the Internet — *for free!* You just have to put up with the ads that Juno displays while you're reading your mail, and you have to be in the United States. Unlike other free e-mail services, Juno does not require that you have Internet access. You need a computer that can run Windows 95 or later or NT 4.0 or greater, as well as a 9,600 bps or faster modem (14,400 is recommended). Juno has more than 2,300 access numbers throughout the United States. You have to pay for any long-distance telephone charges if you can't connect through a local access number.

Getting and installing Juno software

To use Juno, you have to install special Juno software on your PC. This chapter describes Juno Version 5.0 with the free Juno basic service. You can download the Juno software from www.juno.com or borrow the CD from a friend who has Juno — the company encourages this method. Juno mails you a disc if you call 800-654-JUNO (in the United States), but this disc isn't free.

To install Juno, follow these steps:

1. **Follow the directions that come with Juno or double-click the file** junoinst.exe.

2. **Make sure that your modem is turned on and not in use or that your LAN or cable connection to the Internet is working.**

3. **Click the Create New Account button to set up your user profile.**

   You can choose between Juno basic service (e-mail only, for free) or Juno Web (e-mail and Juno as your ISP, for about $10 per month).

Juno asks you to answer roughly 20 questions about your tastes, interests, and demographics to help it select which advertisements to show you. Juno says: "While we make available to our advertisers a great deal of statistical information about our member base, we never share information about any individual member without that member's permission." Permission can be implied by your responses to ads, however.

Reading incoming mail

To check for incoming mail, follow these steps:

1. **To see whether you have new mail, make sure that your modem is turned on and not in use.**

2. **Start Juno and click Yes in the Check for New Mail dialog box.**

If Juno is already running, click the Get New Mail button on the Read tab.

If you have outgoing mail waiting to be sent, Juno asks whether you want to send it while you're online. When Juno is finished getting your mail, it displays a count of what it received (and sent).

3. **Click Close.**

If you have e-mail waiting for you, you see a count of how many unread messages are in the folder information window. A scrolling list of messages appears below that, showing the sender, subject, date, and status of each message.

4. **Click a listed message to see its text in the lower-right part of the Juno window.**

Composing and sending new mail

Normally, you compose messages on your computer and then dial in to Juno to send them.

To compose a message and send it, follow these steps:

1. **Start Juno and click the Write tab.**

2. **Type the recipient's Internet address or alias in the Send To box.**

3. **If you want, type additional recipients' Internet addresses or aliases in the Cc box.**

4. **Fill in the Subject box.**

5. **Type your message in the large text box.**

You can send an attachment by using the Attach File button.

6. **Click the Spell Check button if you want to check your spelling.**

7. **Click the Send Mail button.**

   You can either save the message in your Outbox for later transmission by clicking Put Message in Outbox, or click Get and Send Mail Now for immediate gratification.

   If you decide not to send a message that you've composed, click the Clear button rather than the Send Mail button.

If you want to keep a copy of all the messages you send, choose Options⇨ E-mail Options from the Juno menu and select Save All Sent Mail. Otherwise, Juno discards outgoing mail after sending it.

Using the address book

Juno gives you a personal address book that can automatically store the addresses of everyone who sends you e-mail. To open the address book, click the Address Book button on the Read or Write tab. In the Address Book window, click the New Name button to add an entry. Juno asks for the person's first name, last name, e-mail address, and an alias. You use the alias in the Send To or Cc field as a nickname in place of the person's e-mail address. When you're finished looking at the address book, click OK.

When you're composing a message or addressing a message that you're forwarding, click the Address Book button, select a name, and click the Add buttons under Send To and Cc. Juno automatically enters the person's address in the appropriate field of your message. Click OK to return to your message.

You can sort the address book by name, e-mail address, or alias by clicking the gray bar at the top of the appropriate column. To create a list of people to whom you send messages, enter each person into the address book, click New List, and choose the people to include on the list.

Replying to messages

To reply to an e-mail message, follow these steps:

1. **When you're reading a message, click the Reply button.**

2. **Choose whether you want your reply to go to only the sender or to all recipients. Select whether Juno should include in your reply the text of the original message.**

   Juno displays a new message window, with the address and subject lines already filled in. If you asked to include the original message, it appears preceded by the address of sender.

3. **(Optional) Type your reply and click the Spell Check button.**

4. **Click the Send Mail button.**

Forwarding messages

To forward a message to another person, follow these steps:

1. **When you finish reading the message, click the Forward button.**

   Juno displays a new message window with the subject already filled in. The original message appears at the bottom of the window.

2. **Type the address of the recipient in the To box.**

3. **Type any additional text that you want to include.**

4. **Click the Send Mail button.**

Saving messages in a folder

To save a message into a folder, follow these steps:

1. **When you finish reading the message, click the Move to Folder button.**

2. **Select an existing folder or create a new one by typing its name in the Move Message Into box.**

3. **Click OK.**

The Copy to Folder button lets you save a message in more than one folder. To read the messages in a folder, choose its name from the Folder drop-down list.

Free E-Mail with Hotmail

Hotmail is another free e-mail service supported by advertising. As long as you have Internet access and a Web browser, such as Internet Explorer, you can use Hotmail anytime and anywhere. You don't need any special e-mail software. And because Hotmail e-mail is Web based, you can access your e-mail from any computer. Even more, you can get multiple e-mail accounts for free.

In addition, if you're one of those people who frequently changes Internet Service Providers, you may want to consider Hotmail or another Web-based e-mail program. No matter how many times you change ISPs, your e-mail address is always the same. (Your friends will thank you.)

Getting started with Hotmail

Signing up with Hotmail is easy. Just launch your Web browser, and go to www.hotmail.com (see Figure 4-1).

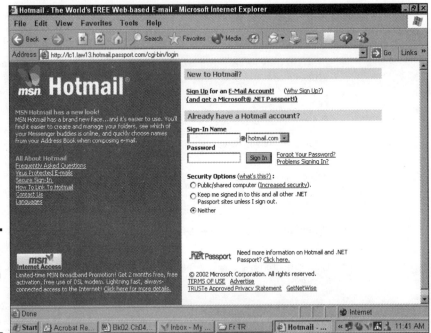

Figure 4-1:
Go to www. hotmail.com to sign up for free e-mail.

If you already have a Hotmail account, simply type your sign-in name and password and click Sign In. You're ready to e-mail!

If you're a new user, follow these steps:

1. **Click <u>Sign Up</u>.**

   The Registration page appears.

2. **Complete the registration screen and then click Sign Up.**

   If you chose a sign-in name that is already taken, you're asked to choose another one. If you're determined to create your own sign-in name because you don't like any of the suggestions offered, keep in mind that it may take you several attempts to succeed.

   After you've successfully chosen your new sign-in name, the Sign Up Successful screen appears.

3. **Click Continue at Hotmail.**

   The Terms of Service page appears.

4. **Read over the terms and click I Accept or I Decline.**

   If you click I accept, a page giving you the option between paid e-mail and free e-mail appears.

5. **Click Free E-Mail.**

   You're invited to sign up for free WebCourier subscriptions.

6. **Click the subscriptions that you're interested in and then click Continue.**

   A new screen appears, confirming the subscriptions that you chose. If you're not interested in any subscriptions, don't click any subscriptions.

7. **Click the Continue to E-Mail button.**

   You're ready to use your e-mail account.

Using the address book

Want to send a message fast? Use the address book. Enter the recipient's information once, and you don't have to do it again (unless, of course, your friend gets a new e-mail address).

The address book holds as much information about a person as you want to enter — but most importantly, it contains her e-mail address so that you only have to type her name when you're ready to send a message.

To add a person to your address book, follow these steps:

1. **Click the Address Book tab.**

   The Address Book appears, as shown in Figure 4-2.

2. **Click the Individuals tab.**

   If you're adding addresses for a group, click the Group tab.

3. **Click Create New.**

   The Create New Individual screen appears.

4. **Type the information into the text boxes and then click OK.**

   Make sure that you enter information into the categories that appear next to an asterisk; these areas are required fields.

5. **Click OK.**

   This person's information is now in your address book.

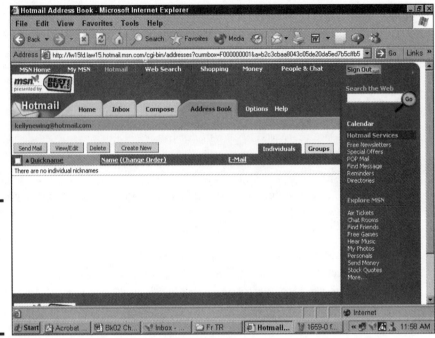

Figure 4-2:
Adding
addresses
to your
address
book saves
you time
and effort.

If the person that you'd like to add to your address book has sent you an e-mail, simply open the message, click Save Address(es) and then click OK. The address is in your address book — and you didn't have to type anything!

Reading incoming mail

Reading mail is easy. Simply click Inbox, click the sender's name for the message that you want to see and read the message that appears.

Composing and sending mail

If you've got big news you want to share, Hotmail lets you write and send e-mail quickly and efficiently. Follow these steps:

1. **Click the Compose tab.**

2. **Type the recipient's name or e-mail address in the To box and add a subject if you want.**

3. **Type your message in the blank box in the middle of the screen.**

4. **When you're finished writing your message, click Send.**

   A Sent Message Confirmation appears.

5. **Click OK to acknowledge the confirmation.**

Replying to and forwarding messages

If a message is on-screen and you want to respond to it, simply click the Reply button. You see the same screen that appears when you create new mail. Simply type your response and click Send. Again, a Sent Message Confirmation appears (unless you turned off that option).

Likewise, if you have a message open and you want to forward it to a friend, click the Forward button (instead of the Reply button) and type the recipient's name. Then follow the same steps that you used to reply to a message.

Saving messages in a folder

If you receive lots of e-mail or if you signed up for a bunch of WebCourier subscriptions, you may find that using folders to organize your Inbox is a wonderful idea.

To create a folder, follow these steps:

1. **Click the Create Folder button.**

2. **Type the new folder name and click OK.**

   Congratulations! Your new folder appears in the folder list.

To actually use your new folder, follow these steps:

1. **In the Inbox, click to place a check mark in the box next to the message that you want to move.**

   You can click to select more than one box and move multiple messages at one time.

2. **From the Put in Folder drop-down list, choose the name of the folder that you want to move the message into.**

   Your message no longer appears in your Inbox; it now appears in its new home.

Free E-Mail with Yahoo! Mail

Yahoo! Mail is another free e-mail service supported by advertising. Like Hotmail (discussed in preceding section), Yahoo! Mail is Web-based, so you can access your e-mail from any computer that has Internet access and a Web browser.

Like Hotmail, your Yahoo! Mail account remains the same address no matter how many times you switch ISPs.

If you sign up for any Yahoo! service, you also gain access to all other Yahoo! services, including Mail and Messenger. (See the section "Instant messaging with Yahoo! Messenger," later in this chapter, to find out how to use the Messenger feature.)

Getting started with Yahoo! Mail

Yahoo! Mail is extremely user-friendly, and you'll be up and running in no time. To sign up for Yahoo! Mail, follow these steps:

1. **Go to** www.yahoo.com.

The familiar Yahoo! home page appears.

2. **Click the Check Email icon at the top of the page.**

You're prompted to sign up for Yahoo! Mail or to sign in.

3. **If you're a new user, click Sign Up Now to obtain a user ID and password; otherwise, type your Yahoo! ID and password to sign in.**

If you've not used the Yahoo! e-mail service before, you're first asked to choose the type of service you want: Free, Custom, or Business.

4. **Click Sign Me Up! in the Free Edition box.**

5. **Complete the registration form, shown in Figure 4-3, and then click Submit This Form.**

If someone has already chosen your name, you're asked to select another.

After you've successfully chosen a name and password, you see the Yahoo! Mail welcome screen.

6. **Select any newsletters and special offers you'd like and then click Continue to Yahoo! Mail.**

You don't have to select any newsletters or offers if you don't want to.

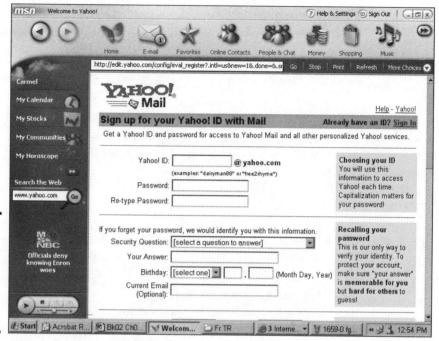

Figure 4-3:
Complete
this form for
your free
Yahoo!
e-mail
account.

Using the address book

Using the Yahoo! Mail address book, like everything else in Yahoo! Mail, is
fairly intuitive.

To add an address to your address book, follow these steps:

1. **Click Addresses.**

Your address book appears.

2. **Click the New Contact button.**

The Add Contact screen appears.

3. **Complete the contact information for the person you want to add to
your address book; then click Save.**

Congratulations! You've made your first addition to your address book.

Reading incoming mail

To read incoming mail, simply click Check Mail. Your messages appear in
your Inbox window. Then click the Subject column of the message you'd like
to read. Your message appears on-screen.

Composing and sending new mail

If you can't wait to send your first message, get ready — composing and sending mail is just a click away. Simply click Compose, add your recipient's e-mail address and a subject, and type your message. Then click Send, and you're done. You even receive a confirmation saying that your message has been sent.

Replying to and forwarding messages

If your message is open on-screen, you're just a step away from replying to or forwarding your message. If you want to send a reply to the sender, click the Reply button, type your message, and click Send. If multiple people appear on the original e-mail and you want to reply to everyone, click the Reply All button.

To forward a message that you have open on-screen, click the Forward button, type the address of the person you want to forward it to, and click the Send button.

Saving messages in a folder

If you're an organization freak, you won't be able to tolerate your Inbox unless you set up folders. Fortunately, Yahoo! Mail makes that task a simple one.

To set up folders for storing your messages, follow these steps:

1. **Click Folders.**

A list of the default folders provided by Yahoo! Mail appears, as shown in Figure 4-4.

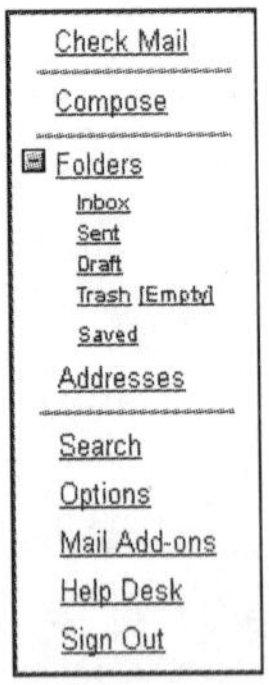

Check Mail

Compose

⊟ Folders
   Inbox
   Sent
   Draft
   Trash [Empty]
   Saved

Addresses

Search

Options

Mail Add-ons

Help Desk

Sign Out

Figure 4-4:
You need
some more
folders!

2. **In the Folder Name text box under Create a Personal Folder, type a new folder name and click the Create Folder button.**

This new folder appears in your folder list.

To move a message into a folder, simply click the box to the left of the message you want to move, choose the folder into which you want to move it, and click Move. Your message disappears from your Inbox and appears in the folder.

Instant messaging with Yahoo! Messenger

After you sign up for Yahoo! Mail, you have access to all its services, including Yahoo! Messenger. This instant messaging service enables you to send messages back and forth to your friends in real time. To use Messenger, you first need to download its software. To download the Messenger software, follow these steps:

1. **From the Yahoo! home page, click the Messenger icon at the top.**

   You're taken to the Messenger page.

2. **Click the appropriate format (Windows , Macintosh, and so on) for the Messenger software that you want to download.**

   The program starts downloading automatically.

3. **Click the Next button as necessary to continue the installation.**

4. **When the Install Options page appears, click Install Yahoo! Messenger Only and then click Next.**

5. **Read the terms that appear; then, assuming that you agree to them, click I Accept.**

   The Select Destination Directory dialog box appears.

6. **Accept the default directory by clicking Next.**

7. **Continue clicking Next.**

   Messenger quickly installs.

To send an instant message after you're online, follow these steps:

1. **Click the Messenger icon at the top of the Yahoo! home page.**

2. **Click Invite a Friend to Use Messenger.**

   The Invite a Friend to Use Messenger Window appears.

3. **Complete the information and click Invite Friend.**

   You're ready to start talking.

If you're shy, are feeling unsociable, or just don't want to be bothered, try out Messenger's Invisible Mode. You can still send and receive messages in real time, but your name doesn't show up for everyone to see. Simply choose Login⇨Change My Status⇨Invisible Mode.

Chapter 5: Mailing Lists

In This Chapter

- ✔ **Finding a mailing list**
- ✔ **Getting on and off a mailing list**
- ✔ **Sending messages to a mailing list**
- ✔ **Receiving mailing-list messages**
- ✔ **Starting your own mailing list**
- ✔ **Using filters**

An e-mail *mailing list* offers a way for people with a shared interest to send messages to each other and hold a group conversation. Mailing lists differ from newsgroups in that a separate copy of the mailing list message is e-mailed to each recipient on the list. Mailing lists are generally smaller and more intimate than newsgroups. Lists can be very specific, tend to be less raucous, and are less infested with spam.

Imagine a mailing list that would keep you up to date in an area vital to your work or one that would let you exchange views with people who share your fondest passions. That list probably already exists. We give you hints on how to find it and how to start it if it doesn't exist.

Addresses Used with Mailing Lists

Each mailing list has its own e-mail address; on most lists, anything sent to that address is remailed to all the people on the list. People on the list respond to messages and create a running conversation. Some lists are *moderated,* which means that a reviewer (moderator) skims messages and decides which to send out.

Every mailing list, in fact, has *two* e-mail addresses:

- ✦ **List address:** Messages sent to this address are forwarded to all the people who subscribe to the list.

- ✦ **Administrative address:** Only the list's owner reads messages sent to this address. Use it for messages about subscribing and unsubscribing. Messages to the administrative address often are processed entirely by a computer, called a *mailing list server, list server,* or *MLM* (mailing list manager). In that case, you have to type your message in a specific format, as described throughout this chapter. ***Note:*** This address may also be called the *request address.*

For matters such as subscribing to or unsubscribing to a list, always send e-mail to the administrative address, not to the list address. If you use the list address, everyone on the list sees your request *except* for the person or computer that needs to act on it. Proper use of the administrative address is the most important thing you need to know about using mailing lists.

You can usually figure out the administrative address if you know the list address:

✦ **Manually maintained lists:** Add *request* to the list address. If a manual list is named `unicycles@blivet.com`, for example, the administrative address is almost certainly `unicycles-request@blivet.com`.

✦ **Automatically maintained lists:** The administrative address is usually the name of the type of list server program at the host where the list is maintained. Look for the server name in a message header to determine how a list is maintained. The most common list server programs are ListProc, LISTSERV, Mailbase, Lyris, and Majordomo.

✦ **Web-based lists:** A number of companies run Web sites that host mailing lists for free in exchange for placing an ad at the end of each message. These firms accept administrative requests at their Web site, and some allow you to read list messages and archives there, too. Popular Web-based list servers include

```
www.coollist.com
groups.yahoo.com
www.topica.com
```

Some mailing list servers don't care whether your administrative request is in uppercase or lowercase — others may care. In this chapter, we show all commands in uppercase, which generally works with all servers.

Finding a Mailing List

An excellent Web site that maintains extensive indexes to mailing lists is `paml.taronga.com`.

In many cases, the best way to find out about mailing lists is to ask colleagues and friends who share your interests. Many lists are informally maintained and are not indexed anywhere.

Subscribing and Unsubscribing

The way you subscribe and unsubscribe depends on how the list is maintained. Subscribing to a mailing list (unlike subscribing to a magazine) is almost always free.

Lists maintained manually

Send a mail message (such as "Please add me to the unicycles list" or "Please remove me from the unicycles list") to the administrative address. Keep these tips in mind:

**Book II
Chapter 5**

✦ Include your real name and complete e-mail address so that the poor list owner doesn't have to pick through your e-mail header.

✦ Because humans read the messages, no fixed form is required.

✦ Be patient. The person maintaining the list is probably a volunteer and may have a life — or be trying to get one.

Mailing Lists

Lists maintained automatically

To join a list, send an e-mail message to its administrative address with no subject and the following line as the body of the message:

```
SUBSCRIBE listname your-name
```

Replace *listname* with the name of the mailing list, and *your-name* with your actual name. You don't have to include your e-mail address because it's automatically included as your message's return address. For example, George W. Bush would type the following line to subscribe to the leader_support mailing list:

```
SUBSCRIBE leader_support George W. Bush
```

✦ For Mailbase lists, replace SUBSCRIBE with JOIN.

✦ For Majordomo lists, don't include your name.

To get off a list, send e-mail to its administrative address with no subject and the following line as the body of the message:

```
UNSUBSCRIBE listname
```

The command SIGNOFF works with most mailing lists too.

For Mailbase lists, replace UNSUBSCRIBE with LEAVE.

When you're subscribing to a list, be sure to send your message from the e-mail address to which you want list messages mailed. The administrator of the list uses your message's return address as the address he adds to the mailing list.

When you first subscribe to a list, you generally receive a welcome message via e-mail. Keep this message! You may want to keep a file of these messages because they tell you what type of server is being used and how to unsubscribe.

Many list servers e-mail you back for confirmation before processing your request. If you plan to unsubscribe from a bunch of lists before going on vacation — a good idea to keep your mailbox from overflowing — be sure to allow enough time to receive and return the confirmation requests.

Web-based lists

You usually join or leave Web-based lists by going to the list company's Web site, although you can often use e-mail, too. Most services ask you to append `-subscribe` or `-unsubscribe` to the list name. For example, send e-mail to `gerbils-subscribe@onelist.com` to join the Gerbils list at ONElist.

Sending Messages to a Mailing List

To send a message to a mailing list, just e-mail it to the list's address. The message is automatically distributed to the list's members.

If you respond to a message with your mail program's Reply button, check to see — before you click Send — whether your reply will be sent to the list address. Edit out the list address if you're replying only to the message's author.

Some lists are moderated — in other words, a human being screens messages before sending them out to everybody else, which can delay messages by as much as a day or two. Mail servers usually send you copies of your own messages to confirm that they were received.

Special Requests to Mailing Lists

Depending on which list server manages a list, various other commands may be available. Read on to find out more about these commands.

Archives

Many mailing lists store their messages for later reference. To find out where these archives are kept, send the following message to the administrative address:

```
INDEX listname
```

Some lists make their archives available on a Web site: Read the message that you received when you joined the list.

Subscriber list

To get a list of (almost) all the people who subscribe to a list, you can send a message to the administrative address. The content of the message depends on the type of server the list uses. See Table 5-1.

**Book II
Chapter 5**

Mailing Lists

Table 5-1	Getting a List of Subscribers
Server	*Message*
ListProc	RECIPIENTS *listname*
LISTSERV	REVIEW *listname*
Mailbase	REVIEW *listname*
Mailserve	SEND/LIST *listname*
Majordomo	WHO *listname*

Privacy

ListProc and LISTSERV mail servers don't give out your name as just described if you send a message to the administrative address. To find out how to hide your name or show it again, see Table 5-2.

Table 5-2	Setting Your Privacy Preference	
Action	*Server*	*Message*
Conceal your name	ListProc LISTSERV	SET *listname* CONCEAL YES SET *listname* CONCEAL
Unconceal your name	ListProc LISTSERV	SET *listname* CONCEAL NO SET *listname* NOCONCEAL

Going on vacation

If you subscribe to a busy mailing list, you probably don't want mailing list messages to flood your inbox while you're on vacation. To stop messages from a list temporarily and continue receiving messages when you get back, see Table 5-3.

Table 5-3	**Managing Messages During Your Vacation**	
Action	*Server*	*Message*
Stop Messages Temporarily	ListProc	SET *listname* MAIL POSTPONE
	LISTSERV	SET *listname* NOMAIL
Resume receiving messages	ListProc	SET *listname* MAIL ACK or SET *listname* MAIL NOACK or SET *listname* MAIL DIGEST
	LISTSERV	SET *listname* MAIL

Open and Closed Mailing Lists

Most mailing lists are *open*, which means that anyone can send a message to the list. Some lists, however, are closed and accept messages only from subscribers. Other lists accept members by invitation only.

If you belong to a closed list and your e-mail address changes, you must let the list managers know so that they can update their database.

Receiving Digested Mailing Lists

As soon as you join a list, you automatically receive all messages from the list along with the rest of your mail.

Some lists are available in digest form with all the day's messages combined in a table of contents. To get the digest form, send an e-mail message to the list's administrative address with no subject and one of the lines shown in Table 5-4 as the body of the message. Table 5-4 also shows how to undo the digest request.

Table 5-4	**Digest Requests**	
Action	*Server*	*Message*
Receive digest form	ListProc	SET *listname* MAIL DIGEST
	LISTSERV	SET *listname* DIGEST
	Majordomo	SUBSCRIBE *listname*-digest, UNSUBSCRIBE listname
Undo digest request	ListProc	SET *listname* MAIL ACK
	LISTSERV	SET *listname* MAIL
	Majordomo	UNSUBSCRIBE *listname*-digest, SUBSCRIBE listname

Using Filters

Joining even one mailing list can overwhelm your e-mail inbox. Some e-mail programs can sort through your incoming mail and put mailing list messages in special mailboxes or folders that you can look at when you have time.

If you use Eudora, choose Tools⇨Filters, click New, click the Incoming check box, and then copy the From line from the mailing list message and paste it into the first `contains` box. (You also can use the second `contains` box if you want to specify another condition.) Then, in the Action section, specify the mailbox to which you want the messages transferred.

If you use Outlook Express, you can use the Rule Editor to organize your incoming e-mail messages. See Book 2, Chapter 2, for more information on setting up e-mail rules.

Starting Your Own Mailing List

Maybe you've decided that you've got some extra time on your hands (don't you wish!), and you need a new hobby. Or maybe you want to promote your rock band, create a support group for parents, or share your expertise on a topic. Whatever the reason, starting a mailing list may be just what you need.

Here are some tips for starting a new mailing list:

✦ Before you start a new list, see "Finding a Mailing List," earlier in this chapter, to see whether a list that meets your needs already exists.

✦ You can start a simple manual list with nothing more than an e-mail program that supports distribution lists (such as Outlook Express, Netscape Messenger, or Eudora). When a message comes in, just forward it to the distribution list.

✦ Put manual distribution lists in the Bcc address field if you don't want every message to include all recipients' names in the header. You can put your own address in the To field, if you want.

✦ You will soon tire of administering your list manually. Some Internet Service Providers let you use their list server, or you can use one of the ad-supported, Web-based services (`www.coollist.com`, `groups.yahoo.com`, and `www.topica.com` are all popular). If someone in your group has a university affiliation, that person may be able to have the list maintained there for free.

✦ Creating a Web page for your list makes it easy to find by using the Internet's search engines.

✦ For public lists, inform the Web sites listed under "Finding a Mailing List" (earlier in this chapter) about your list. Each site has instructions for adding your new mailing list to their collections.

Index

Book III

Web Browsing with Internet Explorer 6

The 5th Wave   By Rich Tennant

"This afternoon, I want everyone to go online and find out all you can about Native American culture, history of the old west, and discount airfares to Hawaii for the two weeks I'll be on vacation."

Contents at a Glance

Chapter 1: Web Basics

The *World Wide Web* (or *WWW* or just *the Web*) is a system that uses the Internet to link vast quantities of information all over the world. At times, the Web resembles a library, newspaper, bulletin board, and telephone directory — all on a global scale. "The vision I have for the Web," says its inventor, Tim Berners-Lee, "is about anything being potentially connected to anything." Still very much a work in progress, the Web is destined to become the primary repository of human culture.

The Web has become the first place to look for answers to almost any question under the sun. This chapter explains all you need to know about the basics of the Web.

If your browser of choice is Netscape Navigator, check out Book IV after you review the Web basics in this chapter. Otherwise, if you're using Internet Explorer, continue with Chapter 2 in this minibook after you complete this chapter.

ABCs of the Web

To start using the World Wide Web, all you need is an Internet connection and a program called a Web browser, such as Internet Explorer or Netscape Navigator. A *Web browser* displays, as individual pages on your computer screen, the various types of information found on the Web and lets you follow the connections — called *hypertext links* — built into Web pages.

Here are some basic Web concepts:

✦ **Hypertext:** A type of electronic document that contains pointers to other documents. These links (often called *hyperlinks*) appear in a distinct color or are highlighted when your browser displays the document. When you click a hypertext link, your Web browser displays the document to which the link points, if the document is available.

✦ **Uniform Resource Locator (URL):** The standard format used for hypertext links on the Internet, such as `http://www.microsoft.com`. They're also called *URIs* (for Universal Resource Identifiers); in fact, the inventor of the Web, Tim Berners-Lee, prefers this term. For more information, see the next section, "Uniform Resource Locators (URLs)."

✦ **Web site:** A collection of Web pages devoted to a single subject or organization.

✦ **Webmaster:** The person in charge of a Web site.

✦ **Surfing:** The art and vice of bouncing from Web page to Web page in search of whatever.

Common Web browsers and the computer systems for which they're available include the following:

✦ **Internet Explorer:** A graphical browser, developed by Microsoft, that works with any SLIP or PPP account or with a direct connection to the Internet. Internet Explorer comes with new Macs and is built into Microsoft Windows. You can download Internet Explorer 6 for free from `www.microsoft.com`. (See Chapter 2 of this minibook to find out about browsing with Internet Explorer.)

✦ **Netscape Navigator:** A graphical browser developed by Netscape Communications Corporation (and now owned by America Online). As with Internet Explorer, Netscape works with a SLIP or PPP account or with a direct connection to the Internet. The browser is available in versions for Microsoft Windows, Unix, and the Macintosh. A free version is available for download at `home.netscape.com`. Navigator comes as part of Netscape 6.2, a suite of programs that includes a powerful HTML editor for making your own Web pages, an e-mail program, and a newsreader. (See Book IV for information on browsing with Netscape Navigator.)

✦ **Lynx:** A browser available on Unix systems and from Internet providers with Unix shell accounts. Because Lynx presents only the text portion of Web documents, it's handy for people with special needs or older computers that can't keep up with graphical browsers.

Web browsers can handle most, but not all, types of information found on the Net. You can add software called *plug-ins* and *ActiveX controls* to extend your browser's capabilities.

Uniform Resource Locators (URLs)

One of the key advances that Web technology brought to the Internet is the Uniform Resource Locator, or URL. URLs provide a single, standardized way of describing almost any type of information available in cyberspace. The URL tells you what kind of information it is (such as a Web page or an FTP file), what computer it's stored on, and how to find that computer.

URLs are typically long text strings that consist of three parts:

✦ The document access type followed by a colon and two slashes (://)

✦ The host name of the computer on which the information is stored

✦ The path to the file that contains the information

Table 1-1 describes the parts of the following URL:

```
http://www.microsoft.com/windows/ie/newuser/default.asp
```

Table 1-1	Parts of a URL
Example	*What It Indicates*
http	Indicates a hypertext document (a Web page)
www.microsoft.com	Indicates the host computer on which the Web page is stored (www indicates that the site is located on the World Wide Web)
/windows/ie/newuser/default.asp	Indicates the path and filename of the file

Be careful to type URLs exactly as they're written, and be especially cautious when you use uppercase and lowercase letters. Many Internet host computers run Unix, in which capitalization counts in directory names and filenames. To ensure proper capitalization, copy and paste URLs or use bookmarks or favorites whenever you can. (Refer to Chapter 2 of this minibook to find out how to use the Favorites feature in Internet Explorer. Book IV, Chapter 1, covers how to use bookmarks in Netscape Navigator.)

E-mail addresses are structured a bit differently than URLs. See Book II, Chapter 1, for more about e-mail addresses.

Some browsers can fill in missing information, such as the http:// prefix, if you leave it out. Some browsers go even further by letting you type **hungry minds** rather than the complete **http://www.hungryminds.com** to go to the Hungry Minds Web site. Typing the complete address may load the page a little more quickly, however. Because many companies use their corporate name as their host name, you can often type **sony**, for example, in the URL text box; press Enter; and expect to end up at the Sony Corporation Web site.

Common document access types include the following:

✦ **http:** For hypertext (the Web)

✦ **https:** For hypertext with a secure link

✦ **ftp:** For File Transfer Protocol files

✦ **gopher:** For Gopher files

✦ **mailto:** For e-mail addresses

The following list includes other mysterious things that you see in URLs:

✦ **.html** or **.htm:** The filename extension for a hypertext document; html stands for HyperText Markup Language, the set of codes used to build Web pages.

✦ **index.html** or **default.html:** The master page of a Web site (the actual file name depends on the server).

✦ **.txt:** A plain-text document without links or formatting.

✦ **.gif, .jpg, .jpeg, .mpg, .png,** and **.avi:** Pictures, graphics, or video. (Refer to Book VI, Chapter 3, for more information on these file formats.)

✦ **.mp3, .mid (MIDI), .wav, .snd,** and **.au:** Music files. You can even get a Walkman-size unit that accepts and plays these files. (See Book VI, Chapter 3, for more information on using these formats.)

✦ **.zip, .sit, .hqx, .gz, .tar,** and **.z:** Filename extensions for files that have been compressed to save downloading time.

✦ **.class:** A Java applet.

✦ **~george:** As suggested by the tilde (~) character, probably a Unix account belonging to someone with the account name of george.

✦ **www:** Short for World Wide Web.

Not all Web sites have www at the beginning of their host name. For example, net.gurus.com takes you to the Internet Gurus Web site — a neat site where you can find, among other things, updates to *The Internet For Dummies,* 8th Edition, published by Hungry Minds, Inc. (The book's authors, not the publisher, maintain the site.)

Finding Your Way around the Web

The Web displays pages of information with hypertext links that take you to other pages. Browsers usually **highlight the links** to make them easy to spot by using a different color for the item and underlining it. By default, the color of a text hyperlink that you've not yet followed is blue. If you return to a page after clicking hyperlinked text, the hyperlinked text color changes from blue to purple. You can customize the colors that a Web browser uses to indicate links to pages that you've already visited and links to pages that you have yet to view. (For information on customizing hyperlinks, see Chapter 4 of this minibook for Internet Explorer or see Book IV, Chapter 3, for Netscape Navigator.)

Some links are just areas you click inside an image or photograph. Currently, three different graphics file formats are used to display images on a Web page: GIF (Graphics Image Format), JPEG (Joint Photographic Experts Group), or PNG (Portable Network Graphics). You can always tell when one of these types of graphics contains a hyperlink and when it doesn't. Only graphics with hyperlinks cause your mouse pointer to assume the shape of a hand, as shown in Figure 1-1.

Graphic with hyperlink   Text with hyperlink

Figure 1-1:
Web pages
use both
text
hyperlinks
and
graphics
hyperlinks.

Here are some tips for using hyperlinks:

✦ On a system that uses windows and a mouse, and browsers such as Internet Explorer or Netscape Navigator, use the mouse to click the link. If the page doesn't fit on-screen, click the scroll bar (or drag the scroll box) to scroll up and down.

✦ On a text system, such as Lynx, press the up- and down-arrow keys to move the cursor to the link that you want and then press Enter.

✦ Many mail programs, including Eudora, automatically detect and high-light URLs in e-mail messages. You can activate these links by clicking them in the mail program.

You can bring up a page on your browser in ways other than following a link:

✦ Select a page from your browser's list of bookmarks or favorites.

✦ Type a URL in the address field on your browser's screen and press Enter.

✦ If you have the page stored as a file on a disk or CD-ROM on your computer, most browsers let you open it by choosing the File➪Open (or similar) command.

Web page components that appear in your browser can take on other functions, such as the following:

✦ **File items containing text, pictures, movies, or sound:** If your Web browser can handle the file, the browser displays or plays the file. If not, the browser just tells you about the file. If an image or element is missing, the browser displays a broken link icon.

✦ **Search query items that let you type one or more key words:** A Web page displays the results of your search.

✦ **Forms you fill out:** The answers are sent as a long URL when you click Done, Submit, or a similar button on the form.

✦ **Small computer programs called *Java applets*:** You download and run them on your computer. (See Book VI, Chapter 4, for more on Java tools.)

Web style versus Classic style

Just when the whole world finally got the hang of the rule of double-clicking to *open* a Windows object (such as a program, folder, or file icon) and single-clicking to *select* such an object, here comes Internet Explorer 5 and 6 with their Web style integration. Now all bets are off.

When you first install Internet Explorer, the program selects a Custom style of desktop integration. This converts all program, folder, and file icons that have been placed on the desktop into hyperlinks. Otherwise, it leaves all single-clicking and double-clicking mouse actions as normal. You can, however, modify the mouse actions for the Custom style by selecting Web-style desktop integration.

In Web-style mode, program, folder, and file icons look and act like hyperlinks on a Web page. In this topsy-turvy Windows world, you have to follow a new rule: Point to a Windows object to highlight (select) it; single-click a Windows object (such as a program, folder, or file icon) to open it.

If you have any amount of experience with the old style (what Microsoft refers to as the *Classic style*) of dealing with desktop icons, you'll find that this new system has its definite pros and cons:

✔ On the pro side, it's easier to launch desktop shortcuts and open folders in the My Computer window with a single click of the mouse.

✔ On the con side, it requires a light touch to select a group of folder or file icons when performing such routine tasks as copying or moving items to a new location on your computer system. Even after spending awhile using the Web-style integration mode, you may still occasionally click a file icon (thereby launching the application and opening the file itself) when you merely meant to select it. Remember, in Web-style integration mode, you select an object simply by hovering the mouse pointer over its icon without clicking the mouse button.

More ambiguous aspects of this new mouse technique for selecting desktop items become evident only when you try to select multiple desktop icons — for example, a series of files that you want to copy to another disk. Traditionally, when selecting a series of adjacent files in a list, you click the first file in the list to select it and then press and hold down the Shift key while you click (Shift+click) the last file to highlight the entire series. Likewise, when you select a series of nonadjacent files in a list, you press and hold down Ctrl while you click (Ctrl+click) each file separately.

With Web-style integration in force, the Shift+click technique becomes Shift+point, and Ctrl+click turns into Ctrl+point. For an adjacent list, this means that you must be patient enough to hover the mouse pointer over the first file icon until it's highlighted, and then press and hold down the Shift key as you position the mouse pointer over the last file icon in the list. And when selecting icons in a nonadjacent list, you must hold down the Ctrl key as you highlight each icon by positioning the mouse pointer over it.

Under the Web style integration, don't even think about clicking a folder or file icon with the I-beam pointer to insert a cursor and type in a new name. The only way to rename a folder or file is to right-click its icon (which doesn't select it) and then choose the Rename command on the icon's shortcut menu. Choosing this command selects the name of the folder or file and inserts the cursor at the end of its characters.

To get rid of the Web-style integration mode and restore the old look of the Windows desktop in Windows 95/98/XP, open Windows Explorer and choose Tools⇨Folder Options. On the General tab of the Folder Options dialog box, click the Classic Style option button and click OK.

**Book III
Chapter 1**

Web Basics

Some Web browsers, including Netscape Navigator and Internet Explorer, can also access older Internet information systems, such as FTP, Gopher, Archie, and WAIS databases. (See Book V, Chapter 3, for more information on FTP and Gopher.)

Another way of accessing information on the Web is by using *channels*. Channels allow a Web site to deliver content to your computer whenever the site has new information for you. You can read the information at another time. (See Chapter 2 of this minibook for more information on channels.)

A Potpourri of Pointers

As in all Windows programs, the mouse pointer takes on many forms in a Web browser. The shape of the mouse pointer indicates two things: where you are in the Web page and why you're there. Table 1-2 shows the default mouse pointers that you may encounter when using a Web browser.

Table 1-2	Mouse Pointer Shapes	
Mouse Pointer	*What It's Called*	*What It Does*
I	I-beam pointer	This is the mouse pointer you see when your mouse encounters editable text on a Web page. (Note that editing text in Web pages is limited to changing the size of the text and copying it for pasting into a non-Web document.)
↖	Arrow pointer	This pointer shape appears when you pass over an item that you can select by clicking.
↖⧗	Busy pointer	An hourglass appears alongside the arrow pointer when you ask your Web browser to perform a task that it can't perform instantly.
👆	Hand pointer	The mouse pointer takes on this pointing-hand shape whenever you pass over a hyperlink. When you see this pointer, you know that you can click the text or graphic beneath it to transport yourself to another location on the Web. Looking for this pointer is the best way to find hyperlinks in a Web page.
👆⊘	Hand pointer with International No symbol	The mouse pointer turns into a hand accompanied by this world-recognized No symbol when you're browsing offline and you pass over a hyperlink to a page that's not available locally on your hard drive.
↕	Vertical Resize	This pointer appears when you pass over the top or bottom edge of an object whose height can be resized.
↔	Horizontal Resize	This pointer appears when you pass over the left or right edge of an object whose width can be resized.

Mouse Pointer	What It's Called	What It Does
↗	Diagonal Resize	This pointer appears when you pass over the corner of an object whose height and width can be resized.
✛	Move	This pointer appears when you pass over an object that can be moved to a new location on the screen.

TIP

Zooming and scrolling with the IntelliMouse

The Microsoft IntelliMouse has done wonders for making the scrolling process a little less tedious. In Internet Explorer, the IntelliMouse makes scrolling downright fun, letting you literally zoom around a Web page by using a new feature called *datazooming*. To datazoom, press and hold down the Shift key while you rotate the IntelliMouse wheel button forward or back. Use the IntelliMouse (or another brand of wheel mouse, such as Logitech) to perform these functions:

✔ Jump to any linked Web page by pointing to the hyperlink and then datazooming forward. To return to the previous topic, datazoom back.

✔ Scroll through a Web page by rotating the wheel button forward or back.

✔ Continuously scroll through the current Web page by clicking the wheel button and then moving the mouse in the direction you want to scroll. Click the wheel button again (or press Esc) to disable the scrolling.

**Book III
Chapter 1**

Web Basics

Chapter 2: Using Internet Explorer 6 to Browse the Web

In This Chapter

✔ Launching Internet Explorer 6

✔ Understanding the Internet Explorer 6 screen elements

✔ Using Internet Explorer 6 to navigate the Web

✔ Keeping track of your favorite Web sites

✔ Viewing Web pages offline

✔ Viewing channels and pages from the History folder

*T*his chapter takes you on a tour of Microsoft's Web browser — Internet Explorer 6. You find out how to launch Internet Explorer, get to know the elements of the screen, and use the browser to begin your travels on the Web. In addition, this chapter shows you how to add links to the sites that you can't possibly live without and how to surf the Web channels and offline favorites that you add to your Favorites list. Now boarding Internet Explorer 6. The next stop in cyberspace is totally up to you!

For more detailed help on the Internet and getting connected, refer to *The Internet For Dummies*, 8th Edition, by John Levine, Carol Baroudi, and Margaret Levine Young (published by Hungry Minds, Inc.).

If your browser of choice is Netscape Navigator, refer to Book IV.

Getting Started with Internet Explorer

Internet Explorer owes its existence to a single type of document — the *Web page* (also known as an *HTML document*). At first glance, a Web page looks like any other nicely formatted document containing graphics and text. What differentiates a Web page from a regular document? In a Web page, text and graphics elements can be used as hyperlinks. When you click a *hyperlink,* you're transported to another Web page.

Many Web sites now include *frames,* which display multiple Web pages on-screen at one time. The Web site shown in Figure 2-1 provides an example of frames.

Information/navigation frame   Contents frame   Logo frame

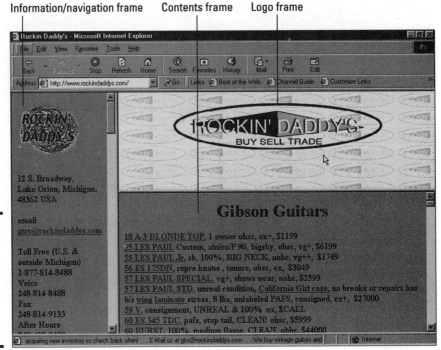

Figure 2-1:
This Web site uses frames to show three different Web pages at once.

The three frames on this page are used for the following purposes:

✦ A *logo frame* with the company name and its logo.

✦ An *information/navigation frame* that gives contact and ordering information about the business. The hyperlinks in this frame take you to different sections of the company's inventory.

✦ A *contents frame* that lists all the items in the company's current inventory.

Launching Internet Explorer

The Windows desktop includes several doorways to the Internet Explorer 6 browser, as shown in Figure 2-2.

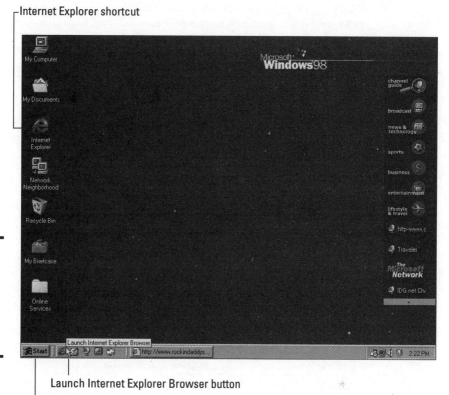

Internet Explorer shortcut

Figure 2-2:
You launch
Internet
Explorer in
several
different
ways.

Launch Internet Explorer Browser button

Start button

Although you could probably hold a contest to find out exactly how many
ways Microsoft has provided for starting Internet Explorer 6, the following
three are the most useful:

✦ Double-click the Internet Explorer shortcut on your desktop.

✦ On the Windows taskbar at the bottom of the screen, choose
   Start➪All Programs➪Internet Explorer.

✦ Click the Launch Internet Explorer Browser button on the Quick Launch
   toolbar located on the taskbar. (If the Quick Launch toolbar is not displayed, right-click the taskbar and choose Toolbars ➪Quick Launch.)

Accessing a Web site

After you start Internet Explorer, you can tell it which Web site you want to
go to. If you haven't saved the Web site in your Favorites list (see the section

"Keeping Track of Your Favorite Web Sites," later in this chapter), you must type the Web site's URL or choose it from a list of Web sites you've recently viewed.

To access a Web site, follow these steps:

1. **Choose File⇨Open.**

The Open dialog box displays.

2. **In the Open text box, type the URL of the site you want to visit or click the drop-down arrow and select a site from the list.**

3. **Click OK.**

You also can access a Web site by positioning the cursor in the Address box of the Internet Explorer window, typing the URL of the Web site you'd like to go to, and pressing Enter or clicking the Go button.

Elements of the Internet Explorer window

Each of the launch methods covered in the preceding section opens Internet Explorer, as shown in Figure 2-3. Table 2-1 provides a rundown of the various parts of the Internet Explorer screen.

Table 2-1	Internet Explorer Screen Elements
Part of the Screen	*What It Is*
Address bar	A text box that displays the URL (Web address) of the current Web page, and in which you type the URL that you want to visit. If you click the down arrow on the right of the box, a drop-down list of the addresses you've previously visited appears.
Menu bar	The standard Windows 95/98/XP menu bar with the addition of the Favorites menu.
Standard Buttons toolbar	A set of tools for navigating Web pages and accessing some of the more often used features of Internet Explorer 6.
Links bar	The choices on the Links bar of the Internet Explorer toolbar contain standard links to various pages on the Microsoft Web site.
Windows taskbar	The standard Windows 95/98/XP taskbar contains the Start button and the Quick Launch toolbar, along with icons for all open programs.
Quick Launch toolbar	A set of tools automatically added to the Windows taskbar when you install Internet Explorer 6. It provides buttons for launching the browser, minimizing all open windows, viewing channels, and launching Outlook Express.
Web page browsing area	The space where the current Web page actually appears.
Status bar	Provides information on your whereabouts as you travel the Web and also the status of Internet Explorer as it performs its functions.

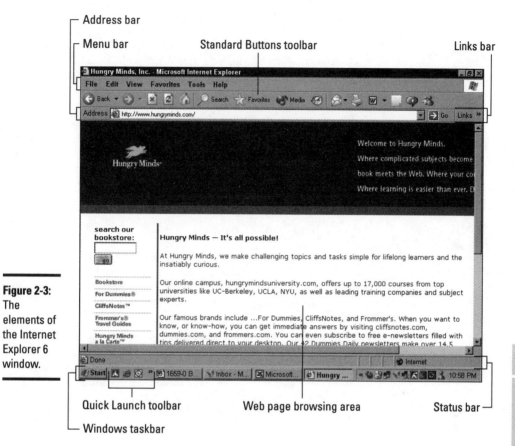

Figure 2-3:
The
elements of
the Internet
Explorer 6
window.

**Book III
Chapter 2**

**Using Internet
Explorer 6 to
Browse the Web**

The Explorer bar

The Explorer bar is a frame that appears on the left side of the Internet
Explorer screen when you want to perform a search, work with your Favorites
list, or display a history of recently viewed Web pages. Click the Search,
Favorites, or History button on the Standard Buttons toolbar to display the
Explorer bar and additional options for each of these functions. The contents
of the current Web page appear in the area (frame) on the right.

If the need should arise, you can change the width of both frames by positioning the mouse pointer on the border that the two frames share. When you do
this, the mouse pointer changes to a double-headed arrow (the horizontal
resize pointer). You can then modify the widths of the two frames by clicking
and dragging the border to the right (to make the Explorer bar wider) or to
the left (to make the Explorer bar narrower).

The Internet Explorer 6 Explorer bar comes in five different flavors:

✦ **Search bar:** The Search bar gives you access to the various search engines that you can use to search the World Wide Web for particular topics. To open the Search bar, click the Search button, choose View➪Explorer Bar➪Search, or press Ctrl+E. (See "Searching the Web," later in this chapter.)

✦ **Favorites bar:** The Favorites bar contains links to all the Web pages that you have marked as your favorites. To open the Favorites bar, click the Favorites button, choose View➪Explorer Bar➪Favorites, or press Ctrl+I. (See "Viewing pages from the Favorites folder," later in this chapter.)

✦ **Media bar:** The Media bar gives you easy access to buttons that let you play music of your choice, whether it be your favorite radio station or CD. You can also use the rest of the bar to read up on the latest audio and video news.

✦ **History bar:** The History bar gives you access to links of all the Web pages that you've visited in the last 20 days. To open the History bar, click the History button, choose View➪Explorer Bar➪History, or press Ctrl+H. (See "Viewing Pages from the History Folder," later in this chapter.)

✦ **Folders bar:** The Folders bar displays a map (in outline form) of the elements of your computer. If you click the icon for a drive or folder in the Folders bar, the contents of that drive or folder appears in the right pane of Internet Explorer. To get back to surfing the Internet, click the Internet Explorer icon in the Folders bar. To open this Explorer bar, choose View➪Explorer Bar➪Folders (the Standard Buttons toolbar doesn't contain a Folders button).

To remove the Explorer bar from the browsing area when you no longer need access to its links, click the Close button (the X) in the upper-right corner of the Explorer bar.

The toolbars

Internet Explorer 6 includes several varieties of toolbars to help you accomplish tasks quickly. The following list describes these toolbars. (Refer to Figure 2-3 to see where these toolbars are located.)

✦ **Menu bar:** As with all standard Windows menu bars, the Internet Explorer menu bar consists of a group of pull-down menus (File, Edit, View, Favorites, Tools, and Help) that you can click to reveal a list of options and submenus.

✦ **Standard Buttons toolbar:** This toolbar contains the tools that you use most often for navigating and performing tasks, such as the following:

- **Back:** Enables you to return to any Web sites you may have previously visited during your Web session.

- **Forward:** Takes you to any available pages in the History listing.

- **Stop:** Lets you stop a page from loading.

- **Refresh:** Reloads or updates the current Web page.

- **Home:** Displays the Web page you designate as the home page.

- **Search:** Displays or hides the Search Explorer bar.

- **Favorites:** Displays or hides the Favorites Explorer bar.

- **Media:** Displays or hides the Media Explorer bar.

- **History:** Displays or hides the History Explorer bar.

- **Mail:** Opens a menu with options for sending e-mail or for reading e-mail or news.

- **Print:** Prints the current Web page without opening the Print dialog box.

- **Edit:** Opens the current Web page in a text editor.

- **Discuss:** Displays the Discussions toolbar so that you can review and add comments about the Web page.

- **Messenger:** Opens the Windows Messenger window.

✦ **Address bar:** This bar shows you the URL of the Web page currently displayed in the Internet Explorer browsing area. You can go to a new Web page by typing in a new URL in the Address bar's text box and pressing Enter (or clicking Go). (If the Address bar is hidden by the Links bar, double-click the word Address to reveal the full Address bar.) When you're entering a URL, the autocomplete feature helps you correctly complete the address. (For more details on autocomplete and how to customize this feature, see Book III, Chapter 4.)

As you visit different pages during a Web browsing session, Internet Explorer adds the URL of each site that you visit to the drop-down list attached to the Address bar. To revisit one of the Web pages that you've seen during the session, you can click the drop-down button at the end of the Address box and click its URL or its page icon in the drop-down list.

The Address bar also includes an autosearch feature that lets you search for Web sites that meet your search criteria. Click the Address box and type a descriptive term or terms that you think describes the site (such as **computer books**). Internet Explorer 6 opens the Search Explorer bar with a list of possible links to sites that meet your search criteria.

**Book III
Chapter 2**

Using Internet Explorer 6 to Browse the Web

✦ **Links bar:** This button contains a drop-down list of shortcuts to various Microsoft Web pages — RealPlayer, Customize Links, and various other pages. (If the Links bar is hidden by the Address bar, double-click the word Links to reveal the full Links bar.) You can, however, change the shortcuts listed on the Links bar to reflect the Web pages that you visit most often.

To add a Quick Link button for the Web page that you're currently viewing, drag its Web page icon (the icon that precedes the URL in the Address bar) to the place on the Links bar where you want the Quick Link button to appear. To remove a button from the Links bar, right-click the button and choose Delete from the shortcut menu.

✦ **Discussions bar:** This toolbar appears below the main browsing area when you click the Discuss button on the Standard Buttons toolbar. The Discussions bar contains buttons for taking part in online discussions. You can add your own comments and reply to other people's comments pertaining to the current Web page.

✦ **Quick Launch toolbar:** The Quick Launch toolbar provides one-click access to the Internet Explorer browser and other applications or features. This toolbar, which appears next to the Start button on the Windows taskbar, includes a variety of buttons, depending on the programs you have on your computer.

 If you're having trouble seeing the Quick Launch toolbar, don't panic. You just need to unlock the taskbar to get these options to appear. Simply right-click an empty part of the toolbar and choose Lock the Taskbar from the submenu. Then, stretch the toolbar to view all its icons.

 You can quickly display or hide toolbars by right-clicking the menu bar and selecting the toolbar that you want to display or hide from the shortcut menu. In this shortcut menu, a check mark appears next to toolbars that are currently displayed.

Getting Help

The Help feature in Internet Explorer 6 is written in HTML so that it looks and acts like a Web page. To open Internet Explorer 6 Help, click Help on the menu bar and then choose from the following options:

✦ **Contents and Index:** Opens the Help window for Internet Explorer, which is divided into two panes. The left pane shows the categories available on the Contents tab or, in the case of the Index tab, an alphabetical list of subjects; the window on the right serves as a viewing area. You also can use the Search tab to search for specific keywords.

Customizing the Quick Launch toolbar

You can do quite a bit in terms of customizing the appearance of the Quick Launch toolbar. For example, you can display it in a floating dialog box by dragging it off the Windows toolbar. You can also reposition it after the other icons on the taskbar simply by dragging the toolbar control handle (the vertical line on the left part of the toolbar).

In addition, the Quick Launch toolbar shortcut menu (which appears when you right-click an empty part of the Quick Launch toolbar) contains, among other things, these choices for customizing the toolbar:

✔ **View⇨Large:** Increases the size of the icons used on the buttons (not recommended unless the toolbar is floating on the desktop). Note that the Small setting on the View menu is the setting that is usually used.

✔ **Show Text:** Adds the names of each of the buttons to the toolbar, which spaces it out so much that not all the Quick Launch buttons can be displayed at once, even when you have no other buttons on the taskbar.

✔ **Show Title:** Adds the title of the Quick Launch toolbar immediately following the toolbar control handle.

✦ **Tip of the Day:** Provides a useful tip about Internet Explorer 6 at the bottom of the program window. Click the Close button to remove the tip.

✦ **For Netscape Users:** Opens the Help window and displays information on making the transition from Netscape Navigator to Internet Explorer.

✦ **Online Support:** Takes you to a Microsoft Web site page where you can search a database, download software, find information according to product, post questions to newsgroups, and find contact phone numbers.

✦ **Send Feedback:** Takes you to Microsoft's Contact Web page, where you can choose various types of feedback to send to Microsoft.

✦ **About Internet Explorer:** Displays an About Internet Explorer dialog box with the version number, copyright and licensing information.

Book III
Chapter 2

Using Internet Explorer 6 to Browse the Web

Searching the Web

The World Wide Web holds an enormous wealth of information on almost every subject known to humanity, but you need to know how to get to that information. To help Web surfers like you locate sites containing the information that you're interested in, a number of so-called *search engines* have been designed. Each search engine maintains a slightly different directory of the sites on the World Wide Web (which are mostly maintained and updated by automated programs called *Web crawlers, spiders,* and *robots*).

Starting the search

Internet Explorer 6 gives you access to all the most popular search engines through the Search bar, a special Explorer bar for searching the Web (for details on the Explorer bars in Internet Explorer 6, see "The Explorer bar," earlier in this chapter). You can open the Search bar in one of three ways:

✦ Click the Search button on the Standard Buttons toolbar.

✦ Choose View⇨Explorer Bar⇨Search.

✦ Press Ctrl+E.

In this window, you find a text box where you can type the kind of Web page to look for. After you enter the keyword or words (known affectionately as a *search string* in programmers' parlance) to search for in this text box, you begin the search by clicking the Search button.

Internet Explorer then conducts a search for Web sites containing the keywords by using the first search engine (the one listed in the Search bar). If that search engine finds no matches, Internet Explorer then conducts the same search by using the next search engine in its list.

To change the search engine you're using, simply scroll down and click Change Preferences. From the list that appears, choose Change Internet Search Behavior. Scroll down and from the list, choose the search engine that you'd like to be the default and then click OK. When the search engine finishes processing your search string, it returns a list of hyperlinks in the Search bar that represent the top ten matches, as shown in Figure 2-4. You can then click any of the hyperlinks in the list to display that Web page in the area of the browser window to the right of the Search bar. If you aren't interested in the page that appears, try another of the hyperlinks to see whether it leads to a Web page that's of more interest.

Note that at any time during the process of checking out the matches to your search, you can temporarily remove the Search bar so that the Web page is displayed full-screen. To do so, click the Search button on the Standard Buttons toolbar or press Ctrl+E. Then if you decide, after browsing the page's content, that you want to check out another of the pages in the results list, you can restore the Search bar by clicking the Search button or pressing Ctrl+E again.

After exhausting the links in the top-ten list, you can display links to the next ten matching pages returned by the search engine by clicking some sort of next button. Note that in some search engines, this button appears as a page number in a list of the next available result pages at the bottom of the Search bar.

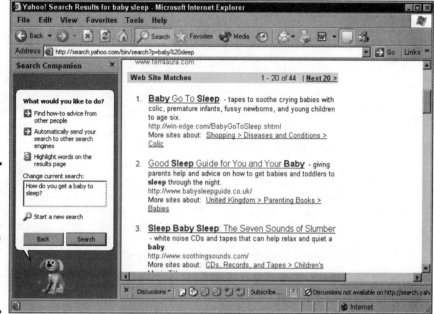

Figure 2-4:
The top-ten matches for weary parents who want to find out how to get Baby to sleep.

After you're convinced that you've seen all the best matches to your search, you can conduct another search with the same search engine by using slightly different terms. You can also switch to another search engine to see what kinds of results it produces by using the same search string.

Limiting your searches

To avoid getting back thousands of irrelevant (or at the very minimum, uninteresting) search results, you need to consider telling the search engines to return links only to sites that contain all the terms you enter in the search string. For example, say that you want to find sites that deal with koi (the ornamental carp that are very popular in Japan) ponds. If you type the search string **koi ponds** in the Find a Web Page Containing text box, the search engines will return links to Web sites with both *koi* and *ponds* (without any reference to the fish) in their descriptions, as well as sites that contain both *koi* and *ponds* in their descriptions. The problem with this approach is that it can give you far too many extraneous results because many search engines search for each term in the search string independently as well as together. It's as though you had asked for Web sites with descriptions containing koi *and/or* ponds.

The easiest way to tell the search engines that you want links to a Web site returned only when *all* the terms in your search string are matched in their descriptions is to enclose all the terms in double quotation marks. In the case of the *koi ponds* search string, you can find more Web sites that deal only with koi ponds (as opposed to frog ponds or other ponds containing just garden plants), by typing **"koi ponds"** in the Find a Web Page Containing text box. Taking this little extra step often brings you fewer, but more useful, results.

Browsing in full screen mode

One of the biggest drawbacks of Web surfing is the amount of scrolling that you have to do to see all the information on a particular Web page. To help minimize the amount of scrolling, Internet Explorer 6 offers a full screen mode that automatically minimizes the space normally occupied by the menu bar, Standard Buttons toolbar, Address bar, and Links bar. In full screen mode, only a version of the Standard Buttons toolbar with small buttons is displayed at the top of the screen, as shown in Figure 2-5.

To switch to full screen mode, press F11 or choose View⇨Full Screen. To get out of full screen mode and return to the normal view, press F11 again.

Figure 2-5:
Press F11 to enter full screen mode and see more of the Web page.

Displaying Previously Viewed Web Pages

As you browse different Web sites, Internet Explorer keeps track of your progression through their pages. You can then use the Back and Forward buttons on the toolbar, or the equivalent commands on the View⇨Go To menu, to move back and forth between the pages that you've visited in the current work session.

If you use the Back and Forward buttons on the Standard Buttons toolbar, you get the added benefit of being able to tell in advance which page will be redisplayed when you click the button. Simply position the mouse pointer on the Back or Forward button and hold it there until the title of the Web page appears in a little ScreenTip box.

Both the Back and Forward buttons have drop-down menus attached to them. When you display these drop-down menus (by clicking the drop-down arrow to the immediate right of the Back or Forward button), they show a list, in most-recent to least-recent order, of the nine most recent Web pages visited in the work session before (Back) or after (Forward) the current Web page.

By using the drop-down menu attached to the Back button, you can avoid having to click Back, Back, Back, Back, and so on, to revisit a page that you saw some time ago during the current Web surfing session. Likewise, should you go back some ways in the queue of pages, you can use the drop-down menu attached to the Forward button to jump forward right to the desired page without incessantly clicking the Forward button.

When the Back or Forward buttons are grayed out on the toolbar, this means that you're already viewing the first or the last of the Web pages that you visited in the current Internet Explorer session. You cannot go further back or forward.

(See "Viewing Pages from the History Folder," later in this chapter, for information on revisiting pages opened in the last few weeks.)

Viewing Channels

Channels are Web pages with content that is updated regularly, such as stock market information, news, or any current information. Channels not only enable you to download updated Web contents on a schedule of your choosing (avoiding peak periods of heavy Internet traffic), but also give you easy access to this information.

Book III
Chapter 2

Using Internet
Explorer 6 to
Browse the Web

The easy access to the updated information is primarily due to these factors:

✦ Channels do not require you to deal with the traditional URL system to get to their Web pages.

✦ Internet Explorer 6 enables you to access the updated Web pages offline so that you can view their contents even when you can't connect to the Internet (see "Browsing Web Pages Offline," later in this chapter).

Unfortunately, you can access channels only if you upgraded to Internet Explorer 6 from Version 4 or Windows 98.

Keeping Track of Your Favorite Web Sites

As you browse the Web with Internet Explorer 6, you may come across interesting Web sites that you want to revisit later. To make finding a site again easy, you can recall its home page (or any of its other pages) by placing a reference to the page in the Internet Explorer Favorites folder. You can then revisit the page by selecting its title from the Favorites pull-down menu or from the Favorites bar. (See "Viewing pages from the Favorites folder," later in this chapter.)

Adding Web pages to your Favorites folder

To add a Web page to the Favorites folder, follow these steps:

1. **Go to the Web page that you want to add to your Favorites.**

2. **Choose Favorites➪Add To Favorites.**

   The Add Favorite dialog box opens. The name of the Web page displayed in the title bar of the Internet Explorer browser window also appears in the Name text box.

3. **(Optional) You can edit the Web page title that appears in the Name text box.**

   Keep in mind that this text is listed on the Favorites menu, so you want to make it as descriptive as possible, while, at the same time, keeping it brief.

4. **(Optional) To make the Web page that you're adding to your Favorites available for offline browsing, click to select the Make Available Offline check box.**

(See the next section, "Making pages available for offline viewing," for information on how to control when new content is downloaded for offline viewing.)

5. **(Optional) To add the favorite to a subfolder of Favorites, click the Create In button to expand the Add Favorite dialog box (if the files and folders aren't already displayed in the list box); then click the icon of the appropriate subfolder (see Figure 2-6) or click the New Folder button to create a new folder in which to add your new favorite.**

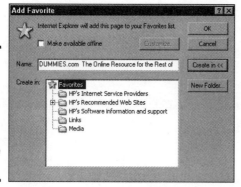

Figure 2-6:
You can specify the folder where you want to add your favorite pages.

6. **Click OK to add the Web page to your Favorites.**

   If you clicked the Make Available Offline checkbox in Step 4, a synchronization box appears and automatically configures your settings. You're all done!

Making pages available for offline viewing

You may want to make a Web page in your Favorites folder available for offline viewing. As discussed in the preceding section, you can do so by clicking the Make Available Offline check box when you add the page to your Favorites folder. When you click OK with this check box selected, Internet Explorer 6 downloads the page into your computer's Favorites folder. This enables you to view the page's contents in the browser when you aren't connected to the Internet.

Thereafter, you can have Internet Explorer 6 go online and check the page on the World Wide Web against the page downloaded into your Favorites folder. If Internet Explorer finds that the page on the Web contains updates that aren't included in the page in your Favorites folder, the browser replaces the Favorites page with the updated Web version. This process of checking the online page for updates and replacing the one downloaded in the Favorites folder with a newer version is called *synchronization*.

To synchronize the contents of a Favorites page marked for offline viewing, you open the page in Internet Explorer and then choose the Tools⇨ Synchronize command on the menu bar. If you want, you can customize how often and under what conditions Internet Explorer synchronizes a Web page marked for offline viewing.

To customize your synchronization settings, follow these steps:

1. **Go to the Web page that you want to add to your Favorites folder for offline viewing.**

2. **Choose Favorites⇨Add to Favorites.**

3. **Click to select the Make Available Offline check box and then click the Customize button.**

The first dialog box of the Offline Favorite Wizard appears, describing its purpose, which is to help you set up a page for offline viewing.

4. **Click the Next button.**

The second Offline Favorite Wizard dialog box asks whether you want to make the page's links to other pages available offline.

5. **Choose No if you don't want pages linked to the Favorite page downloaded for offline viewing. Choose Yes if you know that the links on this page are important to you, and you want them to be downloaded and synchronized along with this favorite.**

By default, Internet Explorer downloads only the pages linked to the current page (one link deep), which can be several pages. You can increase the number of pages downloaded by increasing the number of pages in the Download Pages text box (three is the maximum).

6. **Click the Next button; then select the option that describes how you would like to synchronize the Web page.**

In the third wizard dialog box, leave the Only When I Choose Synchronize from the Tools Menu option button selected if you always want to manually determine when the Favorite page is synchronized. Choose the I Would Like to Create a New Schedule option button if you want to create a customized automated schedule.

7. **(Optional) If you selected the I Would Like to Create a New Schedule option button in the previous dialog box, the next wizard dialog box lets you create the custom schedule and name it.**

8. **Click the Next button. The last wizard dialog box lets you enter your user name and password if your new Favorite requires them. If this is the case, choose the Yes, My User Name and Password Are option button and type the name in the User Name text box and the password in both the Password and Confirm Password text boxes.**

9. **Click the Finish button to close the Offline Favorite Wizard and put your new custom schedule into effect.**

Viewing pages from the Favorites folder

The Favorites folder contains hyperlinks to all the Web pages that you've marked during your Cyberspace travels on the World Wide Web, as well as all the channels and local folders and files on which you rely. From the Favorites list, you can open Web pages that you want to revisit, go to a channel home page, or open a favorite file with its native application (such as Word 2002 if it's a Word document, or Excel 2002 if it's an Excel workbook).

To display the links in your Favorites folder, you can select the links directly from the Favorites pull-down menu, click the Favorites button on the Standard Buttons toolbar, or press Ctrl+I. When you click the Favorites button or press Ctrl+I, Internet Explorer presents the subfolders and links of your Favorites folder in the Favorites bar (a frame on the left side of the screen). The current Web page appears in a frame on the right.

To display the links in one of the Favorites subfolders, click the folder icon containing the link in the Favorites bar. Then click the desired hyperlink to display a Web page (if it's a Web hyperlink), a list of folders and files (if it's a link to a local disk), or to open a document in its own program (if it's a link to a particular file).

Organizing your favorites

The Organize Favorites dialog box, shown in Figure 2-7 (which you open by choosing Favorites➪Organize Favorites), lets you arrange the links in your Favorites folder (see "Adding Web pages to your Favorites folder," earlier in this chapter), as well as those in your Channels and Links folders.

**Book III
Chapter 2**

**Using Internet
Explorer 6 to
Browse the Web**

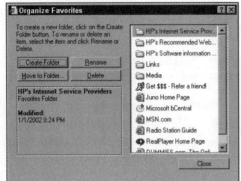

Figure 2-7:
Arrange
your links in
your folders.

Organizing your favorites and links into folders

One of the best methods for organizing favorites is to group them together
into folders, maybe even using subfolders within those folders. After you
have a folder structure, you can then move the links to your favorite pages
into the appropriate folders, renaming them if you so choose.

Use the following options in the Organize Favorites dialog box to group the
links in your Favorites and Links folders:

✦ To create a new folder, click the Create Folder button, type a new name
   for the folder icon, and press Enter.

✦ To move a link to a favorite page, click its icon to highlight it and then
   click the Move to Folder button to open the Browse for Folder dialog
   box. Click the destination folder in the Browse for Folder dialog box and
   click OK.

✦ To rename a link to a favorite page, click its icon to select it and then
   click the Rename button. Edit the description and then press Enter.

✦ To delete a link to a favorite page, click its icon and then click the Delete
   button. Then click Yes to confirm the deletion.

Don't delete or rename the Links folder in the Organize Favorites dialog box.
Internet Explorer 6 needs the Links folder so that it knows what buttons to
display on the Links bar.

Organizing your favorites, channels, and links with drag-and-drop

You can also use the drag-and-drop method to reorganize the links to
your Favorites and Links folders from the Favorites Explorer bar in

Internet Explorer 6. Click the Favorites button on the Standard Buttons toolbar and then perform one of the following actions:

✦ To open a folder to display the folder's contents, click its folder icon in the Favorites bar. Internet Explorer then shows a series of icons for each of the links that it contains. To close a folder and hide its contents, click the folder icon again.

✦ To move an icon to a new position in its folder, drag its icon up or down until you reach the desired position. As you drag, Internet Explorer shows you where the item will be inserted by displaying a heavy horizontal I-beam. The program also shows you where you can't move the icon by displaying the International No symbol.

✦ To move an icon to another (existing) folder, drag its icon to the folder icon. When the folder becomes highlighted, you can drop the icon and it goes into the highlighted folder.

The Favorites bar can display not only your favorite Web links but also local folders that contain your favorite files. When you click one of the local folders displayed in the Favorites bar, Internet Explorer shows all the subfolders and files in that folder in the frame to the right of the Favorites bar. In addition, Internet Explorer removes buttons associated specifically with Web browsing (such as Search, Favorites, and History) from the Standard Buttons toolbar and adds those associated with file browsing (such as Up, Cut, Copy, and Paste). But as soon as you click a hyperlink to a Web page on the Favorites bar (or choose one on the Favorites pull-down menu, if you closed the Explorer bar), the buttons associated with Web browsing reappear on the Standard Buttons toolbar, and the buttons associated with file browsing disappear.

Browsing Web Pages Offline

Offline browsing (as opposed to normal *online* browsing) lets you view pages in your Favorites folder when you're not connected to the Internet (see the earlier section, "Adding Web pages to your Favorites folder," for details on making Favorite pages available offline). You can set up schedules so that updated content for your favorite Web pages is automatically downloaded to your hard drive. Offline browsing enables you to view the updated Web content at your leisure.

To turn offline browsing on and off, choose File➪Work Offline. This command acts as a toggle — a check mark appears next to the Work Offline command when you are working offline. In addition, the words Working Offline appear in the title bar. When you're ready to resume some serious online surfing, you need to begin by choosing File⇨Work Offline again to turn off the offline mode.

Knowing what links are not available offline

When you're working in offline mode (indicated by the words Working Offline in the title bar), Internet Explorer 6 doesn't attempt to connect to the Internet, and you can browse only pages stored locally on your computer, such as those downloaded into the cache on your computer's hard drive. The *cache,* also known as the Temporary Internet Files, contains all Web pages and their components that are downloaded when you set up your synchronization schedules for Web sites or channels. Note that the Internet Explorer 6 cache is stored in a Windows subfolder called, appropriately enough, Temporary Internet Files.

When you browse a Web site offline from a local disk, you have none of the wait often associated with browsing online while connected to the Internet. You may, however, find that some of the links — especially those to pages on another Web site that you haven't added to your favorites — are not available for viewing. Internet Explorer lets you know when a link is not available by displaying it as grayed out and adding the International No symbol (you know, the circle with a backslash in it) to the hand-shaped mouse pointer. If you click a grayed out hyperlink, Internet Explorer presents a dialog box that gives you the option to connect to the Internet.

Opening Web pages offline

Most of the time when browsing offline, you do your local Web surfing in a couple of ways:

+ **Visit updated Web pages stored in the cache as Favorites marked for offline viewing.** You open these pages by choosing the Favorites menu and then selecting the particular folder with the page or pages that you want to see.

+ **Revisit Web pages stored in the cache as part of the History folder.** You open these pages by clicking the History button on the toolbar and then selecting them from the History bar. (See the next section, "Viewing Pages from the History Folder.")

Viewing Pages from the History Folder

The History folder contains a list of links to the Web pages that you visited within the last 20 days (unless you've changed this default setting, as explained in Book III, Chapter 4). These hyperlinks are arranged chronologically from least recent to most recent, grouped by days for the current week, and then by weeks for all days further back.

 To display the links in your History folder, click the History button on the Standard Buttons toolbar or press Ctrl+H. Internet Explorer 6 shows the folders for each Web site that you visited on a particular day or during a particular week in the History bar (a pane on the left side of the screen). The current Web page appears in a pane on the right.

To revisit a Web page in the History folder, click the Web site's folder icon in the History bar to display the links to its pages; then click the hyperlink for the particular page that you want to go to (see Figure 2-8).

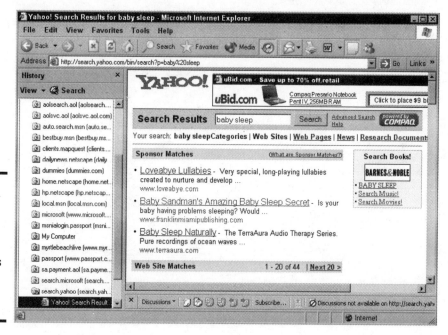

Figure 2-8: Use the History folder to quickly locate sites that you've recently visited.

Book III
Chapter 2

Using Internet
Explorer 6 to
Browse the Web

Creating a shortcut to a Web page

Instead of adding a Web page to the Favorites folder, you can create a shortcut to the Web on your computer's desktop. That way, you can open the Web page (and launch Internet Explorer 6 at the same time, if it's not already open) simply by clicking the shortcut icon.

To place a shortcut to a Web page on your desktop, follow these few steps:

1. **In the Internet Explorer 6 browser, open the Web page to which you want to create a shortcut.**

2. **Choose File⇨Send⇨Shortcut to Desktop.**

   Internet Explorer creates a shortcut to the current Web page, with the title of the page beneath a Web icon.

3. **To rename the Web page shortcut, click the Show Desktop button on the Quick Launch toolbar to display the desktop and then right-click the new shortcut icon and choose Rename from its shortcut menu.**

4. **After editing characters or replacing the entire name, press Enter.**

If the Internet Explorer browsing window isn't full size (as is the case when you click the Restore button in the upper-right corner of the window), you can create a shortcut to the Web page that you're currently viewing by dragging the Web page icon to the desktop. (This icon appears at the beginning of the Address bar, in front of the URL of the current Web page.)

Chapter 3: Printing and Saving Web Information

In This Chapter

✔ Printing the contents of a Web page

✔ Saving a Web page or graphic to your hard drive

✔ Copying a Web graphic to your hard drive

✔ Viewing the HTML contents of a Web page

✔ Turning a Web graphic into your desktop's wallpaper

*W*ith Internet Explorer 6, you can print and save all or part of a favorite Web page. You can even save an interesting Web graphic or photo and set it as your desktop's wallpaper. To understand what makes a Web page tick, take a look behind the scenes to examine the HTML code used to create the Web page. This chapter provides details on the various aspects of storing and reusing the information that you uncover in your travels with Internet Explorer 6.

Printing a Web Page

Although you can save a Web page to your hard drive (as you discover how to do in the next section, "Saving a Web Page on Your Computer"), you may prefer to just print its contents. Internet Explorer 6 makes it easy to print the contents of the Web page you're currently browsing. Just remember that a Web page (in spite of its name) can produce multiple printed pages due to the amount of information contained on that "page."

When you want to print the contents of the Web page currently displayed in your Internet Explorer 6 browser, you can choose from a couple of methods:

✦ Click the Print button on the Standard Buttons toolbar.

✦ Choose File⇨Print or press Ctrl+P to open the Print dialog box (see Figure 3-1); then click Print or press Enter.

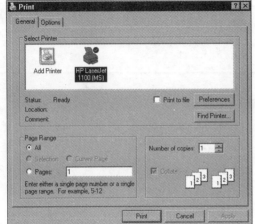

Figure 3-1:
Specify print settings for the current Web page in the Print dialog box.

Printing pages on a site that uses frames

Many of the Web sites that you're sure to visit in the course of your cyber-travels use frames as a way to divide your browser window into separate panes, each displaying content from different HTML documents. (For more information on frames, see Book VI, Chapter 2.)

When you print a Web page that uses frames, the Print dialog box (accessed by choosing File➪Print or by pressing Ctrl+P) gives you the options to print all the frames on the page as they appear in the browser, to print each one individually, or to print just a particular frame of your choice (refer to Figure 3-1):

✦ To print the contents of all frames as they appear on the Web page, click the Options tab and then click to select the As Laid Out on Screen option button.

✦ To print all frames on separate, successive pages, click to select the All Frames Individually option button in the Options tab of the Print dialog box.

✦ To print only the frame that you selected (by clicking the mouse pointer in the frame before opening the Print dialog box), click to select the Only the Selected Frame option button in the Options tab of the Print dialog box.

You can also print a selected frame by right-clicking in the frame and then selecting Print from the shortcut menu that appears. The Print dialog box opens with the Only the Selected Frame option button already selected. If you click the Print button on the Standard Buttons toolbar, Internet Explorer prints whatever frame is selected at the time. (When you first open a Web page, the frame selected initially is determined by the person who designed the page.)

Changing the setup of a page you're printing

Before you print from Internet Explorer, you should check the page settings. You can change page settings from the Page Setup dialog box (see Figure 3-2), which you open by choosing File⇨Page Setup.

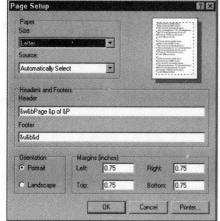

Figure 3-2:
The Page Setup dialog box lets you adjust the default page settings.

Book III
Chapter 3

Printing and Saving Web Information

To change the page size, select a new size setting from the Size drop-down list. To change the orientation of the printing from Portrait (vertical) to Landscape (horizontal), click the Landscape option button. To change any or all of the page margins, enter a new value (in inches) in the Left, Right, Top, and Bottom text boxes.

To change the information that appears at the top of each page as a header or the bottom of each page as a footer, you need to modify the codes in the Header and Footer text boxes. Each of these printing codes begins with an ampersand (&), followed by a single character. You can use any of the printing codes shown in Table 3-1.

Table 3-1	Printing Codes
Printing Code	*What It Prints*
&w	Title of the Web page as it appears in the title bar of the browser window
&u	URL (Web address) of the Web page
&d	Current date using the short date format specified in the Regional Settings control panel (for example: 11/6/00)
&D	Current date using the long date format specified in the Regional Settings control panel (for example: Monday, November 6, 2000)

(continued)

Table 3-1 *(continued)*

Printing Code	What It Prints
&t	Current time as specified in the Regional Settings control panel (for example: 9:41:35 PM)
&T	Current time using a 24-hour clock (for example: 21:41:35)
&p	Page number of the current printout
&P	Total number of pages in the printout
&&	Ampersand character (&) in the header or footer text

When setting up a custom header or footer, you can intersperse the preceding printing codes with standard text. For example, if you want the footer to say something like *Page 2 of 3*, you need to intersperse the codes &p and &P between the words *Page* and *of* in the Footer text box, like this:

```
Page &p of &P
```

All the printing codes and text that you enter in the Header and Footer text boxes in the Page Setup dialog box are automatically left-justified at the top or bottom of the page. To have some of the text or codes right-justified in the header or footer, type the code **&b&b** immediately before the text and codes that you want to right-justify in the printout. If you want text or codes centered in the text, type **&b**.

To prevent Internet Explorer 6 from printing a header or footer in the Web page printout, delete all the text and printing codes from the Header and Footer text boxes in the Page Setup dialog box.

Printing all linked pages or a table of all links

The Options tab of the Print dialog box (refer to Figure 3-1) in Internet Explorer 6 incorporates a couple of nifty check box settings that enable you to print all the pages linked to the current Web page (along with the current page) or a table of the links to other pages from the current page (that appears at the end of the printout). If you select either of these check boxes, the printouts also include links from any advertisements included on the Web page(s):

✦ Click the Print All Linked Documents check box to tell Internet Explorer to print all the pages linked to the current page.

✦ Click the Print Table of Links check box to tell Internet Explorer to print a table showing all the hyperlinks and URLs of the pages linked to the current page. (This table appears at the very end of the printout of the current page.)

Saving a Web Page on Your Computer

You can save to your computer's hard drive any Web page that you visit. Then you use Internet Explorer 6 to view the page offline. (For more on viewing Web pages when you're not connected to the Internet, see Book III, Chapter 2.)

To save a Web page to your hard drive, follow these steps:

1. **Use Internet Explorer 6 to display the Web page that you want to save to your hard drive; then choose File⇔Save As.**

The Save Web Page dialog box opens, as shown in Figure 3-3.

2. **Select the folder on your hard drive where you want to save the Web page.**

The folder name appears in the Save In drop-down list box.

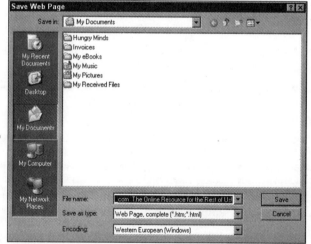

Figure 3-3:
The Save Web Page dialog box in Internet Explorer 6.

Book III
Chapter 3

Printing and Saving
Web Information

3. **(Optional) If you want to change the filename under which the Web page is saved, you need to edit or replace its current name in the File Name text box.**

4. **Click the Save button to close the Save Web Page dialog box.**

Internet Explorer downloads the Web page and saves it on your computer's hard drive.

After the Web page is saved on your hard drive, you can view its contents offline by choosing File⇨Work Offline and then opening it from the Internet Explorer Address bar or from the Open dialog box (choose File⇨Open or press Ctrl+O).

Saving a Web Graphic on Your Computer

Internet Explorer 6 makes it easy to save any still graphic images in the GIF or JPG (JPEG) graphics file format. (If you want to save a Web graphic as desktop wallpaper, see "Wallpapering Your Desktop with a Web Graphic," later in this chapter.)

To save a Web graphic on your computer, follow these steps:

1. **Use Internet Explorer to go to the Web page that contains the graphic that you want to save on your computer.**

2. **Right-click the Web graphic to display its shortcut menu and choose Save Picture As.**

    The Save Picture dialog box opens.

3. **In the Save In drop-down list box, select the folder on your hard drive into which you want to save the graphic.**

4. **(Optional) If you want to change the filename that the Web graphic is saved under, you need to edit or replace its current name in the File Name text box.**

5. **(Optional) By default, Internet Explorer 6 saves the Web graphic in the GIF graphics file format or JPEG graphics file format (depending on which format the Web designer used). To save the graphic in the BMP (bitmapped picture) graphics file format — which Windows uses extensively for such things as buttons and desktop backgrounds — choose Bitmap (*.bmp) in the Save As Type drop-down list box.**

6. **Click Save to close the Save Picture dialog box.**

    Internet Explorer 6 downloads the Web graphic and saves it on your computer's hard drive.

Copying Web Page Information

When surfing the Internet, you may encounter a Web page that contains information that you want to access offline. In those situations, you can use the Windows Copy and Paste features to incorporate the section of Web page text of interest into a document on your hard drive.

To copy text of a Web page into a local document, follow these steps:

1. **With the Web page displayed in the Internet Explorer 6 browsing window, position the I-beam mouse pointer at the beginning of the text that you want to copy; then click and drag through the characters or rows until all the text you want to copy is selected (highlighted).**

   When you drag through the text, all the graphics that appear between or to the side of the paragraphs that you're selecting are highlighted for copying as well. If you don't want to include a particular graphic in your selection, you must copy the text before and after it in separate actions.

   If you want to copy everything on the page (including all text and graphics) choose Edit⇨Select All or press Ctrl+A.

2. **Choose Edit⇨Copy or press Ctrl+C.**

   The selected text is copied onto the Windows Clipboard.

3. **Switch to the word processor (for example, Microsoft Word), text editor (such as Wordpad or Notepad), or e-mail editor (such as Outlook Express) that contains the destination document or e-mail message into which you want to copy the selected text.**

   If your computer doesn't have sufficient memory to have both applications open at once, you can close Internet Explorer and then launch the word processor, editor, or e-mail program.

   If you want to copy the selected text into an existing document, open that file with a word processor or text editor. Otherwise, open a new document.

4. **Click the I-beam mouse pointer at the place in the document or e-mail message where you want the selected text to appear and then choose Edit⇨Paste or press Ctrl+V.**

To copy graphics without surrounding text, you use another copy technique covered in the section "Saving a Web Graphic on Your Computer," earlier in this chapter.

Depending on the capabilities of the program into which you are pasting the copied Web text, you may find that the copied text retains some or, in rare cases, all of its original formatting (created by using the Web-based computer language HTML). For example, if you copy a section of text formatted in HTML as a bulleted list into a Word document, Word retains the bullets and properly indents the text items.

When copying text from a Web page, you usually copy hyperlinks that the author has included within that text. Some word-processing programs (such as Word) and e-mail editors (such as Outlook Express) retain the correct HTML tags for these hyperlinks, making them functioning links within the destination document. Be forewarned, however, that seldom, if ever, do these hyperlinks work properly when clicked. This problem most often occurs because you don't have the pages to which these links refer copied to your hard drive. You also may end up with extra line breaks or spaces (due to the HTML formatting) when you copy text from a Web page.

 When copying information from a table on a Web page, you can retain its tabular format by copying entire rows of the table into Word 2002 documents or Outlook 2002 and Outlook Express e-mail messages. For the best results in copying tables from Web pages, copy the entire table into the Word document or Outlook e-mail message. You can now copy information from a Web table into an Excel 2002 worksheet simply by dragging the copied table cells to the blank worksheet cells and releasing the mouse button!

Viewing the HTML Source of a Web Page

A Web page is no more than a special type of text document that makes extensive use of HTML (HyperText Markup Language) tags to format its contents. If you're a Web page designer (or have any inclination to become one), you can figure out a lot about Web design by viewing the HTML contents of the really cool pages that you visit.

To see the HTML codes behind any Web page displayed in the Internet Explorer 6 browsing window, choose View⇨Source. When you select this command, Internet Explorer launches the Windows Notepad utility, which displays a copy of the *HTML source page* (the page containing all the HTML tags and text) for the current Web page, as shown in Figure 3-4.

Figure 3-4: The HTML source code appears in the Notepad window.

```
dummies[1] - Notepad
File  Edit  Format  View  Help
<!DOCTYPE HTML PUBLIC "-//W3C//DTD HTML 4.0 Transitional//EN">
<html><head>
<script src="javascript/dummies.js" language="JavaScript"></script>
<script language="JavaScript">
<!--
var lnk = '<LINK REL=STYLESHEET TYPE="text/css" HREF="stylesheet/';
var v = navigator.appVersion;
var a = navigator.appName;
var useNN = false;
if (a.indexOf('Netscape')> -1 )
{
        if (v.indexOf('3')> -1 | v.indexOf('4')> -1)
        {
                useNN = true;
        }
}
lnk += (useNN) ? 'nn_style_scott.css' : 'ie_style_scott.css';
lnk += '">';
document.writeln(lnk);
//-->
</script>
<link rel="STYLESHEET" type="text/css" href="stylesheet/style_scott.css
<title>DUMMIES.com | The Online Resource for the Rest of Us!</title>
</head>
<body bgcolor="#FFFF00" topmargin="0" bottommargin="0" marginwidth="0"
```

You can then print the HTML source page by choosing File⇨Print within Notepad.

If you want to save the temporary text document with Notepad, follow these steps:

1. **In Notepad, choose File⇨Save As.**

2. **In the Save In drop-down list box, select the folder in which you want to save the page.**

3. **(Optional) In the File Name text box, rename the document.**

Notepad automatically changes the file extension from .htm to .txt. To prevent this, type **.htm** at the end of the filename.

4. **Click Save.**

Wallpapering Your Desktop with a Web Graphic

Internet Explorer 6 makes it a snap to copy a favorite graphic from a Web page and save it as a wallpaper file. You can then use the wallpaper file as the background for your Windows desktop.

To turn a Web graphic into wallpaper for your desktop, follow these steps:

1. **Use Internet Explorer to go to the Web page that contains the graphic that you want to save as wallpaper.**

2. **Right-click the Web graphic to display its shortcut menu and click the Set As Background command.**

As soon as you click Set As Background, Internet Explorer 6 makes the graphic the wallpaper for your desktop and copies the selected graphic onto your hard drive, placing it in the Windows folder. The graphic is given the filename `Internet Explorer Wallpaper.bmp`.

To remove the Web graphic wallpaper, right-click the desktop and select Properties from the shortcut menu that appears. The Display Properties dialog box opens. On the Desktop tab (the Background tab in Windows 98), choose a new graphic or HTML file for the wallpaper in the Select an HTML Document or a Picture list box. If you no longer want any graphic displayed as the wallpaper, select the (None) option at the top of the list.

If you're using Windows 95, your Display Properties dialog box looks a little different. On the Background tab, you can either choose a standard background pattern from the Pattern box or choose to wallpaper your desktop with a graphic chosen from the Wallpaper box. If you want a simple, plain background, select None from both boxes.

Chapter 4: Customizing Internet Explorer 6

In This Chapter

✓ Choosing a home page

✓ Customizing the display of Web pages and personalizing your toolbars

✓ Using the Content Advisor

✓ Adding Active Channels and Active Desktop Items

✓ Working with the cache of Temporary Internet Files

✓ Adjusting History settings

✓ Speeding up your browser

✓ Synchronizing Web pages for offline viewing

✓ Using AutoComplete

In preparation for your extensive travels on the World Wide Web via Internet Explorer 6, you may need to make some minor adjustments. This chapter is the place to look for information on everything from how to change the way Web pages are displayed on your screen, to customizing your toolbars, to ways to tweak your browser's performance.

This chapter also provides information on adding Active Channels and Active Desktop Items so that the latest and greatest Web information automatically finds its way from Cyberspace to your computer desktop, with no World Wide Wait.

Changing Your Home Page

 Each time you start the Internet Explorer browser, it opens a specially designated page, which it calls the home page. The home page is also where Internet Explorer goes when you click the Home button on the toolbar.

If your computer isn't connected to the Internet when you click Home, Internet Explorer loads the home page locally from the cache. The *cache* is an area of a computer's hard drive used to store data recently downloaded from the Internet so that the data can be redisplayed quickly. If the page doesn't happen to be in the cache at the time (because you deleted its files before quitting the browser the last time), Internet Explorer gives you an error message and then displays an empty Web page called about:blank. To return to your home page, you must go online again and click the Home button.

To change the home page on your computer, follow these steps:

1. **Launch the Internet Explorer browser and go to the Web page that you want to make the new home page.**

2. **Choose Tools⇨Internet Options.**

   The Internet Options dialog box appears. Click the General tab if it isn't already selected.

3. **In the Home Page section of the dialog box, click the Use Current button to make the current page your new home page.**

   You can also type the URL of the page that you want to designate as your home page in the Address text box.

4. **Click OK to close the Internet Options dialog box.**

After you designate the page of your choice as your home page, you can return there anytime by clicking the Home button.

If, for the sake of speed, you want a blank Web page to be used as the home page, click the Use Blank button. Internet Explorer then enters about:blank (the name of its standard blank page) in the Address text box. You also can click the Stop button on the navigation bar as soon as Internet Explorer starts loading the page.

Changing the Way Web Pages Look

A Web page, depending on the computer displaying it, can appear in a variety of fonts and colors and can use various characters and symbols for different languages of the world. The combination of the Web browser settings and the design of the individual pages controls how Web pages look in Internet Explorer.

The changes that you make to the Internet Explorer settings only affect the way Web pages look on your screen. You don't have to worry that you're actually changing somebody's Web page.

Changing the text size

You can customize your copy of Internet Explorer 6 so that you get larger, easier-to-read text, or you can choose a smaller font size that lets you see more text at a time on the screen.

To change the display size of text in Web pages, follow these steps:

1. **Choose View⇨Text Size.**

A submenu appears with the following size options: Largest, Larger, Medium, Smaller, and Smallest. The Largest, Larger, Smaller, and Smallest font sizes are all relative to the Medium font size (which is the default size used by Internet Explorer 6).

2. **Choose the Largest or Larger option to make the text on the current Web page appear bigger. Choose the Smaller or Smallest option to make the text appear smaller.**

Selecting a different font

Many Web pages do not specify a font for the proportional and fixed-width (or monospaced) text on the Web page, leaving that determination to Internet Explorer. When you first start browsing the Web with Internet Explorer 6, it uses Times New Roman to render nonspecifically defined proportional text and Courier New for all fixed-width text.

If you prefer other fonts for rendering the proportional and fixed-width text, you can modify one of the Internet Explorer 6 character sets (different styles of the alphabet and other symbols).

To choose other fonts, follow these steps:

1. **Choose Tools⇨Internet Options.**

The Internet Options dialog box appears. Click the General tab if it isn't already selected.

2. **Click the Fonts button.**

The Fonts dialog box opens, as shown in Figure 4-1.

Figure 4-1: You can change the default proportional and fixed-width fonts via the Fonts dialog box.

3. **To change the font used to render proportional text, choose a font in the Web Page Font list box.**

   Your particular choices depend upon which fonts you have installed on the computer.

4. **To change the font used to render fixed-width text, choose a font in the Plain Text Font list box.**

5. **Click OK twice to close the Fonts dialog box and the Internet Options dialog box.**

Changing the text and background colors

If you have problems reading the text on a Web page due to its text color and background, you may be able to modify these colors (assuming that the Web page author hasn't specified his or her own colors). By default, Internet Explorer 6 chooses black for the text color and battleship gray for the background (page) color.

To set custom colors for your Web page background and text, follow these steps:

1. **Choose Tools⇨Internet Options.**

   The Internet Options dialog box appears. Click the General tab if it isn't already selected.

2. **Click the Colors button.**

   The Colors dialog box appears, as shown in Figure 4-2. In this dialog box, you can set colors for the text and background as well as the colors for visited and unvisited hyperlinks.

Figure 4-2:
You can change the color of Web page text and the background color.

3. **In the Colors section of the Colors dialog box, click the Use Windows Colors check box to remove its check mark.**

   Deselecting this check box enables you to specify your own colors.

4. **To change the text color, click the Text button in the Colors dialog box to open the Color dialog box and then select a new color from the Basic Colors palette. Then click OK.**

5. **To change the background color of the page, click the Background button in the Colors dialog box to open the Color dialog box and then select a new color from the Basic Colors palette. Then click OK.**

6. **When you finish setting the text and background colors that you want to use, click OK twice to close the Colors dialog box and the Internet Options dialog box.**

When the Internet Options dialog box closes, Internet Explorer displays the current Web page in the text and background colors that you selected. If it doesn't, this means that the author of this Web page has explicitly set a style for the page, which takes precedence over the browser default settings that you set.

Changing the way your browser displays hyperlinks

Hypertext links (*hyperlinks*) are a special form of text that, when clicked, take you to a new location on the current page or to another page altogether. Traditionally, blue underlined text on-screen indicates the hypertext links that you haven't yet followed. When you follow a hypertext link and then return to the original page, Internet Explorer 6 lets you know that you've followed the link by displaying the same hypertext in purple underlined text. People often refer to these links as *unvisited* and *visited* links.

To modify the color of hypertext links in Internet Explorer 6, follow these steps:

1. **Choose Tools⇨Internet Options.**

   The Internet Options dialog box appears. Click the General tab if it isn't already selected.

2. **Click the Colors button.**

   The Colors dialog box appears.

3. **To change the color for visited hyperlinks, click the Visited button and choose a new color from the palette in the Color dialog box. Click OK to close the Color dialog box.**

4. **To change the color for unvisited hyperlinks, click the Unvisited button and choose a new color from the palette in the Color dialog box. Click OK to close the Color dialog box.**

   In addition to customizing the visited and unvisited hypertext colors, you can choose to assign a *hover* color (that is, the color that hyperlinked text becomes when you position your mouse pointer over it).

Book III
Chapter 4

**Customizing
Internet Explorer 6**

5. To have text hyperlinks turn a special color whenever your mouse pointer hovers above them, click the Use Hover Color check box to put a check mark in it. If you don't like the default color of red, click the Hover button and choose a new color from the palette in the Color dialog box. Click OK to close the Color dialog box.

6. When you're finished changing the link colors, click OK twice to close the Colors dialog box and the Internet Options dialog box.

Selecting a language

If you're multilingual and really want to experience the World Wide Web (with the emphasis on World), you may want to enable Internet Explorer to display the characters, currency signs, and conventions for expressing decimals used in various languages.

To select a new language for Internet Explorer 6, follow these steps:

1. **Choose Tools⇨Internet Options.**

The Internet Options dialog box appears. Click the General tab if it isn't already selected.

2. **Click the Languages button.**

The Language Preference dialog box appears.

3. **Click the Add button.**

The Add Language dialog box appears.

4. **Click to select the language that you want to add.**

5. **Click OK to place the language in the Language list box of the Language Preference dialog box.**

In addition to adding languages, you can set the priority order that Internet Explorer 6 uses in displaying material from a multilingual Web site. Internet Explorer 6 switches the language it uses, using the order of the languages as they appear in the Language Preference dialog box.

6. **(Optional) To boost a language's priority in the Language Preference dialog box, click the language and then click the Move Up button until the language appears at the desired place in the list box. To lower a language's priority, click the language and then click the Move Down button until the language appears at the desired place in the list box.**

7. **When you finish adding languages and changing their priority order, click OK twice to close both the Language Preference and Internet Options dialog boxes.**

Customizing Toolbars

Internet Explorer 6 contains several toolbars, which you can customize to your liking. You can change the display size of toolbars, move toolbars, hide toolbars, and add buttons to toolbars. Refer to Chapter 1 of this minibook if you need a refresher on the toolbars included with Internet Explorer 6.

Changing the size of toolbars

You can minimize the amount of space that the toolbar takes up by putting Internet Explorer in full-screen view. To do so, choose View➪Full Screen or press F11. The full-screen view shrinks the amount of space given to the toolbars — Internet Explorer hides all the toolbars except the Standard Buttons toolbar, which now uses smaller icons.

When Internet Explorer is in full-screen mode, the browser adds an Auto-Hide command to the shortcut menu that appears when you right-click the remaining Standard Buttons toolbar. Selecting the Auto-Hide command causes the entire toolbar to slide up until it's off the screen. To redisplay the toolbar, move the mouse pointer up to the top of the Internet Explorer window. When the mouse pointer rolls over the area where the toolbar would normally be, the toolbar magically (and temporarily) reappears.

To again fix the Standard Buttons toolbar on the screen, choose the Auto-Hide command from the toolbar's shortcut menu. You can also take Internet Explorer 6 out of full-screen mode by pressing F11.

Moving a toolbar

When you first start browsing with Internet Explorer 6, the toolbar components are arranged so that the menu bar appears in a row of its own at the top, the Standard Buttons toolbar appears in a row immediately below the menu bar, and the Address bar and Links bar share the third row. You can, however, customize this arrangement:

✦ You can move any toolbar to a new row by dragging its control handle (the vertical bar that appears in front of the first option or button on the bar) up or down.

 If the control handle isn't showing, simply choose View➪Toolbars and then click to remove the checkmark next to Lock the Toolbars.

✦ You can lengthen or shorten the toolbar when two (or more) toolbars share the same row by dragging the toolbar control handle to the left or right.

Hiding and unhiding a toolbar

You can hide the Standard Buttons toolbar, the Address bar, or the Links bar. To do so, choose View⇨Toolbars. From the submenu that appears, click to remove the check mark next to the toolbar that you want to hide. You can also right-click any empty area of the toolbar and choose the appropriate name (Standard Buttons, Address bar, or Links) from the toolbar shortcut menu. To display the hidden toolbar again, reverse this procedure.

Adding a button to the toolbar

You can add a button to the Standard Buttons toolbar to make the button's command more accessible. Follow these steps:

1. **Choose View⇨Toolbars⇨Customize or right-click the Standard Buttons toolbar and choose Customize from the shortcut menu.**

   The Customize Toolbar dialog box appears.

2. **In the Available Toolbar Buttons list box, click the button you want to add to the toolbar and then click Add.**

   Internet Explorer adds the button to the end of the list in the Current Toolbar Buttons list box.

3. **(Optional) To change the position of the newly added button on the toolbar, click the button in the Current Toolbar Buttons list box; then click the Move Up button one or more times.**

4. **Click the Close button to close the Customize Toolbar dialog box.**

Screening Web Content with the Content Advisor

The Internet contains an enormous amount of material on all kinds of matters. The topics, however, that seem to raise the most interest, at least for top government executives and senators and evening news anchors, are the subjects of sex, nudity, violence, and adult language.

Microsoft has responded by endowing Internet Explorer 6 with an automated Content Advisor that works with a national rating system. You may want to use this system to prevent computer users from accessing Web sites that contain material that fails to meet particular rating standards.

Setting a password and enabling the Content Advisor

To set up the Content Advisor, you have to supply a password, thereby making you its supervisor. If you're very concerned about screening Web content, be sure to provide a password that's hard to guess or crack. To keep your password secure, you should provide one that contains a completely random combination of letters, numbers, and special characters (such as $ and @ signs).

Never lose your password. You need your password to change any of the settings, including setting a new password. Memorize your password or write it down and store it somewhere secure, such as a fire-resistant safe or a safety deposit box at a bank.

After you decide on your password, follow these steps to get the Content Advisor up and running:

1. **Choose Tools⇨Internet Options and click the Content tab.**

You see the dialog box shown in Figure 4-3.

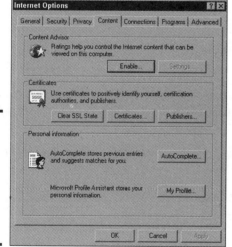

Figure 4-3: Click the Enable button to begin setting up the Content Advisor.

Book III
Chapter 4

Customizing
Internet Explorer 6

2. **Click the Enable button.**

The first time you attempt to set a password, the Content Advisor dialog box opens at this point. If you have set a password previously and want to change it, skip to the next section, "Changing the Supervisor password."

3. **Click the General tab.**

4. **In the User Options section, select one or both of the following options:**

- **Supervisor Can Type a Password to Allow Users to View Restricted Content:** Select this option if you want the Supervisor password to be used by default.

- **Users Can See Sites That Have No Rating:** If you select this option, the Create Supervisor Password dialog box appears. Enter your password in the Password text box and click OK. This enables the Settings button.

Again, be sure to remember your password. Internet Explorer requires it any time you want to change Content Advisor settings.

5. **Click OK to close the Content Advisor dialog box.**

You can now begin using the Content Advisor with its default settings. If you want to change the Ratings and General options in the Content Advisor dialog box, refer to the section "Modifying the level of the ratings," later in this chapter.

Changing the Supervisor password

If you want to change your Supervisor password, follow these steps:

1. **Choose Tools⇨Internet Options and click the Content tab.**

2. **Click the Settings button.**

   The Supervisor Password Required dialog box appears.

3. **Type your existing password in the Supervisor Password Required dialog box and click OK.**

   The Content Advisor dialog box appears.

4. **Click the General tab and then click the Change Password button to open the Change Supervisor Password dialog box.**

5. **Type your existing password in the Old Password text box, type your new password in the New Password text box, and type your new password again in the Confirm New Password text box.**

6. **Click OK to complete the process of changing the password.**

7. **Click OK two more times to close the Content Advisor and Internet Options dialog boxes.**

Modifying the level of the ratings

When you first enable the Internet Explorer 6 Content Advisor, the ratings are set to the maximum levels of content screening in all four of the following categories: Violence, Nudity, Sex, and Language. Internet Explorer 6 uses the RSAC (Recreational Software Advisory Council) rating system, which has four levels. Level 0 is the most stringent and Level 4 is the most permissive, as shown in Table 4-1.

Table 4-1		Rating Levels		
Level	*Language*	*Nudity*	*Sex*	*Violence*
0	Inoffensive slang	None	None	None
1	Mild expletives	Revealing attire	Passionate kissing	Fighting
2	Moderate expletives	Partial nudity	Clothed sexual touching	Killing
3	Obscene gestures	Frontal nudity	Nonexplicit sexual touching	Killing with blood and gore
4	Explicit or crude language	Provocative frontal nudity	Explicit sexual activity	Wanton and gratuitous violence

When you first enable the Content Advisor, all levels are set to the most restrictive (Level 0), by default.

To change the level of any of these ratings, follow these steps:

1. **Choose Tools⇨Internet Options; then click the Content tab.**

2. **Click the Settings button, type your password in the Password text box of the Supervisor Password Required dialog box, and then click OK.**

The Content Advisor dialog box appears, with the Ratings tab displayed. A list box contains the four categories: Language, Nudity, Sex, and Violence.

3. **In the list box of the Content Advisor dialog box, click the category for which you want to set the rating levels.**

4. **Drag the slider control to reset the level for that category.**

5. **Repeat Steps 3 and 4 for each category that you want to reset and then click the Apply button.**

6. **Click OK when you have made all necessary changes.**

The Content Advisor dialog box closes, and the new ratings settings are put into effect.

Disabling the Content Advisor

You may want to disable the Content Advisor at some point. (Hey, someday the kids are going to grow up and move away.) Just keep in mind that as soon as you enable the Content Advisor, its Enable button magically turns into a Disable button. To permanently turn off the cyberthought police, click the Content tab of the Internet Options dialog box and then click the Disable button. Now you're just a password away from disabling the Content Advisor. You can always use the Enable button at a later time if you find the need to use the Content Advisor again.

Active Channels and Active Desktop Items

Active Channels (also known simply as *channels*) are Web sites that use a technology called *Webcasting*. This technology makes it possible for Internet Explorer 6 to automatically download updated content from the Active Channel's Web site to your computer's *cache* (temporary storage area) on a regular schedule. This enables you to browse the new content even when you're not connected to the Internet (known as *offline viewing*).

Many channels offer a more condensed experience of their online information, known as Active Desktop Items. *Active Desktop Items* are World Wide Web components that appear directly on your Windows desktop and give you immediate access to the information that you want to see without having to browse through Web page after Web page. Active Desktop Items often give you instant access to highlights or headlines of the Web site, which you can click to open into full-screen Web pages.

Adding Active Channels or Active Desktop Items

After initially installing Internet Explorer 6, you have access to only one Active Desktop Item — the Internet Explorer Channel bar. The Internet Explorer Channel bar provides an easy way to access the Active Channels that you add to your computer as well as to sign up for new channels.

To display this built-in Active Desktop Item, you need to right-click the desktop and then choose Active Desktop➪Show Web Content from the shortcut menu. Of course, if you decide that you want more Active Desktop goodies adorning your desktop, you have to go and get them.

To add additional Active Desktop Items and channels, you need to go online and install them from the Windows Active Desktop Gallery Web page. To connect to this page, follow these steps:

1. **Right-click the desktop.**

   A shortcut menu appears.

2. **Choose Active Desktop➪Customize My Desktop.**

   The Display Properties dialog box appears with the Web tab selected.

3. **Click the New button to open the New Active Desktop Item dialog box. If the New button is not available (grayed out), click the Show Web Content on My Active Desktop check box and then click the New button.**

4. **Click Visit Gallery in the New Active Desktop Item dialog box to close both the New Active Desktop Item and the Display Properties dialog boxes.**

   This launches Internet Explorer 6 and opens the Windows Active Desktop Gallery Web page.

5. **Find the specific Active Desktop Item or channel that you want to add and then click the Add to Active Desktop button.**

6. **Click Yes in the Internet Explorer dialog box to confirm that you want to add the selected Active Desktop Item to your desktop.**

   The Add Item to Active Desktop dialog box appears, listing the name of the item you selected in Step 5.

7. **Click OK to confirm the selected channel.**

   After you click OK, a Downloading dialog box appears, keeping you apprised of the download progress of the Active Channel or Desktop Item that you selected.

If you download a new Active Desktop Item, you need to return to the desktop to check out your new toy. Click the Close box in the title bar of the Internet Explorer window to return to the desktop. If you don't see your new Active Desktop Item right away, right-click the desktop to display the shortcut menu and then choose the Refresh command.

Viewing channels with the Channels folder

You can easily display the content of the channels that you add by opening the Favorites Explorer bar in the browser (by clicking the Favorites button on the Standard Buttons toolbar) and then clicking the Channels folder icon.

The default channels in the Channels folder are arranged into the following categories (you may see additional channels, depending on your setup):

+ Microsoft Channel Guide
+ News and Technology
+ Sports
+ Business
+ Entertainment
+ Lifestyle and Travel

If you add a channel to a particular category, click its name in the Favorites Explorer bar. When you see the name of the channel whose contents you want to view, click its hyperlink in the Favorites Explorer bar. The channel's opening page then appears in the right frame of Internet Explorer, and hyperlinks to linked channel pages appear in the Favorites Explorer bar (the frame on the left side of Internet Explorer).

To update the contents of the channel that you want to view, right-click the channel's hyperlink and click the Refresh command on the shortcut menu.

Removing an Active Channel or Active Desktop Item

If you decide that you want to remove a channel and its contents from your computer, you can do so via the Favorites Explorer bar.

To delete an Active Desktop Item, follow these steps:

1. **Right-click your desktop and choose Active Desktop⇨Customize My Desktop from the shortcut menu.**

   The Display Properties dialog box appears.

2. **Click the Web tab, if it isn't already selected.**

3. **Click the item that you want to delete in the View My Active Desktop as a Web page list box and then click the Delete button.**

   The Active Desktop Item dialog box appears.

4. **Click Yes to confirm that you want to delete this item.**

5. **Click OK to close the Display Properties dialog box.**

Adjusting Your Cache Settings

When you connect to the Internet and browse a Web site, Internet Explorer 6 downloads the pages and their embedded content into a special place on your hard drive. This place is known as the *cache* or the *Temporary Internet Files* (because they reside in a folder called Temporary Internet Files in the Windows folder on your hard drive).

The Internet Explorer 6 cache stores all the Web pages you visit to speed up the performance of the browser when you go back and forth between the pages online and to enable you to see these pages when you browse offline (see Book III, Chapter 2). The only drawback to this arrangement occurs when the contents of a Web page are updated. You see only the stale, old contents of the page from your cache (thus, the purpose of the Refresh button on the Internet Explorer toolbar).

You may need to increase your cache size if you're going to view movies and other multimedia content that take up loads of room.

Clearing your cache

To clear out old, unwanted Temporary Internet Files from your cache, follow these steps:

1. **Choose Tools⇨Internet Options.**

The Internet Options dialog box appears. Click the General tab if it isn't already selected.

2. **Click the Delete Files button.**

The Delete Files dialog box opens. In the Delete Files dialog box, you can delete not only your cached Temporary Internet Files, but also your offline content that is stored locally on your hard drive.

3. **Click OK two times to close the Delete Files and Internet Options dialog boxes.**

Setting your cache size

Your cache size is important: Too small a cache doesn't allow proper display of multimedia content; too large a cache takes up too much room on your hard drive. Although the Internet Explorer 6 installation program automatically sets the cache to 1 percent of the size of your hard drive, you may want to change this amount later — for example, to free up space as your hard drive fills up, or to increase your cache size for better browser performance.

To change the size of the Internet Explorer 6 cache, follow these steps:

1. **Choose Tools⇨Internet Options.**

The Internet Options dialog box appears. Click the General tab if it isn't already selected.

2. **Click the Settings button.**

The Settings dialog box opens, as shown in Figure 4-4.

Book III
Chapter 4

**Customizing
Internet Explorer 6**

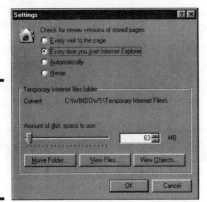

Figure 4-4:
Use the slider control to change the size of your cache.

3. **In the Amount of Disk Space to Use area, drag the slider control to the left or right to change the size of the cache.**

As you move the control to a new location, the amount of space in megabytes (MB) appears in the text box. You may also type a value into the text box or use the arrows next to the text box to increase or decrease the value.

4. **Click OK to put the new cache size into effect.**

Changing when the browser checks for newer versions of pages

Normally, Internet Explorer 6 checks for newer versions of the pages in the cache only when you launch the browser and connect to the Internet — in other words, at the very beginning of a browsing session.

This means that when you revisit a Web page during the same browsing session (that is, without closing and restarting Internet Explorer), the browser loads that page from the cache rather than downloading a possibly newer version. Internet Explorer assumes that if the address is the same, then the contents of the page are the same.

You can, however, change the setting for when Internet Explorer checks for newer versions of a cached page. To change the setting, follow these steps:

1. **Choose Tools⇨Internet Options.**

The Internet Options dialog box appears. Click the General tab if it isn't already selected.

2. **Click the Settings button. The Settings dialog box appears, presenting four choices:**

   - **Every Visit to the Page:** Selecting this setting forces Internet Explorer to check for changes every time you visit a page — even if you're using the Back button to return to a page that you were at two seconds ago. Using this setting can slow your browser down considerably.

   - **Every Time You Start Internet Explorer:** This setting updates pages in your cache each time you begin a new surfing session, but uses the cached version of pages you visited in the current session.

   - **Automatically:** This setting uses your synchronization schedule to update pages. (See "Synchronizing Offline Web Pages," later in this chapter, for more details.)

   - **Never:** Selecting this setting prevents Internet Explorer from ever checking for new versions of the pages in the cache. This is the choice for trying to get the most speed out of a slow Internet connection. But it completely sacrifices any attempt to check for changed content — even if you haven't been to that address for weeks.

Regardless of what setting you choose under Check for Newer Versions of Stored Pages, you can always force Internet Explorer to download a new copy of any Web page that you're viewing (thereby replacing any older version in your cache with the new one). Here are three ways to do so:

✦ Choose View➪Refresh from the Internet Explorer menu bar.

✦ Press the F5 key on your keyboard.

 ✦ Click the Refresh button on the Internet Explorer toolbar.

Changing the History Settings

When you come across a wonderful Web page, you can save the page to your Favorites list or create a shortcut to the page to make returning there easy (see Book III, Chapter 2, for more details). However, if you forgot to save a Web page to your Favorites list at the time it was displayed in the Internet Explorer 6 browsing window, you can still get back to it by finding its link in the History folder.

By default, the Internet Explorer 6 History folder retains links to the pages that you visited during the last 20 days. But you may want to change the length of time that links remain in your History folder. For example, you can increase the time so that you have access to Web pages visited in the more distant past, or you can decrease the time if you're short on hard drive

**Book III
Chapter 4**

**Customizing
Internet Explorer 6**

space. You can also purge the links in the History folder to free up space on your hard drive and restore all hyperlinks to pages that you've visited to their unvisited state (and colors).

To change the History settings, follow these steps:

1. **Choose Tools⇨Internet Options.**

   The Internet Options dialog box appears. Click the General tab if it isn't already selected.

2. **In the History section, type a new value in the Days to Keep Pages in History text box or click the up or down arrows to select the desired value.**

3. **Click OK.**

To purge the links in the History folder, follow these steps:

1. **Choose Tools⇨Internet Options.**

   The Internet Options dialog box appears. Click the General tab if it isn't already selected.

2. **Click the Clear History button.**

3. **Click OK in the Internet Options alert box that appears, which asks if you want to delete all items from your History folder.**

4. **Click OK to close the Internet Options dialog box.**

Specifying Mail, News, and Internet Call Programs

Internet Explorer 6 can work with other programs to add to its functionality and capabilities. Microsoft has created certain programs that it intends to work so closely with Internet Explorer 6 that it refers to them as *members of the Internet Explorer Suite.*

The auxiliary programs that are included with Internet Explorer 6 as part of the suite depend upon which type of installation you perform:

+ **Custom:** This installation lets you select which auxiliary programs are installed along with the browser and Outlook Express.

+ **Minimal:** This installation gives you the Microsoft Internet Connection Wizard along with Internet Explorer 6.

+ **Typical:** This installation includes the browser plus Outlook Express, Windows Media Player, and a few multimedia enhancements.

One of the most practical of these many auxiliary programs is Microsoft Outlook Express, which adds e-mail and news-reading capabilities to Internet Explorer 6. If you do the typical installation and your computer is equipped with sound and video hardware, such as a microphone and video camera, you can use NetMeeting to make Internet calls or set up video conferencing. Even if you don't have such hardware, you can use Chat (originally known as Comic Chat) as part of NetMeeting to participate in online chat sessions.

To see which programs are configured to run from Internet Explorer (such as the Mail, News, and Internet call programs) and, if necessary, change them, follow these steps:

1. **Choose Tools⇨Internet Options; then click the Programs tab (see Figure 4-5).**

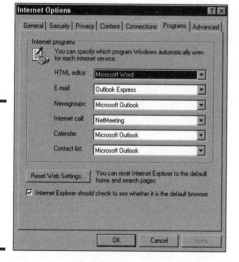

Figure 4-5:
Use the
Programs
tab to view
or select
programs
used with
Internet
Explorer.

2. **To change the program listed in the HTML Editor, E-Mail, Newsgroups, Internet Call, Calendar, or Contact List text boxes, select a new program by using the drop-down list boxes.**

3. **After you finish checking over the programs and making any changes to them, click OK.**

If you have installed another Web browser, such as Netscape Navigator, after installing Internet Explorer 6, you can click the Reset Web Settings button in this dialog box to restore your original Internet Explorer default settings for search pages and your home page. Clicking this button also restores the prompt to ask you whether you want to make Internet Explorer 6 your default browser each time you launch Microsoft's browser.

Speeding Up the Display of Web Pages

You can speed up the display of Web pages on your computer, but unless you do it by getting a faster connection (with a modem upgrade, a DSL or ISDN line, or a cable modem), the increase in speed comes at the expense of hard drive space or viewing content. You can get some increase in speed by increasing your cache size or decreasing how often Internet Explorer 6 checks for new content posted on Web pages (see "Adjusting Your Cache Settings," earlier in this chapter).

You can also dramatically speed up the display of Web pages by turning off the display of most pictures, animations, videos, and sounds. To make this kind of change to Internet Explorer 6, follow these steps:

1. **Choose Tools⇨Internet Options; then click the Advanced tab.**

2. **In the Multimedia section of the Settings list box, click to remove the check mark from the check boxes of as many of the items as you want to disable to get a sufficient speed boost.**

   These items include Play videos, Play sounds, Smart image dithering, Show pictures, and Play animations.

3. **Click OK to add the new settings and close the Internet Options dialog box.**

 Now when you open new Web pages, weird (but fast) generic icons replace the multimedia contents that you've disabled. If you still see graphics on the Web pages that you visit, click the Refresh button on the Internet Explorer toolbar to remove their display.

After disabling the Show Pictures and Play Videos settings, you can still choose to display a particular graphic or play a particular video. Just right-click the icon placeholder and choose Show Picture from its shortcut menu. Internet Explorer 6 then downloads and displays the particular graphic or video that you selected.

To restore the multimedia items that you disabled, click the Advanced tab of the Internet Options dialog box again and click the check boxes to select the desired Multimedia items. Then click OK to save your changes and close the Internet Options dialog box. Remember that you have to use the Refresh button on the Internet Explorer toolbar to see and hear multimedia items on pages that were downloaded to the cache when these items were disabled.

Synchronizing Offline Web Pages

To make sure that you have the most current data from an Active Channel or a Favorites Web site that you've made available for browsing offline, you may want to update the contents of your cache — a process known as *synchronization*. (For related information, see Book III, Chapter 2, and the section "Adding Active Channels and Active Desktop Items," earlier in this chapter.)

To synchronize individual Active Channels or favorite Web sites, follow these steps:

1. Choose Tools⇨Synchronize.

The Items to Synchronize dialog box appears.

2. In the Select the Check Box for Any Items You Want to Synchronize list box, make sure that the check box for each offline Web page you want updated contains a check mark. Remove the check mark from the check box of any offline Web page whose contents you don't want updated.

3. Click the Synchronize button.

Internet Explorer then connects you to the Internet and begins the process of checking each selected offline Web page for updated content, which is then automatically downloaded into your computer's cache. Synchronizing enables you to browse the updated contents (using the Favorites Explorer bar) when you're not connected to the Internet.

If you connect to the Internet over a LAN (local area network) or via a cable modem, DSL, or ISDN connection (you can therefore go online at anytime), you may want to specify when and under what conditions particular offline Web pages are synchronized. To do this, choose Tools⇨Synchronize. Then with the Offline Web Pages folder selected, click the Setup button. When you click this button, Internet Explorer opens the Synchronization Settings dialog box.

**Book III
Chapter 4**

**Customizing
Internet Explorer 6**

The Synchronization Settings dialog box contains three tabs: Logon, On Idle, and Scheduled.

✦ **Logon tab:** Use this tab to select the offline pages that you want synchronized whenever you log onto a networked computer. Click the check boxes for the offline pages to be synchronized when you log onto your computer; then click the When I Log On to My Computer check box.

✦ **On Idle tab:** Use this tab to select the offline pages that you want synchronized whenever your computer is idle for a particular period of time. Click the check boxes for the offline pages to be synchronized when your computer is idle for a particular period and then click the Synchronize the Selected Items When My Computer Is Idle check box. To specify how long an idle period to use, click the Advanced button and then change the settings in the Idle Settings dialog box.

✦ **Scheduled tab:** Use this tab to set up a custom schedule by which selected offline pages are routinely synchronized. To create a new schedule to be used, click the Add button and then use the Scheduled Synchronization Wizard to take you through the steps of creating and naming a new custom schedule for certain offline Web pages. To edit the settings for a particular default schedule, click the name of the schedule (such as CNN Desktop Scores Recommended Schedule); then click the Edit button to open a dialog box in which you can modify the current settings (the name of the dialog box and its tabs and options vary depending on the particular synchronization schedule that you're editing).

Customizing Your AutoComplete Settings

The AutoComplete feature makes it easier to fill out addresses, forms, and passwords by providing a drop-down list of suggestions as you type, based on your previous entries. Internet Explorer 6 has added the capability to customize the AutoComplete settings.

To customize your AutoComplete settings, follow these steps:

1. **Choose Tools⇨Internet Options and click the Content tab.**

2. **Click the AutoComplete button.**

The AutoComplete Settings dialog box appears.

3. **Select the check boxes for the items for which you want to use AutoComplete.**

Select the Web Addresses check box to have AutoComplete suggest URLs for previously visited Web pages. Select the Forms check box if you want AutoComplete to match the field values from the most recently submitted form. Select User Names and Passwords on Forms if you want AutoComplete to retain your user ID and password for sites that require them.

4. **(Optional) To delete the form information that AutoComplete retains, click the Clear Forms button. To delete the list of user IDs and passwords that AutoComplete retains, click the Clear Passwords button.**

To delete the list of Web addresses that AutoComplete keeps on file, you must click the Clear History button on the General tab of the Internet Options dialog box.

5. **Click OK twice to close both dialog boxes.**

Index

Book IV

Web Browsing with Netscape Navigator

The 5th Wave   By Rich Tennant

"It's a free starter disk for AOL."

Contents at a Glance

Chapter 1: Using Navigator to Browse the Web

In This Chapter

✔ Browsing with Navigator

✔ Knowing where to get help

✔ Finding what you need

✔ Marking your favorite sites

✔ Viewing pages offline

✔ Using Smart Browsing

✔ Understanding the History file

*N*avigator is the world famous browser from Netscape that many Web surfers use to go globetrotting. In addition, because your company intranet works on the same principle as the Internet, you can also use Navigator for browsing your company's intranet, assuming, of course, that the intranet has not been designed to be used with Internet Explorer alone. In this chapter, we tell you what you need to know to successfully use Netscape Navigator.

If your browser of choice is Internet Explorer, see Book III, Chapter 2. If you need a refresher on Web basics, refer to Book III, Chapter 1.

Getting Started with Netscape Navigator

Who said you had to know how to type to use a computer? Navigator disproves that theory. If you can use a mouse, you can see the online world with Navigator. Netscape Navigator is extremely easy to use, and it has an interface that even a child can master within a few minutes.

Launching Netscape Navigator

The first thing you need to do is launch Netscape Navigator. To do so, double-click the Netscape Navigator icon on your desktop or choose Start⇨ All Programs⇨Netscape 6.2⇨Netscape 6.2.

Accessing a Web site

When you first fire up Navigator, you have to tell it which Web site you want to go to. If you don't have the Web site bookmarked (see the section "Keeping Track of Your Favorite Web Sites," later in this chapter), you must type the Web site's URL.

To type the URL of a Web site that you want to visit, follow these steps:

1. **Choose File⇨Open Web Location.**

The Open Web Location dialog box appears, as shown in Figure 1-1.

Figure 1-1:
Type the
URL in the
Open Web
Location
dialog box.

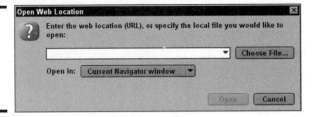

2. **Type the URL of the site you want to visit.**

3. **Select the Open Location or File in Navigator option button.**

4. **Click Open.**

Alternatively, you can simply position the cursor in the Location text box and type the URL of the Web site you'd like to go to. Press Enter and voilà! Your Web page appears.

Elements of the Navigator window

If you're a first-time Navigator user, you may wonder what's what in the Navigator window. Figure 1-2 shows you the various elements of the Navigator window. The following list describes what you can do with each item.

✦ **Menu bar:** The menu bar in Navigator works like the menu bars in virtually all Windows-based programs.

✦ **Navigation toolbar:** Use the buttons on the Navigation toolbar to get around quickly.

   • **Back:** Enables you to return to any Web sites that you may have previously visited during your Web session.

   • **Forward:** Takes you to any available pages in the History listing.

Personal toolbar

Navigation bar   Menu bar   Location box   Maximize/Restore button   Close button

Figure 1-2:
Use these
shortcuts to
navigate
around
Navigator.

Component bar   Status bar   Scroll bar

- **Reload:** Refreshes the current page. (Sometimes, the information on a page may not download to your computer properly the first time. *Reloading* the page downloads the entire page a second time.)

  Keep in mind that sometimes you have to hold the Shift key and click the Reload button to refresh not only the window, but also any Java or ActiveX components.

- **Stop:** Lets you stop a page from loading.

- **Location box:** The Location box shows the URL for the page being viewed. You can type a Web site's URL directly in the Location text box to go to that Web site.

- **Search:** Displays a page containing a collection of search engines.

- **Print:** Prints the current page.

**Book IV
Chapter 1**

Using Navigator to
Browse the Web

The Component bar

You can set the Component bar to be visible at all times, regardless of the Navigator application that you're using. This bar gives you immediate, one-click access to all the Navigator components.

You can set the Component bar so that it is visible as a tiny bar at the bottom-right corner of the Navigator window.

To make the Component bar appear and reappear, simply choose View⇨Show/Hide⇨ Component Bar.

✦ **Personal toolbar:** Use this customizable toolbar to create buttons for the URLs that you want to visit often. These URLs can be for Web sites, discussion groups, mail folders, and Address Book entries. The buttons shown in Figure 1-2 include Home, My Netscape, Search, Shop, Bookmarks, and Net2Phone.

✦ **Maximize/Restore button:** When this button resembles a square (Maximize), click it to enlarge the page to fill the entire screen. When this button resembles two overlapping documents (Restore), click it to reduce the page to a less-than-full-size view.

✦ **Close button:** Click this button when you're finished using Navigator.

✦ **Scroll bar:** Use the vertical scroll bar on the right side of your page to view the various areas of your screen. Occasionally, you may also see a horizontal scroll bar at the bottom of the Web page.

✦ **Status bar:** This bar tells you the status of your Web page.

✦ **Component bar:** The Navigator Component bar gives easy access to the browser, the mailbox messages, newsgroups messages, instant messages, the Address Book, and the Composer window, via a set of icons.

Think of the toolbars collectively as the steering wheel with which you control your journey on the Web. Among other things, you use the toolbars to move around, find information, and print what you see on the screen.

Getting Help

Navigator features an extensive set of online help files, called NetHelp; each of the components described in this section has a link to NetHelp. To access it, just choose Help⇨Help and Support Center on the menu bar at the top of the screen at any point to bring up the Help and Support Center window, shown in Figure 1-3.

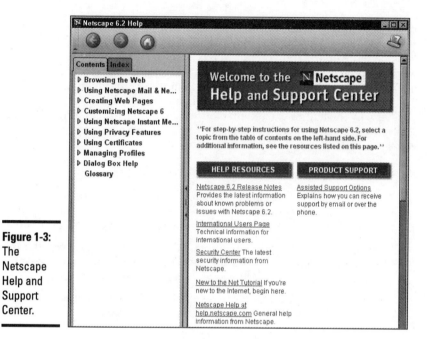

Figure 1-3:
The
Netscape
Help and
Support
Center.

To locate information on a particular component, follow these steps:

1. **Click any of the components in the left pane of the Help and Support Center window.**

On the right side of the Help window, a list of topics within the component you selected is displayed.

2. **In the list of topics, click the topic on which you need help.**

To view an alphabetical listing of all help topics, follow these steps:

1. **Click Index.**

An alphabetical list of all topics appears.

2. **Scroll down the list.**

3. **When the topic you want help on appears in the list, click it.**

To exit from the Help and Support Center, click the Close button in the upper-right corner of the window.

**Book IV
Chapter 1**

**Using Navigator to
Browse the Web**

Searching the Web

You find more information on the Web than in any library or museum in the world. At last count, 150 million home pages were on the Web, and the number is increasing at an amazing rate. Some of the information is useful — other information, utterly useless. Some information is so useless, you wonder why the author wasted precious time putting it up. But the information is there if you want it, and Navigator provides an easy way to find what you want. Follow these steps:

1. **On the Navigation toolbar, click the Search button.**

The Netscape Net Search site appears, as shown in Figure 1-4. At this site, you can access a variety of *search engines* — software that finds the information you want — to look up people, businesses, and products.

2. **To begin a search, type your query in the text box under Search the Web and then click a button that says something like Go or Search or Go Get It!, depending on the search engine that you're using.**

If you are not satisfied with the results from a search engine, try another, and another, and another, and . . . you get the picture.

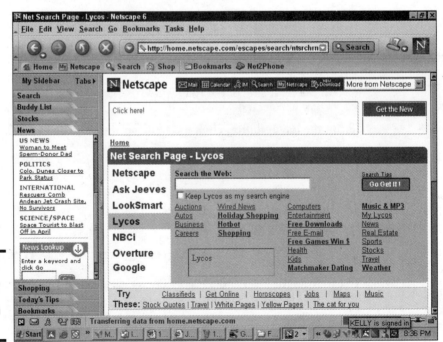

Figure 1-4:
The
Netscape
Net Search
site.

Using the Location text box

Using the Location text box, you can return to any site you've recently visited with one click of the mouse. To do so:

1. **Click the arrow at the end of the Location text box.**

The URLs of the sites you've visited recently are displayed.

2. **Click the URL of the site to which you want to return.**

Whoosh! You're on your way.

Clearing this list of URLs from the Location text box takes just a few clicks of the mouse. Follow these steps:

1. **Choose Edit➪Preferences.**

You should see the Preferences window, as shown in Figure 1-5. Navigator should be selected in the Category pane on the left side of the window. If it isn't, click it to select it.

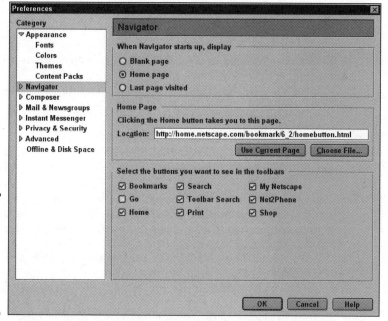

Figure 1-5:
The Navigator section of the Preferences window.

2. **From the drop-down list that appears, click History.**

3. **Click the Clear Location Bar button in the Location Bar History section, near the bottom of the window.**

4. **Click OK.**

The URLs in the Location text box are deleted, and you're back to the Navigator window.

Reloading a Web page

Reloading a page simply means asking Navigator to download the most current information available on the Web site. This feature is helpful when you're viewing a page that provides rapidly changing information — for example, a page providing running stock quotes. Because the page is constantly updated at its source, you want to make sure that the version of the page you're viewing is the most recent one. To ask Navigator to go out and get the current version of the page, click the Reload button on the Navigation toolbar.

Returning to a previously visited Web page

To return to a Web site that you visited earlier in your Web session, you can do one of the following things:

✦ Click the Back button on the Navigation toolbar until you get to the Web site. Positioning the mouse pointer on the Back button for a second or two shows you the URL of the Web page to which you will return by clicking that button.

✦ Click the arrow next to the Back button. A drop-down menu listing the most recently visited pages is displayed. Scroll down to the page that you want to visit again and then let go of the button.

✦ Right-click and choose <u>B</u>ack.

✦ Press Alt+←.

✦ Choose <u>G</u>o in the menu bar. From the list that appears, select the Web site to which you want to go.

Sometimes, you may click the Back button once too often in your hurry to get back to a particular page and then realize that you've gone too far back — like when you want to listen to a song one more time on your cassette player. You rewind the cassette for a little too long and then realize that you've gone way past the beginning. To get back to the song, you must press the Fast Forward button. The Forward button on the Navigation toolbar serves the same purpose. You can go forward to a site you've visited in any of the following ways:

✦ Click the Forward button on the Navigation toolbar. Positioning the mouse pointer on the Forward button for a second or two shows you the URL of the Web page to which you will return by clicking that button.

✦ Click the arrow next to the Forward button. A drop-down menu listing the most recently visited pages to which you can fast forward is displayed. Scroll down to the page that you want to visit again and then let go of the button.

✦ Right-click and choose Forward.

✦ Press the Alt+→.

✦ Choose Go in the menu bar. From the list that appears, select the Web site to which you want to go.

Keeping Track of Your Favorite Web Sites

You know what a bookmark is. It's a little mark you make in a book to help you find a particular page when you need it, fast. A *bookmark* within Navigator serves the same purpose. When you see a Web site that you think you may want to visit again, you bookmark it. The Bookmark feature is a neat feature and very helpful; if you cruise the Web as much as we do, you'll come across at least a handful of sites every day that you'll want to visit again.

Adding Web pages to the bookmark list

When you're viewing a Web site, adding a URL to the bookmark list is so easy. To mark a site with a bookmark, choose <u>B</u>ookmarks⇨Add <u>B</u>ookmark. or click the Bookmarks button and choose Add <u>B</u>ookmark.

The URL for the current page is added to the bottom of the bookmark list.

Here are other ways to add the URL for the currently displayed page to the bookmark list:

✦ Right-click anywhere on the current page and choose <u>B</u>ookmark This Page.

✦ Press Ctrl+D.

To add a URL to a specific folder within your bookmark list, follow these steps:

1. **Choose <u>B</u>ookmarks⇨<u>F</u>ile Bookmark.**

The Add Bookmark window appears.

2. **From the Create In area, choose the folder in which you'd like to place the bookmark and then click OK.**

The bookmark has now been added to the selected folder. (See the next section, "Creating a new bookmark folder," for more information on using folders.)

**Book IV
Chapter 1**

Using Navigator to
Browse the Web

Creating a new bookmark folder

After a few sessions of cruising the Web, you'll notice that your bookmark file is longer than the tail of Haley's comet (which, incidentally, could sometimes stretch to about 50 million miles). To organize your bookmarks, we recommend that you store them in folders.

To create a folder within the bookmark file, follow these steps:

1. **Choose** <u>B</u>**ookmarks**➪**Manage Book<u>m</u>arks.**

The Bookmarks window appears.

2. **Click the New Folder button.**

The Create New Folder dialog box appears.

3. **Replace the generic name** *New Folder* **with something more descriptive and click OK.**

The new folder now appears in the bookmark list.

Make sure that no two folders have the same name. Navigator doesn't alert you if a folder with the same name already exists within your bookmark list.

Adding (and removing) a URL to your Personal toolbar

The Personal toolbar is one of the great features of Navigator. It gives you the freedom to add links or icons as buttons to the toolbar. Then you can jump to your favorite Web site with just one simple mouse click. If you visit a particular Web site at least once a day, this feature can be a real time-saver!

To add the current Web page to your Personal toolbar, follow these steps:

1. **Choose** <u>B</u>**ookmarks**➪<u>F</u>**ile Bookmark.**

The Add Bookmark window appears.

2. **From the Create In area, choose the folder in which you'd like to place the bookmark — in this case, the Personal Toolbar folder — and then click OK.**

The URL for the current page appears as an icon on your Personal toolbar.

All links on your Personal toolbar are maintained within a folder called the Personal Toolbar folder in your bookmark list. To remove a link from your Personal toolbar, you must remove it from the Personal Toolbar folder.

To remove a link from the Personal Toolbar folder, follow these steps:

1. **Choose Bookmarks⇨Manage Bookmarks.**

2. **Click the Personal Toolbar folder to reveal its contents.**

3. **Within this folder, choose the URL that you want to remove from the Personal toolbar.**

4. **Press the Delete button on your keyboard.**

5. **Exit from the bookmark list by choosing File⇨Close.**

Using a bookmark to view a Web page

To go to a URL listed within your bookmark file, choose Bookmarks and then choose the URL to which you want to go from those listed.

To pick a URL bookmarked within a bookmark folder, hold the mouse pointer over a folder for a second. The contents of that folder are displayed. Then choose your URL.

Finding a bookmark

To perform a search to locate a particular bookmark, follow these steps:

1. **Choose Bookmarks⇨Manage Bookmarks.**

The Bookmarks window appears, listing all your bookmarks.

2. **Choose Edit⇨Find Bookmarks.**

The Find Bookmarks dialog box opens, as shown in Figure 1-6.

Figure 1-6:
The Find
Bookmarks
dialog box.

3. **Type the word(s) you want to find in the Find text box.**

4. **Use the two drop-down lists to specify whether you want to look for this word in the Name of the bookmark, its URL (Location), in its Description, or its Keyword and whether you want the word you typed to be contained in the Name, URL, or Description.**

5. **Click OK.**

   If a bookmark meeting your search criterion exists in your Bookmark file, it is highlighted.

Moving URLs between bookmark folders

To move a URL from one folder to another, follow these steps:

1. **Choose Bookmarks⇨Manage Bookmarks.**

2. **Drag-and-drop the bookmark into your folder of choice.**

Browsing Web Pages Offline

Offline browsing (as opposed to normal *online* browsing) lets you view your bookmarked pages when you are not connected to the Internet. (See "Adding Web pages to the Bookmark list" earlier in this chapter for details on making bookmarks available offline.) Because you can set up schedules for Favorite Web pages that you've made available offline so that updated contents are automatically downloaded to your hard drive, offline browsing enables you to view the updated Web contents at your leisure. To turn offline browsing on and off, choose File⇨ Work Offline on the menu bar.

Knowing what links are not available offline

When you're working in offline mode, you can browse only pages stored locally on your computer, such as those that have been downloaded into the cache on your computer's hard drive.

When you browse a Web site offline from a local hard drive, you have none of the wait often associated with browsing online while connected to the Internet. However, you may also find that some of the links, especially those to pages on another Web site that you haven't added to your bookmarks, are not available for viewing.

Opening Web pages offline

Most of the time when browsing offline, you do your local Web surfing in one of two ways:

✦ **Visit updated Web pages stored in the cache as a bookmark marked for offline viewing.** You open these pages by clicking the Bookmarks button and then selecting the particular folder that contains the page(s) you want to see.

  ✦ **Revisit Web pages stored in the cache as part of the History file.**
    Choose Tasks⇨Tools⇨History.

Internet Keywords

With millions of Web sites out there, it's getting increasingly difficult to find the information you want. Even the best search engines deliver less than half the information that exists on the Web, and often it is irrelevant to what you're looking for. As more Web sites are added to the Internet, your search for information will become even more difficult. Internet Keywords hopes to eliminate this problem.

Using Internet Keywords, you don't need to know the exact URL of the Web site to which you want to go. You just provide Navigator with a word or two by typing them in the Location text box, and Navigator does the rest. It does a behind-the-scenes search within its database, finds a site that is related to those words, and takes you there.

Suppose that you want to go to the Web site of Charles Schwab. You don't know the company's exact URL, so you can either perform a search by using a search engine or take the easy way out:

1. **Type** Schwab **in the Location text box.**

2. **Press Enter.**

    Navigator automatically takes you to the Charles Schwab Web site at www.schwab.com. Isn't that cool? It is, but keep in mind that the feature doesn't always work. Sometimes you get a list of Web sites when you search, and you have to choose which one to go to.

Internet Keywords also give you the convenience of not typing the www. and .com within a URL. Navigator automatically adds these to whatever you type in the Location text box. Follow these steps to get to the CNN Web site:

1. **Type** CNN **in the Location text box.**

2. **Press Enter.**

    Navigator adds the www. in front of CNN, appends .com to it, and takes you to the CNN Web site.

But what if sites have URLs that are identical except for the .com portion of the URL? For example, www.airfares.com, www.airfares.net, and www.airfares.org are three such sites. If you type just **airfares** in the Location text box, which site would Navigator take you to? None of them.

Instead, Navigator alerts you that it has found multiple listings for your query, lists all its findings, and lets you decide which one you want to visit. To see how this works, follow these steps:

1. **Type** airfares **in the Location text box.**

2. **Press Enter.**

    Navigator takes you to the Netscape Netcenter site and offers the results shown in Figure 1-7.

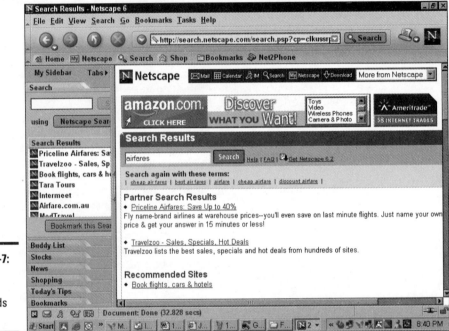

Figure 1-7:
Your
Internet
Keywords
result.

NetWatch and Communicator

NetWatch is Communicator's built-in ratings protection feature. (This feature used to find its home in Navigator in previous versions of the program, but now it's been moved to Communicator.) Parents and teachers may be especially interested in Communicator because it enables them to filter Web content.

Viewing Pages from the History File

Navigator maintains a log of the Web sites that you visit during a Web session. This log is maintained in the History file and is like a set of footprints you leave behind as you cruise the Web. You can ask Navigator to periodically erase this log automatically after a fixed number of days. When Navigator erases the contents of the file, the log stays empty until you start a new Web session.

At any time during a Web session, you can review the History file and directly jump to a Web site listed there — that is, a Web site you have already visited.

To use the History file to get to a Web site, follow these steps:

1. **Choose Tasks➪Tools➪History.**

   The History window appears. The most recent Web site you visited appears at the very top.

2. **Highlight the Web site that you want to revisit and double-click.**

Chapter 2: Printing and Saving Web Information

In This Chapter

✔ Printing and saving Web pages

✔ Checking out the HTML code behind a Web page

✔ Saving graphics to your hard drive

✔ Decorating your desktop with Web graphics

*I*f you already know how to browse, search, and maneuver around Netscape Navigator, then you're probably ready to find out how to do more advanced things. For example, how do all those people get cool graphics from Web pages to show up as wallpaper on their desktops? In this chapter, we not only let you in on the secret to jazzing up your desktop, but also explain how to print, save your favorite Web pages and graphics, and view HTML code.

Printing a Web Page

Navigator can help you find the information you want on the Web, but unless you plan to carry your computer around with you, you may need to print the information you find in order to show it to someone else.

To print a Web page, follow these steps:

1. **Choose File⇨Print, or click the Print button on the Navigation toolbar.**

   The Print dialog box appears, as shown in Figure 2-1.

2. **If you want to print only specific pages, specify those pages in the Print Range section.**

3. **Click Properties to specify the paper size and the print quality of the text and graphics.**

4. **Click OK to begin printing.**

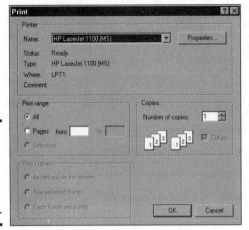

Figure 2-1:
Use the
familiar
Print dialog
box to print
a Web page.

Printing pages on a site that uses frames

Frames are a way to divide your browser window into separate panes, each displaying content from different HTML documents. (To find out more about frames, see Book VI, Chapter 2.)

If you're viewing a page containing frames, you see the Print Frame option area in the Print dialog box. (If the page you're viewing doesn't contain frames, this area of the dialog box is grayed out.) Select the radio button that corresponds to the frame you want to print and then click OK.

Changing the setup of a page that you're printing

When you print a Web page from Netscape Navigator, the program applies default page settings to the printout, such as Letter for Page Size and Portrait for Orientation. If you decide that you want to break out of the mold, you can adjust the page options.

To change the paper size, tray, or orientation, choose File➪Print and then click the Properties button. Adjust your settings in the Paper tab of the Properties dialog box (which differs depending on the printer you're using) and then click OK.

Saving a Web Page on Your Computer

You can save a Web page to your hard drive. Why would you want to do that? Here are a couple of reasons:

✦ After you save a page to your computer, you can view it even if you're not connected to the Internet. This means that when you're cruising the Web and don't have the time to read the entire contents of a lengthy page, you can save it to your hard drive — which usually takes only a few seconds — and then view it at your leisure after you have disconnected from the Internet.

✦ If you come across a page that makes you sit up and take notice, you may want to refer to the HTML code behind it for ideas when you're creating your own page. (See the section "Viewing the HTML Source of a Web Page," later in this chapter.) After you save the page on your computer, you can refer to it whenever you want to.

To save a page to your computer, follow these steps:

1. **Wait until the page has finished loading completely.**

This is usually indicated by the words `Document: Done` on the status bar at the bottom of the screen.

2. **Choose File⇨Save As.**

If you're viewing a page that has frames on it, the Save Frame As option is also available on the menu. Use this option to save the current frame.

The Save As dialog box appears.

3. **In the File Name text box, type a more descriptive name than the one that comes up by default on the screen.**

You'll appreciate this when it's time to look up the file; for some reason, it's hard to remember what is in a file called `chbstr.htm`.

4. **Click Save.**

Saving a page without viewing it

You can also save a page without displaying it on-screen. For example, a page may contain links to other pages. Instead of clicking a link, waiting for the page to appear, and then saving it, you can save the page that the link references without downloading and displaying the page on your screen.

To save a page without downloading and displaying it first, follow these steps:

1. **Right-click the link.**

2. **Choose Save Link As from the shortcut menu.**

3. **In the Save File window, type a name for the file to which you're saving the Web page and then click Save.**

Do not use the following characters in a filename; Navigator uses them to interpret URLs, and you could run into problems if you use them:

+ slash (/)
+ colon (:)
+ number sign (#)

Copying Web Page Information into a Document

If you like the contents of a Web page and want to share it with others, you can copy the text into a document on your hard drive.

To copy Web page information into a document, follow these steps:

1. **Go to the Web page and position the mouse pointer at the beginning of the text that you want to copy.**

2. **Click and drag to highlight all text that you want to copy.**

   If you want to copy *everything* on the page (including all text and graphics), choose Edit⇔Select All.

   When you drag through the text, all the graphics that appear between or to the side of the paragraphs you are selecting are highlighted for copying as well. If you don't want a graphic, you must copy the text before it and after it in separate actions.

3. **Choose Edit⇔Copy.**

   The selected text is copied into the Windows Clipboard.

4. **Switch to the word processor, text editor, or e-mail editor that contains the destination document or e-mail message into which you want to copy the selected text.**

   If you want to copy the selected text into an existing document, open the file with a word processor or text editor. Otherwise, open a new document.

5. **Click the I-beam mouse pointer at the place in the document or e-mail message where you want the copied text to appear and then choose Edit⇔Paste.**

Viewing the HTML Source of a Web Page

Behind every great Web page is a document of great HTML tags that present and format the page's contents. To see the HTML code behind any displayed

Web page, choose View➪Page Source. The HTML source code appears in a separate window, like the code shown in Figure 2-2. To close the window when you're finished, just click the Close button (X) in the upper-right corner of the window.

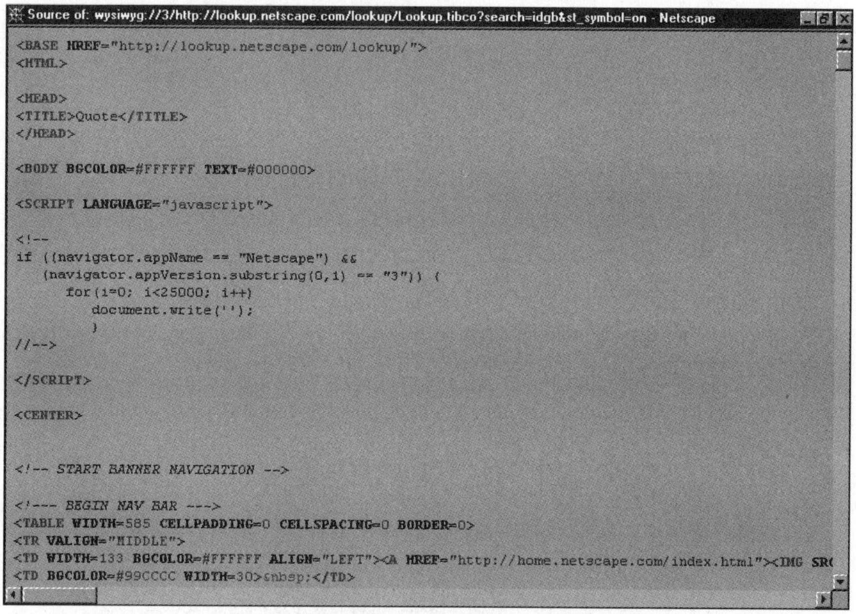

Figure 2-2:
The HTML
source code
for a Web
page.

```
Source of: wysiwyg://3/http://lookup.netscape.com/lookup/Lookup.tibco?search=idgb&st_symbol=on - Netscape

<BASE HREF="http://lookup.netscape.com/lookup/">
<HTML>

<HEAD>
<TITLE>Quote</TITLE>
</HEAD>

<BODY BGCOLOR=#FFFFFF TEXT=#000000>

<SCRIPT LANGUAGE="javascript">

<!--
if ((navigator.appName == "Netscape") &&
    (navigator.appVersion.substring(0,1) == "3")) {
        for(i=0; i<25000; i++)
            document.write('');
            }
//-->

</SCRIPT>

<CENTER>


<!-- START BANNER NAVIGATION -->

<!-- BEGIN NAV BAR -->
<TABLE WIDTH=585 CELLPADDING=0 CELLSPACING=0 BORDER=0>
<TR VALIGN="MIDDLE">
<TD WIDTH=133 BGCOLOR=#FFFFFF ALIGN="LEFT"><A HREF="http://home.netscape.com/index.html"><IMG SR(
<TD BGCOLOR=#99CCCC WIDTH=30> </TD>
```

Saving a Web Graphic on Your Computer

Very rarely will you come across a page that doesn't have a picture or animation on it. Some are worth saving; others are a waste of time. If you run into a jaw-dropping picture and want to save it, it's a simple process.

To save a Web graphic to your hard drive, follow these steps:

1. **Right-click the picture.**

2. **Choose Save Image from the shortcut menu.**

3. **In the Save File window, type a name for the picture and click Save.**

You can save an animation with a GIF extension in exactly the same way. An animation is an image file just like any other graphic.

Wallpapering Your Desktop with a Web Graphic

If you really like a Web page graphic and you'd like to see it more often, why not turn the graphic into wallpaper for your desktop?

To wallpaper your desktop with a downloaded Web graphic, follow these steps:

1. **Go to the Web page that contains the graphic you want to save as wallpaper.**

2. **Right-click the Web graphic and choose Set As Background from the shortcut menu.**

To remove the Web graphic wallpaper when you've grown tired of looking at it, follow these steps:

1. **Right-click the desktop and choose Properties from the shortcut menu.**

The Display Properties dialog box appears, as shown in Figure 2-3.

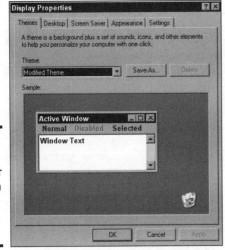

Figure 2-3:
Change or remove your wallpaper in the Display Properties dialog box.

2. **On the Background tab, choose a new graphics or HTML file for the wallpaper in the Select a Background Picture or HTML Document As Wallpaper list box.**

If you no longer want any graphic displayed as wallpaper, select the (None) option at the top of the drop-down list.

3. **Click OK when you're finished.**

Chapter 3: Customizing Netscape 6.2

In This Chapter

✔ **Personalizing your browser**

✔ **Determining what's old and new with your History settings**

✔ **Taking advantage of shortcuts**

✔ **Making Web pages display more quickly**

✔ **Discovering My Netscape**

*A*fter you're comfortable with the Netscape 6.2 Navigator, you're probably ready to add your personal touch to it. Not only can you change the way your pages look when they are displayed, but you can adjust other, less obvious, settings as well. In this chapter, we tell you how to change the way your Web pages look, how to create desktop shortcuts to Web pages, and how to help speed up the display of Web pages on your computer. Enjoy!

Changing Your Home Page

One of the first things you can do to make Navigator your very own is to change your home page. You no longer have to see the standard Navigator page when you launch your browser; now you can load a specific page automatically each time you start it.

To change your home Web page, follow these steps:

1. **Choose Edit⇨Preferences.**

   The Preferences dialog box opens.

2. **In the Category pane on the left side of the dialog box, click Navigator.**

   The Navigator screen appears in the Preferences dialog box, as shown in Figure 3-1.

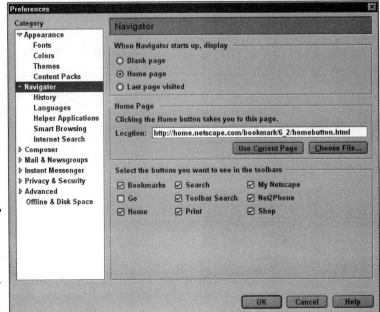

Figure 3-1:
Use the
Navigator
settings to
change your
home page.

3. **In the When Navigator Starts Up Display section, click the Home Page option button.**

   If you don't want to see any page when you start Navigator, click the Blank Page option button and then click OK.

4. **In the Location text box of the Home Page section, type the URL for the page that you want to start with.**

5. **Click OK to apply your changes and close the Preferences dialog box.**

Sometimes you may be in such a rush that you don't want this page to appear when you first start Navigator. Just click the Stop button on the Navigation toolbar as soon as Navigator starts loading this page, and then type the URL of the page you really want to see.

Changing the Way Web Pages Look

You can customize the Navigator screen to your personal tastes. Don't like the background color of the pages as displayed on your screen? Change it.

Don't like the fonts displayed on your screen, either? Change them, too. How about the color of the links? You can customize them to your liking as well.

Changing the color or fonts within Navigator on your computer changes the way pages appear on your computer only; you don't permanently modify the contents of the actual page you are viewing.

Changing the font type and size

Most pages display their text using a proportional font. If the page contains a form in which you can type information, a fixed font type is usually used. You can change this font.

To change the proportional and fixed fonts used to display text on a Web page, follow these steps:

1. **Choose Edit⇨Preferences.**

    The Preferences dialog box opens.

2. **In the Category pane on the left side of the dialog box, click the arrow next to Appearance to expand it; then click Fonts.**

    The Fonts screen appears in the Preferences dialog box.

3. **Make sure that the Fonts For box has Western selected so that you can read the type.**

4. **In the next six boxes, select the fonts that you want Navigator to use.**

    Experiment; try a few different options to see which you like best.

5. **In the Size boxes, select the size that you want to use for each type of font.**

6. **Click the Allow Document to Use Other Fonts option button.**

7. **Click OK to apply your changes and close the Preferences dialog box.**

Changing the text color

The default color for text in Navigator is black. How much more boring can things get?

To add some spice by changing the color that Navigator uses to display text on a Web page, follow these steps:

1. **Choose Edit⇨Preferences.**

The Preferences dialog box opens.

2. **In the Category pane on the left side of the dialog box, click the arrow next to Appearance to expand it; then click Colors.**

The Colors screen appears in the Preferences dialog box, as shown in Figure 3-2.

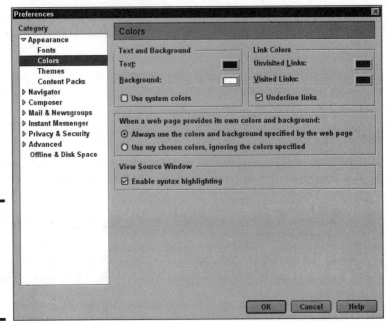

Figure 3-2:
You can change the display colors on the Colors screen.

3. **In the Colors section, click the button to the right of Text.**

The Color palette appears, offering a palette of colors for you to choose from.

4. **Choose a color from the palette.**

The Color palette closes, and you return to the Preferences dialog box.

5. **Click the Use My Chosen Colors, Ignoring the Colors Specified check box.**

6. **Click OK to apply your changes and close the Preferences dialog box.**

Make sure that the color you select for text is not the same as the background color, or you won't be able to read anything. You may think this tip is obvious, but you'd be surprised by how many people choose the same color for both and then wonder what happened.

Changing the background color

Netscape uses gray as the default background color, which you may (understandably) get bored with quickly.

To change the background color that Netscape uses to display Web pages, follow these steps:

1. **Choose Edit⇔Preferences.**

   The Preferences dialog box opens.

2. **In the Category pane on the left side of the dialog box, click the arrow next to Appearance to expand it; then choose Colors.**

   The Colors screen appears in the Preferences dialog box.

3. **Click the Background Color button.**

   The Color palette appears.

4. **Choose a color from the palette.**

   The Color palette closes, and you return to the Preferences dialog box.

5. **Click the Use My Chosen Colors, Ignoring the Colors Specified check box.**

6. **Click OK to apply your changes and close the Preferences dialog box.**

Some pages really want you to see the background in a specific color. For example, a page may contain graphics that look good only when viewed with a specific background color. If the graphics on a page look fuzzy, remove the check mark from the Use My Chosen Colors, Ignoring the Colors Specified check box.

Changing the way your browser displays hyperlinks

Before you change the color of links, you need to know that two kinds of links exist — those that you have followed and those that you haven't. By default, a blue link tells you that you haven't yet visited a link, whereas a purple link usually indicates that you've been there recently. (For information on how to change the time limit used to signify visited links, see "Changing the History Settings" later in this chapter.)

**Book IV
Chapter 3**

**Customizing
Netscape 6.2**

To change the color of both visited and unvisited links, follow these steps:

1. **Choose Edit⇨Preferences.**

   The Preferences dialog box opens.

2. **In the Category pane, click the arrow next to Appearance to expand it; then choose Colors.**

   The Colors screen appears in the Preferences dialog box.

3. **In the Links section, select the type of link that you want to change by clicking the button next to either Unvisited Links or Visited Links.**

   Whichever button you click opens the Color palette, offering you an array of colors to choose from.

4. **Choose a color from the palette.**

   The Color palette closes.

   Most of the time, links appear underlined. However, if you have to march to the beat of your own drum, you can remove the underline by getting rid of the check mark in the Underline Links check box.

5. **Click the check box for Use My Chosen Colors, Ignoring the Colors Specified.**

6. **Click OK to apply your changes and close the Preferences dialog box.**

Selecting a language

If you want to see Web pages in other languages, make sure that you select a new language for Navigator.

To select a new language in Navigator, follow these steps:

1. **Choose Edit⇨Preferences.**

   The Preferences dialog box opens.

2. **In the Category pane, click the arrow next to Navigator to expand it; then choose Languages.**

   The Languages screen appears in the Preferences dialog box.

3. **Click Add.**

   The Add Languages dialog box appears.

4. **Choose the language that you'd like to add and click OK.**

   The Add Language dialog box closes.

5. **Click OK again to apply your new language and close the Preferences dialog box.**

Customizing Toolbars

Depending on whether you're a toolbar clicker, a menu chooser, or a keyboard shortcut user, you may decide to shrink or enlarge your toolbars or make some disappear altogether.

Changing the size of toolbars

Sometimes, you may want to see a little more of the screen and temporarily remove a toolbar from view. To shrink a toolbar, follow these steps:

1. **Move the mouse pointer over the up arrow to the extreme left of the toolbar that you want to shrink.**

2. **Click the arrow.**

The toolbar disappears; in its place, you see a down arrow.

At some point, you may want to use a toolbar that you put out of view earlier. To expand the toolbar, follow these steps:

1. **Move the mouse pointer over the down arrow in the top-left margin of your screen.**

Positioning the mouse pointer over a tab displays a ToolTip indicating which toolbar it is.

2. **Click the arrow of the toolbar that you want to expand.**

The toolbar appears in full view once again.

Displaying toolbars without text

After you get used to the icons on the Navigation toolbar and what they stand for, you may want to display them without their names.

To turn off the names under the toolbar icons, follow these steps:

1. **Choose Edit⇨Preferences.**

The Preferences dialog box opens.

2. **In the Category pane, click Appearance.**

The Appearance screen appears in the Preferences dialog box, as shown in Figure 3-3.

3. **Remove the check mark from the Show Tooltips option button.**

4. **Click OK to apply your change and close the Preferences dialog box.**

**Book IV
Chapter 3**

**Customizing
Netscape 6.2**

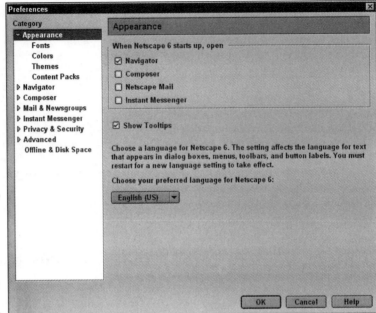

Figure 3-3:
Change
toolbar
settings in
the
Appearance
screen.

Moving a toolbar

To move a toolbar above or below other toolbars, follow these steps:

1. **Position the mouse pointer on the toolbar.**

2. **Press and hold down the left mouse button as you drag the toolbar to the new location (in other words, click and drag the toolbar).**

Hiding (and unhiding) a toolbar

Hiding a toolbar is not the same as minimizing it. When you hide it, you completely remove it from the screen.

To hide a toolbar, follow these steps:

1. **Choose <u>V</u>iew⇨Sho<u>w</u>/Hide.**

   A submenu opens, listing the three toolbars.

2. **Choose the toolbar that you want to hide by clicking it.**

To display a hidden toolbar, follow these steps:

1. **Choose View⇨Show/Hide.**

A submenu appears, listing the toolbars.

2. **Click to select the toolbar that you want to display.**

Adjusting Your Cache Settings

After you visit a Web page, the page is stored in your cache, which is part of your hard drive. Your cache stores the last few Web pages that you've visited. When you visit a Web page, your computer first checks your cache to see if the Web page is stored there. If the page is in your cache, you see the page immediately without waiting for it to load.

Netscape can retrieve a Web page from its memory cache about five to ten times faster than from your hard drive. So, if you're in a hurry, use your cache.

Clearing your cache

The size of your cache is important: Too small a cache, and the multimedia content on Web pages may not be displayed properly; too large a cache, and you're taking up precious room on your hard drive. (The following section explains how to change the size of your cache.) Regardless of the size of your cache, it's important that you regularly clean out old content so that you have room for new Web pages.

To clear out your cache, follow these steps:

1. **Choose Edit⇨Preferences.**

The Preferences dialog box appears.

2. **In the Category pane on the left, click the arrow next to Advanced to expand it; then choose Cache.**

The Cache screen appears in the Preferences dialog box, as shown in Figure 3-4.

3. **Click Clear Memory Cache and/or Clear Disk Cache to clear your memory or disk cache.**

We suggest cleaning both these caches. The memory cache holds such things as Java applets or Shockwave files that can sometimes hang up when they are running. The disk cache holds HTML and graphics files that have been downloaded to the temporary storage area to help Web pages load faster. It's a good idea to occasionally clean out both of these caches.

A dialog box appears to confirm that you really want to delete the cache.

4. Click OK.

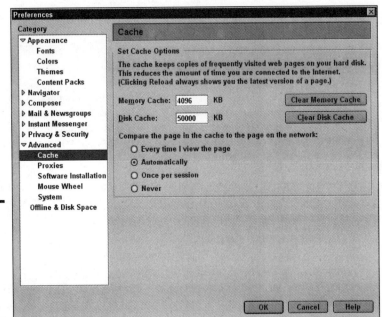

Figure 3-4:
Use the
Cache
screen to
clear the
memory or
disk cache.

Setting your cache size

Navigator's default memory cache of 1024K should fit your needs, but you may decide to increase the amount.

To change your cache size, follow these steps:

1. Choose Edit⇨Preferences.

The Preferences dialog box opens.

2. In the Category pane, click the arrow next to Advanced to expand it; then choose Cache.

The Cache screen appears in the Preferences dialog box.

3. Type the amount of cache you'd like in the Memory Cache text box.

4. Click OK to apply your change and close the Preferences dialog box.

Changing when the browser checks for newer versions of pages

Navigator normally checks for newer versions of pages in your cache at the beginning of a browsing session. If you want Navigator to search for newer versions more often, however, you need to change the setting.

To change how often Navigator checks for new pages in the cache, follow these steps:

1. **Choose Edit⇨Preferences.**

   The Preferences dialog box opens.

2. **In the Category pane, click the arrow next to Advanced to expand it; then choose Cache.**

   The Cache screen appears in the Preferences dialog box.

3. **In the Compare the Page in the Cache to the Page on the Network section, click the option button for how often you'd like Navigator to check for a newer page — Automatically, Once Per Session, Every Time I View the Page (you access a page), or Never.**

4. **Click OK to apply your change and close the Preferences dialog box.**

Changing the History Settings

You can tell whether you have followed a particular link by the color of the link. The color of visited links is different than the color of unvisited links. But visited links don't retain this different color indefinitely. Visited links retain their color temporarily, after which they revert to the color of unvisited links. You can change the time limit for this color change from 30 days to whatever you please. You can even set up Navigator so that it always shows you links you have visited no matter how long ago.

To change the time limit for how Navigator tracks visited links, follow these steps:

1. **Choose Edit⇨Preferences.**

   The Preferences dialog box opens.

2. **In the Category pane, click Navigator.**

   The Navigator screen appears in the Preferences dialog box.

3. In the History section, type a number in the Remember Visited Pages in the Last *X* Days text box that represents the number of days that you want Navigator to keep track of visited links.

4. Click OK to apply your change and close the Preferences dialog box.

If you click Clear History, you empty all the contents of the History file.

Creating a Desktop Shortcut to a Web Page

You don't have to use a bookmark to create a shortcut to a Web page (see Book IV, Chapter 1, for more on bookmarks). If you prefer, you can create a shortcut to a Web page right on your desktop.

To create a desktop shortcut to a Web page, follow these steps:

1. Go to the Web page to which you want to create a shortcut.

2. Position the mouse pointer over the Bookmark icon — the yellow-and-green icon at the left end of the Location toolbar.

3. Click and drag the Bookmark icon to your desktop, and then release the mouse button.

The new shortcut appears on your desktop.

To go to the page, simply double-click the shortcut on your desktop.

Speeding Up the Display of Web Pages

Tired of waiting for all those fancy pictures to download? Then you'll like this feature — you can speed up the display of your pages by turning off the pictures.

To turn off the display of graphics when downloading Web pages, follow these steps:

1. Choose Edit⇨Preferences.

The Preferences dialog box appears.

2. In the Category pane, click Privacy and Security.

The Advanced screen appears in the Preferences dialog box.

3. Click Images.

4. In the Image Acceptance Policy area, click Do Not Load Any Images.

5. Click OK to apply your change and close the Preferences dialog box.

Now, instead of pictures, you see a small icon where the image should be. If you just can't stand the mystery of what's behind that little box, click the image icon to open the image.

Using My Netscape

My Netscape is a news service that Netscape provides and that caters to your personal interests. You tell Netscape what your interests are, and Netscape builds a page for you that contains news items on those topics. If you like to see stock quotes and the day's top business and sports stories every morning, you can set up Netscape so that when you click the My Netscape button, a page appears with the news items you requested.

To create your My Netscape profile, follow these steps:

1. **Click the My Netscape button on the Navigation toolbar.**

The My Netscape page of the Netscape Netcenter site opens, as shown in Figure 3-5.

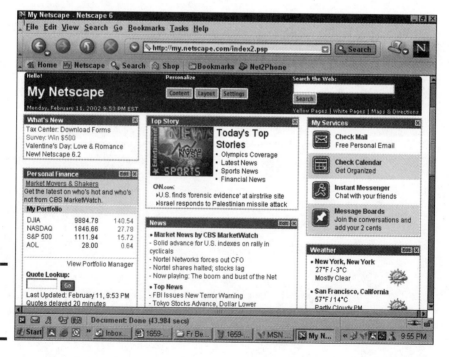

Figure 3-5: The My Netscape page.

2. **Click the Content button.**

   The Express Registration page opens.

3. **Follow the steps provided to indicate your interests and complete the registration.**

After you complete the registration process, a page containing your items of interest appears. Now, whenever you click the My Netscape button, you are presented with this page. You can change your preferences any time by clicking the Personalize button on the My Netscape page.

Index

Book V

Newsgroups, Chats, and Other Internet Communication

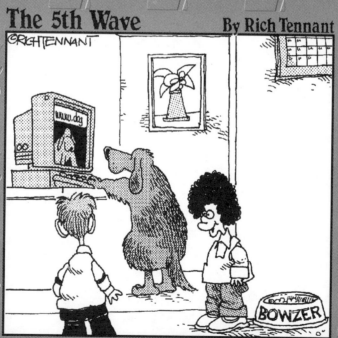

The 5th Wave — By Rich Tennant

BOWZER

"He found a dog site over an hour ago and has been in a staring contest ever since."

Contents at a Glance

Chapter 1: Keeping Up-to-Date with News

The Internet is chock full of information — you just have to know how to access it. One way that you can delve into some of the most current issues is through newsgroups.

A *newsgroup* is a place on the Internet where people gather to discuss a topic of common interest. A newsgroup resembles an electronic bulletin board on which people post questions or comments, and others respond to these questions and comments. Others then respond to the responses and so on, until a string, or *thread,* of discussion about a topic emerges. At any given time, multiple discussions can be in progress in a particular newsgroup.

Usenet, also known as *network news,* is the worldwide distributed group-discussion system that feeds information to newsgroups. Internet users around the world submit Usenet messages to tens of thousands of news-groups with names such as `rec.gardens.orchids` or `sci.space`. Within a day or so, these messages are delivered to nearly every other Internet host that wants them for anyone to read.

Newsgroup Basics

Reading Usenet is like trying to drink from a fire hose. Usenet had more than 55,000 different newsgroups the last time we looked. Here are some tips for maintaining your sanity:

✦ Pick a few groups that really interest you, or use an indexing service, such as Google. (See "Reading Newsgroups with Google," later in this chapter.)

✦ Develop a tolerance for the numerous junk-mail messages that infest many groups.

+ If you feel that you absolutely have to reply to a comment, save the message and sleep on it. If it still seems urgent in the morning, see "Posting messages to a newsgroup," later in this chapter.

+ Don't get into a flame war; however, if ever you do, let the other guy have the last word.

+ Don't believe everything you read on Usenet.

To read newsgroup postings, you use a *newsreader* program, or you can use your browser to read newsgroup postings on the Google Web site. To configure your newsreader program, ask your Internet Service Provider (ISP) for the name of its *news server,* the program that stores newsgroup postings for you to download.

Newsgroup "netiquette"

The e-mail etiquette rules listed in Book II, Chapter 1, apply even more to newsgroup articles because *many* more people read newsgroups. Here are some other suggestions:

+ Don't post to the whole group if you're sending a follow-up intended solely for the author of the original article. Instead, reply via e-mail.

+ Be sure that each article is appropriate for the group to which you post it.

+ Don't post a message saying that another message — a spam ad, for example — is inappropriate. The poster probably knows and doesn't care. The first message wasted enough of everyone's time; your response would waste more. Silence is the best answer.

+ Never criticize someone else's spelling or grammar.

+ Make your subject line as meaningful as possible. If your reply is tangential to an article, change the subject line to reflect the new topic.

+ When you're asking a question, use a question mark:

      Subject: Meaning of Life?

+ Don't post a 2-line follow-up that quotes an entire 100-line article. Edit out most of the quoted material.

+ Don't *cross-post;* that is, don't post the same article to multiple newsgroups, unless you have a good reason. Be especially careful when you're replying to multiple cross-posted messages; your response may be cross-posted too.

+ Watch out for *trolls,* messages calculated to provoke a storm of replies. Not every stupid comment needs a response.

+ Most groups periodically post a list of Frequently Asked Questions (or FAQs). Read the FAQ before asking a question. See "Frequently Asked Questions (FAQs)," later in this chapter.

Newsgroup names

Usenet newsgroups have multipart names separated by dots, such as `comp.dcom.fax`, a data communication discussion group about fax machines. Related groups have related names. Groups about data communication, for example, all start with `comp.dcom`. The first part of a newsgroup name is called its *hierarchy*.

In e-mail addresses and Internet host names, the top-level component (`edu`, for example) is on the *right*. In newsgroup names, the top-level component is on the *left*.

Table 1-1 lists the most popular Usenet newsgroup hierarchies.

Table 1-1	Popular Newsgroup Hierarchies
Newsgroup	*Description*
comp	Computer-related topics
humanities	Discussions relating to humanities
misc	Miscellaneous topics that don't fit anywhere else
news	Topics having to do with the Usenet newsgroup system itself; a few newsgroups with valuable general announcements — otherwise, not very interesting
rec	Recreational groups about sports, hobbies, the arts, and other fun endeavors
sci	Science-related topics
soc	Social groups, both social interests and plain socializing
talk	Long arguments, frequently political
alt	Semiofficial "alternative" to the preceding newsgroup hierarchies (which are often called "the big eight"); alt groups range from the extremely useful to the totally weird

In addition to the popular hierarchies in Table 1-1, you can find regional, organizational, and national hierarchies such as `ne` for New England, `ny` for New York, `uk` for the United Kingdom, and `ibm` for IBM. If you speak another language, you may be interested in hierarchies that serve languages other than English. For example, `de` is for German, `es` for Spanish, `fj` for Japanese, and `fr` for French.

New hierarchies are being started all the time. Lewis S. Eisen maintains a master list of Usenet hierarchies (619, at last count), at

`www.magma.ca/~leisen/mlnh`

Frequently Asked Questions (FAQs)

Many newsgroups periodically post a list of frequently asked questions and their answers, or *FAQs*. They hope that you read the FAQ before posting a message they have answered a dozen times before, and you should.

MIT collects FAQs from all over Usenet, creating, in effect, an online encyclopedia with the latest information on a vast array of topics that is accessible with your Web browser or via FTP, at this URL:

`ftp://rtfm.mit.edu/pub/usenet-by-hierarchy`

FAQs are often quite authoritative, but sometimes they're just a contributor's opinion. Reader beware!

Posting articles to newsgroups

Standard Usenet dogma is to read a group for a few weeks before posting anything. It's still good advice, although Internet newbies generally aren't big on delayed gratification. Here are some tips on your first posting:

✦ Pick a newsgroup whose subject is one you know something about.

✦ Read the FAQ before you post.

✦ Reply to an article with specific information that you know firsthand or can cite in a reference and that is relevant to the topic being discussed.

✦ Read the entire preceding *thread* (a series of replies to the original article and replies to those replies) to make sure that your point hasn't been raised already.

✦ Edit included text from the original article to the bare minimum.

✦ Keep your reply short, clear, and to the point.

✦ Have your facts straight. Your article should contain more than your opinion.

✦ Check your spelling and grammar.

✦ Stay calm. Don't be inflammatory, use foul language, or call people names.

✦ Avoid Netisms, such as ROFL ("rolling on floor laughing"). If necessary, use — at most — one smiley :-).

✦ Use a local hierarchy for stuff of regional interest. The whole planet does not need to hear about your school's bake sale.

✦ Save your message overnight and reread it before posting.

Some newsgroups are *moderated,* which means that

✦ Articles are not posted directly as news. Instead, they're e-mailed to a person or program who posts the article only if he, she, or it feels that it's appropriate to the group.

✦ Moderators, because they're unpaid volunteers, do not process items instantaneously, so it can take a day or two for items to be processed.

✦ If you post an article for a moderated group, the news-posting software mails your item to the moderator automatically.

✦ If your article doesn't appear and you really don't know why, post a polite inquiry to the same group.

Remember that Usenet is a public forum. Everything you say there can be read by anyone, anywhere in the world. Worse, every word you post is carefully indexed and archived. However, Google will let you avoid having your material archived if you type **X-No-archive: yes** in the header or first line of the text. If you forget to do this, you can ask Google to remove the message for you or remove the message yourself by using Google's automatic removal tool.

Reading Newsgroups with Google

Google Groups, the area of the Google site that offers newsgroups, is a great place to find answers to problems that you may be having with your computer and its software. You can find a newsgroup for almost every system out there, including ones that are obsolete.

Google updates its site from time to time, so the details described in this section may change.

Google and Usenet indexes

Usenet has been around almost since the beginning of the Internet and is a bit old and creaky. Google Groups has done much to bring Usenet into the modern Web era. You can use Google Groups to

✦ Do a keyword search for newsgroup articles

✦ Look for newsgroups of interest

✦ Read newsgroup articles

✦ Send e-mail to an article's author

✦ Post a reply article to something you read

✦ Post a newsgroup article on a new topic

Watch out what you post on Usenet newsgroups because anyone can find your posts later by using Google. A simple search for your name displays your e-mail address and a list of every message that you've posted — at least since 1981. If you include your home address, phone number, kids' names, political opinions, dating preferences, personal fantasies, or whatever in any message, that information also is easily retrieved. You have been warned.

Searching Google Groups

The traditional way to read Usenet is to go to a newsgroup and read the recent messages posted there. With tens of thousands of newsgroups, however, this method has become inefficient. Google Groups enables you to search *all* newsgroups by content.

To use Google Groups to search all newsgroups by content, follow these steps:

1. **Open your browser and go to** `groups.google.com`.

   A list of categories appears.

2. **Click a category or type keywords in the text box and click Google Search.**

   In the Related Groups area at the top of your search results, you see a list of related newsgroups that include many articles (or contributor's names) with those keywords. The Activity bar to the left of the group name shows how often the groups have been visited. In the Searched Groups For area, you see a list of newsgroups articles that contain your search terms.

3. **Click a group to see a list of specific articles listed by the most recent date, or click an article to read it.**

   Follow a link that says <u>Next</u> or <u>Next 25 Threads</u> to see more search results.

4. **To save an article, choose <u>F</u>ile⇨Save As in your browser.**

If you don't find what you want in the search results, change your keywords in the search box and click the Google Search button.

If you want to do more advanced searching, check out the Advanced Groups Search. Not only can you search by newsgroup, but you can search by subject, author, message ID, language, and message dates as well.

Replying to an article

You can reply to an article in two ways: by sending a message to the poster's e-mail address and by posting a message to the newsgroup. To reply to a newsgroup article via e-mail, find the person's e-mail address in the article and copy it in the To field of your favorite e-mail program. (See Book II for more information on e-mail.) **Note:** People often add *nospam* or other text to their e-mail addresses to decrease the amount of spam in their inboxes. Watch for this text to make sure that your message reaches the intended recipient.

To post an article following up on a message, click the <u>Post a follow-up to this message</u> link. On the Post a Message page, edit the quoted article to a reasonable size and add your response. You can also edit the list of newsgroups to which your article is posted. Click the Preview Message to preview your reply. You can make changes by clicking the Edit Message button, or you can post the message by clicking Post Message.

Keep in mind that the first time you post a message, you are taken to a registration page where you're asked for your name, e-mail address, and password. Next, you receive a confirmation message. As soon as you reply, you'll be able to post.

Posting a new article

To post a new message to a newsgroup, at the top of the list of threads, click the Post a New Message to Newsgroup Name link. On the Post Message page, type your title in the Subject box. Type the message in the Your Message box. You can also edit the list of newsgroups to which your article is posted. When the message is ready to send, click either the Preview Message or Post Message–No Preview button.

Reading Newsgroups with Outlook Express

Outlook Express, the e-mail program that comes with Internet Explorer and Windows (see Book II, Chapter 2), also works as a newsreader. You can receive (by subscribing) copies of all the messages being sent by the participants of the newsgroup, or you can peruse the chitchat (by not subscribing to the newsgroup). You must first set up a newsgroup account.

You can add and remove News Server accounts or make an account your default account by choosing <u>T</u>ools⇨<u>A</u>ccounts and clicking the News tab of the Internet Accounts dialog box.

Viewing newsgroup messages before you subscribe

To get a feel for a newsgroup by reading some of its messages before actually subscribing to it, follow these steps:

1. From the Internet Explorer 6 toolbar, click the arrow next to the Mail button and then choose Read News.

Internet Explorer opens the Outlook Express window for the News server that you selected when you set up your News account.

2. **Click Yes to display a list of all available newsgroups in the Newsgroup Subscriptions dialog box.**

   This process may take a few minutes if your connection speed is slow.

3. **Select a newsgroup in the list box of the Newsgroup Subscriptions dialog box by clicking it.**

   If you want to limit the list of newsgroups, you can enter a term or series of terms used in the newsgroup's title (if you know that kind of thing) in the Display Newsgroups Which Contain text box.

4. **Click the Go To button to download all the messages from the newsgroup into the Outlook Express window).**

   You can read through the newsgroup messages just as you do your own e-mail messages.

5. **(Optional) If you want to reply to a particular message, click the message in the upper pane; then click the Reply button to reply to the author of the message, or click the Reply Group button to reply to the entire group.**

6. **To return to the list of newsgroups on your News server, click the Newsgroups button on the Outlook Express toolbar.**

7. **When you finish perusing the newsgroups of interest, click OK to close the Newsgroup Subscriptions dialog box and then click the Close button in the Outlook Express window.**

Subscribing to a newsgroup

When you find a newsgroup in which you want to regularly participate, you can subscribe to it as follows:

1. **From the Internet Explorer 6 toolbar, click the Mail button and then choose Read News.**

2. **If you see an alert dialog box telling you that you haven't subscribed to any newsgroups, click Yes.**

   The Newsgroup Subscriptions dialog box opens.

3. **In the list box, click the name of the newsgroup to which you want to subscribe.**

4. **Click the Subscribe button.**

   Outlook Express then adds a newspaper icon in front of the name of the newsgroup to indicate that you are subscribed to it. The program also adds the name of the newsgroup to the Subscribed tab of the Newsgroup Subscriptions dialog box.

5. **Repeat Steps 3 and 4 to subscribe to any other newsgroups of interest.**

6. **When you're finished subscribing, click OK.**

   The Outlook Express window appears, where you now see a list of all the newsgroups to which you have subscribed.

7. **To see the messages in a particular newsgroup, select the newsgroup by clicking its name in the Folders pane. To have Internet Explorer go online and download any new messages for the selected newsgroup, choose Tools⇨Synchronize Newsgroup.**

   The Synchronize Newsgroup dialog box appears.

8. **Select the Get the Following Items check box and then choose the desired option button: All Messages, New Messages Only (the default), or Headers Only; then click OK.**

   After the messages are downloaded, you can get offline and peruse the messages at your leisure.

9. **(Optional) Read and reply to as many of the newsgroup messages as you want. Click the message to display it in the lower pane and then click either the Reply button to reply to the author of the message or the Reply Group button to reply to the entire group.**

10. **When you're finished looking at the newsgroup messages, click the Close button in the upper-right corner of the Outlook Express window.**

After subscribing to a newsgroup, you can click the Mail button on the Internet Explorer 6 toolbar and choose Read News to return to the list of newsgroups in Outlook Express. Remember to click the title of a newsgroup to download its current messages.

Unsubscribing from a newsgroup

Should you decide that you no longer want to participate in a newsgroup to which you're subscribed, you can easily unsubscribe by following these steps:

1. **Click the Newsgroups button on the Outlook Express toolbar.**

   The Newsgroup Subscriptions dialog box appears.

2. **Click the Subscribed tab, and then click the name of the newsgroup to which you want to unsubscribe.**

3. **Click the Unsubscribe button and then click OK.**

Starting your own newsgroup

You can start your own newsgroup, although the process is not for the fainthearted. Most hierarchies have a newsgroup in which proposals for new groups are presented, discussed, and disposed of, by vote or consensus.

Here are some things that you have to do if you want to start a new newsgroup:

- Understand Usenet's and your hierarchy's culture.

- Think about who will want to join your group and how you will let them know about it.

- Spend some time reading news.groups and alt.config.

- Make sure that a suitable group doesn't already exist.

- Pick the right hierarchy and name for your group. The folks who run Usenet groups are really picky about names.

- Write a strong justification.

- Find as many allies as possible.

- Be tenacious.

For more information about starting your own group, see the newsgroup news.groups. questions or visit this Web page:

```
www.geocities.com/Research
    Triangle/Lab/6882/ncreate.
    html
```

Chapter 2: Chat and Other Online Communication

In This Chapter

✔ **Chatting online**

✔ **Using Internet Relay Chat (IRC)**

✔ **Using ICQ**

✔ **Chatting on the Web**

✔ **Using Netscape AOL Instant Messenger**

✔ **Making Internet calls with NetMeeting**

The Internet lets you communicate with people in a more immediate way than sending electronic mail and waiting hours or days for a reply. You can type something, press Enter, and get a reply within seconds — a process called *instant messaging* or *chatting*. Instant messaging enables you to communicate privately and individually with other friends, whereas chatting is generally done in groups that typically include people that you don't know. You can also use the Internet for voice and even video communication. In this chapter, we tell you about the most popular forms of online communication and how to get the most from them.

Chatting Online

Online chat lets you communicate with people live, just as you would on the telephone — except that you type what you want to say and read the other person's reply on your computer screen. Here are some things that you need to know about chat:

✦ In chat, a window shows the ongoing conversation. You type in a separate box what you want to send to the individual or group. When you press Enter or click the Send button, your message appears in the conversation window, along with any responses.

✦ Chat differs from e-mail in that you don't have to address each message and wait for a reply. Though sometimes a small lag occurs in chatting, communication is nearly instantaneous — even across the globe.

✦ You're usually limited to a sentence or two in each exchange. Instant messages, described later in this chapter, allow longer expressions.

✦ You can select a group or an individual to chat with, or someone can ask to initiate a private chat with you. Many chat venues exist on the Net, including IRC (Internet Relay Chat), AOL chat rooms (for AOL users only), Web-based chat, and instant messaging systems like ICQ and AIM (AOL Instant Messenger). (See the "ICQ" section, later in this chapter, for more information about this popular chat service.)

✦ Because tens of thousands of people are chatting at any instant of the day or night, the discussions are divided into groups. Different terms exist for chat groups. AOL and ICQ call them *rooms*. IRC (Internet Relay Chat) calls them *channels*.

✦ The chat facilities of the value-added service providers (such as AOL, CompuServe, and Microsoft Network) are accessible to only that service's members. Only AOL members can use the AOL chat rooms, for example. You can't get to the AOL chat rooms from ICQ or IRC.

✦ People in chat groups can be unruly and even vicious. The online service providers' chat groups usually are tamer because the service provides some supervision.

✦ You may select a special name — called a *screen name, handle,* or *nickname* — to use when you're chatting. This name can and often does differ from your login name or e-mail address.

Although your special chat name gives you some privacy online, someone could possibly find out your real identity, particularly if your online service or ISP cooperates. Don't go wild out there.

Following group conversations

Get used to following a group conversation if you want to make any sense of chats. Here's a sample of what you may see (screen names and identifying content have been changed):

```
BrtG221: hey Zeb!
Zebra795: Hello
ABE904: Where is everyone from...I am from Virginia
Zebra795: Hi Brt!
HAPY F: how should I know
Zebra795: Hi ABE
HAPY F: <—Virginia
ABE904: Hi Zebra!!!
BrtG221: so StC... what
Zebra795: <—was from Virginia!
ABE904: Hi HAPY ! Didn't see ya
BrtG221: is going on in FL?
HAPY F: HI ABE
Zebra795: Hap's been on all night!
Storm17: Brt...what?...i miss our heart to hearts
HAPY F: on and off
```

```
ABE904: Zeb, and wish you were back here!
DDouble6190: im 26 but i like older women
Zebra795: I was over July Fourth!!
Janet5301: Sorry...DD...call me in 10 yrs...
BrtG221: really DD?... where do you live?
BrtG221: lol.. so talk to me Storm..
ABE904: Gee, you didn't call, didn't write...
```

Here are a few tips for getting started:

✦ When you enter a chat group, a conversation is usually already in progress. You can't see what went on before you entered.

✦ Wait a minute or two for a page full of exchanges to appear on-screen so that you can understand some of their context before you start reading, and then determine with whom you want to converse and who you want to ignore.

✦ Start by following the comments from a single screen name. Then follow the people whom that person mentions or who reply to that person. Ignore everything else because the other messages are probably replies to messages that went by before you came in.

✦ After you can follow one thread, try picking up another. It takes practice to get the hang of it.

✦ Some services, such as AOL, let you highlight the messages from one or more screen names. This capability can make things easier to follow.

✦ Many services allow you to indicate screen names to ignore. Messages from these chatters no longer appear on-screen, though other members' replies to them do appear.

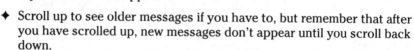

✦ Scroll up to see older messages if you have to, but remember that after you have scrolled up, new messages don't appear until you scroll back down.

✦ Many of the messages are greetings to familiar names as they join or leave the chat group.

✦ A few regulars often dominate the conversation.

✦ The real action often takes place in private, one-on-one side discussions, which you can't see.

Chatting etiquette

Chatting etiquette isn't much different from e-mail (see Book II, Chapter 1), and common sense is your best online guide. Here are some additional chat behavior tips:

✦ The first rule of chat is that a real person with real feelings is at the other end of the computer chat connection. Hurting him or her is not okay.

✦ The second rule is that because you really have no idea who that other person is, being cautious is okay. (See "Safe chatting guidelines," in the following section.)

✦ Read messages for a while to figure out what is happening before sending a message to a chat group.

✦ Keep your comments short and to the point.

✦ Avoid insults and foul language.

✦ Many systems let you create a profile about yourself that other members can access. Having a profile is polite. You don't have to tell everything about yourself in your profile, although what you do say should be truthful.

✦ If you want to talk to someone in private, send a message saying Hi, who you are, and what you want.

✦ More people are out there who you don't want to meet than people who you do, although quite a few potential friends are chatting, too. If the rudeness and banality of the chat turn you off at first, try other groups.

Safe chatting guidelines

Here are some guidelines for conducting safe and healthy chats:

✦ Many people in chat groups are totally dishonest about who they are. They lie about their occupation, age, locality, and, yes, even gender. Some think that they're being cute, and others are exploring their own fantasies; a few are really sick.

✦ Be careful about giving out information that enables someone to find you personally, including phone numbers, mailing address, and the schools that your kids attend.

✦ Pick a screen name or handle that's different from your login name; otherwise, you will receive a great deal of unwanted junk e-mail.

✦ Never give out your password to anyone, even if she says that she works for your service provider, the phone company, the FBI, the CIA, or Dummies Press. Never!

✦ If your chat service offers profiles and a person without a profile wants to chat with you, be extra cautious.

✦ If your children use chat, realize that others may try to meet them. Before your kids log on, spend some quality time talking to them about the guidelines in "Kids, Porn, and the Web," in Book I, Chapter 3.

✦ Don't hesitate to report anyone who you believe is behaving inappropriately on a value-added service's chat group. On AOL, go to keyword **Notify AOL**. On CompuServe, go to keyword **feedback**.

If you choose to meet an online friend in person, use at least the same caution you would use in meeting someone through a newspaper ad:

◆ Don't arrange a meeting until you have talked to that person a number of times over the course of days or weeks.

◆ Have a few phone conversations first.

◆ Meet in a public place.

◆ Bring a friend along, if possible. If not, at least let someone else know what you're doing and agree to call that person at a specified time (a half-hour, for example) after the meeting time.

◆ If you travel a long distance to meet someone, stay in a hotel, not at that person's home.

Smileys, abbreviations, and emoticons

Chat abbreviations are similar to those used in news and e-mail, although some are unique to the real-time nature of chat. Table 2-1 provides abbreviations and emoticons common on AOL and other chat services:

Table 2-1	Common Chat Abbreviations
Abbreviation/Emoticon	*What It Means*
AFK	Away From Keyboard
A/S/L	Age/Sex/Location (response may be 35/f/LA)
BAK	Back At Keyboard
BRB	Be Right Back
BTW	By The Way
FTF	Face To Face
GMTA	Great Minds Think Alike
IC	In Character (playing a role)
ICQ	"I Seek You" (a chat service described later in this chapter)
IM	Instant Message
IMHO	In My Humble Opinion
IRC	Internet Relay Chat (a chat service described later in this chapter)
LTNS	Long Time No See
LOL	Laughing Out Loud
M4M	Men seeking other men
OOC	Out of Character (stepping out of a role)
RL	Real Life (opposite of RP)

(continued)

Table 2-1 *(continued)*

Abbreviation/Emoticon	What It Means
ROFL	Rolling on Floor, Laughing
RP	Role Play (acting a character in a fantasy)
TOS	Terms of Service (the AOL member contract)
TTFN	Ta-Ta for Now!
WB	Welcome Back
WTG	Way To Go!
:) or :-)	Smile
:D	Smile/laughing/big grin
**	Kisses
;)	Wink
{}	Hug
:(or :-(	Frown
:'(	Crying
0:)	Angel
}:>	Devil
:X	My lips are sealed
:P	Sticking out tongue
(_|_)	Moon

Internet Relay Chat (IRC)

Internet Relay Chat (IRC) is the Internet's own chat service. IRC is available from most Internet Service Providers. You can even participate in IRC through most online services, although IRC is completely separate from the service's own chat services. You need an *IRC client program* (or just *IRC program*), which is simply another Internet program, like your Web browser or e-mail software. Freeware and shareware IRC programs are available for you to download from the Net. Most Unix systems come with an IRC program. Two of the best shareware IRC programs are mIRC (for Windows) and Ircle (for Macintosh).

You can download updated versions of these programs and get detailed information about installing them from www.irchelp.org. They're also available from TUCOWS (www.tucows.com). Windows XP comes with Windows Messenger. You can download it from www.microsoft.com/downloads.

Check with your Internet Service Provider for any additional information you may need in order to use IRC. If you have a direct link to the Internet, ask your system administrator whether the link supports IRC.

You use IRC in two main ways:

✦ **Channel:** This is like an ongoing conference call with a bunch of people. After you join a channel, you can read what people are saying on-screen and then add your own comments just by typing them and pressing Enter.

✦ **Direct connection:** This is like a private conversation.

Starting IRC

To start IRC, follow these steps:

1. Connect to the Internet and run your IRC program.

If you're on a value-added service, follow its instructions for connecting to the Internet. If you're using a Unix shell Internet provider that offers IRC, type **ircii** or **irc** at the Unix prompt.

2. Connect to an IRC server.

See the following section, "Picking a server," to find out how to connect.

3. Join a channel.

You're ready to chat! See "IRC channels," later in this chapter, for more about channels.

Picking a server

To use IRC, you connect your IRC program to an *IRC server,* an Internet host computer that serves as a switchboard for IRC conversations. Although dozens of IRC servers are available, many are full most of the time and may refuse your connection. You may have to try several servers, or the same one dozens of times, before you can connect. When you're choosing a server, pick one that's geographically close to you to minimize response lag.

To connect to an IRC server, do one of the following, depending on whether you are using a PC or a Mac:

✦ In mIRC, choose File➪Options or press Alt+O to display the mIRC Options window; then click the IRC Servers arrow for the drop-down box. Double-click a server on the list to attempt to connect to it. If you choose All as your IRC Servers, and one will be selected randomly.

✦ In Ircle, choose File➪Preferences➪Startup. Select a server and choose File➪Save Preferences.

If at first you don't connect, try, try again.

Issuing IRC commands

You control what is happening during your chat session by typing IRC commands. All IRC commands start with the slash character (/). You can type IRC commands in uppercase or lowercase or a mixture — IRC doesn't care.

The most important command for you to know gets you out of IRC:

/QUIT

The second most important command gives you an online summary of the various IRC commands:

/HELP

Table 2-2 provides some of the most useful IRC commands.

Table 2-2	Useful IRC Commands
Command	*What It Does*
/ADMIN server	Displays information about a server.
/AWAY	Enables you to tell IRC that you will be away for a while. You don't need to leave this type of message; if you do, however, it's displayed to anyone who wants to talk to you.
/CLEAR	Clears your screen.
/JOIN channel	Joins the channel you specify.
/PART	Leaves the current channel.
/LIST	Lists all available channels.
/NICK thenameyouwant	Enables you to specify your chat nickname.
/QUERY nickname	Starts a private conversation with nickname.
/TIME	Displays the date and time in case you can't take your eyes off the screen for even a moment.
/TOPIC subject	Changes the topic for the current channel.
/WHO channel	Lists all the people on channel. If you type /WHO *, you see displayed the names of the people on the channel you're on.

If anyone on IRC ever tells you to type commands you don't understand, *don't do it. Ever.* You can unwittingly give away control of your IRC program and even your computer account to another person that way. Everything you type while you're on IRC goes out to the Internet, *except* lines that start with a slash (/).

If you use mIRC or Ircle, you can achieve most of the same effects that are controlled by IRC commands by choosing options from the menu bar or clicking icons on the toolbar. These IRC commands work too, however, and some IRC programs don't have menu bar or toolbar equivalents.

IRC channels

The most popular way to use IRC is through *channels*. Most channels have names that start with the # character. Channel names aren't case sensitive. Numbered channels also exist. (When you type a channel number, don't use the # character.)

Thousands of IRC channels are available. You can find an annotated list of some of the best by visiting www.funet.fi/~irc/channels.html. Each channel listed there has its own linked home page that tells much more about what that channel offers. A searchable list of IRC channels is also available at www.ludd.luth.se/irc/list.html.

Good channels to know about include the following:

+ **#irchelp:** A place to ask questions about IRC. (Read the FAQ first; see "Getting more info," later in this chapter.)

+ **#newbies:** All your IRC questions answered.

+ **#21plus** and **#30plus:** Age-appropriate meeting places.

+ **#41plus:** A more mature channel (many on it are younger).

+ **#teens:** For teenagers — chill and chat.

+ **#hottub:** A rougher meeting place.

+ **#macintosh:** Mac users meet here.

+ **#windows95:** Windows users meet here.

+ **#chat:** A friendly chat channel.

+ **#mirc:** A help channel for mIRC users.

Also, try # followed by the name of a country or major city.

Types of channels

Three types of channels are available in IRC:

+ **Public:** Everyone can see them, and everyone can join.

+ **Private:** Everyone can see them, but you can join only by invitation.

+ **Secret:** They do not show up in the /LIST command, and you can join them only by invitation.

If you're on a private or secret channel, you can invite someone else to join by typing

```
/INVITE nickname
```

If you get an invitation from someone on a private or secret channel and want to join, just type

```
/JOIN -INVITE
```

Some people like to write computer programs that sit on IRC channels and make comments from time to time. These programs are called *bots*, short for *robots*. Some people think that bots are cute; if you don't, just ignore them.

Starting your own channel

Each channel has its own channel operator, or *chanop,* who can control, to some extent, what happens on that channel. You can start your own channel and become its chanop by typing

```
/JOIN #unusedchannelname
```

As with nicknames, whoever asks for a channel name first gets it. You can keep the name for as long as you're logged on as the chanop. You can let other people be chanops for your channel; just make sure that they're people you can trust. A channel exists as long as anyone is in it; when the last person leaves, the channel winks out of existence.

Filing a complaint

Compared to AOL and CompuServe, IRC is a lawless frontier. Few rules, if any, exist. If things get really bad, you can try to find out the offender's e-mail address by using the /whois command — /whois badmother@iecc.com, for example. You can then send an e-mail complaint to the postmaster at the same host name — postmaster@iecc.com, in this case. Don't expect much help, however.

Getting more info

You can discover much more about IRC from these sources:

+ **The official IRC home page:** irchelp.org (where IRC was invented)
+ **The New IRC user's page:** www.newircusers.com
+ **The Usenet newsgroup:** alt.irc

ICQ

ICQ, pronounced "I seek you," is a popular program that lets you chat and exchange messages and files with other ICQ users. Developed by an Israeli company, Mirabilis, and sold to AOL, ICQ has more than 100,000,000 users.

Even though AOL now owns ICQ, you can't use ICQ to communicate with AOL chat or Instant Messenger.

Getting ICQ

ICQ is available for Windows and Macintosh, and a Java version is also available. You can download ICQ from www.icq.com or www.tucows.com.

ICQ asks a number of personal questions for marketing purposes when you first register. You don't have to answer the questions to use ICQ. Parents should review the questions with their kids before letting their kids sign up.

Making contact

Using ICQ is a little complicated at first, compared with e-mail. Here are some of the reasons why:

✦ You have to add a user to your contact list before you can send that person a message.

✦ Each ICQ user is assigned an identification number. Knowing a user's ID number helps when you're building your contact list. After that, you don't need to know the number.

✦ ICQ lets you find another user by name, nickname, or e-mail address as well as by number.

✦ You can chat with other ICQ users whenever you and they are connected to the Internet at the same time. You can send messages and files at any time.

✦ When your ICQ friends are online, ICQ moves their names to the top of your contact list.

To add someone to your contact list, follow these steps:

1. **Click the Add/Invite Users button in the ICQ window.**

You see the Find/Add Users to Your List window, which lists a number of different search methods.

2. **Choose one of the search methods and fill in the requested information.**

3. **Click Search.**

   If the search finds more than one match, you're asked to click the user you want to add to your list. If too many results come up, a dialog box appears. You're asked to narrow down your search, or you can also double-click the result you want.

At the time you register, you can ask ICQ to notify you whenever someone wants to add you to his contact list. It's best to know who your contacts are.

Let's chat

To initiate an ICQ chat session with someone, follow these steps:

1. **Click the person's name on your contact list.**

   Mac users, click the arrow icon to the right of the name.

2. **Choose ICQ Chat from the User menu.**

3. **In the text box, type a brief message that tells what you want to chat about.**

4. **Click the Chat button.**

   Your message is sent to the user you requested, who, we trust, will favor you with a reply.

Taking a message

To send a message to someone on your ICQ contact list, follow these steps:

1. **Open the ICQ window and click the person's name.**

   Mac users, click the arrow icon to the right of the name.

2. **Click Message in the Send area of the User menu.**

3. **Type the message in the text box.**

4. **Click the Send button.**

When an ICQ user wants to contact you, a flashing icon appears next to his name. Double-click this icon to see the message or start a chat session.

Filing a complaint

ICQ has an acceptable-use policy and frowns on various forms of abuse. However, given its huge user base and free service, don't expect a great deal of support. To inform ICQ of a serious problem, visit web.icq.com/help and click Contact Our Support Team.

Web-Based Chatting

A number of sites on the World Wide Web let you chat by using just your Web browser. Sometimes, a Java applet is loaded automatically. Fewer people use Web-based chat than either America Online or IRC, although Web-based chat is becoming more popular. New chat sites appear all the time.

If it's 2 a.m. and you can't sleep, or if you want to find out someone else's opinion about that spiffy new car you can't stop thinking about, consider participating in Web-based chat rooms or discussion boards.

Chat rooms

Web-based chatting is similar to arriving in a crowded room at a party where clusters of people, all in the same room, are following different conversations. When you first join a chat room, like a party, the conversation is already under way. You just need to figure out which *thread* of conversation you'd like to follow, get up to speed on what everyone is saying, and then join in if you'd like. People who respond are interested in commenting or have advice to offer.

No matter what topic you're interested in, you'll probably have no problem locating a chat room. Common topics include autos, computers, family, health, and sports, among many others.

Discussion boards

Discussion boards are slower paced than chat rooms (see preceding section). Like chat rooms, discussion boards revolve around one specific topic, such as relationships, family, or music. Discussion boards differ from chat rooms, however, in that they don't take place in real time. You click a category that piques your interest and a list of subcategories appears. When you choose a subcategory under the main category, you see that the discussion becomes even more focused (see Figure 2-1).

When you reach a discussion that interests you, you can post a message and return to the board at a later time to see how others have responded. Figure 2-2 shows some of the responses posted to this board.

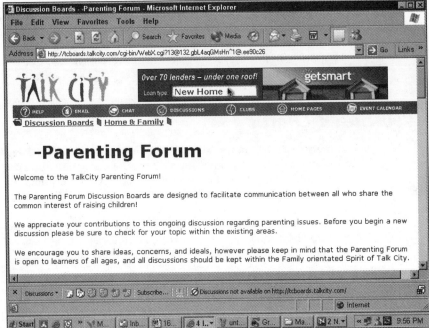

Figure 2-1:
You can find the Parenting subcategory under Home & Family.

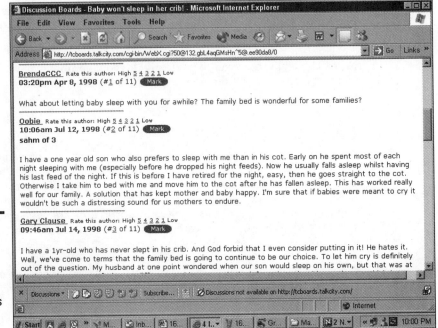

Figure 2-2:
Post your message and return later to see what others had to say.

Accessing via a Web browser

If you've never participated in Web-based chatting and don't know where to begin, this section is for you. You may want to start with one (or all) of these three free communities. Just fire up your Web browser and head to these sites:

✦ **Excite Talk:** Located at `www.excite.com/channel/chat` in the Chat tab, Excite Chat offers chat rooms and message boards on the following topics: Autos, Computers, Education, Entertainment, Family, Games, Health, Home, Lifestyle, Money, People, Politics, Relationships, Shopping, Sports, and Travel. Before you participate in anything, you need to register. To do so, you simply click the Join Now button and follow the on-screen instructions. If you're already a member, you're prompted to sign in.

✦ **Talk City:** Located at `www.talkcity.com`, Talk City offers chat rooms and message boards on about 20 common topics, including Cities & Travel, Ethnic & Lifestyles, and Women. Like Excite Chat, you need to register or sign in before you can participate.

✦ **Yahoo!:** Yahoo! may be better known as a search engine, but it, too, boasts chatting — even voice chatting! — and discussion boards. Go to `www.yahoo.com` and click Chat. After you sign in, you can chat away (see Figure 2-3).

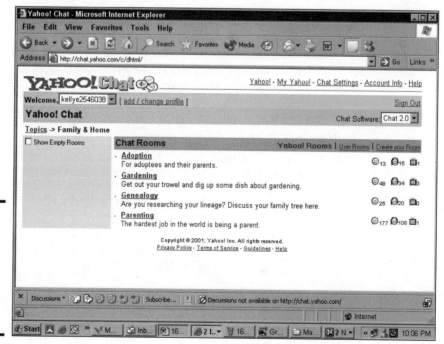

Figure 2-3:
Choose
from a
variety of
chat rooms
in the
Family &
Home area.

Of course, free chatting comes at a price. Occasionally, on any of these three sites, advertising floating across your screen will interrupt you. In addition, advertising usually appears at the top and/or bottom of your screen.

Downloading necessary software

When you first sign up for one of the communities in the preceding section, you probably won't have the necessary software to participate in Web chatting. In those cases, you'll be prompted to download software. If you want to participate — and you trust the source — simply click Yes.

As you go along, you may decide that you need other software to make your Web experience complete. You may decide that you need WinZip (to compress large files and unstuff decompressed files), RealPlayer to listen to audio files, Adobe Acrobat Reader to read PDF (Portable Document Format) files, or Macromedia Shockwave to enjoy video and audio effects.

AOL Instant Messenger

If you're one of the 12 million or so AOL subscribers, you probably already know what Instant Messenger is. If you aren't an AOL subscriber, suffice it to say that it's a tool you'll be addicted to in five minutes flat. Briefly, Instant Messenger is online chat software that makes chatting easy and fun. You can chat with your friends in real time, no matter where in the world they're located, as long as you both use Instant Messenger.

AOL Instant Messenger (often called *AIM*) has some really neat features. It can tell you when your chat buddies sign on, even before they send you an online "Hello." If your chat buddies sign off, you know that, too. This software is a breeze to use, and we bet you'll use it as much as, if not more than, e-mail.

Becoming a registered user

Before you can chat with someone using Instant Messenger, you have to register yourself as a user with a name nobody else has used. This way, you're identified uniquely in the world of Instant Messenger, and only you can have that name. Your permanent online name can be anything you choose: Bob1, Jennie118, Kangaroo — it just has to be unique.

To register to use Instant Messenger, follow these steps:

1. **Go to** www.netscape.com.

2. **Click the Instant Messenger button.**

You see the Instant Messenger page.

3. **Click the <u>Register</u> button.**

The registration screen appears.

4. **Complete the form, scroll down the window, and submit the form by clicking the Register Now button.**

In a few minutes, you receive an e-mail message confirming your registration. You must reply to that message within 48 hours, or your registration becomes null and void.

Logging on to AOL Instant Messenger

To log on to Instant Messenger after you've registered, follow these steps:

1. **Start Instant Messenger in one of the following ways:**

- Within Navigator, choose Tasks⇨Instant Messenger (or press Ctrl+3).

- On your Windows desktop, choose Start⇨Programs⇨Netscape⇨AOL Instant Messenger.

- On your Windows desktop, click the yellow man icon in your Systems Tray.

2. **Replace <New User> in the Screen Name box with the online name you registered with.**

3. **Type your password in the Password box.**

4. **To avoid having to type the password each time you sign on in the future, click in the Save Password box to select it.**

5. **If you want to automatically log in to Instant Messenger each time you sign on to the Internet, click in the Sign On At Launch box to select it.**

6. **Click the Sign On button.**

You see the Instant Messenger Buddy List window, shown in Figure 2-4. This window displays the names of your buddies who are currently online. You're now signed on.

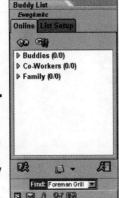

Figure 2-4:
The Buddy List appears after you've successfully signed on.

Starting a chat session

Before you initiate a chat session, you must know the Instant Messenger screen name of the person you want to chat with. To initiate a session, follow these steps:

1. **Click the Send Instant Message at the bottom of the Buddy List window.**

   This displays the Instant Message window.

2. **In the To box, type the screen name of the person you want to chat with or choose their name from the drop-down list.**

3. **Type your message in the message window.**

   If the person you want to chat with is signed on to Instant Messenger, she instantly sees your message pop up on her screen. Your Instant Message window splits into two windows. She, too, sees a similar screen with two windows in it. The top window displays the text of the conversation between you and your friend. The bottom window is where you type your messages.

   If the person you want to chat with is not logged on to Instant Messenger, you see the Information window telling you that your friend is not available.

4. **If your buddy is online, type your message in the bottom window and click Send.**

5. **To end your chat session, click the Close (X) button in the upper-right corner of the Instant Message window or press Esc.**

You can tell which of your buddies is currently signed on by glancing at the Buddy List in your Buddy List window. Click the Online tab in the Buddy List window. The screen names of all those who are currently logged on are displayed there.

Adding/deleting buddies on your Buddy List

The Buddy List within Instant Messenger is like a phone book listing your buddies' screen names, and you can add buddies to the list.

To add a buddy to your Buddy List, follow these steps:

1. **Click the List Setup tab on the Buddy List window.**

2. **Click a folder to select it as the folder to which you want to add your new buddy.**

3. **Click the Add a Buddy button.**

   This creates a *New Buddy* entry within that folder.

4. **Type the Instant Messenger screen name of your buddy and press Enter.**

To start a chat session with a buddy, double-click the buddy's name.

To delete a buddy from your list, select the name you want to delete, and click the Delete icon.

Internet Telephony

The Internet doesn't limit you to communication by typing. Today's powerful personal computers and fast modems let you send voice and even pictures over the Net. Best of all, no long-distance charges apply — even for calls overseas.

You do need a microphone or headset, a fast PC with a sound card or a fast Mac, and a 28.8 Kbps or faster modem. You need the proper phone software, of course, although those packages cost less than a couple of months' worth of phone bills.

So why isn't everyone calling on the Internet yet? Here's the bad news:

✦ Internet phone software is complicated to set up and use.

✦ At best, the sound quality is not that great, and it can be downright poor.

✦ Both parties must have the equipment and have their computers turned on, which can be tricky to arrange.

✦ Internet phone software may not work well if you're behind a firewall (if your computer is connected to a corporate LAN, for example).

✦ Some packages require you to know the other person's IP address to make connections.

✦ Different software packages often don't work with one another.

✦ If Internet telephony is widely adopted, it will place a big strain on the Net and may raise the ire of phone regulators, especially in countries with state telephone monopolies.

Things will get better, though. The technology is improving all the time, with new features such as these:

✦ **Whiteboards:** Special screens that both parties can see and draw on

✦ **Text windows:** Enable you to write notes that others can see, similar to online chat

✦ **Conference calls:** Enable more than two people to talk together

✦ **Voice mail and voice e-mail:** Enable callers to leave a message at the beep

✦ **Video phone:** Displays the other person's image on-screen in a small picture that changes at rates as fast as several times per second

The adoption of standards such as ITU H.323 will let different software and computers talk to each other. Although larger software companies (such as Microsoft, Netscape, Intel, and IBM) are just entering the field, a number of Internet telephony packages are on the market now (see Table 2-3). Most offer a 30-day free trial. (See "Making Internet Calls with NetMeeting," in the next section.)

Table 2-3	Internet Telephony Packages	
Package	*URL*	*Comments*
Internet Phone (VocalTec)	www.vocaltec.com	Mac and Windows
Video Phone (Intel)	www.intel.com/pccamera/index.htm	Supports H.323 standard
NetMeeting 3(Microsoft)	www.microsoft.com/netmeeting	Comes with Windows XP and Internet Explorer 5 and 6

Package	URL	Comments
ClearPhone (Engineering Consulting)	www.clearphone.com	Uses QuickTime for high-quality Mac and Windows connections
Speak Freely (Open Source)	www.speakfreely.org	Offers something the others don't: encryption for real privacy; Windows and Unix
Enhanced CU-SeeMe (White Pine Software)	www.cuseemeworld.com	Pioneering Internet video phone software

You can see up-to-date information about the fast-changing field of Internet telephony at the following Web sites:

✦ **Voice on the Net:** www.von.com

✦ **Iphone:** www.pulver.com/iphone

Making Internet Calls with NetMeeting

Microsoft NetMeeting — which automatically installs with a typical installation of Internet Explorer 6 (and comes with Windows XP) — is a premier online conferencing tool that incorporates Internet "telephone" calls, online chat sessions, whiteboard sessions (where you get to draw with others on a shared whiteboard), and collaborative document editing, as well as video conferencing. Of course, you need not only the necessary hardware (microphone, external speakers, and video camera to name a few), but also a mighty fast Internet connection to make good use of the tools.

To start NetMeeting, choose Start➪Programs➪NetMeeting. Or if you use Microsoft Outlook 2002 as your e-mail program (a program included as part of the Premium version of Office XP), you can run NetMeeting from the Contacts portion. Simply select the name of the person you want to meet with in the Contacts folder and choose Actions➪Call Using NetMeeting from the Outlook menu bar.

See *Microsoft Outlook 2000 For Windows For Dummies Quick Reference* by Bill Dyszel (published by Hungry Minds, Inc.) to find out more about how to use Microsoft Outlook 2000.

The first time you use NetMeeting, you encounter a wizard that guides you through setting up the program and checking out your audio and video equipment.

Thereafter, when you start NetMeeting, you see the NetMeeting window, which is the master control station for your conferencing activities. It's from this window that you place calls and start conferencing utilities, such as Chat and Whiteboard.

Placing a conference call

To make it easier for NetMeeting users to contact each other for conferences, Microsoft maintains directory servers that list users who have logged on to the server and are available for conference calls. By default, NetMeeting is set up to check in with the Microsoft directory service when you start the program. However, you can select a different directory service for startup by using the Directory Server Name setting in the Directory section of the Calling tab of the Options dialog box. In fact, your network administrator may have set up a directory service for your local network. You can change your current Directory Server simply by choosing a different one from the Server drop-down list in the main window.

After NetMeeting makes contact with a directory, you can place a call to someone listed on that directory simply by double-clicking a name in the directory list. NetMeeting places a call to that person using the default settings. If you want to specify call settings, you can click the Call button on the toolbar or choose Call⇨New Call from the menu bar. From the Call dialog box that appears, you can specify the e-mail address, computer name, network address, or telephone number of the modem to which you want to connect in the To drop-down list.

After you make a call and the other conference participant accepts the connection, you can talk with each other as you would when conducting a telephone call. (If the other participant doesn't accept the connection, a dialog box tells you so and tells you what to do next.) The sound quality isn't as good as a telephone connection, and you may need to take turns talking because some sound cards don't allow the microphone and speakers to work simultaneously. But still, the system works pretty well. If you and the other conference participants have those nifty little video cameras attached to your computers, you can even see the person you're talking to.

The person you call may already be in a meeting. If this is the case, a dialog box appears that asks if you would like to join the meeting. If you choose Yes and the person you call grants permission, you can participate in the meeting. Any number of people can participate in a call.

Chatting with the keyboard

After you place a conference call with NetMeeting, the Chat window enables you to type a message and have it appear simultaneously on the other participants' screens.

To use NetMeeting's Chat feature, follow these steps:

1. **From the NetMeeting menu bar, choose Tools⇨Chat.**

Alternatively, you can click the Chat button at the bottom of the NetMeeting window.

The Chat window opens on your desktop. A Chat window also opens on each of the other conference participants' screens.

2. **Type a message into the Message text box at the bottom of the Chat window.**

3. **To send your message to all the other conference participants, press Enter or click the large Send Message button in the lower-right corner of the Chat window.**

Your message appears in the upper panel of the Chat window of all conference participants. Other participants can send messages in the same way. Each message in the Chat window is preceded by the name of the participant who sent the message.

Using the Whiteboard

After you place a conference call with NetMeeting, the Whiteboard window enables conference participants to collaborate on drawings and diagrams.

To use the Whiteboard, follow these steps:

1. **Choose Tools⇨Whiteboard.**

Alternatively, you can click the Whiteboard button at the bottom of the NetMeeting window.

The Whiteboard window opens on each conference participant's screen.

2. **To draw lines and shapes in the Whiteboard window, click a drawing tool in the toolbar on the left side of the Whiteboard window.**

You can choose from a pen, a highlight marker, outline or solid rectangles, or outline or solid ovals.

3. **Click a color in the color palette at the bottom of the Whiteboard window, move the pointer into the drawing area (the large box that occupies most of the Whiteboard window), and press and hold the mouse button as you drag the mouse.**

If you're drawing lines with the pen or marker tools, the lines appear along the path you drag until you release the mouse button. If you're using a rectangle or oval tool, you define the size and position of the shape by starting in one corner and dragging to the opposite corner before releasing the mouse button.

4. **To add text to a Whiteboard drawing, click the text tool in the toolbar (the one with the big letter A) and click a color in the color palette. Then click in the drawing area where you want to position the text. When the flashing cursor appears, type in the text.**

5. **To move or change an item already on the drawing area, click the selection tool in the toolbar (the one that looks like an arrow) and then click the shape or text with the selection tool.**

   A dotted rectangle appears around the object to show that it's selected. You can drag the selected object with the selection tool to move it, or click a color in the color palette to change the color of the object.

As you make changes in the drawing area of the Whiteboard window, NetMeeting replicates those changes on the other conference participants' screens. Likewise, any changes that other participants make in the Whiteboard drawing appear in the Whiteboard window on your screen.

Sending files

Along with everything else you can do in a NetMeeting conference, you can also send files to other conference participants. The easiest way to send files is to drag a file icon from an Explorer window and drop it on the list of conference participants in the NetMeeting window. NetMeeting sends the file to all the conference participants simultaneously. You can also send a file by choosing Tools➪File Transfer➪Send File, pressing Ctrl+F, or clicking the Transfer Files button at the bottom of the NetMeeting window.

Chapter 3: Using Classic Internet Tools

In This Chapter

✔ Transferring files using FTP

✔ Logging in to other computers with Telnet

✔ Taking a quick tour of Unix and Linux commands

✔ Exploring Gopherspace with Gopher

*A*lthough e-mail and the World Wide Web dominate Internet use today, the Internet was originally built from a number of smaller tools that were part of the Unix operating system. Today, Web browsers, such as Netscape Navigator and Microsoft Internet Explorer, perform the functions of many of these tools. You may have to use these tools directly from time to time, however, and understanding a little about how they work can help you use your browser more effectively. We tell you a little about them in this chapter.

Using FTP to Transfer Files

The Internet copies files between your computer and other computers on the Internet by using a facility known as FTP *(file transfer protocol)*. You connect your computer to an *FTP server,* an Internet host computer that stores files for transfer. Many publicly accessible FTP servers enable you to log in and retrieve a wide variety of files, including software, text files, and graphics files. On these systems, rather than log in with your own name and password, you log in as *anonymous* and use your e-mail address or the word *guest* as the password. A common use of FTP is to obtain updated drivers for your printer, video card, and other system components.

Your browser can usually log in as *anonymous* for you, download the file you want, log off, and unpack the file — all automatically. URLs that start with ftp:// take you to an FTP site.

When you transfer a file by using any FTP program, the program has to know whether the file contains text or anything else. If the file contains only text, it transfers the file in ASCII mode; otherwise, it uses Binary or Image mode. Some FTP programs can look at the file you want to transfer and guess the mode; other programs require you to specify.

Using FTP programs

Sometimes, you may want more control over the file transfer process — for example, when you're uploading files to a remote Web server. If your ISP uses a PPP (Point-to-Point Protocol) account, which allows your computer to connect directly to the Internet (most dial-up ISPs use PPP), you can use Winsock or Macintosh TCP/IP-compatible software to move files on the Internet. Here are two such compatible programs:

+ **WS_FTP Pro 7.0 for Windows:** From Ipswitch, Inc. and available at www.ipswitch.com

+ **Fetch for Macintosh:** Written by Jim Mathees and available at www.dartmouth.edu/pages/softdev/fetch.html

On America Online and CompuServe, go to keyword **ftp**.

On Unix systems, type **ftp** followed by the host name of the server. Type your login name and password for that server when prompted.

Navigating files and directories

Most Winsock and Mac TCP/IP programs use a full-screen interface that displays in one window the files in the current directory on the FTP server (the "Remote system") and in another window the files on your own computer (the "Local system"). Before you can transfer files, you want to display in one window the files to transfer and in the other window the directory you want to transfer them to.

To change directories, click the name of the directory you want to move files to in the FTP window. If you want to move to the parent directory of the current directory, click the .. entry on the directory list.

In Unix, you type FTP commands that are similar to standard Unix file-management commands. (If you're familiar with DOS, you may recognize some of them as the DOS commands for these same tasks.) To change to a directory, for example, you type **cd** followed by the name of the directory. To see a list of the files in a directory, type **dir**. To move to the parent directory of the current directory, you can type the **cd ..** command.

Uploading and downloading files

If you use an FTP program with a full-screen interface (such as WS_FTP), click all the names of the files that you want to transmit. Click the ASCII button if the files contain only text; otherwise, click the Binary button. Then click the transfer button that shows the arrow pointing from the system where the files are located to the system where you want to move them.

On Unix, type **ascii** if the files to be transferred contain only text; type **image** or **binary** if the files contain something other than text. To download a file from the other computer to your computer, type **get** followed by the name of the file. To upload a file from your computer to the other computer, type **put** followed by the name of the file.

When you're done copying files, disconnect from the FTP server.

✦ If you're using a graphics FTP program, click the Disconnect button or choose Disconnect from the menu.

✦ If you're using the Unix FTP program, type **quit**.

Using Telnet to Log In to Other Computers

Telnet enables you to log in to other computers on the Net as though you were connected to them directly. Don't worry — it's perfectly legal! Telnet works only if the other computer gives permission.

Using Telnet from a Winsock or MacTCP program

If you use a PPP account or a direct Internet connection, you can use a Winsock or Macintosh TCP/IP-compatible Telnet program, such as the following:

✦ **Telnet:** This program comes with Windows 95/98/2000/XP.

✦ **NetTerm for Windows:** This program is from InterSoft International, Inc., and available at www.securenetterm.com.

✦ **NCSA Telnet:** Visit www.ncsa.uiuc.edu/SDG/Homepage/telnet.html.

✦ **Better Telnet for Macintosh:** Visit www.cstone.net/~rbraun/mac/telnet for a copy.

Winsock and Mac TCP/IP Telnet programs use a graphical interface that includes a window in which you type commands and see the remote computer's responses.

If you're using a Web browser (such as Internet Explorer or Netscape Navigator) and want to Telnet to some site — foo.com, for example — try sending your browser to the URL telnet://foo.com.

Connecting to remote computers

On systems that use a graphical interface (such as Windows and Macintosh — refer to the previous section), you type the host name in the Telnet window after choosing Connect or Open Connection from Telnet's menu bar.

On Unix systems, you type **telnet** followed by the host name of the computer you want to log in to. (Type **tn3270** instead to connect to older IBM mainframes.)

To access remote computers from CompuServe, go to keyword **telnet**.

The remote system usually asks you to enter your username *on that system* and then your password. You may be asked what kind of terminal you're using (common terminal types include VT100, ANSI, and 3101). If you indicate the wrong type, the information on your screen may be scrambled. If Telnet suggests a terminal type, accept it and see what happens.

Disconnecting from remote computers

You end a Telnet session by typing **logout, exit,** or **bye** or pressing Ctrl+D or Ctrl+] (that's the Control key and then the right bracket).

On Windows and Macintosh systems, just close the Telnet window.

Unix and Linux Commands

Telnet may bring you to one of the many Unix or Linux systems on the Internet. Table 3-1 gives a brief guide to some of the most important Unix and Linux commands:

Table 3-1	Unix and Linux Commands
Command	*Description*
`cd directoryname`	Changes the current directory.
`cd ..`	Brings you up one directory level.
`cd`	Returns you to your home directory.
`Control-C`	Terminates most operations.
`cp filename1 filename2`	Copies a file.
`logout`	Terminates your session.
`ls`	Lists the files in the current directory. For more complete information, use `ls -alF`.
`man commandname`	Displays a page of instructions for that command; for example, `man ls`.
`mkdir newdirectoryname`	Makes a new directory.
`more filename`	Displays a text file one page at a time. Press the spacebar to see the next page; press Q to quit.

Command	Description
mv filename1 filename2	Moves a file or changes its name.
pwd	Prints the current working directory.
rm filename	Deletes a file. (**Caution:** Unix, unlike Windows and MacOS, doesn't have a way to undo a file deletion.)
rmdir directoryname	Removes an empty directory.

Unix filenames are similar to Windows filenames, but Unix uses forward slashes (/) rather than backslashes (\). You can use an asterisk (*) as a wild-card in a filename in most commands. Filenames that start with a period (.) are normally hidden and are used to store the settings for various programs.

The tilde character (~) is used as an abbreviation for a home directory path: cd ~ takes you to your home directory, and cd ~arnold takes you to Arnold's home directory.

For more information about using Unix tools, get a copy of *UNIX For Dummies*, 4th Edition, by John R. Levine and Margaret Levine Young (published by Hungry Minds, Inc.).

Using Gopher to Cruise Gopherspace

Gopher is an older Internet filing system that presents information as a series of menus. Gopher preceded the World Wide Web, and it stores mainly text information. A great deal of useful information is still out there in *Gopherspace*. Web browsers can navigate Gopherspace just fine by themselves. Gopher sites have URLs that start with gopher://. On AOL, you can also go to the keyword **gopher**.

Index

Book VI

Creating Web Pages

TARZAN - LORD of the WEB

@RICHTENNANT

Maybe you write memos too long — last one make server traffic move like hippo through mud pit.

What your problem? No can swing link to link? Try going "ahAHahAHahAHah!" real loud next time you click — ahhahahaha

This guy real interesting. Wonder how long it take to call in elephant stampede?

Why you say this not elegant interface? Tarzan work hard to design warthog icons!

Contents at a Glance

Chapter 1: Getting Started with Web Publishing

In This Chapter

✔ Understanding the different kinds of Web sites

✔ Creating a Web site

✔ Determining what to include on a Web site

✔ Finding space for your Web site

This chapter presents some basic information to help you get started with setting up your own Web site. You discover the basic steps for creating a Web site, what you should include on every Web site (and on every *page* in the site), how to effectively organize the pages in your site, and where to find space for your Web site. In addition, this chapter presents recommendations and guidelines for creating a successful Web site.

Understanding the Different Kinds of Web Sites

This section describes three broad categories of Web sites. The site that you intend to publish probably falls into one of these three categories: personal home pages, company Web sites, and special-interest Web sites.

Personal home pages

Just about anyone with access to the Internet can create a personal home page. The simplest personal home pages contain basic information, such as your name, information about your family, your occupation, your hobbies, and any special interests you may have. You can also throw in one or more pictures. Links to your favorite pages on the Web are also commonly included. If you're looking for a job, include your résumé on your site.

Company Web sites

More and more companies are joining the Web bandwagon. Even mom-and-pop pizza parlors are putting up Web pages. The simplest corporate Web pages provide basic information about a company, such as a description of the company's products or services, phone numbers, and so on. A more elaborate corporate Web site can include any or all of the following:

✦ An online catalog that enables users to see detailed information about products and services and that may also include pictures and prices

✦ Online ordering, which enables Internet users to actually place orders over the Internet

✦ Lists of frequently asked questions about the company's products or services

✦ Online support, where a customer can leave a question about a problem he or she is having with a product and receive a reply within a day or so

✦ Articles and reviews of the company's products and press releases

✦ Employment opportunities with the company

✦ History of the company

✦ Biographies of company employees

Special-interest Web sites

Many of the most interesting Web sites are devoted to special interests. For example, if you're involved with a youth soccer league, you may want to create a Web page that includes team rosters, schedules, and standings. Or you can create a Web page that focuses on Christmas decorating. The list of possible topics for a special-interest Web site is limitless.

Guidelines for Creating a Successful Web Site

When you're planning the content, design, and layout of your Web site, keep the following guidelines in mind so that you create a Web site that people will want to visit over and over again:

✦ **Offer something useful on every page.** Too many Web sites are filled with fluff — pages that don't have any useful content. Avoid creating pages that are just steps along the way to truly useful information. Instead, strive to include something useful on every Web site page.

✦ **Check the competition.** Find out what other Web sites similar to yours have to offer. Don't create a "me, too" Web site that offers nothing but information that is already available elsewhere. Instead, strive for unique information that people can find only on your Web site.

✦ **Make it look good.** No matter how good the information at your Web site is, people will stay away if your site looks as if you spent no more than five minutes on design and layout. Yes, substance is more important than style. But an ugly Web site turns people away, whereas an attractive Web site draws people in.

✦ **Proof it carefully.** If every third word in your Web site is misspelled, people will assume that the information on your Web site is as unreliable as your spelling. If your HTML editor has a spell-check feature, use it and proof your work carefully before you post it to the Web. In fact, you may want to consider having someone else proofread it for you; a fresh pair of eyes can catch things that you may have overlooked.

✦ **Provide links to other sites.** Some of the best pages on the Internet are links to other Web sites that have information about a particular topic. In fact, many of the pages we have bookmarked for our own use are pages of links to topics as diverse as hobby electronics, softball, and backpacking. The time you spend creating a directory of links to other sites with information similar or complementary to your own will be well spent.

✦ **Keep it current.** Internet users won't frequent your site if it contains out-of-date information. Make sure that you frequently update your Web pages with current information. Obviously, some Web pages need to be changed more than others. For example, if you maintain a Web page that lists the team standings for a soccer league, you have to update the page after every game. On the other hand, a page that features medieval verse romances doesn't need to be updated often.

If your Web site contains links to other Web sites, frequently check all those links to make sure that they're still valid.

✦ **Don't tie it to a certain browser.** Exploiting the cool new features of the latest and greatest Web browser is a good idea. But don't do so at the expense of users who may be using the *other* browser, or at the expense of users who are still working with an earlier version. Some people still use browsers that don't support frames. Make sure that any pages in which you incorporate the advanced features of newer browsers work well with older browsers as well. In addition, it's always a good idea to include a statement on your home page stating which browser provides the optimum viewing for the pages.

✦ **Don't make hardware assumptions.** Remember that not everyone has a 21-inch monitor and a high-speed cable-modem connection to the Internet. Design your Web site so that the poor sap who is stuck with a 14-inch monitor and a 28.8 Kbps modem can use it, too.

✦ **Publicize it.** Few people will stumble across your Web site by accident. If you want people to visit your Web site, you have to publicize it. Make sure that your site is listed in the major search engines, such as Yahoo! and Lycos. You can also promote your site by putting its address on all your advertisements, correspondence, business cards, e-mail, and so on. For more information about publicizing your site, see Book VI, Chapter 5.

Book VI Chapter 1

Getting Started with Web Publishing

Basic Steps for Creating a Web Site

Although you don't have to be obsessively methodical about creating a Web site, it's a good idea to at least follow the three basic steps described in this section.

Step 1: Planning your Web site

Start by making a plan for your Web site. If all you want to do is create a simple, one-page "Here I Am" personal Web site, you don't really need to make a plan. But for a more elaborate Web site, you should plan the content of the site before you start creating actual pages.

One good way to plan a Web site is to sketch a simple diagram on paper showing the various pages that you want to create, with arrows showing the links between the pages. Alternatively, you can create an outline that represents your entire site. You can be as detailed or as vague as you want.

Step 2: Creating your Web pages

You can take several different approaches to creating the pages that will comprise your Web site. If the mere thought of "programming" gives you hives, you can use a simple Web page editor to create your Web pages. Both Microsoft Internet Explorer and Netscape Navigator come with basic Web page editors that enable you to create simple Web pages without any programming. You can also purchase inexpensive programs for creating complete Web sites. One of the best-known Web site development programs is Microsoft FrontPage 2002.

On the other hand, if you dream in Boolean, feel free to fire up Notepad and start banging away HTML code from scratch. You have to learn the intricacies of using HTML codes to format your Web pages, but you'll gain satisfaction from knowing that you did it the hard way.

If you need help writing HTML code, check out *HTML 4 For Dummies,* by Ed Tittel, Natanya Pitts, and Chelsea Valentine (published by Hungry Minds, Inc.).

For more information about the process of designing and creating Web pages, see Book VI, Chapter 2. For information about using Microsoft FrontPage 2002 or Netscape Composer to create Web pages, see Book VI, Chapter 6, and Book VI, Chapter 7, respectively.

Step 3: Publishing your Web pages

After your Web pages are complete, it's time to publish them on the Internet. First, you have to find a Web server that will host your Web pages.

The section "Finding Space for Your Web Site," later in this chapter, gives you ideas for finding a Web server. Next, you copy your Web pages to the Web server. Finally, you can publicize your Web site by cataloging it in the major search services. For more information about these tasks, see Book VI, Chapter 5.

What to Include on Every Web Site

Although every Web site is different, you can find certain common elements on most Web sites. The following sections describe the items you should consider including on your Web site.

Home page

Every Web site should include a home page that serves as an entry point into the site. The home page is the first page that most users see when they visit your site (unless you include a cover page, as described in the next section). As a result, devote considerable time and energy to making sure that your home page makes a good first impression. Place an attractive title at the top of the page. Remember that most users have to scroll down to see your entire home page. They see just the top of the page first, so you want to make sure that the title is immediately visible.

After the title, include a site menu that enables users to access the content available on your Web site. You can create a simple text menu or a fancy graphics-based menu in which the user can click different parts of the image to go to different pages. However, if you use this type of menu, called an *image map,* be sure to provide a text menu as an alternative for users who don't want to wait for the image map to download or who have turned off graphic downloads altogether. For more on image maps, see Book VI, Chapter 3.

Here are a few other goodies that you may want to include on your home page:

✦ **An indication of new content that is available on your Web site.** Users who return to your site often want to know right away when new information is available.

✦ **The date your site was last updated.** That way, users know right away whether you've added any information since their last visit.

✦ **A copyright notice.** You can include a link to a separate copyright page where you spell out whether others can copy the information you have placed on your site.

✦ **A reminder to bookmark the page.** That way, users can get back to the page easily.

✦ **A hit counter.** If users see that 4 million people have visited your site since last Tuesday, they automatically assume that yours must be a hot site. On the other hand, if they see that only three people have visited since Truman was president, they'll yawn and leave quickly. If your site isn't very popular, you may want to skip the hit counter.

Avoid placing a huge amount of graphics on your home page. Your home page is the first page on your Web site most users see. If it takes more than 15 seconds for your page to load, users may lose patience and skip your page altogether.

Cover page

A cover page is displayed temporarily before your home page is displayed. Cover pages usually feature a flashy logo or an animation. In most cover pages, the user must click the logo or some other element on the page to enter the site's home page. You can also program the page so that it automatically jumps to the home page after a certain amount of time has elapsed — say 10 or 15 seconds.

Cover pages annoy many users, especially pages that take more than a few seconds to download and display. Think carefully about whether the splashy cover page actually enhances your site or is more of an annoyance.

Site map

If your site has a lot of pages, you may want to include a site map. A site map is a detailed menu that provides links to every page on the site. By using the site map, a user can bypass intermediate menus and go directly to the pages that interest him or her.

Contact information

Be sure that your site includes information about how to contact you or your company. You can easily include your e-mail address as a link right on the home page. When the user clicks this link, most Web browsers fire up the user's e-mail program and stand ready to compose a message with your e-mail address already filled in.

If you want to include complete contact information, such as your address and phone number, or if you want to list contact information for several individuals, you may want to place the contact information on a separate page that users can access from the home page.

Help page

If your Web site contains more than a few pages, consider providing a help page that provides information about how to use the site. The help page can include information about how to navigate the site, how you obtained the information for the site, how often the site is updated, how someone can contribute to the site, and so on.

FAQ

Frequently Asked Questions (FAQ) pages are among the most popular sources of information on the Internet. You can organize your own FAQ page on any topic you want. Just come up with a list of questions and provide the answers. Or solicit answers from readers of your page.

Related links

At some sites, the most popular page is the links page, which provides a list of links to related sites. As the compiler of your own links page, you can do something that search engines such as Yahoo! cannot: You can pick and choose the links you want to include, and you can provide your own commentary about the information contained on each site.

Discussion group

A discussion group adds interactivity to your Web site by allowing visitors to post articles that others can read and respond to. Other similar Web page elements that encourage interactivity include a feedback page or a guest book. Those who visit your Web site can use these elements to comment on your site.

What to Include on Every Page

Although every Web page should contain unique and useful information, all Web pages must contain the following three elements.

Title

Place a title at the top of every page. The title should identify not just the specific contents of the page, but also the Web site itself. A specific title is important because some users may not enter your site through your home page. Instead, they may go directly to one of the content pages in your site.

Navigation links

All the pages of your Web site need a consistent set of navigation links. At the minimum, provide a link to your home page on every page in your site. In addition, you may want to include links to the next and previous pages if your pages have a logical sequential organization.

Author and copyright information

Every page should also include author credits and a copyright notice. Because users can enter your site by going directly to any page, placing the authorship and copyright notices on only the home page is not sufficient.

Organizing the Content

The following sections describe several popular ways to organize the information on your Web site.

Sequential organization

In sequential organization, you simply organize your pages so that they follow one after another, like the pages in a book, as shown in Figure 1-1.

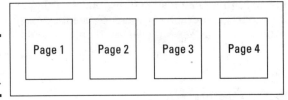

Figure 1-1:
Sequential
organization.

On each page, provide navigation links that enable the user to go to the next page, go to the previous page, or return directly to the first page.

Hierarchical organization

With a hierarchical organization, you organize your Web pages into a hierarchy, categorizing the pages according to subject matter. The topmost page serves as a menu that enables users to access other pages directly (see Figure 1-2).

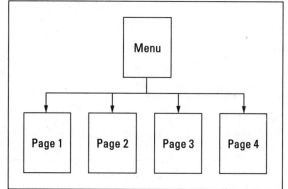

Figure 1-2:
Hierarchical
organization
with one
menu level.

On each page, provide a navigation link that returns the user to the menu.
You can include more than one level of menu pages, as shown in Figure 1-3.
However, don't overdo the menus. Most users are frustrated by Web sites
that have unnecessary menus, in which each menu has only two or three
choices. When a menu has more than a dozen choices, however, consider
splitting the menu into two or more separate menus.

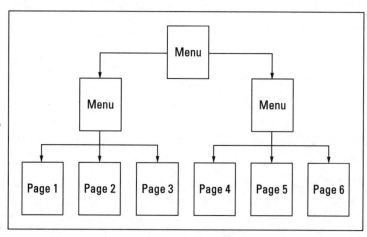

Figure 1-3:
Hierarchical
organization
with
multiple
menu levels.

Combination sequential and hierarchical organization

Many Web sites use a combination of sequential and hierarchical organization, in which a menu enables users to access content pages that contain
sequential links to one another, as in Figure 1-4.

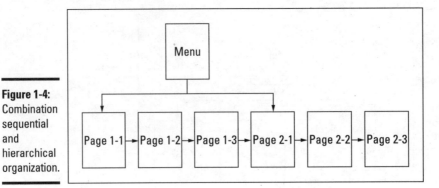

Figure 1-4:
Combination
sequential
and
hierarchical
organization.

In a combination organization style, each content page includes a link to the next page in sequence in addition to a link back to the menu. The menu page contains links to the pages that mark the start of each section of pages.

Web organization

Some Web sites have pages that are connected with links that defy a strict sequential or hierarchical pattern. In extreme cases, every page in the site is linked to every other page, creating a structure that resembles a web, as shown in Figure 1-5.

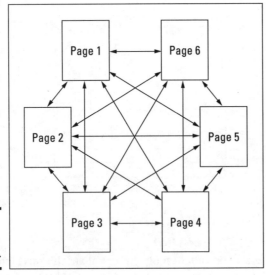

Figure 1-5:
Web
organization.

This is a good style of organization if the total number of pages is limited and you can't predict the sequence in which a user may want to view them.

Finding Space for Your Web Site

If you don't have a home for your Web site, the following sections give you some ideas for where to find space for your Web pages.

Internet Service Providers

If you access the Internet through an Internet Service Provider (ISP), you probably already have space set aside to set up a home page. Most ISPs give each user a small amount of disk space for Web pages included in their monthly service. The space may be limited to a few megabytes, but that should be enough to set up several pages. You can probably get additional disk space if you need it for a modest charge. You may also have to pay additional fees for any type of commercial use on your site. Your ISP can give you step-by-step instructions for copying your Web pages to the ISP's Web server.

Online services

Two of the major online services — CompuServe and America Online — let you publish your own Web pages.

CompuServe (CSi) lets you publish your Web page in an area called *Our World,* which already has more than 100,000 home pages. Our World includes authoring tools that make creating Web pages easy. CSi limits each user to 5MB of disk space. CompuServe also has a service called CSi BusinessWeb that provides 30MB of disk space and your own domain name (such as www.mycompany.com) for $79/month, plus a $50 setup fee.

America Online (AOL) also lets you publish your own Web page in the AOL Hometown. (hometown.aol.com) Each AOL member is limited to 12MB of disk space. (For more information on building a home page in AOL, see Book VII, Chapter 4.)

Unfortunately, the domain name you're assigned when using these services may not be easy to remember or type. Write down your domain name and be careful when you're typing it.

Free Web servers

If you can't find a home for your Web page at your Internet Service Provider or your online service, consider using a free Web server to host your site.

Troubleshooting Web publishing

The following points summarize the most trouble-some aspects of creating high-quality Web pages:

✔ **Too many Web browsers:** Different Web browsers display Web pages differently. The two most popular Web browsers — Netscape Navigator and Microsoft Internet Explorer — offer HTML features. In their efforts to get ahead of one another, both Netscape and Microsoft put the notion of *compatibility* in the back seat. Whenever you use a new HTML feature, you have to make sure that your page looks good no matter which browser a visitor uses to view it.

✔ **Different screen sizes:** Some users have 14-inch monitors that are set to 640 x 480 resolution. Others have giant 21-inch monitors that run at 1280 x 1024. Your pages look different depending on the display resolution of the user's computer. A good middle-of-the-road approach is to design your pages for 800 x 600.

✔ **Different connection speeds:** Some users are connected to the Internet over high-speed T3 lines or cable modems, which can send megabytes of data in seconds. Others are connected over a phone line at 28.8 Kbps, which downloads large graphics files at a snail's pace. To compensate for lack of speed, some 28.8 Kbps users set up their browsers so that graphics are not automatically downloaded. Keep this fact in mind and don't create pages that are overly dependent on graphics.

The best-known free home page service is GeoCities, which hosts more than 1 million home pages. Each free Web site can use up to 15MB of disk space. The only limitation is that you must include a banner advertisement at the top of your Web page and a link to the GeoCities home page at the bottom of your page. (For $8.95 per month plus a one-time setup fee of $15, you can eliminate the advertising and increase your space allotment to 25MB.) For more information, go to www.geocities.com.

Many other free home page services are available, although most cater to specific types of home pages, such as those for artists, churches, chambers of commerce, and so on. To find a good directory of free home page services, go to Yahoo! (www.yahoo.com) and search for *Free Web Pages*.

Chapter 2: Elements of Web Page Design

*T*his chapter presents a primer on the techniques for adding commonly used elements to your Web pages, such as headings, backgrounds, links, tables, and navigation bars.

For more detailed information on the topics presented in this chapter, pick up a copy of *Creating Web Pages For Dummies*, 5th Edition, by Bud Smith and Arthur Bebak (published by Hungry Minds, Inc.).

HTML Basics

All HTML documents contain the following elements, which define the overall structure of the document:

```
<HTML>
<HEAD>
<TITLE>Your title goes here</TITLE>
</HEAD>
<BODY>
The body of your document goes here.
</BODY>
</HTML>
```

As the preceding example shows, HTML tags are generally used in pairs that enclose portions of your document. The beginning tag, such as <BODY>, signals the start of specific formatting for that section; the closing tag, such as </BODY>, includes a slash before the tag name and signals the end of the formatting for that section.

Here is an explanation for each of these tags:

✦ `<HTML>`: This tag must always appear as the very first thing in an HTML document. It tells the browser that the file is an HTML file.

✦ `<HEAD>` **and** `</HEAD>`: These tags enclose the section of the document called the *header,* which contains information that applies to the entire document.

✦ `<TITLE>` **and** `</TITLE>`: These tags enclose the document title. Any text that appears within them is used as the title for your HTML document. This is also the text that appears in the browser's title bar.

✦ `<BODY>` **and** `</BODY>`: These tags mark the beginning and end of the portion of your document that the browser displays when someone views the page. A lot of stuff typically falls between these tags.

✦ `</HTML>`: This tag is always the last tag in your document.

Specifying Font Settings

In the early days of the Web, HTML didn't provide a method that enabled you to precisely control the appearance of type on your Web pages. Now, however, HTML offers several methods for controlling type.

HTML has two tags that let you control font settings: `<FONT>` and `<BASEFONT>`. The `<FONT>` tag enables you to control font settings for an individual block of text, whereas the `<BASEFONT>` tag sets the default font used for an entire document. Both of these tags are immediately followed by one or *more attributes,* which provide specific information for the tag. Here are the most important attributes of the `<FONT>` and `<BASEFONT>` tags:

✦ `FACE`: Sets the typeface.

✦ `SIZE`: Gives the type size on a scale of 1 to 7, where 7 is the largest and 1 is the smallest. The default size is 3.

✦ `COLOR`: Sets the color of the text.

Here is a snippet of HTML that sets the typeface, size, and color used for text:

```
<BODY>
<BASEFONT SIZE=4 COLOR=BLACK FACE="Times New Roman">
<P>This is normal body text using the font set by the BASE-
    FONT tag.
<H1><FONT FACE="Arial">This is a heading</FONT></H1>
<P>After the heading, the text reverts to the BASEFONT set-
    ting.
</BODY>
```

Following guidelines for Web typography

Typography involves more than just setting a font. Here are some pointers for creating text that is both readable and attractive:

✔ **Don't use too many typefaces on a page.** Two or three different typefaces are plenty.

✔ **Use a serif typeface for body text.** *Serifs* are the little "feet" that appear at the end of each stroke on individual letters. Times New Roman is an example of a serif typeface. Serifs make large quantities of type easier to read.

✔ **Use either a larger version of the body text typeface or a sans-serif typeface for your headings.** *Sans-serif* typefaces are typefaces that do not have serifs. The best-known sans-serif typeface is Arial.

✔ **Whichever typeface you use, adjust the point size and the length of each text line to improve legibility.** Small type and long lines make for unreadable text. For the best readability, choose a body text size from 9 to 12 point. Then adjust the page layout so that each text line is long enough to hold about two complete alphabets (52 characters) spelled in lowercase letters using the body text typeface and size, like this:

abcdefghijklmnopqrstuvwxyzabcde-fghijklmnopqrstuvwxyz

When you want to force a line to break down to the next line, you can insert the paragraph (<P>) tag at that point. The <P> tag also inserts an extra blank line of space before the new line of text begins. If you don't want to add the extra blank line, you can use the <BR> tag. This tag also forces a line break but doesn't insert any extra space. Neither the <P> tag nor the <BR> tag requires a closing tag.

Figure 2-1 shows how this HTML code would look if it were displayed in Internet Explorer.

Figure 2-1:
The result of HTML text that uses tags to change font settings.

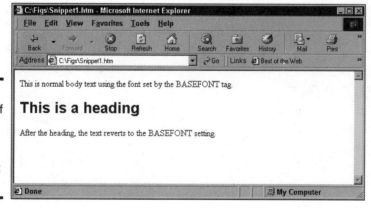

Entering Headings

Don't fill your Web pages with a constant stream of uninterrupted text. Instead, use headings and paragraphs to organize the content on each page. The HTML heading tags make easy work of creating headings that break your text into manageable chunks. You can use up to six levels of headings on your Web pages by using the HTML tags ⟨H1⟩, ⟨H2⟩, and so on through ⟨H6⟩. The following snippet of HTML shows all six heading styles in use:

```
<H1>This is a heading 1</H1>
<H2>This is a heading 2</H2>
<H3>This is a heading 3</H3>
<H4>This is a heading 4</H4>
<H5>This is a heading 5</H5>
<H6>This is a heading 6</H6>
<P>This is a normal text paragraph.
```

Figure 2-2 shows what this HTML code would look like if it were displayed in Internet Explorer.

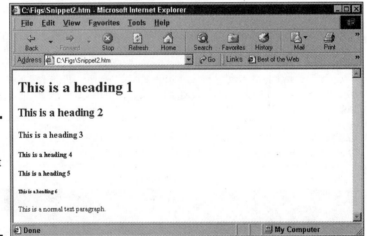

Figure 2-2: Sample heading text as it would look in Internet Explorer 5.

Formatting Text

This section shows you how to insert formatting commands that control alignment and enable you to add bold, italic, and color to your HTML documents.

Alignment

HTML doesn't give you many options for aligning text. By default, text is left-aligned on the page. But you can use the `<CENTER>` tag to specify text to be centered, as in this example:

```
<CENTER>This text is centered.</CENTER>
```

Bold

You can use the `<B>` tag to format your text in boldface type. Add a `<B>` tag immediately before the text you want to appear in boldface. Then turn the boldface off by adding the `</B>` end tag, as shown in the following example:

```
This is <B>bold</B> text.
```

Be stingy in your use of the `<B>` tag. Occasional use of boldface is okay, but if you overuse bold formatting, your text becomes difficult to read.

Italic

You can use the `<I>` tag to format your text in italic type. Add an `<I>` tag immediately before the text you want to appear in italic. Then turn the italic typeface off by adding the `</I>` end tag, as shown in the following example:

```
This is <I>italic</I> text.
```

Occasional use of italic is okay, but try not to overdo it.

Color

You can specify colors in various HTML tags. For example, `<BODY>` has a `BGCOLOR` attribute that lets you specify the background color for your page. The `COLOR` attribute in a `<FONT>` tag sets the text color. Standard HTML defines 14 color names that you can use to set a predefined color: BLACK, SILVER, GRAY, WHITE, MAROON, PURPLE, FUCHSIA, GREEN, LIME, OLIVE, YELLOW, NAVY, TEAL, and AQUA. The easiest way to set color is to use one of these color names. For example, to create yellow text, you could use a `<FONT>` tag like this:

```
<FONT COLOR=YELLOW>This text is yellow.</FONT>
```

Both Internet Explorer and Navigator support additional color names. To be compatible with as many browsers as possible, however, stick to the 14 color names.

Creating Lists

By using HTML, you can create two basic types of lists for your Web page.

✦ **Bulleted lists:** More formally known as *unordered lists*. In a bulleted list, a bullet character (typically a dot) marks each item in the list.

✦ **Numbered lists:** More formally known as *ordered lists*. A number marks each item in a numbered list. The Web browser takes care of figuring out which number to use for each item in the list.

Bulleted lists

A bulleted, or unordered, list requires these three tags:

✦ `<UL>` marks the beginning of the unordered list.

✦ `<LI>` marks the start of each item in the list. No corresponding `</LI>` tag is needed.

✦ `</UL>` marks the end of the entire list.

Here is a snippet of HTML that sets up a bulleted list:

```
<H3>The Inhabitants of Oz</H3>
<UL>
<LI>The Scarecrow
<LI>The Tin Man
<LI>The Cowardly Lion
<LI>Munchkins
<LI>The Wizard
<LI>The Wicked Witch of the West
<LI>Glenda
</UL>
```

Numbered lists

A numbered, or ordered, list requires these three tags:

✦ `<OL>` marks the beginning of the ordered list.

✦ `<LI>` marks the start of each item in the list. No corresponding `</LI>` tag is needed.

✦ `</OL>` marks the end of the entire list.

Here is an HTML snippet that creates a numbered list:

```
<H3>Steps for ordering a pizza</H3>
<OL>
<LI>Pick up phone
<LI>Dial number
<LI>Place order
<LI>Hang up phone
</OL>
```

Creating a Basic Table

Tables are a basic HTML feature that are frequently used to present information in a tabular format. Creating a table requires you to use some complicated HTML tags. For this reason, setting up a table using an HTML editing program, such as Microsoft FrontPage or Netscape Composer, is often easier than trying to code the table manually in HTML.

The following procedure explains how to set up a basic table in which the first row contains headings and subsequent rows contain data:

1. **Type a set of <TABLE> and </TABLE> tags in the Web document where you want the table to appear, like this:**

```
<TABLE>
</TABLE>
```

2. **Add a BORDER attribute to the <TABLE> tag to create a border and establish its width in pixels. For example:**

```
<TABLE BORDER=6>
</TABLE>
```

3. **Create the first table row by typing a set of table row (<TR> and </TR>) tags between the <TABLE> and </TABLE> tags:**

```
<TABLE BORDER=6>
<TR>
</TR>
</TABLE>
```

This first row will hold the headings for the table.

4. **For each column in the table, type a table head (<TH>) tag, followed by the text you want to display for the heading, followed by a </TH> tag. Place each of these column headings between the <TR> and </TR> tags:**

```
<TR>
 <TH>Web Feature</TH>
 <TH>Love It</TH>
 <TH>Hate It</TH>
</TR>
```

5. **Create additional rows for the table by typing additional `<TR>` and `</TR>` tags. Between these tags, type a table data cell (`<TD>`) tag, followed by the text that you want to appear in each column in the row, followed by a `</TD>` tag.**

The following example shows the tags and text that you would type to add a row to show that 62 percent of Web users love tables and 38 percent hate them:

```
<TR>
 <TD>Tables</TD>
 <TD>62%</TD>
 <TD>38%</TD>
</TR>
```

Putting all this HTML code together, here is the HTML for a table with four rows, including the heading row:

```
<TABLE BORDER=6>
<TR>
 <TH>Web Feature</TH>
 <TH>Love It</TH>
 <TH>Hate It</TH>
</TR>
<TR>
 <TD>Tables</TD>
 <TD>62%</TD>
 <TD>38%</TD>
</TR>
<TR>
 <TD>Frames</TD>
 <TD>18%</TD>
 <TD>72%</TD>
</TR>
<TR>
 <TD>Style Sheets</TD>
 <TD>55%</TD>
 <TD>45%</TD>
</TR>
</TABLE>
```

Figure 2-3 shows how this table looks in a Web browser.

Figure 2-3:
Here's how
the table
looks in
a Web
browser.

Web Feature	Love It	Hate It
Tables	62%	38%
Frames	18%	72%
Style Sheets	55%	45%

Inserting Horizontal Rules

Horizontal rules are horizontal lines that you can add to create visual breaks on your Web pages. To add a rule to a page, you use the `<HR>` tag (no closing tag is required). You can control the height, width, and alignment of the rule by using the `SIZE`, `WIDTH`, and `ALIGN` attributes. For example:

```
<HR WIDTH="50%" SIZE=6 ALIGN=CENTER>
```

In this example, the rule is half the width of the page, six pixels in height, and centered on the page.

Many Web designers prefer to use graphic images rather than the `<HR>` tag to create horizontal rules. Because various Web browsers display the `<HR>` tag differently, using an image for a rule allows you to precisely control how your rule appears on-screen.

To use an image rule, follow these steps:

1. **Type an image rule (`<IMG>`) tag where you would normally use an `<HR>` tag to create a horizontal rule:**

```
<IMG>
```

2. **For the source (`SRC`) attribute within the `<IMG>` tag, type the name of the graphics file that contains the image rule that you want to use:**

```
<IMG SRC="grule1.gif">
```

3. **Add a `WIDTH` attribute that specifies the number of pixels you want the rule to span or a percentage of the screen width:**

```
<IMG SRC="grule1.gif" WIDTH="100%">
```

4. **Insert a `<BR>` tag immediately following the rule to force a line break, like this:**

```
<IMG SRC="grule1.gif" WIDTH="100%"><BR>
```

Specifying Page Settings

The following sections explain the importance of page settings — screen size considerations, page length, and page layout — to control how your pages look in a Web browser.

Screen size considerations

Most computer users are used to scrolling up and down to view pages that are longer than the height of the screen. But few users like to scroll left and right to view pages that are too wide. To avoid horizontal scrolling, design your pages so that they fit within the width of the screen.

If you want to target users who run their computers with 800 x 600 screen res-olution (which accounts for a growing number of users now that 15-inch and larger monitors are commonplace), shoot for 780 as the maximum page width.

If your pages consist entirely of text, you don't have to worry about screen size because the user's Web browser automatically adjusts text lines to fit the width of the screen. The only time you have to worry about page width is when you are creating a page that includes elements that have a fixed width, such as tables, images, or frames. The following list explains how to adjust the width for those three elements:

✦ **Tables:** Set the overall width of a table by using the WIDTH attribute in the <TABLE> tag, like this:

```
<TABLE WIDTH=620>
```

✦ **Images:** The size of the image determines how wide the image appears on the page. If the image is too wide, you can change the width by using the WIDTH attribute in the <IMG> tag:

```
<IMG SRC="chick.gif" WIDTH=200>
```

✦ **Frames:** Set the width of side-by-side frames by using the columns (COLS) attribute in the <FRAMESET> tag. For more information, see "Creating Frames," later in this chapter.

Page length

Even though most users don't mind scrolling down to see pages that are longer than the height of the screen, you should still limit the length of your pages. As a general rule, try to limit your pages to two or three times the height of the screen — about the same amount of information that could be printed on a single 8½-x-11-inch sheet of paper.

Page layout

The best way to create an effective design for your Web pages is to set up a basic grid of common elements that will appear in the same or a similar arrangement on all your pages. The following list indicates some of the ele-ments you may need to include in your Web design grid. (Depending on the content of your site, you may not need to provide all these elements.)

✦ **Header area:** The header area appears at the top of each page, indicat-ing the site title, page title, company name, site navigation buttons, and any other elements that you want to place at the top of each page.

✦ **Footer area:** The footer area appears at the bottom of each page, possibly including contact information, a copyright notice, and navigation buttons.

✦ **Main text area:** This area contains the main text and illustrations for each page.

✦ **Sidebar area:** A sidebar occupies a vertical band on the left or right portion of each page. This area can contain elements such as a table of contents or menu for the site.

Figure 2-4 illustrates how these areas may be arranged.

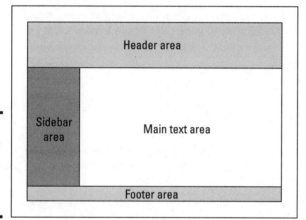

Figure 2-4:
An effective
arrange-
ment for
your Web
pages.

Working with Backgrounds

When creating Web pages, don't make the mistake of using a garish background image that makes your page almost impossible to read. If you want to use a background image for your pages, choose an image that doesn't interfere with the text and other elements on the page.

Setting the background color

To set the background color of your Web page, follow these steps:

1. **Add the background color (**BGCOLOR**) attribute to the** <BODY> **tag.**

2. **Type a color name for the** BGCOLOR **attribute. For example:**

```
<BODY BGCOLOR=WHITE>
```

For more information about using color, see "Color," earlier in this chapter.

Using a background image

To use a background image for your Web page, follow these steps:

1. Add the BACKGROUND **attribute to the** <BODY> **tag.**

2. **Type the name of the image file you want to use for the background as the** BACKGROUND **attribute value, like this:**

```
<BODY BACKGROUND="bgpic.gif">
```

The background image repeats as many times as necessary to fill the page. As a result, the background image file doesn't have to be very large.

Inserting Icons

Most Web pages incorporate one or more graphical icons. Here are some common uses for icons:

+ **Navigation buttons:** Link to specific locations at the site, such as the home page, the help page, or the next or previous page. (See "Using a Navigation Bar," later in this chapter.)

+ **Browser icons:** Indicate which browser(s) the page is designed for.

+ **Menu choices:** Link to other pages on the site.

+ **The ubiquitous "under construction" icon:** Serves as an apology for the unfinished appearance of your Web page.

To include an icon in a Web page, follow these steps:

1. **Find or create an image file that you want to use as an icon.**

2. **Copy the image file into the same folder on the Web server as the document that will contain the icon.**

3. **In your Web document, type an** <IMG> **tag where you want the icon to appear.**

4. **In the** <IMG> **tag, type an** SRC **attribute that names the graphics file that contains the icon image. For example:**

```
<IMG SRC="icon1.gif">
```

Adding Links

Links are an integral part of any Web page. Links let your reader travel to a different location, which can be a part of the same HTML document, a different page located on your Web site, or a page from a different Web site located elsewhere on the Internet. All the user has to do to be transported to a different page is click the link.

Using text links

A *text link* is a portion of text that someone viewing your page can click to jump to another location. To create a text link, follow these steps:

1. **Determine the address of the page that you want the link to jump to.**

2. **Type an `<A>` tag where you want the link to appear on the page.**

   In the `<A>` tag, use an `HREF` attribute to indicate the address of the page that you want to link to. For example:

   ```
   <A HREF="http://www.dummies.com">
   ```

3. **After the `<A>` tag, type the text that you want to appear in your document as a link, and add a closing `</A>` tag, like this:**

   ```
   <A HREF="http://www.dummies.com">The Official For
   Dummies Web Page</A>
   ```

The text that appears between `<A>` and `</A>` is called the *anchor*. The Web address that appears in the `HREF` attribute is called the *target*. The anchor text is displayed on the Web page in a special color (usually blue) and is underlined so that the person viewing the page knows that the text is a link.

If the target refers to another page at the same Web site as the page the link appears on, you can use just the filename as the target. Always enclose the filename or URL in quotation marks. For example:

```
<A HREF="emerald7.html">See the Wizard</A>
```

When a user clicks the <u>See the Wizard</u> link, the HTML file named `emerald7.html` appears on-screen.

Using graphic links

An *image link* is a graphic image that a user can click to jump to another page or a different location on the current page. To create an image link, follow the procedure described in the preceding section, "Using text links." But in Step 3, instead of typing text for the link, type an `<IMG>` tag that contains an `SRC` attribute that identifies the image file to use for the link. For example:

```
<A HREF="emerald7.html"><IMG SRC="emerald.gif"></A>
```

In this example, the graphic image file named `emerald.gif` appears on-screen. If a user clicks it, the browser displays the `emerald7.html` page.

If you use graphic links, remember to provide a text menu as an alternative for users who don't want to wait for graphics to download or who have turned off graphic downloads altogether.

Linking within the same page

To create a link that simply moves the user to another location on the same page, follow these steps:

1. **Assign a name to the section that you want to link to by adding an `<A>` tag with the `NAME` attribute to the first HTML line of that section. Immediately follow the `<A>` tag with an `</A>` end tag.**

2. **Create a text or graphic link to that section, typing the section name preceded by the # symbol in the `HREF` attribute.**

Here is an example of an `<A>` tag that assigns a name to a location in a document:

```
<A NAME="Here"></A>
```

Here is a snippet of HTML that creates a link that jumps to the location named "Here":

```
<A HREF="#Here">Go over there!</A>
```

Creating Frames

Frames enable you to divide a page into separate areas that each display the contents of a separate HTML file. The advantage of using frames is that the user can interact with each frame independently. For example, a frame that contains a long text document can have its own scroll bars so that the user can scroll through the document, and other elements of the page — such as a navigation bar — remain on the screen.

The use of frames is an advanced HTML technique that enables you to create several HTML files for each page. The first HTML file contains a `<FRAMESET>` tag that indicates the arrangement of frames on the page. Between the `<FRAMESET>` and `</FRAMESET>` tags, you use one or more `<FRAME>` tags to create the actual frames. Each `<FRAME>` tag includes an `SRC` attribute that names a separate HTML file that spells out the contents that will be displayed within the frame. The `<FRAME>` tag can also include additional attributes that indicate such things as whether the frame has a visible border, scroll bars, and so on.

A <FRAMESET> tag can include a ROWS attribute to create frames stacked one atop the other, or it can include a COLS attribute to create side-by-side frames. In the ROWS or COLS attribute, you list the pixel size of each frame that you want to create. For the last frame, use an asterisk to indicate that the frame should fill the remainder of the page. For example, the following <FRAMESET> tag creates three frames side by side: The first is 150 pixels wide, the second is 20, and the third fills the rest of the page:

```
<FRAMESET ROWS="150,20,*">
```

In the <FRAME> tags, use the SRC attribute to indicate the name of the HTML file that should be displayed in the frame.

**Book VI
Chapter 2**

Elements of Web
Page Design

The following example shows how you can use frames to set up a grid page layout with four layout areas: a page header area, a page footer area, a left margin area, and a scrolling main text window (refer to Figure 2-4). Five HTML files are required. The main HTML file contains the following lines:

```
<HTML>
<FRAMESET ROWS="75, *, 50" FRAMEBORDER=0 FRAMESPACING=0>
 <FRAME SRC="frtop.html">
 <FRAMESET COLS="150, *">
  <FRAME SRC="frleft.html">
  <FRAME SRC="frright.html" SCROLLING="YES">
 </FRAMESET>
 <FRAME SRC="frbottom.html" SCROLLING="NO">
</FRAMESET>
</HTML>
```

The frtop.html, frbottom.html, frleft.html, and frright.html files contain the HTML used to display the content of each frame.

Frames are a troublesome HTML feature where browser compatibility is concerned. The current versions of both Navigator and Internet Explorer support the <FRAME> and <FRAMESET> tags, but each has several attributes that aren't supported by the other. In addition, Internet Explorer has a simpler method of creating inline frames using an <IFRAME> tag. Although the <IFRAME> tag is easier to deal with than the <FRAMESET> and <FRAME> tags, Navigator doesn't support the <IFRAME> tag.

Using a Navigation Bar

A *navigation bar* is a collection of text or graphic links that enables users to easily work their way through a series of pages on your Web site. The navigation bar appears in the same place on every page in the site so that the user can easily find it.

There are several ways to create a navigation bar. The most common is to create a table, placing a link in each cell of the table. An alternative is to create a single GIF image for the entire navigation bar and then use that image in an image map. (See Book VI, Chapter 3, for more on image maps.)

Depending on the site, a navigation bar can include some or all of the following links:

✦ **Home:** Takes the user to the site's home page

✦ **Next:** Takes the user to the next page in sequence when viewing a series of Web pages

✦ **Previous:** Takes the user to the page that precedes the current page when viewing a series of pages

✦ **Up:** Takes the user to the page at the next level up in the hierarchy of pages

✦ **Help:** Takes the user to a help page

✦ **Site map:** Takes the user to a page that includes links to all the pages on the site

A navigation bar can also contain links to major sections of your Web site, such as a product information section or an online catalog section.

Creating a text-based navigation bar

The easiest way to create a navigation bar is to use text links in a table. Each cell in the table contains a link. The following HTML code shows how to create a navigation bar with links to four pages (home, help, next, and previous). (For more about tables, see "Creating a Basic Table," earlier in this chapter.)

```
<TABLE BORDER="0" CELLSPACING="0" CELLPADDING="0" WIDTH=800>
<TR>
<TD BGCOLOR="SILVER" HEIGHT="25" WIDTH="160" VALIGN="TOP">
<IMG SRC="blank.gif">
</TD>
<TD BGCOLOR="SILVER" HEIGHT="25" WIDTH="100" VALIGN="TOP">
<A HREF="home.html">Home</A>
</TD>
<TD BGCOLOR="SILVER" HEIGHT="25" WIDTH="100" VALIGN="TOP">
<A HREF="help.html">Help</A>
</TD>
<TD BGCOLOR="SILVER" HEIGHT="25" WIDTH="100" VALIGN="TOP">
<A HREF="page3.html">Next</A>
</TD>
```

```
<TD BGCOLOR="SILVER" HEIGHT="25" WIDTH="100" VALIGN="TOP">
<A HREF="page1.html">Previous</A>
</TD>
<TD BGCOLOR="SILVER" HEIGHT="25" WIDTH="240" VALIGN="TOP">
<IMG SRC="blank.gif">
</TD>
</TR>
</TABLE>
```

This HTML table is set up so that the entire table is 800 pixels in width. The table has a single row, which has six cells. The first and last cells contain the image file blank.gif, which displays a blank cell. These blank cells provide the spacing necessary to precisely position the four middle cells, which contain the text links for the home, help, next, and previous pages.

Remember that you have to modify the HREF attributes in the text links used for the Next and Previous links on each page.

Using images in a navigation bar

You can create a navigation bar using images of the buttons that you would like the user to click to move from page to page. Here is the HTML for a simple navigation bar that uses two images of arrows, one facing left, the other right, to link to the next and previous pages, with a simple two-cell table to position the buttons. The images in this navigation bar are created as links within the cells of a table.

```
<TABLE BORDER="0" CELLSPACING="0" CELLPADDING="0" WIDTH=50>
<TR>
<TD HEIGHT="25" WIDTH="25">
<A HREF="page1.html"><IMG SRC="larrow.gif" BORDER="0"
    HEIGHT="25" WIDTH="25"></A>
</TD>
<TD HEIGHT="25" WIDTH="25">
<A HREF="page3.html"><IMG SRC="rarrow.gif" BORDER="0"
    HEIGHT="25" WIDTH="25"></A>
</TD>
</TR>
</TABLE>
```

In this example, both larrow.gif and rarrow.gif are 25 x 25 GIF images that show a left and right arrow.

Chapter 3: Working with Graphics, Sounds, and Videos

In This Chapter

✔ Understanding formats for image, sound, and video files

✔ Working with images and using image maps

✔ Adding background sounds to a Web page

✔ Adding video to a Web page

This chapter presents the techniques for adding graphics, sounds, and video elements to your Web pages. We show you how to add images and image maps to your Web pages, link and embed sound and video files, and use a background sound that plays when your Web page displays.

File Formats for Image, Sound, and Video

You can choose from many different file formats for images, sounds, and videos. Fortunately, you can construct most Web pages using only the formats that we describe in the following sections.

Image file formats

Although dozens of different image file formats exist, only two are widely used for Web page images: GIF and JPEG.

GIF images: GIF, which stands for Graphics Interchange Format, was originally used on the CompuServe online network and is now widely used throughout the Internet. GIF image files have the following characteristics:

✦ GIF images can have a maximum of 256 different colors.

✦ GIF files are compressed to reduce their size. The compression method GIF uses doesn't reduce the image quality.

✦ A GIF image can include a transparent color, which, when displayed in a Web browser, allows the background of the Web page to show through.

✦ GIF images can be interlaced, which allows the Web browser to quickly display a crude version of the image and then display progressively better versions of the image.

✦ GIF supports a simple animation technique that enables you to store several distinct images in the same file. The Web browser displays the animation by displaying the images one after the other in sequence.

The GIF format is the best choice for most Web graphics that were created with drawing or paint programs and that do not contain a large number of different colors. It is ideal for icons, buttons, background textures, bullets, rules, and line art.

A format called PNG (Portable Network Graphics) was developed in 1995 as a successor to the GIF format. PNG (pronounced *ping*) supports all the features of GIF and then some, and supports more colors than GIF. PNG hasn't really caught on, though, so GIF remains the most widely used image format.

JPEG images: JPEG, a format developed by the Joint Photographic Experts Group, is designed for photographic-quality images. It has the following characteristics:

✦ JPEG images can have either 16.7 million or 2 billion colors. Most JPEG images use 16.7 million colors, which provide excellent representation of photographic images.

✦ To reduce image size, JPEG uses a special compression technique that slightly reduces the quality of the image while greatly reducing its size. In most cases, you have to carefully compare the original uncompressed image with the compressed image to see the difference.

✦ JPEG supports progressive images that are similar to GIF interlaced images.

✦ JPEG doesn't support transparent background colors as GIF does.

✦ JPEG doesn't support animation.

Other image file formats: Many other image file formats exist. Here are just a few:

✦ **BMP:** Windows bitmap

✦ **PCX:** Another bitmap format

✦ **TIF:** Tagged Image File

✦ **PIC:** Macintosh picture file

Sound file formats

Following are the most commonly used sound file formats:

✦ **WAV:** The Windows standard for sound recordings. WAV stands for Wave.

✦ **SND:** The Macintosh standard for sound recordings. SND stands for Sound.

✦ **AU:** The Unix standard for sound recordings. AU stands for Audio.

✦ **MID:** MIDI files, which aren't actually sound recordings. MIDI files are music stored in a form that a sound card's synthesizer can play. MIDI stands for Musical Instrument Digital Interface.

Don't confuse sound files with sound you can listen to in real time over the Internet, known as *streaming audio*. The most popular format for streaming audio is RealAudio. RealAudio enables you to listen to a sound as it is being downloaded to your computer, so you don't have to wait for the entire file to be downloaded before you can listen to it. To listen to RealAudio sound, you must first install a RealAudio player in your Web browser. (You can download it from www.real.com.)

Video file formats

Three popular formats for video clips are used on the Web:

✦ **AVI:** The Windows video standard. AVI stands for Audio Video Interleaved.

✦ **QuickTime:** The Macintosh video standard. QuickTime files usually have the extension MOV.

✦ **MPEG or MP3:** An independent standard. MPEG stands for Motion Picture Experts Group. MP3 is short for MPEG level 3, an adaptation of MPEG used to send music files over the Net.

Although AVI is known as a Windows video format and QuickTime is a Macintosh format, both formats — as well as MPEG and MP3 — have become cross-platform standards. Both Netscape Navigator and Microsoft Internet Explorer can play AVI, QuickTime, and MPEG videos.

Working with Graphics

You've decided which graphic to include on your Web pages, so what's next? This section shows you how to insert your graphics files and how to use image maps. First, here are some guidelines for using images:

✦ Don't add so many images or such large images that your page takes too long to download.

✦ Use the ALT attribute with the <IMG> tag to provide text for users who view your page with images turned off. For example:

```
<IMG SRC="chicken.gif" ALT="Picture of a chicken">
```

✦ Use the HEIGHT and WIDTH attributes with the <IMG> tag to preformat your pages for the correct image dimensions.

```
<IMG SRC="chicken.gif" HEIGHT=100 WIDTH=50>
```

✦ Use BORDER=0 in the <IMG> tag to eliminate the border that appears around your images (unless you want the borders to appear), like this:

```
<IMG SRC="chicken.gif" BORDER=0>
```

✦ Use transparent GIFs to create images that blend seamlessly with your page background. (See the sidebar "Using transparent GIF images," later in this chapter.)

✦ If you want to make large image files available for download on your Web site, provide smaller, thumbnail versions of the images that people can preview before deciding whether to download the full-size image.

✦ Keep in mind that many of the images you see displayed on the Web are copyrighted materials that you can't simply copy and use on your own Web site without permission from the copyright holder. Similarly, photographs, artwork, and other images that appear in magazines and books are copyrighted. You can't legally scan copyrighted images and post them on your Web site without the copyright owner's permission.

For more information about working with images, see *Creating Web Pages For Dummies*, 5th Edition, by Bud Smith and Arthur Bebak (published by Hungry Minds, Inc.).

Inserting a graphic

To insert an image on a Web page, follow these steps:

1. **Obtain an image file that you want to include on your page.**

If necessary, use a graphics program to convert the file to the format that you want to use (probably GIF or JPEG). Store the image file in the same directory as the HTML document that displays the image. Alternatively, you may prefer to store all images for your Web site together in a separate Images folder.

2. **In the HTML file, add the <IMG> tag at the point in the document where you want the image to appear. Use the SRC (source) attribute to provide the name of the image file. For example:**

```
<IMG SRC="image1.gif">
```

3. **(Optional) To remove the border around the image, add a** BORDER **attribute, as follows:**

   ```
   <IMG SRC="image1.gif" BORDER=0>
   ```

4. **(Optional) To provide text that will be displayed for users who have turned off graphics in their Web browsers, use an** ALT **attribute:**

   ```
   <IMG SRC="image1.gif" BORDER=0 ALT="Mountains">
   ```

5. **(Optional) To preformat the Web page with the correct dimensions of the image, use the** HEIGHT **and** WIDTH **attributes, as follows:**

   ```
   <IMG SRC="image1.gif" BORDER=0 ALT="Mountains"
   HEIGHT=200 WIDTH=100>
   ```

Using image maps

An *image map* is a graphic in which specific regions of the graphic serve as links to other Web pages. For example, if you're creating a Web site about *The Wizard of Oz,* you can use an image map showing the characters to link to pages about these characters.

To create an image map, you must use several HTML tags: <MAP> and its companion </MAP>, <AREA>, and <IMG>.

To create an image map, follow these steps:

1. **Find or create a graphic that can serve as an image map.**

   The image should have distinct regions that will serve as the map's links.

2. **Use a graphics program to display the image; then determine the rectangular boundaries of each area of the image that will serve as a link. Write down the pixel coordinates of the left, top, right, and bottom edges of these rectangles.**

   Most graphics programs display these coordinates in the program's status bar as you move the mouse around or when you use the selection tool to select an area. For example, Figure 3-1 shows an area selected in Microsoft Photo Editor.

   For the chicken and egg image, the following coordinates define the rectangular areas for the links:

	Left	*Top*	*Right*	*Bottom*
Egg	0	40	39	79
Chicken	40	0	109	79

Figure 3-1:
The graphic's coordinates typically appear in the status bar.

Coordinates for selected portion of graphic

3. **Type a set of** `<MAP>` **and** `</MAP>` **tags. In the** `<MAP>` **tag, use the NAME attribute to provide a name for the image map, like this:**

```
<MAP NAME="IMGMAP1">
</MAP>
```

4. **Between the** `<MAP>` **and** `</MAP>` **tags, type an** `<AREA>` **tag for each rectangular area of the image that will serve as a link. In the** `<AREA>` **tag, include the following attributes:**

```
SHAPE=RECT
COORDS="start left, start top, end x from left, end x
   from top"
HREF="url"
```

For example:

```
<MAP NAME=IMGMAP1>
 <AREA SHAPE=RECT COORDS="0,40,39,79" HREF="egg.html">
 <AREA SHAPE=RECT COORDS="40,0,109,79"
   HREF="chick.html">
</MAP>
```

5. **Type an** `<IMG>` **tag. Use the** `SRC` **attribute to name the image file and the** `USEMAP` **attribute to provide the name of the image map listed in the** `<MAP>` **attribute, like this:**

```
<IMG SRC="chickegg.gif" USEMAP="#imgmap1">
```

Be sure to type a number sign (#) before the image map name in the `<IMG>` tag's `USEMAP` attribute. But don't use the # symbol when you create the name in the `<MAP>` tag's `NAME` attribute.

Putting it all together, here is a complete HTML document to set up an image map:

```
<BODY>
<H1>Which came first?</H1>
<MAP NAME=IMGMAP1>
 <AREA SHAPE=RECT COORDS="0,40,39,79" HREF="egg.html">
 <AREA SHAPE=RECT COORDS="40,0,109,79" HREF="chick.html">
</MAP>
<IMG SRC="chickegg.gif" USEMAP="#imgmap1">
</BODY>
```

Figure 3-2 shows how this page appears when displayed.

Book VI
Chapter 3

Working with Graphics, Sounds, and Videos

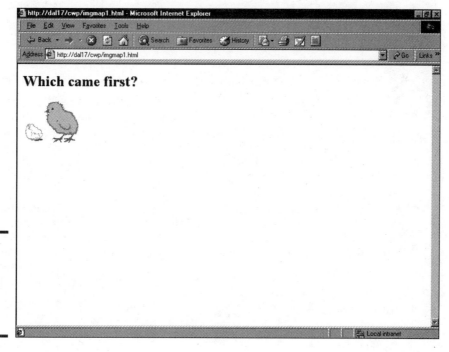

Figure 3-2:
The image map as it appears in a Web browser.

Using transparent GIF images

Most graphics programs can create transparent GIF images, in which one color is designated as transparent. When the image is displayed on your page, the background color of the page shows through the transparent area.

The procedures for setting the transparent color are similar in most graphics programs. The following procedure works for the new version of Microsoft Paint that comes with Windows XP:

1. **Open the GIF file for which you want to create a transparent color.**

2. **In the toolbox, click Select (rectangle shape) to select a rectangular area or click Free-Form Select (star shape) to select a free-form area.**

3. **Drag the pointer to define the area of the picture size.**

4. **Click the button in the bottom-left corner of Paint to apply a transparent background.**

5. **To change the background color, click Pick Color (the eyedropper icon).**

6. **Click the color that you want to use as the image's transparent background color.**

7. **Click Fill with Color and then click the area to the change color.**

8. **Choose File➪Save to save the file with the transparent color information.**

To use a transparent background color, make sure that the image's background consists of a single color and that the background color doesn't appear elsewhere in the image. You may need to fiddle with your program's painting tools to adjust the background of the image accordingly.

If you don't own Windows XP, you can use other graphics programs, such as Microsoft PhotoDraw or Paint Shop Pro, to create transparent GIF images.

Use the `<TITLE>` attribute in the `<AREA>` tags to create ToolTips that are displayed when the user pauses the mouse pointer briefly over an image map area. For example:

```
<AREA SHAPE=RECT COORDS="0,40,39,79" HREF="egg.html"
    TITLE="The Egg">
<AREA SHAPE=RECT COORDS="40,0,109,79" HREF="chick.html"
    TITLE="The Chicken">
```

Remember that some people configure their browsers so that they don't download and display images. Whenever you use an image map, be sure to also provide text links as an alternative to the image map. Otherwise, users who visit your page with images turned off won't be able to navigate your site.

Adding Sounds

You can insert a sound file on a Web page as a link, as an embedded sound, or as a part of the page's background (so that the sound is played automatically whenever the page is displayed). The following sections show you how to use the HTML tags necessary for each method.

Inserting a link to a sound file

The advantage of linking to a sound file is that the sound file is not downloaded to the user's computer until the user clicks the sound file link. To insert a link to a sound file, follow these steps:

1. **Obtain a sound file that you want to link to your Web site and place the sound file in the same directory as the HTML document that will contain the link.**

Alternatively, you may prefer to store all sound files for your Web site in their own folder.

2. **Add an <A> tag, some descriptive text, and an </A> tag to the HTML file as follows:**

```
<A HREF="sound.wav">Click here to play the
sound.</A>
```

Be sure to type the name of your sound file in the HREF attribute.

Embedding a sound file

You can embed a sound on a Web page by using an <EMBED> tag:

```
<EMBED SRC="sound.wav">
```

The SRC attribute provides the name of the sound file. The Web browser displays the sound controls necessary to enable the user to play the sound.

Using background sounds

A background sound is played automatically whenever a user displays your Web page. To add a background sound to a page, follow these steps:

1. **Obtain a sound file that you want to use as a background sound and place the sound file in the same directory as the HTML file.**

2. **Add a** `<BGSOUND>` **attribute following the** `<BODY>` **tag. Use the** `SRC` **attribute to name the sound file that you want to be played:**

```
<BODY>
<BGSOUND SRC="music.mid">
```

3. **If you want the sound to repeat several times, add the** `LOOP` **attribute like this:**

```
<BGSOUND SRC="music.mid" LOOP=3>
```

You can type any number in the `LOOP` attribute to indicate how many times the sound should be repeated. Or you can type `LOOP=INFINITE` to play the sound repeatedly as long as the page is displayed.

Some people would rather listen to fingernails dragged across a chalkboard than annoying background sounds that play over and over again. If you want people to visit your site more than once, avoid using `LOOP=INFINITE`.

Working with Videos

You can insert a video file on a Web page as a link or as an embedded object. The following sections show you each method.

Inserting a link to a video file

To insert a link to a video file, follow these steps:

1. **Locate a video file that you want to add a link to on your Web page.**

2. **Add an** `<A>` **tag, some descriptive text, and an** `</A>` **tag to the HTML file as follows:**

```
<A HREF="movie.avi">Click here to download a movie.</A>
```

Provide the name of the video file in the `<A>` tag's `HREF` attribute. When the user clicks the link, the Web browser downloads the file and plays the video.

Embedding a video

Use the `<EMBED>` tag to embed a video on a Web page. Follow these steps:

1. **Locate a video file that you want to embed on a Web page.**

2. **In the HTML document for the Web page, add an** <EMBED> **tag specifying the name of the video file in the** SRC **attribute, like this:**

    ```
    <EMBED SRC="movie.avi">
    ```

3. **If you want to change the size of the area used to display the video, add the** HEIGHT **and** WIDTH **attributes, like this:**

    ```
    <EMBED SRC="movie.avi" HEIGHT=200 WIDTH=200>
    ```

4. **If you want the video to play automatically as soon as it finishes downloading, add** AUTOSTART=TRUE **to the** <EMBED> **tag:**

    ```
    <EMBED SRC="movie.avi" AUTOSTART=TRUE>
    ```

Chapter 4: Building Your Web Workshop

In This Chapter

✔ **Examining Web browsers**

✔ **Selecting an HTML editor**

✔ **Choosing a graphics program**

✔ **Opting for office suites**

✔ **Perusing Java tools**

*T*his chapter presents the various types of tools that should be in your Web toolbox. Some of these are commercial programs that you must purchase, and others are programs that you can download for free from the Internet.

Web Browsers

Two Web browsers are in widespread use on the Internet: Internet Explorer and Netscape. If you are a serious Web developer, you should have both of them so that you can make sure that your Web pages work well with both browsers.

Internet Explorer 6

Internet Explorer 6 features the latest Web technologies from Microsoft: Dynamic HTML, Visual Basic Scripting Edition (VBScript), channels, ActiveX, and more. The IE6 suite includes the following components:

✦ **Internet Explorer 6:** For Web browsing

✦ **Outlook Express 6.0:** For e-mail and newsgroups

✦ **Chat:** For online chatting

✦ **NetMeeting:** For online conferencing

You can download Internet Explorer 6 for free from the Microsoft Web site at www.microsoft.com/windows/ie.

Netscape 6.2

Netscape is the complete package of Internet access tools from Netscape, including the following major components:

+ **Navigator:** For Web browsing

+ **Messenger:** For e-mail and newsgroups

+ **Composer:** For creating Web pages

+ **Conference:** For online conferencing

You can download Netscape for free from the Netscape Web site at www.netscape.com/browsers.

HTML Editors

You can create HTML documents with a simple text editor such as Notepad, but for serious work, you should invest in a sophisticated HTML editor. Most HTML editors let you work in two modes: WYSIWYG (What You See Is What You Get) lets you create Web pages by dragging and dropping; HTML mode lets you work directly with HTML tags and attributes.

FrontPage 2002

FrontPage 2002 is Microsoft's full-featured Web site development tool. The FrontPage 2002 WYSIWYG HTML editor enables you to use advanced HTML features, such as frames and tables, and it enables you to directly edit HTML tags and attributes. In addition, FrontPage 2002 includes tools that let you manage and coordinate all the pages that make up your Web site, including a feature that automatically maintains your hyperlinks. FrontPage 2002 retails separately for $169, but it's included with the Office XP Professional or Office XP Developer. See www.microsoft.com/frontpage for more information.

Netscape Composer

Composer is a free HTML editor that is bundled with Netscape. Composer includes a nifty feature called Design Assistant that helps you quickly create pages for your Web site. To download Composer (as part of Netscape 6.2), go to www.netscape.com/browsers.

HotDog Professional

HotDog Professional, made by a company called Sausage Software (www.sausagetools.com), is a sophisticated code-based HTML editor that uses wizards to create HTML tags for your documents. Unlike most HTML editors, HotDog Professional lets you utilize advanced features, such as style sheets, Java, and push channels using Microsoft, PointCast, or Netscape channel technologies. This product sells at a retail price of $99.95 (U.S.).

Graphics Programs

Graphics programs are an essential part of your Web toolkit. You need a graphics drawing program that can create images in either GIF or JPEG format, and the program should be able to handle advanced features, such as GIF transparent backgrounds, interlaced images, and animations. This section lists several graphics programs that you can use to create Web pages.

**Book VI
Chapter 4**

**Building Your Web
Workshop**

CorelDRAW

CorelDRAW is one of the best suites of graphics programs available. The comprehensive CorelDRAW package includes the CorelDRAW drawing program, Corel PHOTO-PAINT, and Corel R.A.V.E. (Real Animated Vector Effects). Corel R.A.V.E. is designed for animations. See www.corel.com for more information on CorelDRAW. CorelDRAW 10 Graphics Suite is available for $549, or you can download CorelDRAW ESSENTIALS, which includes CorelDRAW 9 and Corel PHOTO-PAINT 9 for $109.

Paint Shop Pro

Paint Shop Pro 7.0, from JASC, Inc. (www.jasc.com), is a powerful yet inexpensive painting program that you can download from the Internet to use free for a 30-day evaluation period. If you like it, you can purchase it for only $99. Paint Shop Pro has just about everything you could possibly want in an image drawing program: It supports more than 30 image formats and includes sophisticated features, such as gradient fills, blur effects, and textured brush effects for creating stunning images. Paint Shop Pro also comes with Animation Shop 3 for creating GIF animations.

Windows XP Paint

Paint is the free image-drawing program that comes with Windows. With Windows 3.1 and Windows 95, Paint is hardly adequate for creating images for the Web. The only image formats supported by older versions of Paint are BMP and PCX, neither of which is widely used on the Web. With Windows 98 and XP, however, Microsoft has beefed up Paint to make it suitable for working with Web images by supporting the GIF and JPEG file formats. Paint can handle transparent background colors for GIF images, but it can't create interlaced GIF images or GIF animations.

Office Suites

All three of the popular Office suites — Microsoft Office, Corel WordPerfect Suite, and Lotus SmartSuite — include Web-authoring features. These features enable you to use a word processor, spreadsheet, or desktop presentation program to create Web pages.

Microsoft Office XP

Microsoft Office XP comes in several versions; the most popular are the Home Edition and the Professional Edition. The Office XP Home Edition includes the following programs:

+ **Word processing:** Word 2002

+ **Spreadsheet:** Excel 2002

+ **Desktop presentations:** PowerPoint 2002

+ **E-mail and Personal Information Manager:** Outlook 2002

In addition to the Home Edition features, the Professional Edition includes the database program Access 2002.

All the Office XP programs include features for creating Web pages. You can use Word 2002 as a simple WYSIWYG HTML editor, or you can convert existing documents to HTML pages. With Access 2002 and Excel 2002, you can publish database or spreadsheet data on the Web. The Home Edition of Microsoft Office XP retails for $479; the Professional Edition sells for $579; and the Developer retails for $799. For more information, visit the Web site at www.microsoft.com/office.

Lotus SmartSuite Millennium Edition

Lotus SmartSuite Millennium Edition includes the following programs:

+ **Word processor:** Lotus Word Pro

+ **Spreadsheet:** Lotus 1-2-3

+ **Desktop presentations:** Lotus Freelance Graphics

+ **Database:** Lotus Approach

+ **Internet information manager:** Lotus SmartCenter

+ **Time and contact manager:** Lotus Organizer

+ **Intranet publisher:** Lotus FastSite

All the SmartSuite programs can be used for Web publishing. SmartSuite programs can automatically convert documents, presentations, and spreadsheets to HTML format and publish them on the Web. SmartSuite is especially useful if you're doing collaborative work, because it enables you to electronically distribute documents to other Internet users and automatically consolidate multiple versions of a document to create a final edited document. The retail price of Lotus SmartSuite is $224 (see www.lotus.com for details).

Corel WordPerfect Office 2002

The Corel WordPerfect Office 2002 Standard Edition suite features these programs:

✦ **Word processing:** Corel WordPerfect 10

✦ **Spreadsheet:** Corel Quattro Pro 10

✦ **Desktop presentations:** Corel Presentations 10

You can use these programs to create new Web pages or to convert existing documents or data to HTML. The Professional Edition also includes a database, Paradox, which you can use to publish database data on a Web page, and Dragon Naturally Speaking, a speech recognition tool. You'll pay $389 for the Standard Edition of WordPerfect Office 2002 or $489 for the Professional Edition. For more information, see www.corel.com.

Java Tools

If you're into *Java* — the cross-platform programming language that lets you write programs that can run on most modern Web browsers — you may want to invest in one of the following Java development tools.

VisualCafé for Java

VisualCafé for Java, from WebGain, is a rapid development environment for creating Java-based Web sites. Serious Java developers will love it. It's available in two editions: Enterprise and Expert. If you're a serious Java developer, you want either the Enterprise or Expert edition. For casual or first-time Java users, the Standard edition was a great way to get started with Java, but it was discontinued in early 2002. Prices for VisualCafé are $995 (Expert) or $2,995 (Enterprise). Unfortunately, this tool might be a bit expensive for most users.

Visual J++ 6.0

Visual J++, from Microsoft, is the complete development environment for creating Java applications. Visual J++ features support for ActiveX components, database connectivity, and VBScript support. Visual J++ is priced at $109 for the Standard Edition and $549 for the Professional Edition. For more information, see msdn.microsoft.com/visualj.

Chapter 5: Publishing on the Web

In This Chapter

✔ Using the Personal Web Server to test your Web pages

✔ Working with Microsoft's Web Publishing Wizard

✔ Using FTP to post your Web files

✔ Using the RSACi rating service to rate your site

✔ Telling the world about your site

This chapter presents the procedures that you must follow to make your Web pages available so that others can see them. You find out how to test your Web pages, publish your Web pages with the Web Publishing Wizard, and use FTP to post Web files. Finally, we show you how to attach a rating to your site and announce your site via the major search services.

Previewing Your Web Pages

Before you post your Web pages to a Web server, it's a good idea to test them. You can preview your Web pages from your hard drive with a Web browser by typing **C:\FolderName\filename.html** in the Address bar of the browser. (Note that you need to tailor the directory path to what's on your computer by replacing *Foldername* and *filename.html* with the names of your folder and file. Add any subfolders, too.) Alternatively, you can save the files to a disk, choose File➪Open from the menu bar in the browser, and then click the Browse button to open the file and view the page. You'll want to preview your page using both Internet Explorer and Netscape.

In addition, FrontPage has a preview feature. Simply click the Preview in Browser button to see your page.

When you're testing your page, don't forget to check your links.

Using the Web Publishing Wizard

The Microsoft Web Publishing Wizard simplifies the task of transferring files from your computer to your Web server. The Web Publishing Wizard comes with Internet Explorer 4 and later, Windows 98 or later, and FrontPage 2000 and later.

To set up the Web Publishing Wizard for your Web site and to copy the Web files to your Web server for the first time, follow these steps:

1. **In Windows XP, click a document that you want to publish to the Web.**

Normally, your document will be in your My Documents folder. If not, then go find the document by using Windows Explorer.

2. **In the left window pane, click Publish This File to the Web.**

The Web Publishing Wizard begins.

3. **Click Next.**

4. **Continue following along with the wizard, changing options and clicking Next as necessary.**

You're asked about where you want to publish your file and what your e-mail address and password are. See Figure 5-1.

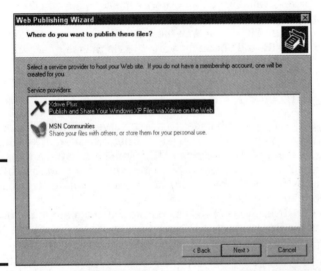

Figure 5-1:
Answer all the Web Publishing Wizard's questions.

5. **Click Finish.**

Next, you're asked to choose the folder you want the file published in.

6. **Choose the folder (or create a new one) and then continue clicking Next.**

More than likely, you'll probably save your files in My Webs, which is a folder located in My Documents. If you don't like that location, simply create a new folder.

7. **Click Finish.**

   The Enter Network Password dialog box appears.

8. **Enter the User Name and Password and click OK.**

   Wait a moment while the Web Publishing Wizard connects to the FTP server and transfers your files.

9. **Click OK and celebrate — you're finished!**

The Web Publishing Wizard stores most of the information that it gathers from you the first time you run it so that you don't have to retype everything each time you use the wizard.

Understanding FTP

FTP, or *file transfer protocol*, is a commonly used method of posting your Web files to a Web server. To use FTP in this manner, you need to obtain the following information from your Internet Service Provider:

✦ **The host name for the FTP server:** This usually, but not always, starts with `ftp`, as in `ftp.yourwebserver.com`.

✦ **The user ID and password that you must use to sign on to the FTP server:** This is probably the same user ID and password that you use to sign on to your service provider's Web, e-mail, and news servers.

✦ **The name of the directory into which you can copy your Web files:** A directory on an FTP server is similar to a folder in Windows 95/98/XP.

The Windows 95/98/XP FTP Client

If you are a Windows 95/98/XP user, you already have the software you need to access an FTP server. The following procedure describes the steps for transferring files to a Web server using the FTP program that comes with Windows 95/98/XP:

1. **Collect all the files required for your Web site in one folder.**

   If you have lots of files — say, 50 or more — you may want to consider using several subfolders to organize the files. Just be sure to keep the folder structure as simple as possible.

2. **Open an MS-DOS command window by choosing Start⇨All Programs⇨ Accessories⇨Command Prompt (see Figure 5-2).**

Figure 5-2:
You need
to work in
MS-DOS to
FTP files.

3. **Use the CD (Change Directory) command to change to the folder that contains the Web files that you want to transfer to the Web server.**

   For example, if your Web files are stored in a folder named Webfiles, type the following command:

   ```
   cd \Webfiles
   ```

4. **Type ftp followed by the name of your FTP host, like this:**

   ```
   ftp ftp.yourwebserver.com
   ```

5. **When prompted, type your user-ID and password.**

   After you have successfully logged in to the FTP server, you see an FTP prompt that looks like this:

   ```
   ftp>
   ```

   This prompt indicates that you are connected to the FTP server, and the FTP server — not the DOS command prompt on your own computer — processes any commands you type.

6. **Use the CD command to change to the directory to which you want to copy your files. For example:**

   ```
   cd directory_name
   ```

   Remember that the FTP server processes this command, so it changes the current directory on the FTP server, not on your own computer. The current directory for your own computer is still set to the directory you specified back in Step 3.

7. **Use the following MPUT command to copy all the files from the current directory on your computer (which you set back in Step 3) to the current directory on the FTP server (which you set in Step 6):**

   ```
   mput *.*
   ```

You are prompted to copy each file in the directory, like this:

```
mput yourfile.html?
```

8. **Type** Y **and then press Enter to copy the file to the FTP server. Type** N **and then press Enter if you want to skip the file.**

After all the files have been copied, the FTP> prompt is displayed again.

9. **Type** exit **to disconnect from the FTP server.**

Windows 95/98/XP and Macintosh use the terms *folders* and *subfolders*. FTP uses the terms *directories* and *subdirectories* to refer to the same concept.

If you have files stored in subfolders on your computer, you must copy those files to the FTP server separately. Just follow these steps:

1. **If needed, use** MKDIR **to create the subdirectories on the FTP server.**

For example, to create a subdirectory named IMAGES, change to the directory in which you want to create the new subdirectory, then type a command like this:

```
mkdir images
```

2. **Use the** CD **command to change to the new directory:**

```
cd images
```

3. **Copy files to the new directory by using the** MPUT **command.**

You must specify the name of the subfolder that contains the files on your computer in the MPUT command, like this:

```
mput images\*.*
```

You are prompted to copy the files in the IMAGES folder one at a time.

FTP command summary

Table 5-1 lists the FTP commands that you're most likely to use when you store your Web files on an FTP server.

Remember that the FTP> prompt indicates that you're logged on to the FTP server and it's processing your commands.

**Book VI
Chapter 5**

**Publishing
on the Web**

Table 5-1	Useful FTP Commands
Command	*Description*
exit	Disconnects from the FTP server and exits the FTP program.
cd	Changes the current FTP server directory.

(continued)

Table 5-1 *(continued)*

Command	Description
del	Deletes a file on the FTP server.
dir	Displays the names of the files in the current FTP server directory.
copy	Copies a single file from the FTP server to your computer.
mget	Copies multiple files from the FTP server to your computer.
mkdir	Creates a new directory on the FTP server.
mput	Copies multiple files from your computer to the FTP server.
put	Copies a single file from your computer to the FTP server.
rename	Renames a file on the FTP server.
rmdir	Removes (deletes) a directory on the FTP server.

Rating Your Site

Many Web users activate their Web browsers' content filtering features to ban access to sites that contain offensive material. For example, Internet Explorer includes a Content Advisor feature that allows users to prevent access to offensive Web sites.

Content Advisor uses a system of ratings similar to ratings used for movies, but the Web site ratings are more detailed. Web publishers voluntarily assign ratings to their Web pages for four categories: violence, nudity, sex, and language. The ratings are stored in special HTML tags that appear in the <HEAD> section of Web pages.

If you fail to provide a rating for your Web site, your site may be banned even if it doesn't contain offensive material. So it's a good idea to provide ratings for your site, even if your site is G-rated.

An organization called the Recreational Software Advisory Council on the Internet, or RSACi, oversees Internet ratings. RSACi has an online service that simplifies the task of rating your site, and best of all, it's free.

To use RSACi to rate your site, follow these steps:

1. **Go to the RSACi home page at** www.rsac.org.

2. **Follow the links to register your site.**

3. **Type the site information requested by RSACi (your Web page URL, contact name, phone number, and so on).**

   This information is kept private, so you don't have to worry about your address being sold to junk mailers.

4. **Answer the questions about the content level of your Web site for language, sex, nudity, violence, and chat.**

   When you're finished, the RSACi Web page displays a snippet of HTML that contains the appropriate tags to add to your Web page.

5. **Use the mouse to highlight the HTML lines that are displayed; then choose Edit⇨Copy to copy them to the Clipboard.**

6. **Next, open your home page in your favorite HTML editor, switch to HTML view so that you can see the actual HTML code, and choose Edit⇨Paste to paste the RSACi tags into the <HEAD> section of the page.**

7. **If you want to let people know that you have rated your site, flip back to the RSACi page that contains the HTML tags that you copied in Step 5. On that page, you can find a "We rated with RSACi" graphic. Save this graphic to your hard drive and then insert it into your Web page.**

Announcing Your Site

Publicizing your page in the major search services helps Web surfers find your site. Try to get your page listed in as many search services as possible. Table 5-2 describes how to add your site to several of the popular Web search services. To list your Web site in the search service, go to the URL and click the link indicated in the last column of the table (some of these are difficult to find, but they're there — most are near the bottom of the page).

Table 5-2	Adding Your Site to a Search Service	
Search Service	*URL*	*Click This Link*
AltaVista	www.altavista.com	Add URL
Excite	www.excite.com	Add URL
GO.com	www.go.com	Add URL
Lycos	www.lycos.com	Add Your Site to Lycos
Yahoo!	www.yahoo.com	How to Suggest a Site

You can save yourself some time by submitting your Web site to a submission service called Submit It at www.submit-it.com. This service can submit your Web site to more than 400 search engines for a modest fee.

For more information about getting your Web site noticed, check out *Creating Web Pages For Dummies*, 5th Edition, by Bud Smith and Arthur Bebak (published by Hungry Minds, Inc.).

Chapter 6: Creating Web Pages with Microsoft FrontPage 2002

In This Chapter

✔ Creating FrontPage Webs and Web pages

✔ Using FrontPage themes to format your Webs

✔ Working with the basic Web page elements

✔ Using advanced FrontPage elements, such as hit counters and marquees

Microsoft FrontPage 2002 is one of the most popular — and most powerful — Web development tools around. With FrontPage 2002, you can create attractive Web sites without knowing the first thing about HTML. This chapter presents the basics of using FrontPage 2002.

For more information, consult *FrontPage 2002 For Dummies* by Asha Dornfest (published by Hungry Minds, Inc.).

Creating a New Web

A FrontPage Web is a collection of HTML documents and other supporting files, such as image files and document files, which together make up a Web site.

To create a new FrontPage Web, follow these steps:

1. **Choose File➪New➪Page or Web.**

   On the right side, a New Page or Web toolbar appears. Click the Empty Web button. This brings up a Web Site Template window.

   The Web Site Template, as shown in Figure 6-1, lists the Web templates and wizards that you can use to create new FrontPage Webs.

2. **Choose the wizard or template that you'd like to use to create the new Web.**

   In Figure 6-1, the Personal Web template has been selected.

3. **(Optional) In the Specify the Location of the New Web text box, change the server and Web name that appear, if necessary.**

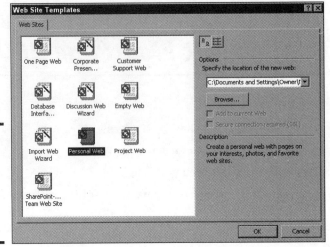

Figure 6-1:
Select a
template or
wizard to
begin
creating
your Web.

4. Click OK.

FrontPage grinds and churns for a moment and then displays your new
Web, as shown in Figure 6-2.

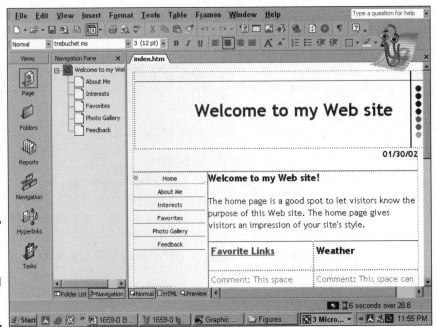

Figure 6-2:
A Web page
based on
the Personal
Web
template.

If the default home page for your Web doesn't appear in Page view as shown in the figure, double-click `index.htm` in the Folder List.

5. **To add text to a page in your Web site, double-click the page in the Folder List, click in the page where you want the text to appear, and begin typing.**

6. **Gather any image files that you want to include in your Web site and import them into your Web by choosing File⇨Import.**

   (See "Importing Files" later in this chapter for more information.)

7. **Edit each of the pages in your Web any way you want. To edit a Web page, double-click the page in the Folder List while in Page view.**

   For more information, see "Editing a Web Page," later in this chapter.

8. **To add a page to the Web, click the New Page button or choose File⇨New⇨Page or Web to open the New Page or Web pane. Select the template that you want to use for the new page.**

   You also can right-click in the Folder List and choose New Page from the shortcut menu. (See the next section, "Adding a Page to a Web," for additional details.)

9. **After your Web is ready for prime time, choose File⇨Publish Web to transfer your Web's files to your Web server so that the Web can be accessed from the Internet.**

   See "Publishing a FrontPage Web" later in this chapter for more information.

Book VI
Chapter 6

Creating Web Pages with Microsoft FrontPage 2002

FrontPage 2002 comes with two Web wizards that help you to create customized Web sites by asking you questions about which elements to include in the Web.

✦ **Corporate Presence Wizard** creates a Web for your company or organization. The Web includes a home page and one or more of the following optional pages: What's New, Products/Services, Table of Contents, Feedback Form, and Search Form. The wizard also enables you to select a theme and information that you want to appear on each page, such as a company logo and navigation links.

✦ **Discussion Web Wizard** creates a Web that features a discussion forum. The discussion forum is similar to an Internet newsgroup: It enables users to post articles, read articles posted by other users, and post replies to articles.

Adding a Page to a Web

The following sections describe several methods that you can use to create a new page to add to a FrontPage Web. If you have not yet created a

FrontPage Web, you should first read the preceding section, "Creating a New Web."

Creating a blank page

To create a blank page and integrate it into an existing Web's navigation structure, follow these steps:

1. **Choose File⇨Open Web to open the Web to which you want to add a page.**

2. **Click the Navigation icon (in the left pane, called the Views bar) to switch to Navigation view.**

   If this icon is not visible, choose View⇨Views Bar to display the Views bar.

3. **Click the page to which you want the new page to be subordinate.**

4. **Click the New Page button.**

   This action inserts a new page beneath the page that was selected. For example, the Interests page was selected when a new page was inserted, as shown in Figure 6-3.

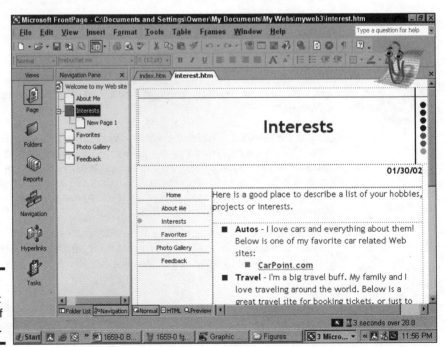

Figure 6-3: The current hierarchy of Web pages.

5. **Right-click the new page and choose Rename from the shortcut menu that appears. Type a new name for the page and press Enter.**

6. **Double-click the new page to open it in Page view so that you can edit the page.**

Creating a page from a template

To create a new page using one of the built-in FrontPage templates, follow these steps:

1. **Switch to Page view by clicking the Page icon in the Views bar.**

2. **Choose File➪New➪Page or Web.**

   This displays the Page Templates dialog box, which lists about 25 different templates that you can use to create your new page.

3. **Choose the template that you want to use for the new page.**

   Note that the Preview in the Page Templates dialog box shows how the page appears.

4. **Click OK.**

   A new page is created from the template that you selected. The new page uses the theme and shared borders that you've set up for the Web. (For more information about themes and shared borders, see the "Choosing Themes" and "Using Shared Borders" sections, later in this chapter.)

5. **Choose File➪Properties.**

   The Page Properties dialog box opens.

6. **In the Title text box, type a title for the page and click OK.**

7. **Edit the page any way you want.**

8. **Choose File➪Save to save the new page.**

   The Save As dialog box opens and displays as a default filename the title that you gave the page in the Page Properties dialog box in Step 6.

9. **Click Save to save the file to the FrontPage Web.**

   If the template you used to create the page contains images that you haven't yet imported into the Web, a Save Embedded Files dialog box appears.

10. **If prompted, click OK to save the images.**

After you've created a new page based on a template, the page is not integrated into the Web's navigation structure. That is why the top border displays the message Add this page to the Navigation view to display a page banner here and the left border displays the message

Add this page to the Navigation view to display hyperlinks here. (See the "Using a Navigation Bar" section for the procedure to follow to add the page to the navigation structure.)

Editing a Web Page

To edit a Web page, switch to Page view and double-click the page that you want to edit in the Folders List.

If you want more room on the screen to edit your Web pages, you can hide the Views bar and Folder List. To hide the Views bar, choose View⇨Views Bar. To hide the Folder List, choose View⇨Folder List.

If you have hidden the Folder List, you can still open a page for editing by choosing File⇨Open or by clicking the Open button. This brings up a dialog box listing all the files in the current Web. Choose the file that you want to edit and click Open.

You can also follow a hyperlink while you're editing a page to edit the page indicated by the hyperlink. To follow a hyperlink, hold down the Ctrl key while you click the link.

Notice the three tabs at the bottom of the screen in Figure 6-2. They allow you to switch among three editing modes:

 ✦ **Normal:** The normal editing mode.

 ✦ **HTML:** Displays the HTML source code for the Web page. Click this tab if you're an HTML guru and you want to edit the HTML directly.

 ✦ **Preview:** Displays the page as it will appear when viewed in a browser.

Choose View⇨Reveal Tags to display icons that represent the HTML tags on a page. Choose View⇨Reveal Tags again to hide the tags.

Choosing Themes

Themes are one of the most powerful features of FrontPage 2002. Themes enable you to set the overall appearance of all the pages in your Web with just a few keystrokes. Here are just some of the elements of Web page design that are set automatically after you choose a theme for your FrontPage Web:

 ✦ Page background

 ✦ Text styles, including fonts and sizes for text elements such as headings and lists

+ Image bullets and lines
+ Color schemes
+ The position and appearance of navigation bars

To change the theme for a Web or to override the Web's theme for an individual page, follow these steps:

1. **Open the Web and switch to Page view.**

2. **If you want to change the theme for a specific page, open that page.**

   Otherwise, it doesn't matter what page is open in Page view.

3. **Choose Format⇨Theme.**

   The Themes dialog box opens, as shown in Figure 6-4.

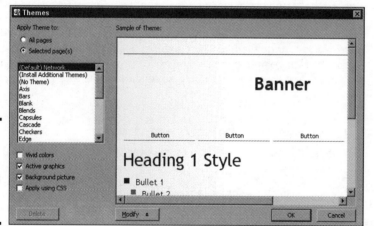

Figure 6-4:
Select the
desired
theme in the
Themes
dialog box.

4. **To set the theme for the entire Web, select the All Pages option. To change the theme for a single page, choose Selected Page(s) instead.**

5. **Choose the theme that you want to use from the list box at the left side of the Themes dialog box.**

   A preview of the theme appears in the Sample of Theme area.

6. **To vary the color scheme of the theme, you can check or uncheck the Vivid Colors check box.**

7. **Check the Active Graphics check box to use an alternate set of graphic banners, buttons, and images for the theme.**

8. **Uncheck the Background Picture check box if you don't want to use the theme's background image.**

9. **Check the Apply Using CSS check box if you're a fan of style sheets. If you don't know what style sheets are, don't check this button. (What you don't know won't hurt you.)**

   As you check or uncheck the options described in Steps 6 through 9, you can see the results immediately in the Sample of Theme window.

10. **Click OK.**

 If you prefer to control all the formatting options for your Web, you can remove the Web's theme by choosing (No Theme) in the list box at the left side of the Themes dialog box.

Using Shared Borders

Shared borders are predefined areas of a Web's pages and may contain elements that appear on every page in the Web. Every FrontPage Web page has four shared borders: top, bottom, left, and right. However, all four of the shared borders are not usually visible. For most Webs, only the top and left borders are made visible. The top border contains a banner that appears on every Web page and a navigation bar to provide basic site navigation, whereas the left border contains a navigation bar that provides automatic links to each page's child pages.

Setting shared borders for a Web

To set the shared borders that appear by default on the Web's pages, follow these steps:

1. **Choose Format⇔Shared Borders.**

   The Shared Borders dialog box appears.

2. **Select the All Pages option.**

3. **Select the borders that you want to appear by default on each page in the Web.**

   The choices are Top, Left, Right, and Bottom.

4. **If you want to include a navigation bar for the top or left border, select the Include Navigation Buttons check box below the Top or Left check boxes.**

   (See the "Using a Navigation Bar" section, later in this chapter, for more information.)

5. **Click OK.**

Changing shared borders on a page

By default, each page in a Web shows the shared borders that you set for the Web. You can, however, override the default shared borders for any page by following these steps:

1. **Switch to Page view and open the page whose shared borders you want to override.**

2. **Choose Format⇨Shared Borders.**

   The Shared Borders dialog box appears.

3. **Make sure that the Current Page option is selected.**

4. **Select the borders that you want to appear on this page.**

   The choices are Top, Left, Right, and Bottom.

5. **If you want to include a navigation bar for the top or left border, select the Include Navigation Buttons check box below the Top or Left check boxes.**

   (See "Using a Navigation Bar," later in this chapter, for more information.)

6. **Click OK.**

Book VI
Chapter 6

**Creating Web Pages
with Microsoft
FrontPage 2002**

To revert to the default shared borders for the page, choose Format⇨Shared Borders and choose the Reset Borders for Current Page to Web Default option.

Editing shared border content

To change the content of a shared border, follow these steps:

1. **In Page view, open any page that uses the border.**

2. **Click anywhere inside the border to activate the border.**

   A solid line appears around the shared border to show that the border is activated.

3. **Make changes to the content of the shared border.**

4. **After you're finished, click outside the shared border so that you can continue editing the page.**

5. **Choose File⇨Save to save the changes that you made to the border.**

   The changes then appear on every page that uses the border.

Using a Navigation Bar

When you create a new Web using a template or wizard, FrontPage automatically adds *navigation bars* to each page in the Web to enable users to easily go from page to page in your Web site. These navigation bars are located in the shared borders of each Web page. (See "Using Shared Borders," earlier in this chapter.)

FrontPage navigation bars rely on the navigation structure that you create for your Web site using the FrontPage Navigation view. Navigation view enables you to organize your Web site's pages into a hierarchy, with the home page at the topmost level of the hierarchy. Any page can have one or more *child pages*, which are at the next level down in the hierarchy. A page that has child pages is referred to as a *parent page*.

FrontPage actually adds two navigation bars to Webs you create using templates or wizards:

✦ The first navigation bar appears in the top shared border. It contains links to the home page, to the current page's parent page, and to any other pages that are at the same navigation level as the current page. For the home page, this navigation bar is blank.

✦ The second navigation bar appears in the left shared border. It contains links to each of the current page's child pages. If the current page has no child pages, this navigation bar is blank.

The navigation bars don't appear quite right when you view them in FrontPage. To see how your navigation bars really appear, choose File⇨ Preview in Browser to view the Web site using an actual Web browser.

Adding a new page to the navigation structure

When you create a new page while working in Page view, that page will be added to the Web but won't be added to the Web's navigation structure. To add the page to the navigation structure so that it appears in the navigation bars, follow these steps:

1. **Click the Navigation icon in the Views bar. (If the Views bar is not visible, choose View⇨Navigation instead.)**

2. **Drag the new page from the list of Web pages that appears in the Folder List into the Web navigation structure. (If the Folder List isn't visible, activate it by choosing View⇨Folder List.)**

3. **Move the new page around the navigation structure until the page latches on to the page that you want to serve as the parent for the new page.**

4. **Release the mouse button.**

   The new page is added to the navigation structure and appears in the Web's navigation bars.

Changing navigation bar properties

The Navigation Bar Properties dialog box enables you to set several important properties for a navigation bar. To set these properties, follow these steps:

1. **In Page view, click anywhere in the shared border that contains the navigation bar to select the shared border.**

   Because the navigation bar is contained in a shared border, it doesn't matter what page you are editing in Page view. Any changes made to the navigation bar properties will apply to the entire Web, not just the page you are editing.

2. **Double-click the navigation bar.**

   The Link Bar Properties dialog box appears.

3. **Choose the hyperlinks that you want to appear on the navigation bar.**

   You can select one of the following six options. The diagram on the left side of the dialog box changes, depending on which option is selected:

   - **Parent Level:** Creates links to all pages that are at the parent level to the current page.

   - **Same Level:** Creates links to all pages that are at the same level as the current page.

   - **Back and Next:** Creates links to the previous page and the next page at the same level as the current page.

   - **Child Level:** Creates links to any children of the current page.

   - **Global Level:** Creates links to all pages at the top level of the Web.

   - **Child Pages Under Home:** Creates links to all of the home page's child pages.

   In addition, you can select either or both of the following pages:

   - **Home Page:** Creates a link to the Web's home page.

   - **Parent Page:** Creates a link to the current page's parent page.

4. **Click the Style tab and then choose the Orientation and Appearance options.**

   You can select one of two options for the navigation bar's orientation: Horizontal or Vertical.

5. **Click OK.**

You cannot change the name that appears on the navigation bar links from Page view. Instead, you must go to Navigation view. Right-click the box representing the page whose title you want to change, and then choose the Rename command from the shortcut menu. Type a new name for the page, and then press Enter.

Inserting a navigation bar

Although FrontPage automatically creates navigation bars for you when you create a Web using a template or wizard, you can also create navigation bars of your own.

To insert your own navigation bar, follow these steps:

1. **In Page view, open the page to which you want to add the navigation bar.**

2. **Move the insertion point to the location where you want the navigation bar inserted.**

3. **Choose Insert➪Navigation.**

   The Insert Web Component window appears.

4. **Select the options that you want to use for the navigation bar.**

5. **Click OK.**

   The navigation bar is inserted on the page.

When you insert a navigation bar on a page, the navigation bar is visible only on that page. If you want the same navigation bar to appear on several pages, you have to insert the navigation bar separately on those pages. Keep in mind, however, that every FrontPage Web can have up to four shared border areas: top, left, bottom, and right. FrontPage automatically creates navigation bars in the top and left shared borders, but you can insert additional navigation bars in the bottom and right shared borders. Then you can turn the bottom and right borders on and off to control which pages these navigation bars appear on.

Formatting Text

FrontPage gives you many different ways to format your text. The following sections present the more common formatting procedures.

Keyboard shortcuts and toolbar buttons

You can set character formats by using the keyboard shortcuts or toolbar buttons shown in Table 6-1.

Table 6-1	Formatting Shortcuts	
Shortcut	**Button**	**What It Does**
Ctrl+B	**B**	**Bolds** text
Ctrl+I	*I*	*Italicizes* text
Ctrl+U	U	Underlines text
	A	Sets the text color
		Formats as a numbered list
		Formats as a bulleted list
Ctrl+M		Increases indent
Ctrl+Shift+M		Decreases indent
Ctrl+Shift+>		Increases text size
Ctrl+Shift+<		Decreases text size
Ctrl+spacebar		Removes character formatting

Changing font settings

You can change font settings by following these steps:

1. **Select the text to which you want to apply the formatting.**

2. **Choose Format⇨Font.**

   The Font dialog box appears.

3. **Select the desired font options.**

Keep your eye on the Preview area of the Font dialog box: As you select various font settings, the sample text in this area changes to show how the text will appear.

4. **Click OK when you're finished.**

Paragraph formatting

To apply paragraph formatting, follow these steps:

1. **Click anywhere in the paragraph that you want to format.**

You don't need to select the entire paragraph, as long as the insertion point is somewhere in the paragraph that you want to format. If you want to format several adjacent paragraphs at once, drag the mouse to select text in all the paragraphs that you want to format.

2. **Choose Format⇨Paragraph.**

The Paragraph properties dialog box opens.

3. **Choose the alignment for the paragraph.**

The choices are Default, Left, Right, Center, and Justify.

4. **Set the paragraph indentation and spacing options you want.**

5. **Click OK.**

To change the HTML style that is assigned to a paragraph, follow these steps:

1. **Click anywhere in the paragraph.**

2. **Choose Format⇨Style.**

The Style dialog box appears.

3. **Choose the style that you want from the Styles list.**

4. **Click OK.**

Refer to Book VI, Chapter 2, for specific information on commonly used HTML styles.

Inserting Horizontal Lines

FrontPage enables you to insert horizontal lines in your Web pages. If you have selected a theme to format the page, an image file supplied by the theme is used to create the line. If the page doesn't use a theme, the line is created using the HTML <HR> tag, and you're able to choose the <HR> formatting options to control the format of the line.

To insert a horizontal line, follow these steps:

1. **Place the insertion point where you want to insert the line.**

2. **Choose Insert➪Horizontal Line.**

3. **To modify the appearance of the line, double-click the line.**

   The Horizontal Line Properties dialog box appears.

4. **Choose the formatting options that you want for the line.**

   If the page doesn't use a theme, you can change the line's width, height, alignment, and color. However, if you've chosen a theme to format the line, you can change only the line's alignment.

5. **Click OK.**

Creating Lists

FrontPage enables you to create bulleted or numbered lists. The following sections show you how.

Creating a simple bulleted or numbered list

To create a simple bulleted or numbered list, follow these steps:

1. **In Page view, type one or more paragraphs that you want to make into a list.**

2. **Select the paragraphs by dragging the mouse over them.**

3. **To create a bulleted list, click the Bullets button; to create a numbered list, click the Numbering button.**

4. **To add additional items to the list, position the cursor at the end of one of the list paragraphs and press Enter.**

   FrontPage automatically adds a bullet or number to the new paragraph. In the case of a numbered list, FrontPage renumbers any paragraphs following the inserted paragraph.

The Bullets and Numbering buttons work like toggles: Click the button once to add bullets or numbers, and click the button again to remove them. To remove bullets or numbers from an entire list, select all the paragraphs in the list and click the Bullets or Numbering button.

Changing the bullet symbol

To change the symbol or image used for a bullet, place the cursor in the paragraph whose bullet you want to change and choose Format➪Bullets and Numbering. You can opt to use the bullet images from the page's theme, or you can check the Specify Picture option and then type the URL of an image file that you want to use for the image (or click the Browse button to locate an image file to use).

Changing the number style

To change the number style used for a numbered list, place the insertion point anywhere in the list and choose Format⇨Bullets and Numbering. Then choose the numbering option that you want to use and click OK.

Inserting Tables

Tables are commonly used in Web documents to organize information into a gridlike arrangement or to control the layout of elements on a page. FrontPage 2002 provides you with two ways to create tables: the Table⇨Insert⇨Table command or the Table⇨Draw Table command. This section covers the first method only.

To create a table, follow these steps:

1. **In Page view, move the insertion point to the desired table location.**

2. **Choose Table⇨Insert⇨Table.**

   The Insert Table dialog box appears.

3. **Select the size of the table that you want to create by setting the Rows and Columns fields.**

4. **Select the layout settings that you want to use from the following choices:**

   - **Alignment:** Default, Left, Right, or Center.

   - **Border Size:** The width of the table border in pixels. To create a table with no border, set this field to 0.

   - **Cell Padding:** The number of pixels to leave between the cell borders and the cell content.

   - **Cell Spacing:** The number of pixels to leave between cells.

5. **Specify the width of the table, either in pixels or as a percentage of the page width, using the Specify Width field.**

6. **Click OK to create the table.**

After you create a table, you can select a cell by clicking it. Then you can type text into the cell or insert elements such as images, buttons, and even other tables into the cell.

Importing Files

When you create a FrontPage Web, FrontPage creates a series of folders that it then uses to store the files that make up your Web. Initially, these folders contain the HTML files, images, and other FrontPage components for the Web pages created when you use a template or wizard to create a Web and when you apply a theme to the Web. The HTML documents themselves are stored in the main folder for the Web. Image files are stored in a second folder called, predictably, *images*. Other folders are also created for various types of FrontPage components used by the Web.

If you want to include other files, such as images, sounds, or videos in your Web, first import them into the FrontPage Web's folders so that the files can be accessible to the Web. Usually, you want to store image, sound, and video files in the images folder. However, you can also create additional folders for files that you import, if you prefer.

To import an image, sound, or video file (or multiple files) into a FrontPage Web so that you can use it on a Web page, follow these steps:

1. **Choose File➪Open Web to open the Web to which you want to add the file or files.**

2. **Choose File➪Import.**

The Import dialog box opens.

3. **Click the Add File button.**

The Add File to Import List dialog box appears.

4. **Use the Add File to Import List dialog box controls to locate the file that you want to import into the FrontPage Web.**

5. **When you find the file that you want to import, click the file to select it and then click Open.**

You're returned to the Import dialog box, which shows the file that you selected in the list of files to be imported.

6. **Repeat Steps 3 through 5 for each file that you want to import.**

7. **After you've selected all the files that you want to import, click OK.**

Inserting Images

The following sections describe various procedures for working with images in FrontPage 2002.

Inserting an image file

To insert an image file into a FrontPage Web, follow these steps:

1. **Obtain the image file that you want to use and import it into your Web.**

   (See the preceding section, "Importing Files," if you need help importing your files.)

2. **Call up Page view to edit the page on which you want to insert the image.**

3. **Move the insertion point to the location on the page where you want the image to be inserted.**

4. **Choose Insert⇨Picture⇨From File.**

   The Picture dialog box appears, as shown in Figure 6-5.

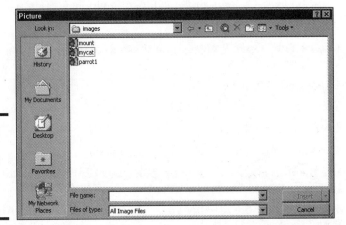

Figure 6-5:
Select the image that you want to add to your Web.

5. **Select the image file that you want, and then click OK.**

Inserting a clip art image

FrontPage 2002 comes with a large collection of clip art and a fancy program called Microsoft Clip Art Gallery to manage your clip art. The clip art images that you find when you display the Clip Art Gallery depend on what other Microsoft programs you have on your computer.

To use a clip art picture on a Web page, follow these steps:

1. **In Page view, move the insertion point to the location where you want to insert the clip art.**

2. **Choose Insert⇨Picture⇨Clip Art.**

   The Insert Clip Art pane appears.

3. **Click Clip Organizer.**

   The Microsoft Clip Organizer appears, as shown in Figure 6-6.

Book VI
Chapter 6

Creating Web Pages with Microsoft FrontPage 2002

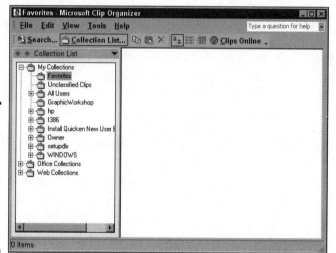

Figure 6-6:
Use the Microsoft Clip Organizer to add a picture to your Web page.

4. **Click one of the categories in the Microsoft Clip Organizer Collection List.**

   Clicking one of the categories displays the clip art images that are in that category. The Clip Organizer shows several images at a time, but you can see other images from the same category by scrolling through the images. When the image that you want to use comes into view, click it.

   If you can't find an image that you want to use in the category you selected, you can return to the list of categories by clicking the Back button.

5. **Click the image that you want to use.**

   A pop-up menu appears next to the image that you clicked.

6. **Click the Insert Clip button to insert the image.**

   The image is inserted into the Web page.

 Notice that the Clip Organizer has tabs for sounds and motion clips as well as clip art. You can use these tabs to add sounds and movies to your Web pages, following the same steps shown here.

Adding Hyperlinks

A *hyperlink* is a bit of text or a graphic image that you can click to display another page. FrontPage does more than just enable you to add hyperlinks to your Web pages: It can also keep track of your links and verify them to make sure that each link points to an actual page within your Web or on someone else's Web site.

Inserting a hyperlink

To insert a hyperlink, follow these steps:

1. **Type the text that you want to use for the hyperlink. Or, if you prefer to use an image for the link, insert the image.**

 2. **Select the text or image, and choose Insert⇨Hyperlink or click the Hyperlink button.**

   The Edit Hyperlink dialog box appears, as shown in Figure 6-7.

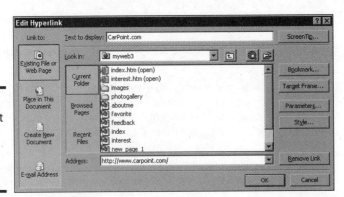

Figure 6-7: Use the Edit Hyperlink dialog box to insert a hyperlink.

3. **Select the page to which you want to link.**

   If the page doesn't appear in the Edit Hyperlink dialog box, you can type the URL of the page you want to link to directly into the URL field. Or, you can click one of the following buttons:

Button	Function
![browse internet icon]	Enables you to browse the Internet to locate and then link to the page.
![browse file icon]	Enables you to browse your hard drive to create a link to an existing file or Web page.
![email icon]	Creates a link that sends an e-mail message.
![new page icon]	Creates a new FrontPage Web page, and makes a link to the new page.

4. **Click OK.**

Verifying hyperlinks

Web sites come and go, so it's a good idea to periodically check the links in your Web to make sure that they remain valid. Use these steps to verify the status of your hyperlinks:

1. **Choose View➪Reports.**

   The Reporting toolbar is displayed.

2. **Click the Verify Hyperlinks button.**

3. **In the Verify Hyperlinks dialog box, click Start.**

   FrontPage attempts to locate the page linked to by each hyperlink. When all the pages have been verified, FrontPage switches to Report view and displays the Broken Links report, as shown in Figure 6-8. The Broken Links report lists every hyperlink in the Web along with the link's status: either OK or Broken.

4. **Double-click a broken hyperlink.**

   The Edit Hyperlink dialog box pops onto the screen.

5. **Correct the broken hyperlink by using one of the following methods:**

   • Type the correct URL for the hyperlink in the Replace Hyperlink With field, and click Replace.

   • Click Browse to browse the Web for a valid hyperlink. When you find the page you want to link to, return to FrontPage and click Replace.

- Click Edit Page to edit the page in FrontPage Editor. Here, you can change or remove the link, save the file, and return to FrontPage.

6. **Repeat Steps 4 and 5 until you have no more broken hyperlinks.**

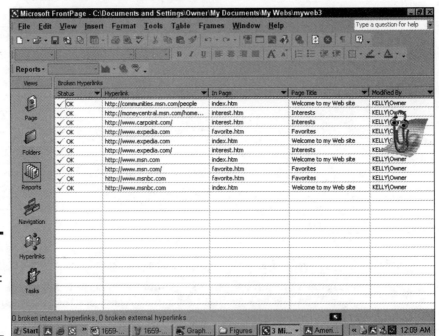

Figure 6-8:
The Broken Links report: All hyperlinks are OK.

Using Image Maps

An *image map* is an image displayed on a Web page in which one or more regions of the image serve as hyperlinks to other Web pages. In FrontPage terms, the hyperlink regions of an image map are called *hotspots*. FrontPage includes tools that enable you to easily create hotspots for any image. Here's the procedure:

1. **Insert the image that you want to use as an image map.**

   See the "Inserting Images" section earlier in this chapter for details.

2. **Click the image that you inserted in Step 1 to select it.**

   The Image toolbar appears at the bottom of the FrontPage window.

3. **To mark a hotspot, click one of the following buttons in the Image toolbar to activate the appropriate hotspot drawing tool:**

Button	Function
	Marks a rectangular hotspot.
	Marks a circular hotspot.
	Marks an irregularly shaped hotspot (a polygon).

**Book VI
Chapter 6**

Creating Web Pages
with Microsoft
FrontPage 2002

4. **Draw the region that you want to act as a hotspot, as follows:**

   - To draw a rectangular hotspot, point the mouse to one corner of the rectangle, press and hold the mouse button, and drag the mouse to the opposite corner.

   - To draw a circular hotspot, point the mouse to the center of the circle and press and hold the mouse to expand the circle's radius.

   - To draw a polygon hotspot, click the mouse at one corner of the polygon. Move the mouse to the next corner and click again to draw a segment of the polygon. Keep clicking to add new segments until the polygon is complete. To finish the polygon, click again at the starting point.

   After you finish drawing the hotspot, the Create Hyperlink dialog box appears.

5. **Select the page to which you want to link.**

   If the page doesn't appear in the Edit Hyperlink dialog box, you can type the URL of the page that you want to link to directly into the URL field, or you can click one of the following buttons:

Button	Function
	Enables you to browse the Internet to locate the page to link to.
	Enables you to browse your hard drive to create a link to a document file.
	Creates a link that sends an e-mail message.
	Creates a new FrontPage Web page, and makes a link to the new page.

    6. **Click OK.**

    7. **Repeat Steps 3 through 6 to create more hotspots for the image map.**

 To display all the hotspots that you've created for an image map, click the image to select it. Then click the Highlight Hotspots button. The image temporarily vanishes so that you can see the highlighted hotspots. To restore the image, click the Highlight Hotspots button again.

 You can change the shape of an existing hotspot by clicking in the hotspot to select it and then dragging on one handle of the hotspot. To delete a hotspot, click the hotspot to select it and then press Delete.

Adding a Hit Counter

A *hit counter* is a special FrontPage component that you can insert on your Web pages to display the number of times a page has been retrieved by Internet users. The hit counter itself is a graphic image that displays the hit count in one of several formats.

To insert a hit counter on a page, follow these steps:

    1. **Switch to Page view to edit the page on which you want to insert the hit counter.**

        Usually, it's best to place a hit counter on your Web site's home page.

    2. **Type some text to precede and follow the hit counter, such as "This page has been visited (*counter*) times" or "You are visitor number: (*counter*)."**

    3. **Place the insertion point where you want the hit counter to be inserted, such as between the words "visited" and "times" for the text "This page has been visited times."**

    4. **Choose Insert➪Web Component➪Hit Counter.**

        The dialog box shown in Figure 6-9 appears.

    5. **Choose the graphic style for the hit counter image by selecting one of the choices listed under Choose a Counter Style.**

    6. **If you want the counter to start at a number other than 1, click the Reset Counter To option and then type the starting counter number in the adjacent text box.**

    7. **If you want the counter to always display a fixed number of digits including leading zeros, click the Fixed Number of Digits option and then type the number of digits in the adjacent text box.**

    8. **Click OK to insert the hit counter.**

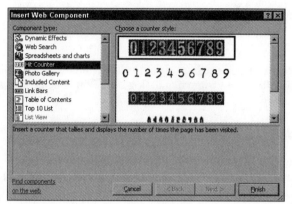

**Book VI
Chapter 6**

Creating Web Pages
with Microsoft
FrontPage 2002

Figure 6-9:
Select the
style of hit
counter
that you
want to use.

After the hit counter is inserted into your document, you won't see the graphic counter image in FrontPage. Instead, you see this:

```
[Hit Counter].
```

Don't worry. When you call up the page with your Web browser, the hit counter displays properly.

Using Marquees

A *marquee* is a line of text that scrolls across the screen as the user views the page. This feature creates an interesting appearance and definitely draws attention to the page.

To create a marquee, follow these steps:

1. **In FrontPage Editor, move the insertion point to the location where you want to insert the marquee.**

2. **Choose Insert➪Component➪Marquee.**

   The Marquee Properties dialog box appears.

3. **In the Text field, type the text that you want to scroll across the screen.**

4. **Change the other marquee settings if you want the marquee to do anything other than scroll repeatedly at a moderate pace from the right of the page to the left.**

5. **Click OK.**

TIP

To see how the marquee will appear when displayed in a browser, switch to Preview mode by clicking the Preview tab at the bottom of the FrontPage window.

To change the marquee settings, double-click the marquee in Normal view to display the Marquee Properties dialog box. Edit the settings and click OK.

Displaying Reports

Reports view is designed to give you information that will help you manage your Web site. To display FrontPage reports, click the Reports icon in the Views bar. This brings up the FrontPage Site Summary report, shown in Figure 6-10.

The Site Summary report gives you valuable overview information about your Web site, such as the total number and size of all the files that make up your Web site, the number of pages that will take more than 30 seconds to download, the number of files that are included in your Web but aren't used anywhere, and so on.

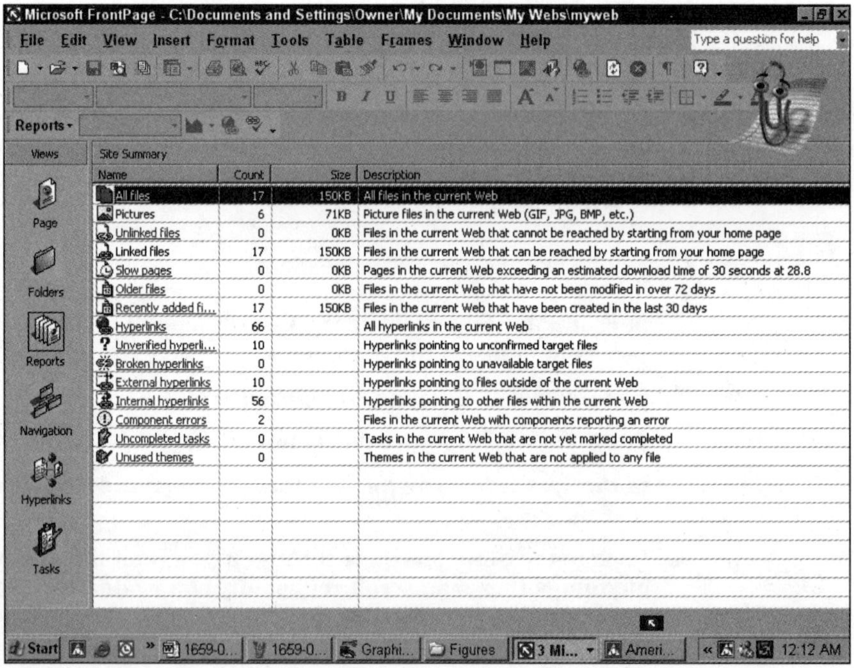

Figure 6-10:
The
FrontPage
Site
Summary
report.

Name	Count	Size	Description
All files	17	150KB	All files in the current Web
Pictures	6	71KB	Picture files in the current Web (GIF, JPG, BMP, etc.)
Unlinked files	0	0KB	Files in the current Web that cannot be reached by starting from your home page
Linked files	17	150KB	Files in the current Web that can be reached by starting from your home page
Slow pages	0	0KB	Pages in the current Web exceeding an estimated download time of 30 seconds at 28.8
Older files	0	0KB	Files in the current Web that have not been modified in over 72 days
Recently added fi...	17	150KB	Files in the current Web that have been created in the last 30 days
Hyperlinks	66		All hyperlinks in the current Web
Unverified hyperli...	10		Hyperlinks pointing to unconfirmed target files
Broken hyperlinks	0		Hyperlinks pointing to unavailable target files
External hyperlinks	10		Hyperlinks pointing to files outside of the current Web
Internal hyperlinks	56		Hyperlinks pointing to other files within the current Web
Component errors	2		Files in the current Web with components reporting an error
Uncompleted tasks	0		Tasks in the current Web that are not yet marked completed
Unused themes	0		Themes in the current Web that are not applied to any file

You can get a more detailed report about any specific item in the Site Summary report by double-clicking on that item. For example, if your Site Summary report shows that you have pages that will download slowly, double-click on the Slow Pages line to find out which pages are slow.

Another way to work with reports is by using the Reporting toolbar. To display the Reporting toolbar, choose View⇨Toolbars⇨Reporting. The Reporting toolbar includes a drop-down list that lets you select a report to view. In addition, many reports add a field that lets you customize the report somewhat. For example, the Reporting toolbar lets you specify how slow a file must be to be included in the Slow Files report.

**Book VI
Chapter 6**

**Creating Web Pages
with Microsoft
FrontPage 2002**

Publishing a FrontPage Web

FrontPage has several built-in features that make publishing your FrontPage Webs to the Internet easy.

When you are ready to publish your Web, follow these steps:

1. **Switch to Reports view, and check the Web reports to make sure that everything is in order (see the preceding section).**

2. **Preview the Web by choosing File⇨Preview in Browser.**

    This opens your Web browser and allows you to see how the Web will appear when actually viewed.

3. **When your Web is ready to be published, click the Publish button or choose File⇨Publish Web.**

    The Publish Web dialog box opens.

4. **Click Publish in the Publish Web dialog box.**

    FrontPage posts your Web files to your Web server.

In the Publish Web dialog box, you can select the Publish Changed Pages Only option to post only those files that have changed since the last time you published your Web. Alternatively, you can choose the Publish All Pages option to copy all your Web's pages to the server.

If some of the pages on your Web are still under construction and you do not want them posted when you publish the rest of your Web, you can mark those pages so that they won't be published.

To mark the pages that you don't want to publish at this time, follow these steps:

1. **In the Folder List, right-click the file that you do not want to publish and choose the Properties command from the shortcut menu.**

2. **Click the Workgroup tab.**

3. **Check the Exclude This File When Publishing the Rest of the Web check box.**

4. **Click OK.**

When you have finished the page and want it to be published, repeat the procedure, but uncheck the Exclude check box in Step 3.

Chapter 7: Creating Web Pages with Netscape Composer 4.7

In This Chapter

✔ Creating and editing Web pages with Netscape Composer 4.7

✔ Applying basic formatting to text and paragraphs

✔ Working with basic Web page elements

✔ Publishing pages to the Web

*N*etscape Communicator comes with a Web page editor called Netscape Composer 4.7. At press time, Composer 4.7 was still the version used in Netscape 6.2. Although Composer doesn't have all the bells and whistles of a more advanced program, such as FrontPage 2002, it is more than adequate for creating basic Web pages. This chapter presents the basic procedures for working with Composer.

Creating a Web Page

The following sections describe several methods that you can use to create a new Web page with Netscape Composer 4.7 by using a blank page or a template.

Starting with a blank page

You have several ways to create a new, blank page in Composer. Here are the most common methods:

✦ Start Composer from Netscape Navigator by choosing Communicator⇨Composer.

✦ Another way to start Composer from Navigator is by choosing File⇨New⇨Blank Page, or its keyboard shortcut, Ctrl+Shift+N.

✦ If you are already in Netscape Composer, you can create a new blank page by choosing File⇨New⇨Blank Page or by clicking the New button and then choosing Blank Page from the dialog box that appears.

Composer displays an empty page upon which you can compose any information you want, as shown in Figure 7-1.

Figure 7-1:
The
Composer
window
awaits your
input.

After you finish composing your page, be sure to save your work to a file by choosing File⇨Save, clicking the Save button, or pressing Ctrl+S.

Using a template

The Netscape Web site houses a collection of Web page templates that you can use as a starting point for your own Web pages. To create a new Web page with one of these templates, follow these steps:

1. **In Navigator, choose File⇨New⇨Page from Template.**

2. **Click the Netscape Templates button.**

   Navigator takes you to a special page at the Netscape Web site containing a list of the Netscape Web page templates.

3. **Scroll down the page to view the complete list of Web page templates; then click the one that you want to use.**

   The template page opens. For example, the basic My Home Page template looks like Figure 7-2.

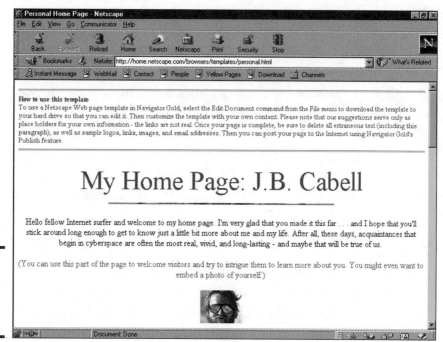

Figure 7-2:
The My
Home Page
template in
Composer.

4. Choose File⇨Edit Page.

This action transfers the page to a temporary resting spot on your computer's hard drive and opens the page in Composer rather than in the Navigator browser.

5. Edit the page any way you want.

6. Choose File⇨Save As.

The Save As dialog box opens.

7. Select the location where you want to save the Web page files and click Save.

This action saves not only the HTML file for the Web page, but also any images or other files included on the page.

You can also create a Web page by using the Netscape Page Wizard. The Page Wizard asks for information about the Web page that you want to create and then creates a customized Web page based on your specifications. To use the Page Wizard, choose File⇨New⇨Page From Wizard and follow the instructions that appear on the screen.

Editing a Web Page

You can edit a Web page that you have saved to your hard drive by following these steps:

1. **In Netscape Composer, click the Open button or choose File⇨Open Page.**

   The Open Page dialog box appears.

2. **Click the Choose File button.**

   The standard Open dialog box appears.

3. **Select the file that you want to edit and click the Open button.**

You can also edit a Web page that has already been published on the Internet by following these steps:

1. **In Navigator, browse to the page that you want to edit.**

2. **Choose File⇨Edit Page.**

   A copy of the Web page opens in Netscape Composer for editing.

3. **After you finish editing the page, choose File⇨Save As to save the page to your hard drive, or choose File⇨Publish to publish the edited page to a Web site.**

   See "Publishing a Web Page," later in this chapter, for more information about this process.

Checking Your Spelling

Composer can check the spelling of every word in your Web page to spare you the embarrassment of publishing a page rife with spelling errors.

To check the spelling of your page, follow these steps:

1. **Choose Tools⇨Check Spelling, or click the Spelling button.**

   Composer begins its spell check. When Composer finds a spelling mistake, the dialog box shown in Figure 7-3 appears.

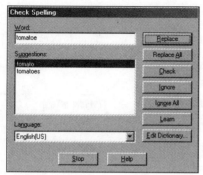

Figure 7-3:
Check your
spelling
before you
publish your
Web pages.

2. **Depending on whether the word is misspelled, take one of the following actions:**

   • If the word is misspelled, select the correct spelling from the list of suggested spellings and click the Replace button.

   • If the word is misspelled and the correct spelling doesn't appear among the suggestions, type the correct spelling in the Word text box and click the Replace button.

   • If the word is spelled correctly, click the Ignore button. Or click Ignore All to ignore any subsequent occurrences of the word.

3. **Repeat Step 2 for any other misspellings that the spell checker finds.**

4. **Click Done to close the Check Spelling dialog box.**

5. **Now carefully read the page and make sure that it doesn't contain any spelling errors that weren't detected by the spell checker.**

Because spell checkers aren't perfect, you still have to carefully proofread your pages before publishing them.

Formatting Text

Netscape Composer enables you to apply the HTML basic formatting options to your text, as described in the following sections.

Keyboard shortcuts and toolbar buttons

You can set character formats by using the keyboard shortcuts or toolbar buttons in Table 7-1.

Table 7-1	Formatting Shortcuts	
Shortcut	*Button*	*What It Does*
Ctrl+B		**Bolds** text
Ctrl+I		*Italicizes* text
Ctrl+U		<u>Underlines</u> text
Ctrl+Shift+C		Sets the text color
		Formats as a numbered list
		Formats as a bulleted list
Ctrl+=		Increases indent
Ctrl+-		Decreases indent
Ctrl+Shift+K		Removes character formatting
Ctrl+L*		Aligns text at the left margin
Ctrl+E*		Centers text
Ctrl+R*		Aligns text at the right margin

* These buttons are located on the Alignment menu. You must first click the Alignment button to make this menu visible.

Character formatting

To apply character formatting to text on your Web page, follow these steps:

1. **Select the text to which you want to apply the formatting.**

2. **Choose Format⇨Character Properties.**

   The Character Properties dialog box opens, as shown in Figure 7-4.

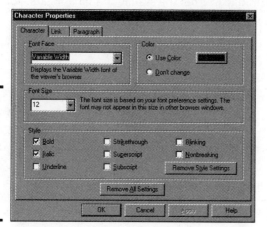

Figure 7-4:
Choose the formatting options that you want to apply to the selected text.

Book VI
Chapter 7

Creating Web Pages with Netscape Composer 4.7

3. **Select the formats that you want to use.**

4. **Click OK when you're finished.**

You can apply character formatting directly by using toolbar buttons or by choosing the following menu commands:

Menu Command	What It Does
Format⇨Font	Selects the typeface
Format⇨Size	Selects the type size
Format⇨Style	Selects the text style (bold, italic, and so on)
Format⇨Color	Selects the text color

To remove all character formatting from selected text, you can choose Format⇨Remove All Styles.

Paragraph formatting

To apply paragraph formatting, first move the insertion point to the paragraph that you want to format (you don't need to select the entire paragraph). If you want to format several adjacent paragraphs at once, drag the mouse to select text in all the paragraphs that you want to format. Then use any of the following techniques to apply the formatting that you want to use.

To format a paragraph as a heading, choose Format⇨Heading and select the heading level (1 through 6) from the submenu that appears. For example, to create a Heading 1, choose the command Format⇨Heading⇨1.

To apply a nonheading paragraph format, use one of the following commands:

✦ Format⇨Paragraph⇨Normal

✦ Format⇨Paragraph⇨Address

✦ Format⇨Paragraph⇨Formatted

✦ Format⇨Paragraph⇨Block Quote

✦ Format⇨Paragraph⇨Description Title

✦ Format⇨Paragraph⇨Description Text

To set a paragraph's alignment, use one of these methods:

✦ Choose Format⇨Align; then click Left, Center, or Right.

✦ Click the Alignment button on the Formatting toolbar to reveal the alignment buttons; then click the button for the type of alignment that you want.

Creating Lists

To create a bulleted or numbered list in Composer, follow these steps:

1. **Type one or more paragraphs that you want to make into a list.**

2. **Select the paragraphs that you want to make into a list by dragging the mouse over them.**

3. **To create a bulleted list, click the Bulleted List button. To create a numbered list, click the Numbered List button.**

4. **To add additional items to the list, position the cursor at the end of one of the list paragraphs and press Enter.**

   Composer automatically adds a bullet or number to the new paragraph. In the case of a numbered list, Composer also renumbers subsequent paragraphs.

The Bulleted List and Numbered List buttons work like toggles: Click the button once to add bullets or numbers and click the button again to remove them. To remove bullets or numbers from an entire list, select all the paragraphs in the list and click the Bulleted List or Numbered List button.

Creating Tables

The Insert⇨Table command enables you to create a table by first specifying the number of rows and columns in the table, the table layout to use, and the size of the table.

To create a table, follow these steps:

1. **Move the insertion point to the desired table location.**

2. **Choose Insert⇨Table⇨Table, or click the Table button.**

    The New Table Properties dialog box appears, as shown in Figure 7-5.

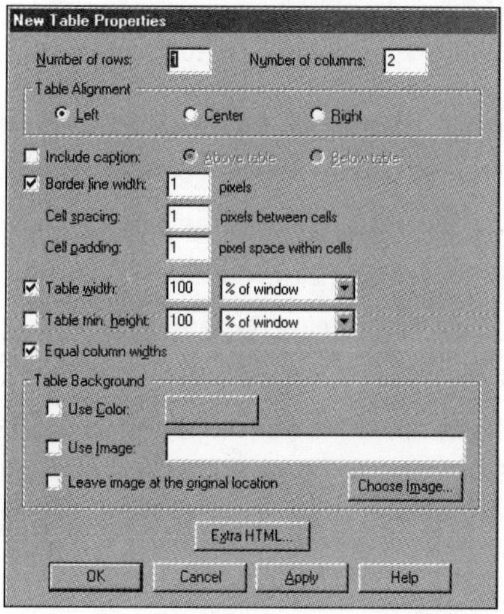

Figure 7-5:
Specify the
options for
your table.

3. **Select the size of the table that you want to create by setting the Number of Rows and Number of Columns fields.**

4. **Select the alignment: Left, Center, or Right.**

5. **Choose any additional options for the table.**

6. **Click OK to insert the table.**

Book VI
Chapter 7

Creating Web Pages
with Netscape
Composer 4.7

After you create a table, you can select a cell by clicking it. Then you can type text into the cell or you can insert elements, such as images, buttons, and even other tables into the cell.

To edit the properties of a cell, click the cell and then choose Format⇨Table Properties. Click the Cell tab, choose the options that you want to use, and then click OK. To edit the properties of a row, select any cell in the row, choose Format⇨Table Properties, and click the Row tab.

To insert a new row, column, or individual cell into an existing table, select the cell where you want the new row, column, or cell inserted and choose one of the following commands:

✦ Insert⇨Table⇨Row

✦ Insert⇨Table⇨Column

✦ Insert⇨Table⇨Cell

Inserting Horizontal Lines

To insert a horizontal line into your document, follow these steps:

1. **Place the insertion point where you want to insert the line.**

2. **Choose Insert⇨Horizontal Line to insert a basic horizontal line.**

3. **Click the line that was inserted to select the line.**

4. **Choose Format⇨Horizontal Line Properties.**

   The Horizontal Line Properties dialog box appears.

5. **Choose the formatting options for the line.**

   You can change the line's height, width, alignment, and 3-D shading.

6. **Click OK.**

Inserting Images

To insert an image file into a Composer page, follow these steps:

1. **Find an image file that you want to insert in your page.**

2. **In Composer, move the insertion point to the location on the page where you want to insert the image.**

3. **Choose Insert↵Image.**

The Image Properties dialog box appears, as shown in Figure 7-6.

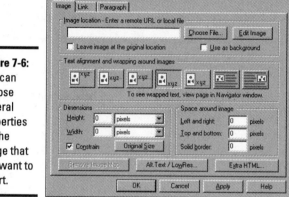

Figure 7-6:
You can
choose
several
properties
for the
image that
you want to
insert.

4. **Click the Choose File button.**

This displays the Choose Image File dialog box, which lets you select image files from your hard drive.

5. **Choose the image file that you want to insert, and then click Open.**

This closes the Choose Image File dialog box and returns you to the Image Properties dialog box, with the Image Location field set to the file location of the image file you selected.

6. **In the Text Alignment and Wrapping Around Images area, click the button representing the alignment and wrapping option you want.**

7. **Type the desired height and width in the Height and Width fields.**

8. **Click the Alt Text/LowRes button.**

The Alternate Image Properties dialog box appears.

9. **In the Alternate Text field, type a message that you want to display for users who view your Web page with their browsers set to disable images.**

10. **Click OK twice to close both dialog boxes and insert the image.**

To change the properties of an image that you've already inserted, double-click the image. This action opens the Image Properties dialog box.

Creating Hyperlinks

A *hyperlink* is a bit of text or a graphic image that you can click to display another page. Follow these steps to create a hyperlink:

1. **Type the text that you want to use for the hyperlink. Or, if you prefer to use an image for the link, insert the image (see the previous section).**

2. **Select the text or image; then choose Insert⇨Link or click the Link button.**

The Link tab in the Character Properties dialog box opens.

3. **In the Link to a Page Location or Local File text box, type the URL for the page to which you want to link.**

4. **Click OK.**

You can edit the page referred to in a link by holding down the Ctrl key and clicking the link. This action starts a separate Composer editing window for the linked page. To return to the page that you're editing, press Alt+Tab.

Publishing a Web Page

Composer can publish a Web page to the Internet by uploading the page's HTML files and other files to an HTTP Web server or an FTP server. You have to obtain information such as the address of your HTTP or FTP server from your Internet Service Provider.

To publish your page to the Internet, follow these steps:

1. **Choose File⇨Publish, or click the Publish button.**

The Publish dialog box appears, as shown in Figure 7-7.

2. **In the Page Title text box, type a name for the page.**

3. **In the HTML Filename text box, type a name for the page's HTML file.**

4. **In the HTTP or FTP Location to Publish text box, type the address of the Web server to which you want to upload the page.**

If you're uploading directly to an HTTP Web server, the address begins with http://. If you're uploading to an FTP server, the address begins with ftp://.

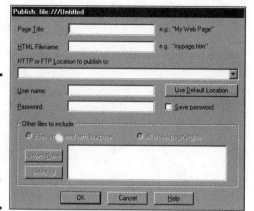

Figure 7-7:
Use the
Publish
dialog box
to specify
options for
uploading to
a server.

5. **If your Web server requires that you enter a user-ID and password to log on before you can upload Web files, type this information in the User Name and Password fields.**

6. **Click OK.**

   Composer connects to your Web server and uploads the Web page and any image or other files included in the page.

Chapter 8: Creating Web Pages with Microsoft Office XP

In This Chapter

✔ Creating Web documents with Word

✔ Using Excel's Web features

✔ Posting PowerPoint presentations on the Web

✔ Publishing Access database data on the Web

Microsoft Office XP — the popular suite that includes Word, Excel, Outlook, and (in the Professional Edition) Access, PowerPoint, and FrontPage — sports many features for creating Web pages. This chapter shows you how to use these Web publishing features to your advantage. (For more on FrontPage specifically, see Chapter 6.)

Word 2002

Word 2002 includes enough HTML formatting features that you can use it as your HTML editor if you don't want to get too elaborate with your Web pages. The following sections describe the procedures for converting an existing Word document to HTML format and for using Word to create a new HTML document.

Converting a document to HTML

To convert an existing Word 2002 document to HTML format so that it can be published on the Web, follow these steps:

1. **Choose File⇨Open, select the document that you want to open, and click Open.**

2. **Choose File⇨Save As.**

   The Save As dialog box appears.

3. **If desired, choose a new location and name for the file.**

4. **From the Save As Type drop-down list, choose Web Page.**

5. **Click the Save button.**

Keep in mind that many differences exist between Word documents and HTML documents. When you save a document as a Web page, Word does its best to convert the formatting you've applied to the Word document into HTML formats. However, some Word formatting features have no HTML equivalents.

Using the Web templates

Word 2002 comes with a nice collection of templates that helps you create various types of Web pages. To use a Web template, follow these steps:

1. **Choose File⇨New.**

   The New Document task pane appears on the right side of your screen.

2. **In the New from Template category, click the General Templates tab.**

3. **Make sure the Web Pages tab is selected and then click the template that you want to use (see Figure 8-1).**

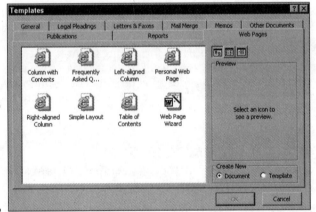

Figure 8-1:
You have several templates to choose from.

4. **Click OK.**

   Word creates a new document based on the template that you selected. For example, Figure 8-2 shows a new document based on the Personal Web Page template.

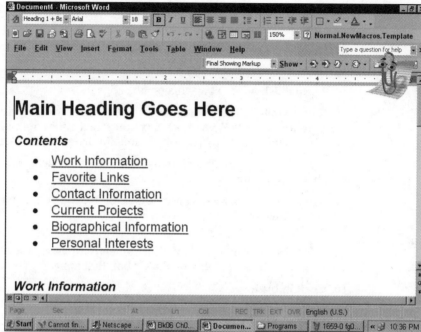

Figure 8-2: You're ready to begin creating your personal Web page.

Excel 2002

Excel 2002 includes a Save As Web Page command that converts an Excel 2002 worksheet to an HTML table that can be published on the World Wide Web. You can use this command in two ways. The first creates a new HTML document that includes the worksheet data in an HTML table. The second inserts the worksheet data as a spreadsheet component in an HTML document, which enables users to edit the spreadsheet data by using their Web browsers.

Publishing worksheet data as a Web page

To publish data from an Excel worksheet to a Web document, follow these steps:

1. **Open the worksheet that you want to publish as a Web page.**

2. **Select the portion of the worksheet that you want to be converted to HTML.**

3. **Choose File⇨Save As Web Page.**

The Save As dialog box appears.

4. **In the Save In list box, select the drive and folder to which you want to save the Web page.**

5. **In the Save area, choose the Selection option button.**

6. **Click the Publish button.**

   The Publish As Web Page dialog box appears.

7. **If you want the user to be able to edit the spreadsheet, check the Add Interactivity With check box and select either Spreadsheet Functionality or PivotTable Functionality from the drop-down list box.**

   If you leave the Add Interactivity With option unchecked, the spreadsheet is published as an HTML table.

8. **(Optional) If you want to provide a title for the published spreadsheet, click the Change button. Type a title in the dialog box that appears and then click OK.**

9. **Click Browse; then select the location and filename for the HTML document from the Publish As dialog box that appears. Then click OK.**

10. **Click Publish.**

After grinding and churning for a moment, Excel successfully completes its work, and you have a Web page ready to be included in your Web site.

Inserting worksheet data into an existing document

When you publish an Excel worksheet as a Web page, Excel creates a new HTML file that contains the spreadsheet and nothing else. Using another method, however, you can insert Excel worksheet data into the middle of an existing HTML document.

To insert your Excel worksheet data into an existing HTML document, follow these steps:

1. **Use an HTML editor to insert the following line at the location where you want the worksheet data to be inserted:**

   ```
   <!--##Table##-->
   ```

   For example, here is a complete HTML document that includes some text, followed by a placeholder for an Excel table, followed by some more text:

   ```
   <HTML>
   <BODY>
   <H1>Here is the Excel data:<H1>
   <!--##Table##-->
   <H1>This is after the Excel data</H1>
   </BODY>
   </HTML>
   ```

2. **Save the HTML file; then close it and exit the HTML editor.**

3. **In Excel, open the worksheet that contains the data that you want inserted into the Web document and highlight the data that you want to publish; then choose File⇨Save As Web Page.**

   The Save As dialog box appears.

4. **Click the Publish button.**

   The Publish As Web Page dialog box appears. The data you selected in Step 3 appears in the Choose text box.

5. **In the File Name text box, type the path and name of the HTML document that you modified and saved in Steps 1 and 2 (or use the Browse button to locate the file).**

6. **To view the Web page in your browser after you publish it, select the Open Published Web Page in Browser check box.**

7. **Click the Publish button; then click the Add to File button.**

The page displays in your browser, and the Excel table appears in the location you specified with the `<!--##Table##-->` statement in the HTML file. Figure 8-3 shows the result of these steps.

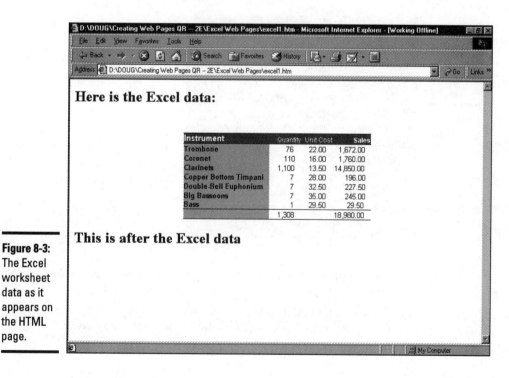

Figure 8-3:
The Excel worksheet data as it appears on the HTML page.

If you use FrontPage to create your Web pages, you can use FrontPage's Insert⇨File command to insert an Excel worksheet into your Web page.

PowerPoint 2002

PowerPoint 2002 includes a Save As Web Page command that publishes your presentation in a format that can be viewed on the Web. PowerPoint uses frames to display the presentation's outline on the left edge of the browser window and the current slide on the right. Navigation buttons appear at the bottom of the browser window.

To publish a presentation to the Web, follow these steps:

1. In PowerPoint, open the presentation you want to publish to the Web; then choose File⇨Save As Web Page.

The Save As dialog box appears.

2. Click Publish.

The Publish As Web Page dialog box opens, as shown in Figure 8-4.

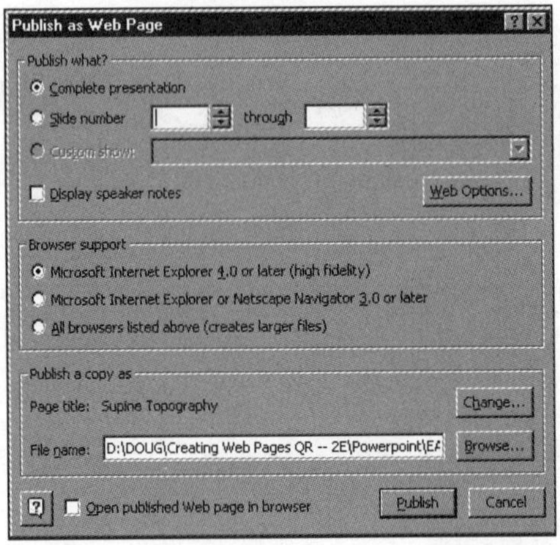

Figure 8-4: Specify the options that you want for your published presentation.

3. Choose whether you want to publish the entire presentation or just a range of slides.

4. (Optional) Check the Display Speaker Notes check box if you want your speaker notes to be published along with the slides.

5. **Click Browse; navigate your way to the location where you want your presentation to be published, and click OK.**

6. **Click Publish.**

PowerPoint saves your presentation as a series of HTML and graphics files in a separate folder created just for your presentation.

 Previous versions of PowerPoint saved each slide as a huge GIF or JPEG image file, resulting in presentations that were painstakingly slow to download. Not so with PowerPoint 2000 and 2002. The Save As Web Page command creates HTML documents that can be efficiently viewed over the Web.

Access 2002

Access 2002 includes many features for accessing database data from the Web. The following sections explain how to use two of the most useful Web publishing techniques: converting an Access database report to an HTML document, and using the Page Wizard to convert an Access database to Web format.

Converting an Access report to HTML

The easiest way to make database information available on your Web site is to convert your Access 2002 report to an HTML file.

To convert an existing Access 2002 report to HTML, follow these steps:

1. **Create an Access 2002 report that includes the information you want to make available on your Web site.**

2. **In the database window (the window that lists all the objects in a database), click Reports in the Objects list and select the report that you want to convert to HTML format.**

3. **Choose File⇨Export.**

   The Export Report dialog box appears.

4. **In the Save As Type drop-down list box, choose HTML Documents.**

5. **In the Save In drop-down list box, choose the drive and folder where you want to save the HTML document.**

6. **In the File Name text box, type the filename that you want to use for the HTML document.**

7. **Select the Autostart option.**

This option will automatically run your Web browser and display the saved HTML document.

8. **Click Save.**

The HTML Output Options dialog box appears. This dialog box asks if you want to use an HTML template file, which is a special file you can create to govern the layout of the HTML document. If you want to use a template file, consult Access 2002 Help for more information.

9. **Click OK.**

Access 2002 exports each page of the report to an HTML document. If the report is large, this process can take a while.

After Access 2002 finishes converting the report to HTML format, your Web browser fires up to display the converted report. Each page of the report is saved as a separate HTML document, with links at the bottom of each page to the First, Previous, Next, and Last pages of the report.

The filename for the first page of the HTML report document is the name you specified in Step 6. For additional report pages, Access 2002 simply adds the page number to the end of the name. For example, if the first page of the report is `Report.html`, the second page is `ReportPage2.html`, the third page is `ReportPage3.html`, and so on.

Data access pages

Access 2002 introduces a new type of database object, called a *data access page*, which lets you create Web pages that can be used to access the information in an Access database. Each data access page is actually a separate HTML document that includes the necessary scripts and other goodies to provide a connection to your Access database.

Access 2002 comes with a Page Wizard that can create a basic data access page for you. The Page Wizard can create two types of data access pages:

✦ **Data-entry pages** work much like an Access form, enabling you to view database records one at a time and enter new records.

✦ **Report pages** work like Access reports, enabling you to view database records sorted and grouped however you wish.

To create a data access page using the Page Wizard, follow these steps:

1. **Choose File⇨Open.**

The Open dialog box appears.

2. **Open the database for which you want to create a data access page.**

3. **In the database window, click Pages in the Objects list.**

4. **Double-click Create Data Access Page by Using Wizard to start the Page Wizard.**

   The Page Wizard dialog box appears, as shown in Figure 8-5.

Book VI
Chapter 8

Creating Web Pages with Microsoft Office XP

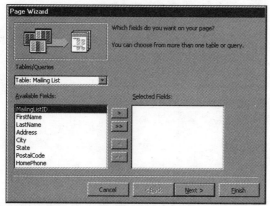

Figure 8-5:
The Page Wizard walks you through the steps for creating a data access page.

5. **From the Tables/Queries drop-down list box, select the table or query on which you want to base the page.**

6. **In the Available Fields list, click to select each field that you want to include on the page, followed by the > button.**

   To quickly add all of the table or query fields to the page, click >.

7. **Click Next.**

8. **If you want to create a report page, decide which field you want to group your report by and select that field in the list box; then click >.**

   To create a data entry page, do not choose a grouping field.

9. **Click Next to proceed to the next page.**

10. **If you want the data to be sorted, use the drop-down list boxes to choose the fields by which to sort the data.**

11. **Click Next.**

12. **Type a suitable name for your data access page in the text box.**

13. **Click Finish.**

   Access grinds and whirs a moment, and then displays your new data access page in Design view, as shown in Figure 8-6.

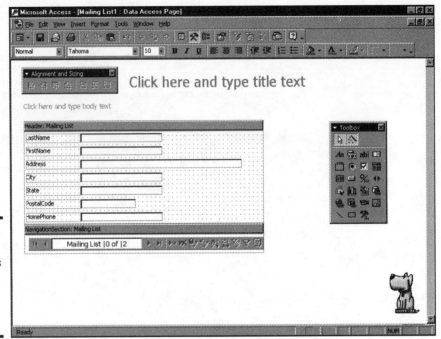

Figure 8-6:
The new
data access
page, as it
appears in
Design
view.

14. Make changes to the page design, if necessary.

At the minimum, you'll want to type a decent title and body text for the page (just click the "Click here . . ." placeholder text and start typing). You may also want to change the field names.

15. Click the Close button at the top-right corner of the Design window to close the page. When Access asks if you want to save your design changes, respond Yes.

You're done! Note that in order to access a data access page from the Web, you need to store the data access page on a Web server. You don't, however, have to store the data access page on the same server as the database itself.

Index

Book VII

America Online

©RICHTENNANT

"...so if you have a message for someone, you write it on a piece of paper and put it on their refrigerator with these magnets. It's just until we get our e-mail system fixed."

Contents at a Glance

Chapter 1: Getting Started with America Online

In This Chapter

✔ Getting into the system and starting the software

✔ Setting and maintaining your password

✔ Finding your way through the menus and toolbars

✔ Understanding screen names

✔ Setting the America Online preferences

✔ Getting help and using Parental Controls

✔ Getting offline and closing AOL

This chapter is your pre-online checklist of the basics you need to know to get into (and out of) America Online Version 7.0. Your new America Online account works pretty well right from the start, but with a few tweaks here and there, it becomes a high-performance technology machine. From account preferences to custom news wires, this chapter also explores the available tools and services that you can use to make America Online uniquely yours.

Starting AOL and Signing On

If you haven't installed the America Online software yet, insert the CD-ROM that came with your AOL information packet into the CD-ROM drive. (You can also download the software from AOL's Web site at www.aol.com.) Follow the installation instructions that appear on-screen and enter the registration number and password (also from your packet) when AOL prompts you to do so. During installation, AOL asks you to choose your own screen name and password — follow the guidelines provided. You'll use this screen name and password each time you log on to AOL. When you've finished installing and registering the software, AOL displays help information to get you started with the program. When you're done using AOL, you sign off and exit the program (see "Signing Off and Exiting AOL" later in this chapter for more information).

Because you can't step into AOL's cyberworld without your America Online software, running the program and signing on is the first order of business. Follow these steps:

1. **If you have an external modem (or a PC Card modem in a laptop), turn it on and do whatever else is necessary to get the modem ready.**

2. **Find the America Online icon and double-click it to start the software.**

   The icon is usually on your desktop or inside an area called America Online 7.0. At this point, you're ready to sign on to America Online. The Sign On dialog box appears, as shown in Figure 1-1

Figure 1-1: Before you can begin using AOL, you must sign on.

3. **If you have more than one screen name, pick the screen name you want to use this time. Click the down arrow in the Select Screen Name box, and then click a screen name.**

4. **Press Tab to move the cursor into the Password box, and then carefully type your password.**

   If you're accessing America Online from your home computer, continue to Step 5. If you want to connect to the service from some other location, select that location from the Select Location box.

5. **Take a moment to make sure that your modem is turned on and nobody else in the family is using the phone line. When you're ready, press Enter or click Sign On.**

   A series of cool graphics shows your progress toward a finished connection. America Online may also have a few commercials for you; click Cancel if you just want to get on with the show. When the Welcome screen appears (see Figure 1-2), you're ready to use America Online.

Every now and then, your connection attempt doesn't quite go through. When that happens, click Cancel and try again. If the connection still doesn't work, wait a few minutes and then give it one more attempt before you seek help from the America Online toll-free support line (800-827-6364).

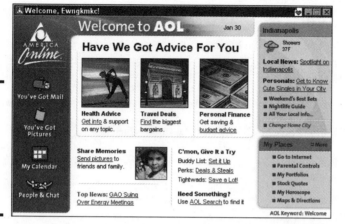

Figure 1-2:
The AOL
Welcome
screen
greets you
after a
successful
logon.

**Book VII
Chapter 1**

**Getting Started with
America Online**

Discovering how AOL works

The online world sounds pretty cool, but how does it work? What's happening behind the scenes? Good questions. Basically, America Online's corner of the online world involves your computer, a couple of modems, the local phone company, a national communications system, and a bunch of computers in Dulles, Virginia. Here are the details:

1. Your computer, with the help of the America Online special software, tells your modem to dial an access phone number. Thanks to a large communications network, America Online access numbers are local calls for more than 80 percent of the country's population.

2. A modem in the America Online communication system answers the call and, if you have a dial-up connection, begins an entertaining round of *I can whistle more obnoxiously than you* with your modem. In just a moment, the modems agree on such things as communication speed, error correction, and other details. The technowizards call this step *feature negotiation*.

3. After the modems settle into a nice conversation, your software tells the communications system to build a link to America Online. In a few seconds, the America Online computers in Dulles, Virginia, respond to your call.

4. Your America Online software tells the master computers in Dulles who's calling (your screen name) and then passes along your password (to prove that it's really you who is calling). If you misspelled your password, America Online asks you to try again.

5. The Welcome window pops onto the screen, ushering you into America Online.

Sometimes, either your modem or the America Online modem gets confused and stops talking. This situation doesn't happen often, but when it does, it's frustrating. The common symptoms include a message saying `A request to the host has taken longer than expected` — or perhaps a single, terse `Lost carrier` message that arrives just after your computer signs itself off the system.

Changing Your Password

Your password is the key to your account. To keep your account safe, change the password every month or so. Pick a password that's hard for other people to guess. For example, try making your password from two unrelated words and a number. Things like `coincard3`, `cow8box`, and `clock4pad` may look silly, but they're examples of good passwords.

To change your password, follow these steps:

1. Press Ctrl+K, type the keyword Password **in the text box, and then press Enter.**

See Book VII, Chapter 2, for information on using keywords.

2. Click Change Password.

3. Type your current password into the Current Password box, and then press Tab.

The password appears as asterisks on-screen.

4. Carefully type your new password into the two boxes at the bottom of the screen.

Capitalization doesn't matter, but spelling does.

5. When you finish, click Change Password.

If the two new password entries match, AOL changes your password. If they don't match, AOL asks you to try again.

Understanding the AOL Interface

Before diving into your AOL session, you should familiarize yourself with the elements of the interface. In this section, you find out about AOL's menus, the toolbar, and the navigation bar.

Menus

The *menu bar* decorates the top of your America Online window. The menu bar is your main tool for controlling the software and communicating your desires to America Online itself. Table 1-1 describes the menu bar choices.

Table 1-1	Menus Available on the AOL Menu Bar
Menu	*Description*
File	Deals with printing, saving, and using online information, text, and graphics files on your computer. This menu also covers the Filing Cabinet.

Menu	Description
Edit	Includes the ever-popular text-editing commands, plus a Capture Picture command. Whether you need to check spelling or have a quick glance at a dictionary or thesaurus, you find those options listed here.
Print	Control your printer and its setup from this menu.
Window	Focuses on window management and offers an option that adds the top window to your Favorite Places list. This menu's most important (and arguably coolest) feature is the list of open windows that fills the bottom of the menu.
Sign Off	Switches between your account's screen names. This menu item also lets you exit the program when you finish playing online.
Help	Comes in handy when you have a general America Online question (or want handy reading material to overcome a bout of insomnia). Get comfy and click AOL Help.

Toolbar buttons

Although the toolbar buttons do add a dash of color to an otherwise utilitarian screen, their main goal is to make your online life easier. The toolbar buttons function in two ways. Buttons *without* a downward-pointing triangle provide a shortcut to either an America Online command, such as Write, or an online area, such as Quotes. Buttons that do sport such triangles reveal a pull-down menu when you click them; they function much like the menu bar items mentioned in the "Menus" section. Use the toolbar buttons to save time and frustration. Table 1-2 provides a description of the buttons on the AOL toolbar.

**Book VII
Chapter 1**

Getting Started with America Online

My AOL

As part of their ongoing effort to make life easier, the America Online programmers created My AOL. This feature ties several customizable areas together into a single dialog box. To get into My AOL, click the arrow next to the Settings tab and then choose My AOL. Of course, keyword **My AOL** works just fine, too.

My AOL is organized around five main areas:

✔ **Daily:** Explore My News, My Calendar, My Portfolios, Favorite Places, and My Places.

✔ **Interests:** Look at News Profiles, Interest Profiles, the Reminder Service, Portfolio Direct, and Newsletters.

✔ **Controls:** Set Preferences and alter screen names, passwords, Mail Controls, and Parental Controls.

✔ **People:** Try out features such as My Pictures, Member Profile, My Home Page, Buddy List, and the Address Book.

✔ **Services:** Access the Billing Center, Quick Checkout, Banking Center, Brokerage Center, and Phone Services.

For new members, My AOL is a great starting point for learning about the system. More advanced members may discover some new features or get reacquainted with old favorites they haven't used in a while.

Table 1-2	AOL Toolbar Buttons	
Button	*Name*	*Description*
Mail ▼	Mail	Use this drop-down menu to look at e-mail you've sent, change e-mail preferences, create a signature file for your e-mail messages, run Automatic AOL, or open your online Address Book. (Some portions of the Mail Center are available offline.)
Read	Read	Open a window full of your incoming mail.
Write	Write	Write a new e-mail message. (This option is available offline.)
People ▼	People	Chat, talk, giggle, and laugh in a chat room, or locate other members online.
IM	IM	Send an instant message to a friend.
Chat	Chat	Chat with a friend.
Services ▼	Services	Find what you want quickly. Shop AOL or find information on a favorite topic, such as car buying or movie showtimes.
Shop	Shop	Click this button to start shopping immediately.
Internet	Internet	Surf the Internet's worldwide information network: Explore newsgroups, search the Web, or jump quickly to the online White Pages or the Yellow Pages.
Settings ▼	Settings	Make AOL your own with this drop-down menu. Change your preferences, create or delete screen names or passwords, set Parental Controls, or design news profiles (see the sidebar nearby). With News Profiles, AOL drops interesting news stories directly into your e-mail box. (Some selections are available offline.)
? AOL Help	AOL Help	Opens the Help window.

Button	Name	Description
Favorites ▼	Favorites	In this area, you can open the Favorite Places window (although click the next button is faster), as well as access hotkeys and keywords.
💟 My Favorites	My Favorites	Open the Favorite Places window, edit shortcut keys to your favorite AOL areas, open the Keyword window, or visit some of the general top areas online. (Some selections are available offline.)
Calendar	Calendar	Schedule outings and appointments with friends, keep your finger on the pulse of upcoming events, and remind yourself of the special days in your life with the AOL Calendar. (You may not see this button if your screen resolution is set at less than 800 x 600.)
Radio	Radio	Listen to news, sports, and radio music.
$ Quotes	Quotes	Track (and potentially cry over) your favorite stocks.

Book VII
Chapter 1

Getting Started with
America Online

Navigation bar

Nestled right under the toolbar resides a thin bar with two text fields in it. This navigation bar (shown in Figure 1-3) helps you navigate the online service and the Internet in one fell swoop. After you figure out how to use it, you'll never want to see the Keyword window again.

Figure 1-3: The navigation bar appears just below the toolbar.

Navigator bar

Table 1-3 describes the items on the navigation bar.

Table 1-3	Items Available on the AOL Navigation Bar	
Tool	*Name*	*Description*
[BACK]	Back	Look at the last window you saw. Keep clicking it to go backward one window at a time.
[FORWARD]	Forward	Go forward through the windows you've already opened online.
[STOP]	Stop	Stop your Web browser from loading the current page.
[RELOAD]	Reload	Reload the current Web page to update what you see.
Type Keywords or Web Addresses here	Address box	Enter a keyword or URL to view that area or Internet site.
[▼]	Arrow	See the online areas or Web pages you already viewed during this online session.
[Go]	Go	Go to the area or Internet site high-lighted in the address box.
[Search]	Search	Fire up the system-wide Search service and go looking for stuff.
[Hide Channels]	Hide Channels	Hides the channels on the left.
[Keyword]	Keyword	Opens the Keyword window so that you can enter key-words directly into the Keyword window rather than using the address box on the navigation bar.

Using Screen Names

Part of the fun on America Online is creating cool screen names that contribute to your online identity. Many people use more than one screen name, often using one for work and another for play. If your kids are online and you want to use the Parental Controls to limit their activities, the kids need individual screen names, too.

Each account has space for a primary screen name (the name you create when you sign up for America Online) and up to six secondary names. America Online allows you to create more than one master screen name for an account, in case you have more than one adult in a household. Your primary screen name automatically classifies as a master screen name. All master screen names have the capability to change America Online billing options and set Parental Controls for all the other screen names on the account. If you already have seven screen names in the account, you can't make a new one until you delete an old one.

Creating a screen name

To create a screen name, follow these steps:

1. **Before signing on to America Online, think up a few possible screen names and write them down.**

   That way, if someone else snarfed the name you wanted, you won't waste online time trying to think up another, equally cool name to replace it.

2. **Sign on to the system with a master screen name.**

   Only a user bearing the master screen name can create new screen names.

3. **Press Ctrl+K, type the keyword** Screen Names, **and press Enter.**

   The Screen Names dialog box appears.

4. **Click Create a Screen Name.**

   The Create a Screen Name dialog box appears, asking whether you're creating this name for a child.

5. **Click No to continue.**

   The Create a Screen Name dialog box appears.

6. **Click Create Screen Name.**

7. **Carefully type the screen name you want in the box at the bottom of the screen.**

8. **Double-check the spelling; then click the Continue button.**

   If the name is available, congratulations! The Choose a Password dialog box pops up to announce your success. On the other hand, if someone else already has that screen name, AOL informs you that the specific name is already in use. Whip out that list of backup names and keep trying until something works.

   If nothing you come up with is available, try asking AOL to suggest a name. Simply select this option, type three words you'd like it to use, and click OK. Who knows? You might like one of the suggestions. (Or you may be too tired of coming up with backup names to say no.)

9. **Type a password for the new screen name, press Tab, and type it again.**

10. **Click the Continue button.**

    If you typed the same password in both boxes, AOL congratulates you by presenting yet another dialog box. If you mistyped one of the pass-words, AOL asks you to try doing the password thing one more time.

11. **Select the age range of the screen name's owner, and America Online automatically installs its Parental Controls on that screen name. Click the Continue button.**

    If you select 18+ as the age range for the new screen name, AOL asks whether you want the new screen name to function as a master screen name, complete with the power to change billing options and set Parental Controls for all other screen names on the account. If you don't want the new screen name holder to exercise that much freedom, select No. (See "Parental Controls" later in this chapter.)

12. **Select Yes or No and then click Continue.**

13. **A final Confirm Your Settings dialog box appears, listing your new screen name and the access features that go along with the age range you selected. If everything looks okay to you, click Accept Settings to accept the settings and create your new screen name.**

    America Online then creates the screen name and adds it to your access software. It appears in the AOL Screen Names window, taking its place as the last created name in the Your Current Screen Names list. Congratulations — you're now the owner of a new, unique AOL screen name.

Deleting a screen name

When the time comes to bid a fond farewell to a screen name, don't get too sentimental — just delete the little fellow. You can delete any of the six secondary screen names on your account. However, you can't delete the primary screen name (you're stuck with that one).

1. **Sign on to AOL with the master screen name.**

Only a user bearing the master screen name can delete another screen name.

2. **Press Ctrl+K, type the keyword** Screen Names, **and press Enter.**

The Screen Names dialog box hops into action.

3. **Click Delete a Screen Name; then click Continue in the Are You Sure? dialog box.**

The Delete dialog box takes the stage, displaying only your account's secondary screen names. (*Remember:* You can't delete the primary screen name.)

4. **Click the screen name you want to delete; then click Delete.**

After a moment, a dialog box pops up and announces the screen name's demise.

Restoring a screen name

You deleted a favorite screen name by mistake, and five minutes later, you decide you want it back. Not so long ago, you were out of luck. However, America Online now provides a way to reactivate those hasty (or erroneous) screen name deletions. You can recover your screen name for up to six months after you delete it.

1. **Sign on to AOL with the master screen name.**

2. **Press Ctrl+K, type the keyword** Screen Names, **and press Enter.**

3. **Click Restore a Screen Name.**

If you recently deleted one or more screen names from your account, the Recover Previous Screen Name window hops onto the screen, helpfully listing the deleted screen names.

4. **Highlight the screen name you want to recover and click Recover.**

The system reinstates your screen name and updates your screen name list.

Changing Your Preferences

The preferences settings fine-tune your America Online experience. Almost every aspect of online life includes some preferences settings. Whether you want to make file copies of e-mail messages automatically, turn off the system sound effects, or manage the Filing Cabinet, the preferences settings cover your needs.

**Book VII
Chapter 1**

Getting Started with
America Online

To change your preferences settings, choose Settings⇨Preferences from the toolbar. When the Preferences window appears, click the link of the item you want to change. The following sections cover the options that appear in the Preferences window, as shown in Figure 1-4.

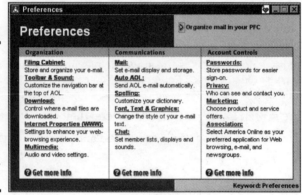

Figure 1-4:
This window is a handy place to set all your preferences for your AOL account.

You don't need to sign on to America Online to use the Preferences window — it's always available.

Association

You can use Association to select America Online as your default application for Internet access. Selecting AOL as your Internet application can save you a lot of frustration if AOL is the only Internet service you use. Then, when you click a link in a document and you're not currently online, instead of watching Microsoft Internet Explorer open and then tell you it can't reach the Internet, you watch AOL open and load the Web site.

Auto AOL

Auto AOL is short for Automatic AOL. Auto AOL enables you to download new e-mail messages onto your computer, send e-mail you've written offline, or get and send any new newsgroup postings that wait for your attention.

You probably want to set your Auto AOL preferences so that AOL sends mail and gets unread mail. We generally leave the Download Files option unchecked, and download each attached file by hand as we need it. That way, we don't mistakenly download and open a hacker's contribution to our hard drives.

Chat

Chat options control the chat room window itself. They change the way you see all chat rooms on the whole system. The most useful settings here are Alphabetize the Member List (turn this option on — it simplifies your life) and Enable Chat Room Sounds (turn this option off when someone won't stop playing sounds).

Download

Downloading cool stuff from the file libraries makes life worth living. To make downloading even easier, turn on Automatically Decompress Zip Files When I Sign Off. This choice automatically expands Zip files after you sign off — it's pretty cool stuff.

Two options to turn off are Delete Zip Files After They Are Decompressed and Confirm When I Add Files to My Download List. If you want downloads to go to a specific place (other than the regular AOL Download folder), this window is where you change the download destination directory.

Filing Cabinet

The most useful preferences in this tab are the *retain* options: Retain All Mail I Read in My Personal Filing Cabinet and Retain All Mail I Send in My Personal Filing Cabinet. If you do business through America Online e-mail, turn these options on — no doubt about it. A copy of every message you send or receive automatically lands in your Filing Cabinet on your computer's hard drive, in the cleverly named Incoming/Saved Mail and Mail You've Sent folders.

Two other options are also worth mentioning: Confirm Before Deleting Single Items and Confirm Before Deleting Multiple Items. If you're confident of your editing skills, turn these options off and save some time. On the other hand, if your life includes small children ("What does the Del key do, Dad?"), leave these options turned on to protect your carefully filed Information.

Font, Text & Graphics

Font preferences give you the flexibility to change the fonts you see in chat rooms, e-mail, and instant messages. Be aware, however, that America Online has gone to great lengths to use fonts that are readable. If you choose some esoteric font for your chat rooms, reading the text may become more of a challenge — but hey, that's half the fun!

If you have trouble reading the text in chat rooms or online articles, consider adjusting the Text Size option in the Font, Text & Graphics Preferences window.

Another useful item in this window is Maximum Disk Space to Use for Online Art. If you're low on drive space, try reducing this setting to 10MB. (Getting a bigger hard drive would be a *really* good idea, though.)

If you open and close several windows while you're online, you may come close to the maximum space amount you set. When that happens, every window you attempt to open brings a warning dialog box explaining that a graphic on the window can't be displayed due to low memory. Don't panic or run out to purchase a new hard drive — simply return to the Graphics window and increase the Maximum Disk Space to Use for Online Art. Poof! No more annoying dialog boxes.

Internet Properties (WWW)

The Web settings resemble a cross between a 747 cockpit and the control room of your local nuclear power plant. When you tweak the Windows Web preferences, you're actually altering the Microsoft Internet Explorer settings.

Depending on your level of comfort with complexity, you may want to change several settings in the AOL Internet Options window. Any alterations here actually change the Microsoft Internet Explorer settings, rather than the America Online software itself. Use the tabs at the top of the window to flip among the setting topics. Look under the General tab to customize link colors and specify the Web page that you want to use as your home page. This tab also lets you clear the History folder — the list of Web page links you've visited. If you surf the Web often, you'll want to click Clear History every now and then to empty the folder. The Security tab, Privacy tab, and Content tab let you set Internet safety preferences. The default setting for general Internet surfing is set at medium; with a medium setting, the software gives you a warning dialog box when you attempt to download files from Web sites. You also can include specific Web sites as Trusted Sites or Restricted Sites by clicking the corresponding icon and then entering the site's Web address in the dialog box that appears. (We recommend that you take the easy way out and set Web preferences in the AOL Parental Controls if you want to shield the kids from harmful content.)

Web Graphics is another important tab in the Windows AOL Internet Options window. Inside, you find one lonely option that offers to Compress Web Graphics as they load. We leave that one marked. It trims a little delay off the World Wide Wait.

Finally, on the Shopping Assistant tab, you can indicate whether you'd like the Shopping Assistant to appear.

Mail

This area is now divided into three sections: Reading Mail, Writing Mail, and Sending Mail. You can choose the options you want for each section, such as showing addresses as Buddy Info links, using your Address Book to auto-suggest e-mail addresses, and performing a spell check before sending mail.

On a related note, we recommend turning off Confirm That Mail Has Been Sent. If you send more than two e-mail messages each month, this option gets very old very fast.

On the left side of the window, you see Keep My Old Mail Online X Days After I Read It. The default is set to three days; we recommend setting it to seven days, which is as high as the setting goes. The system zaps read e-mail messages by the send date rather than the first-read date, so if you read a message that arrived in your box four days ago and then want to reread it from your Read Mail list the next morning, that message will be history unless you increase the number of days the system keeps your old mail.

Marketing

Call us hermits-in-the-making, but we're burned out on junk mail and *have we got an offer for you* phone calls. If you're like us, then run — don't walk — to the Marketing Preferences window. Here is your chance to strike a blow for empty mailboxes and quiet phone lines.

In addition to the Marketing option in the Preferences window, you can find the Marketing Preferences window at keyword **Marketing Prefs**. In the Marketing Preferences window, click the button next to your pet peeve. Your choices are U.S. Mail from Other Organizations, U.S. Mail from AOL, Telephone, E-Mail, Pop-Up, and Additional Information. *Pop-up* is America Online's term for those advertising dialog boxes that appear occasionally when you sign on to the system. When you select a topic, a brief dialog box appears that explains why this particular type of junk mail is desirable. Click Continue and then choose either Yes I Do Want . . . or No I Don't. Then click OK to make it so.

Two other options deserve a quick mention as tools of a dedicated anti-annoyance crusader. Take a look at the Direct Marketing Association Mail Preference Service and Telephone Preference Service choices for details on how to truly remove yourself (at least temporarily) from the world of junk communications. You can find addresses for both these organizations under the Additional Information button.

**Book VII
Chapter 1**

Getting Started with America Online

Multimedia

This tab contains two sections: Player preferences and Accessibility preferences. In the former, you only need to decide whether you want to use AOL Media Player for supported types and as your default CD player. In the latter section, your only option is whether you want to display captions when available.

Passwords

If you're tired of typing a screen name and password every time you sign on to America Online, use this preference setting to fix the problem once and for all. Type the password next to its associated screen name, and America Online won't ever ask you about it again. Unfortunately, anyone who wanders by your computer can then sign on to your account without knowing the password, so use this option only if your computer is in a secure area.

Privacy

Decide who you want to be able to contact you and make your preferences known in the Privacy Preferences window. By default, the preference is set to allow all AOL members and Instant Messenger users to see you on their Buddy Lists and send you instant messages. If you want to exclude a few select people or you want to welcome only a designated group of screen names into your online world, you can do that, too. (You can also get to this window by clicking Setup in your Buddy List window and then clicking Preferences. Open the window with keyword **Buddy**.)

Spelling

The Spelling Preferences dialog box enables you to set your America Online software to capitalize the first word in a sentence, notify you if you type the same word twice, and choose a preferred dictionary (instead of the default AOL U.S. English dictionary) for spell checking. Click the Advanced button to see additional settings. All spelling preferences are turned on; if you really know your grammar and want a challenge, turn off any of them. Otherwise, leave them on — you now have one less thing to worry about.

Toolbar & Sound

With Toolbar & Sound preferences, you can change how the toolbar looks (icons and text or text only) and where it appears (at the top or bottom of your screen). One of its most useful features is that you can set the preferences to clear your history trail each time you sign off the system. Doing so deletes that long list of windows you opened while online — which America Online diligently keeps track of, in case you want to return to a window you saw yesterday (or even last week). Check Clear History After Each Sign Off or Switch Screen Name if you want the software to clean the slate each time you leave. To delete the list yourself, click the Clear History Now button, and then click Yes when it asks whether you really want to erase your trail.

You also have one lone sound option you can set. If you enjoy the AOL sounds you hear when you log on and when instant messages arrive, leave the option checked. If not, make sure that you remove the check mark.

Getting Help

Although the online world is a great deal of fun, it also provides more than a few confusing moments. That's why America Online offers many places to turn for help and consolation in your time of trouble. Most Help options listed here are free of connect charges if you subscribe to an hourly usage plan.

Member Services area

America Online provides free help to members in the AOL Help area (keyword **Help**). If you have questions about online accounts, billing, or America Online itself, you can find answers in AOL Help (see Figure 1-5). Plus, you can find information on everything from downloads to chat areas and from online safety to the Internet. Free of connect time charges, this area offers members information about AOL by giving you the following options:

✦ Under the Get Help With heading, choose any of the links to open a window filled with articles about the corresponding topic or, depending on the subject, another window that provides more choices. Sooner or later, you reach a window with article listings.

✦ Type one or more words in the Search text box and then click the Search button to open a dialog box that starts a search of Member Services information. Double-click an entry to read the article.

**Book VII
Chapter 1**

**Getting Started with
America Online**

Figure 1-5:
Member
services
provides
help info on
a multitude
of topics.

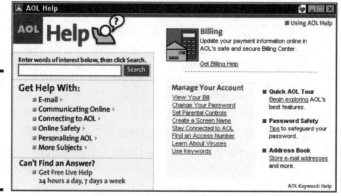

To find out about any system-wide information you should know, such as scheduled maintenance downtimes, a list of cities receiving additional capacity or access numbers, and any new phone numbers that you might need (such as the additional toll-free access number), use the keyword **AOL Update.**

Billing problems

If you need to check your current bill and find the answers to billing questions, keyword **Billing** takes you to the window shown in Figure 1-6. Time spent in this area is free of online charges.

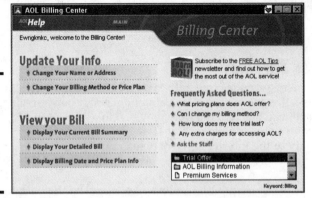

Figure 1-6: Go to the Billing area for questions about your account.

Use the Billing area to perform any of these tasks:

✦ Check your current bill summary.

✦ Change your name or address with America Online.

✦ Change your billing method and information.

✦ Read the answers to questions most often asked about America Online billing.

To request credit for a download that went awry or an evening when the America Online computers didn't feel like talking to you, type the keyword **Credit**. Only members who use America Online's measured service would ever need to use the Credit window.

Free help from other members

Who knows America Online better than your fellow members? Nobody! Some of the best help on the whole system is available from other people, like yourself, in the Members Helping Members area. This area is only a key-word away — and it won't cost you a penny to access it.

Follow these steps to browse the Members Helping Members message board for answers to questions on billing, e-mail, uploading files, and more:

1. **Press Ctrl+K, type the keyword** MHM, **and press Enter.**

The Members Helping Members window opens.

2. **Click the Message Boards.**

The Members Helping Members message board opens.

You also can get help with your computer and America Online through the Computing channel's Get Help Now window. Here you can link to nightly Help Desk chats, where live volunteers answer your computer questions. Open any folder or document you find here to learn about everything from creating a new folder in Windows to online safety and security. Use keyword **Get Help Now** to open the window.

Insider Tips window

Turn to the AOL Insider Tips window (keyword **AOL Insider**) for tips on viruses, ideas for fun and useful areas online, suggestions for making your AOL experience faster, and tips on using AOL like a pro. Whether you're a beginner or a veteran at AOL, you find some good information here (see Figure 1-7). You also have the option to sign up to receive free AOL tips through e-mail.

Use the folders in the item list to read tips organized by subject. Here you find the goodies on navigating the system and enhancing your time on AOL.

Book VII
Chapter 1

Getting Started with America Online

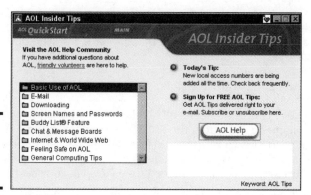

Figure 1-7:
The AOL
Insider Tips
window.

Calling America Online for help

Most of the time, you can find help about America Online while connected to the service. Once in a while, though, connecting to AOL is the problem. In that case, you need some human help. Talk to a technical support staff member live at 800-827-3338. If possible, be near the computer when you call because the technician may need to know some specific info about your computer.

Here are the toll-free numbers you need to contact America Online:

 ✦ For technical help (Windows), call 888-346-3704.

 ✦ For technical help (Mac), call 888-265-8007.

 ✦ For screen name or password problems, call 888-265-8004.

 ✦ For information about access numbers, call 888-265-8005.

 ✦ For billing inquires, use 888-265-8003.

 ✦ To cancel your account, call 888-265-8008.

 ✦ TTY users call 800-759-3323.

Parental Controls

Just as you wouldn't send a child into the bad parts of the city (or into the mall alone with your charge card), you don't necessarily want little eyes to command full access to America Online and the Internet. That's where the Parental Controls come in. The Parental Controls are your tools for steering and blocking an impressionable child's access to online content.

Keeping kids safe today is tougher than ever before, particularly when the kids have online access. That's why America Online created the Parental Controls. These tools help parents delimit simple, enforceable boundaries in the freewheeling cyberworld. (See Book I, Chapter 3, for more on Internet safety and security issues; see Book IX, Chapter 6, for a list of recommended Web sites for kids.)

Three levels of control are available:

 ✦ **Kids Only:** This one-size-fits-all blanket restriction limits your child's screen name to content in the Kids Only channel within America Online, as well as to Kids Only-approved Internet sites. Child Access accounts have no access to America Online's premium games — the games you pay extra to play. For kids under 12, this level is your best option.

 ✦ **Young Teen:** Older children (those in the 13-through-15 age group) need a bit more flexibility to explore the online environment. Young Teen access balances a child's longing for unrestrained command of the world with a parent's goal of not letting the child out of the front yard. AOL's Young Teen controls govern chat areas, download libraries, games, certain Web sites, and the Internet newsgroups.

✦ **Mature Teen:** This setting, designed for mature teens age 16 through 18, allows almost everything on the system. Certain "mature content" Web sites are blocked from these accounts, and the setting also blocks access to premium games (those games that carry a service charge).

Before applying Parental Controls, create a screen name for your child. The child should use his or her own screen name for online access.

1. **Sign on to America Online using your master screen name.**

Only someone using the master screen name has access to the Parental Controls.

2. **Use keyword** Parental Controls **or choose Settings⇨Parental Controls from the toolbar.**

The Parental Controls window appears, as shown in Figure 1-8.

3. **Click the Set Parental Controls button.**

The Set Parental Controls window hops to the screen.

4. **Use the drop-down menu to choose the screen name that's destined for the new controls.**

5. **Choose Kids Only, Young Teen, or Mature Teen, depending on the child's age or maturity.**

To paraphrase the classic warning labels, Parental Controls are not substitutes for parental supervision. We're not saying that you should hover over your children while they're online. Rather, understand how they use America Online, and look for ways to share the experience with them.

Figure 1-8:
The
Parental
Controls
window.

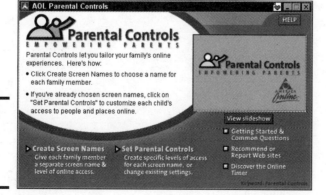

Use the Custom Controls area in the Parental Controls window to set controls on e-mail so that the kids can't send or receive pictures or files. This button also lets you limit instant messages for the child's screen name, as well as specify certain hours and set a time limit for when your child can be online.

Signing Off and Exiting AOL

When you finish visiting America Online, always remember to sign off (signing off keeps AOL from having to do it for you). After you sign off, you exit the America Online program to free up some memory in your computer for other jobs. Follow these steps:

1. **If you started either a chat log or session log, close the log file before leaving America Online. To close the log file, choose File⇨Log Manager and then click Close Log.**

2. **Choose Sign Off⇨Sign Off, and AOL signs you off.**

The Sign On box reappears with a friendly `Goodbye from America Online!` along its top bar.

3. **Choose File⇨Exit.**

The software bids you a fond farewell and closes.

Windows 95/98/XP users can sign off and shut down the software in one motion by clicking the Close box in the upper-right corner of the screen.

Chapter 2: Going Places with AOL

In This Chapter

⤺ Going places with keywords, the Channels list, and more

⤺ Remembering your Favorite Places

⤺ Customizing My Places and Hot Keys with your favorite stops

⤺ Conducting a search with AOL Search

⤺ Saving copies of stuff you find online

Wonderful gems abound on America Online, but you have to know how to find them. This chapter shows you how to locate areas and services on America Online and tells you what to do with a treasure when you find one. For example, you'll discover tools for nabbing online information and tucking it away on your hard drive or saving a copy on paper.

Navigating the Web: The Basics

AOL enables you to find places and move around the Web in a number of ways. To start off, it's helpful to know how to find online places with keywords, the Channel list, the address box, and more.

Using keywords

Many areas on America Online use their own *keywords*. Think of keywords as shortcuts through a city. Instead of navigating menus and windows, you type a word or short phrase, and the window opens.

To use a keyword, follow these steps:

1. **Press Ctrl+K, choose Favorites⇨Go To Keyword from the toolbar, or click the Keyword button on the navigation bar.**

   The Keyword window hops into action.

2. **Type the keyword into the text field.**

3. **Press Enter, or click the Go button.**

With AOL 7.0, you have yet another cool way to use keywords:

1. **Click in the address box at the top of your screen.**

2. **Type the keyword into the address box.**

3. **Click Go or press Enter.**

Most main-menu screens and many individual forums sport their own keywords. Look for keywords in the lower-right corner of the window or on the window's top blue bar. (Sometimes the information hides in another corner, but the lower-right corner is standard.) The text is small and says `Keyword:` (or `KW:`) with the specific keyword after the colon.

To get a current list of all America Online keywords, follow these steps:

1. **Press Ctrl+K, or click the Keyword button on the navigation bar.**

2. **Type** Keywords **into the text field, or click the Keyword List button.**

3. **Click the Go button.**

The Keyword: Keyword window appears, as shown in Figure 2-1.

Figure 2-1:
You can view a list of AOL's keywords alphabetically or by channel.

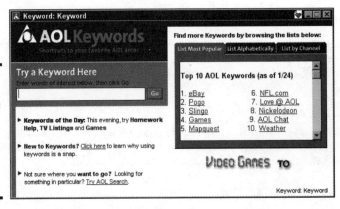

4. **Click the List By Channel tab at the top of the list box on the right side of the window.**

Finding a specific keyword is much easier when you begin with a general topic rather than trying to filter through the alphabetical-by-keyword list.

5. **Choose a channel to explore, and double-click it to see a list of that channel's available keywords.**

When America Online redesigned the keyword area, it removed the ability to download the keyword list. To get a copy for your hard drive, open each channel's window individually, highlight the text, and copy it to a new text file (using File⇨New). Then save the text file(s) under some appropriate name. Unless you're one of those "memorize the keywords in a-b-c order" people, you'll survive quite nicely by accessing the keyword list online.

Keywords change all the time as new keywords appear and nonfunctioning ones phase out. Be prepared for the system to tell you that it can't find the keyword you're looking for.

Browsing through the AOL channels

Automatically opening on the screen each time you sign on to America Online, the Channels list is your doorway to the online world. Channels cover everything in the service from sports to shopping. Click a channel's button to explore. You'll find the channel buttons arranged, in alphabetical order, down the left side of the Welcome screen, as shown in Figure 2-2.

Figure 2-2:
Entertain
yourself by
exploring
the contents
of AOL's
channels.

Book VII
Chapter 2

Going Places with AOL

Looking for an online area dedicated to women? Try the Women channel. Interested in nutrition? The Health channel provides articles, links, and other resources.

Going to a specific Web address

The America Online access software contains a powerful built-in Web browser. If you want to check out a specific site and know the site's Web address, you simply type the Web address into address box on the navigation bar at the top of your AOL screen and click Go. The Web browser appears, displaying the Web site you requested, as shown in Figure 2-3. From there, you can browse the world's Web pages with ease.

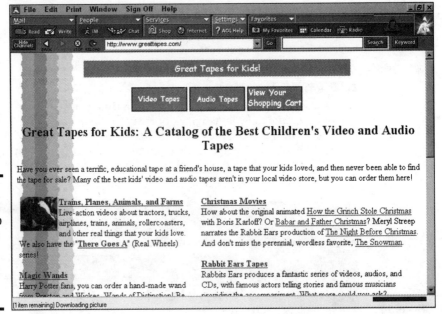

Figure 2-3:
Type a Web address into the address box to access a page on the Web.

Following links

Clicking links can be a great way to find interesting new places online. Navigating the Web by clicking links in each Web page is easy. Links usually appear as colored, underlined text or as a graphic image on a Web page. As you move the mouse pointer over a link, the arrow changes into a pointing hand, indicating that you can click that link to view that Web page or document. (See Book III, Chapter 1, for more information on Web basics.)

After you follow a series of links, you may want to return to a page you visited previously. To do so, simply click the Back button on the navigation bar. After you go back, you can go forward again by clicking the Forward button.

Remembering Your Favorite Online Spots

Returning to neat places becomes half the fun when you cruise AOL. These methods can help you to remember your favorite online spots:

+ Use the Favorite Places list.

+ Set up the My Places feature.

+ Customize the My Hot Keys list.

If you spend a great deal of time online, you may want to customize the Hot Keys list to include the places you visit each time you sign on to America Online, and reserve Favorite Places for really cool places elsewhere online or on the Web. (See "Building Your Own Hot Keys List," later in this chapter.)

Using the Favorite Places list

Favorite Places is the bookmark feature of America Online. Use it to remember an area, window, or chat room that's too good to forget. Put forums, Web pages, chat rooms, or message boards into the Favorite Places list. Any window that contains a Favorite Places icon (that white, dog-eared page with the red heart) in the upper-right corner qualifies as a potential Favorite Place.

Your software comes with several Favorite Places already installed. Open the Favorite Places window, and then double-click any folder to open it, revealing Favorite Places to explore.

Adding something to your Favorite Places list

When something is so neat that you want to remember where you saw it, add it to your Favorite Places list.

To add something to your Favorite Places list, follow these steps:

1. **While looking at an online area or Web site, fall deeply in love with it. Convince yourself that you must be able to return there at any time.**

2. **In the upper-right corner of the window, you see an icon that looks like a heart on a white sheet of paper with the edge turned down. That's the Favorite Places icon. Click it.**

A small dialog box appears, asking whether you want to save this site in your Favorite Places, insert it into an instant message, insert it into an e-mail message, or add it to the toolbar.

3. **Click the Add to Favorites button.**

The online area's address and name are now part of your Favorite Places list.

**Book VII
Chapter 2**

Going Places with AOL

Changing something in the Favorite Places list

Change is part of the online world's nature. Web page addresses change from time to time, forums reorganize, or maybe you just thought of a better name for that folder that holds the miscellaneous best of the best.

Update your Favorite Places list by modifying it:

1. **Choose Favorites⇨Favorite Places or click My Favorites.**

2. **Click the item you want to change.**

3. **Click Edit.**

   If you highlighted a Favorite Place entry, a dialog box appears that contains two text boxes (see Figure 2-4). Alter the place name, the address, or both. If you highlighted a folder, a cursor appears at the end of the highlighted folder name. Use the Backspace key to erase the part of the folder's name that you want to change.

Figure 2-4: You can edit items in your Favorite Places list.

Parenting
Enter the Place's Description:
Parenting
Enter the Internet Address:
www.parents.com
OK

4. **Make the changes to your Favorite Place and click OK. To change the folder name, simply click the folder you want to change and then click the Edit button. Type the new name and then click anywhere else.**

Going to a Favorite Place

After you've found a really cool area and placed it among your Favorite Places, you want to return to that area. Here's how:

1. **Click My Favorites.**

   The Favorite Places window opens, as shown in Figure 2-5.

2. **Double-click the Favorite place from your Favorite Places list (or highlight the place and click the Go button at the bottom of the window).**

Figure 2-5:
AOL's
Favorite
Places
window.

In AOL 7.0, your Favorite Places fall into line at the bottom of the Favorites pull-down menu. For a quick trip to one of your favorite areas, follow these simple steps:

1. **Click the Favorites toolbar button.**

2. **Click your chosen Favorite Place to open its window.**

Any folders you've created appear in the Favorites menu, too. Rest your cursor over the folder, and its contents pop up in a secondary menu for easy selection.

Organizing your Favorite Places

If the Favorite Places list becomes overwhelming, organize it by creating folders that contain *categories* of places.

1. **Choose Favorites⇨Favorite Places or click My Favorites.**

2. **Click the New button at the bottom of the Favorite Places window.**

3. **Click the New Folder option button, and enter a folder name into the text field.**

4. **Click OK.**

The folder appears at the bottom of the Favorite Places list.

5. **Click and drag Favorite Places entries to the folder and drop them in.**

Use the same technique to move the folder itself. Just click and drag it to a new location. (You can even put folders inside other folders!)

**Book VII
Chapter 2**

Going Places with AOL

Deleting items from the Favorite Places list

New things sometimes lose their charm. When a Favorite Place's luster fades, delete it. Follow these steps:

1. **Click My Favorites.**

2. **Click the Favorite Place in question to highlight it.**

3. **Click the Delete button at the bottom of the window, or press the Delete key.**

   A dialog box asks whether you're sure you want to delete the item.

4. **Click Yes to reassure AOL, and kiss that Favorite Place goodbye.**

If the item disappears without asking your permission and that bothers you, then you need to set your Filing Cabinet Preferences to confirm before it deletes single items.

Selecting My Places

Think of AOL's My Places feature as a controlled Favorite Places list. Although you can't select from every keyword on the service, My Places enables you to select from many of the most popular online areas. After you set up your individualized list, you can click one of the buttons in the My Places list to go directly to that area. Look for My Places in the Welcome screen.

You can select up to five favorite online destinations for My Places. Follow these steps to set up My Places:

1. **Click the More button next to the My Places heading at the bottom right of the Welcome screen.**

   The More window appears, containing a list of additional My Places links.

2. **Click the Change My Places button.**

   The Change My Places dialog box appears.

3. **Click the Choose New Place button next to the place you want to change and highlight a channel from the list that appears (see Figure 2-6).**

4. **Click to select an area from the channel you highlight.**

   That area takes its place in the first My Places slot.

5. **(Optional) Continue until all the slots are filled.**

Figure 2-6:
Use My
Places to
store your
favorite
online
destinations.

6. Click Save My Changes to save your changes.

A dialog box appears to tell you that AOL saved your selections.

7. Click OK to close the dialog box.

You can select each of your five favorite areas from different channels, or choose them from the same channel if you like.

Building your own Hot Keys list

If you visit a specific area on AOL so often that you feel like you live there, create a shortcut to the place by including it in your personal Hot Keys list. These items use preset keystroke commands, Ctrl+1 through Ctrl+0.

To customize your Hot Keys list, follow these steps:

1. Choose Favorites➪My Hot Keys.

2. Select Edit My Hot Keys.

The Edit My Hot Keys window opens.

3. Replace the existing Menu Entries with favorites of your own. Enter the area's keyword in the text box appearing next to the area's name (see Figure 2-7).

4. Click Save Changes.

If your hot key doesn't work, check the keyword's spelling. That's the most likely problem.

**Book VII
Chapter 2**

Going Places with AOL

Edit My Hot Keys		
Shortcut Title	Keyword/Internet Address	Key
Buddy List	Buddy View	Ctrl + 1
Chat	chat	Ctrl + 2
Calendar	Calendar	Ctrl + 3
Help	Help	Ctrl + 4
Internet	Internet	Ctrl + 5
Member Rewards	Member Rewards	Ctrl + 6
News	News	Ctrl + 7
Shopping	shopping	Ctrl + 8
Stock Quotes	Quotes	Ctrl + 9
What's New	What's New	Ctrl + 0
Save Changes	Cancel	Help

Figure 2-7: Edit the Hot Keys list to reflect the desired keywords.

Flipping between Windows

Sooner or later, the AOL windows pile up on-screen. Somewhere at the bottom lies the window you seek. To locate the lost window, either look in the Window menu or press Ctrl+Tab:

✦ Choose Window⇨# (where # is 1 through 6) to go directly to a window. If more than six windows lie open on the screen, and none of these six is the window you want, choose Window⇨More Windows.

✦ Press Ctrl+Tab to cycle through the windows one at a time. Each press of that key combination reveals another window.

Finding Almost Anything on AOL

Use the AOL Search feature to locate nearly everything on America Online — channels, window contents, Web links, the Member Directory, and more. Use the search box or click Find at the bottom of most forum windows. (If you want to search for another *person* on AOL, see Book VII, Chapter 6.)

Open the general AOL Search window and begin a search in a jiffy by typing your topic into the text box on the navigation bar and then clicking the Search button. The AOL Search engine returns a list of message boards, AOL areas, and Web sites that meet your search criteria.

Saving Something You Find Online

When you want a copy of something cool that you find online, you can print a paper copy or save an electronic copy on your computer. The following sections explain how.

Printing

Within America Online, you can print text windows and many online graphics, plus most Web pages. You can't print menu lists, though.

To print something, follow these steps:

1. Open the window that you want to print.

2. Choose Print⇨Print.

The Print dialog box appears, as shown in Figure 2-8.

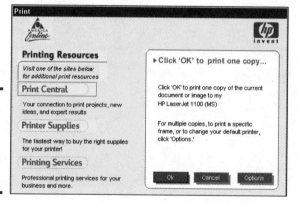

Figure 2-8:
Specify
your print
settings in
the Print
dialog box.

3. Make sure that your printer is online; then press Enter or click OK to print one copy.

If you want to print multiple copies or change your print options, click the Options button.

Unless you're in a text-only window, such as a message board posting, you may receive a surprise when you try to print from the screen. Sometimes, printing gives you the graphic; other times, you receive the text. Often (especially if the top of the window says something like Printing Graphic 1 of 2), you get both.

Saving text from a window

If a news story, information window, e-mail message, or Web site sparks your interest, you can save a copy of the item on your computer. Here's how:

1. Browse through the system until you find some text that looks interesting enough to keep.

2. **Choose File⇨Save or press Ctrl+S.**

   The Save File As dialog box pops up. Unless you specify another file location, America Online saves the file to the My Documents folder on your hard drive.

3. **Type a filename for the text file you're creating in the File Name box.**

4. **When you finish, press Enter or click Save.**

   America Online creates a file for the text and saves it on your computer.

Chapter 3: Using AOL E-Mail

In This Chapter

- ✓ Creating, formatting, and sending e-mail
- ✓ Saving money by reading and writing e-mails offline
- ✓ Addressing e-mail by using the Address Book
- ✓ Sending and receiving file attachments
- ✓ Automating AOL sessions

*W*hat would an online service be without e-mail? This chapter tells you how to send electronic mail to AOL members or to others via the Internet. We explain how you can save some connect time by using the Automatic AOL feature to retrieve your messages so that you can read them offline. You also discover how to use the You've Got Pictures feature in AOL 7.0, which enables you to receive your developed photos online and share them with others.

Creating and Sending E-Mail

Electronic mail makes the Internet go 'round. To put your two cents' worth into the process, create your own e-mail messages and send them to friends and colleagues. Although you can write messages while online, you can shorten your connection time by first writing them offline. If you're feeling creative, you can spice up your e-mail by adding formatting, such as bold-face, italics, different text and background colors, or images.

Writing an e-mail message online

Follow these steps to compose a message while online:

1. **Click the Write toolbar button (or press Ctrl+M).**

    The Write Mail window opens.

2. **Enter the recipient's e-mail address in the Send To text box on the Write Mail window (see Figure 3-1).**

    See the section "Addressing E-Mail by Using the Address Book," later in this chapter to find out how to use the Address Book to quickly insert e-mail addresses.

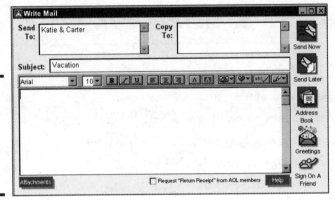

Figure 3-1:
Use the
Write Mail
window to
compose
your e-mail
message.

3. **In the Subject text box below the address, enter a few descriptive words that tell the intent of the message.**

    Keep in mind that a subject line such as Lunch Sunday tells more than Hello.

4. **Press Tab to continue and then write your message in the message text box that takes up most of the Write Mail window.**

5. **(Optional) Dress up your message with some text formatting.**

    Use the buttons at the top of the message box to apply bold, italic, and other highlights to your text. Try clicking the camera icon and inserting an image to spice up your e-mail.

    Right-click in the message text box for several new e-mail options. Use the shortcut menu that appears to insert a background picture, open and insert a saved text file, or create a hyperlink to your favorite Web site.

6. **After you finish writing the message, click the Send Now button on the right side of the Write Mail window.**

    America Online immediately sends the e-mail to its destination.

If you have second thoughts after sending a message to an America Online member, check out the "Unsending e-mail" section later in this chapter. (Also see the "Sending e-mail to an AOL member" and "Sending e-mail to someone on the Internet" sections later in this chapter for additional information on sending e-mails.)

Writing an e-mail message offline

If you use one of America Online's measured service options, writing messages offline saves money by shortening your connection time. As you compose e-mail messages offline, you can ponder word choices without watching the America Online clock tick or needing to click the Yes button in the You've Been Idle — Do You Want to Stay Online? dialog box.

To write an e-mail message offline, follow these steps:

1. **With the America Online software running but not connected by modem, click the Write button on the toolbar.**

2. **Enter the recipient's e-mail address in the Send To text box.**

   See the "Addressing E-Mail by Using the Address Book" section later in this chapter to find out how to use the Address Book to quickly insert e-mail addresses.

3. **In the Subject text box below the address, enter a few descriptive words that tell the intent of the message.**

4. **Press Tab and then write your message in the Message text box.**

5. **After the message is complete, click the Send Later button at the right side of the window.**

   A Send Later dialog box appears and tells you that the mail has been placed in the Mail Waiting to Be Sent folder of your Filing Cabinet.

6. **Click OK.**

7. **Whenever you're ready to send the message, sign on to America Online and begin an Automatic AOL session.**

   When you sign back in to AOL, a Mail Waiting to Be Sent dialog box opens and asks whether you want to Send Now, Review Mail, or Send Later.

8. **Click Send Now.**

   Your message is sent.

See the sections "Automating Your AOL Sessions," later in this chapter, and "Writing an e-mail message online," earlier in this chapter.

Sending e-mail to an AOL member

To send an electronic mail message to another America Online member, use the member's screen name in the Send To text box of the Write Mail window. E-mail that you send from one AOL account to another requires only the member's screen name and not the @aol.com extension that you need on the Internet.

Sending e-mail to someone on the Internet

An Internet e-mail message requires the entire Internet address. Use the person's entire e-mail address, including the @whatever that comes after the name or account name. E-mail that you send to other online services also needs the Internet extension, as in johndoe@whatever.com. Type the Internet address into the Send To text box of the Write Mail window.

Sending e-mail to several addresses

You can send electronic mail to several addresses at once instead of retyping the same message to several people. Type the addresses in the Send To text box of the Write Mail window one after another, separating the addresses with commas, as shown in Figure 3-2.

Figure 3-2: Separate multiple addresses by using commas.

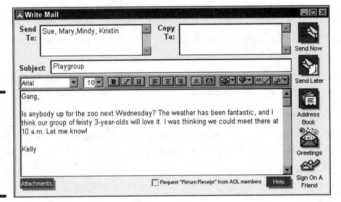

Copying others with CC/BCC

Sending *carbon copies (CC)* or *blind carbon copies (BCC)* of e-mail messages to friends or colleagues is a snap on America Online. Just follow these steps:

1. **To send a carbon copy, type the screen name(s) or Internet address(es) into the Copy To text box on the right side of the Write Mail window (see Figure 3-3).**

2. **To send a blind carbon copy, type the screen name(s) or address(es) in parentheses () in either the Send To text box or the Copy To text box.**

3. **Fill in the Subject and Message text boxes and click Send Now (or Send Later).**

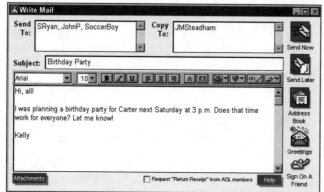

Figure 3-3:
You can
send carbon
copies (CC),
as well as
blind carbon
copies
(BCC).

If you use the BCC option, the original recipient of the e-mail message knows nothing of a carbon copy. A carbon-copied message lists the e-mail address of the additional recipient(s) at the top of the e-mail message, but a message with a blind carbon copy lists nothing.

See the "Writing an e-mail message online" section earlier in this chapter.

Expressing yourself in e-mail

Conveying an entire range of feelings, expressions, and other subtleties can prove difficult if you're communicating via e-mail. To solve this problem, creative e-mailers around the world use several methods of adding a touch of humor, class, and personality to the otherwise dry text of electronic mail. Refer to Book II, Chapter 1, for details on e-mail etiquette and a list of abbreviations (such as BTW, for "By the way") and emoticons, such as the smiley face :-).

Formatting e-mail

Fourteen buttons sit at the top of the Message text box in the Write Mail window. You can use these buttons to format your e-mail message. To format existing text in a message, click and drag across the text to highlight it; then click the buttons for the formatting that you want. To mix and match formatting options, just click more than one button. (To make text both bold and italic, for example, click the Bold button and then the Italic button.) To format new text as you type it, first click the format buttons that you want and then enter the text.

The message shown in Figure 3-4 displays a different font and font size for the word *Kate* in the middle of the message.

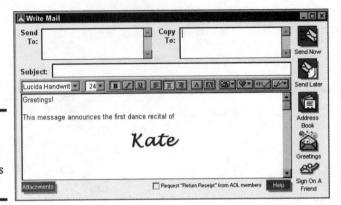

Figure 3-4:
Formatting
text draws
the reader's
attention.

Right-clicking in the Message text box opens a shortcut menu. From here, you can add a hyperlink, insert a text file you previously saved, insert a background picture, and insert a picture into your message.

Adding a hyperlink to an e-mail message

A *hyperlink* enables you to type the name of a really cool Web site and include a link to it in your message; the recipient can simply click the site's name to open it on-screen.

To create a hyperlink, follow these steps:

1. **Right-click in the Message text box.**

2. **Choose Insert a Hyperlink from the shortcut menu that appears.**

   The Edit Hyperlink dialog box appears, awaiting your instructions.

3. **Enter the name of the site into the Description text box of the Edit Hyperlink dialog box.**

4. **Enter the Internet address into the Internet Address text box and click OK.**

   The name that you type into the Description text box appears in the Message text box, wearing underlined blue text (see Figure 3-5).

Checking e-mail status

You can find out what your America Online e-mail correspondents actually do with your messages by using the e-mail status option. This option works only for mail sent to another America Online subscriber. If you try to check the status of an Internet e-mail message, the system reports that status checks are Not applicable.

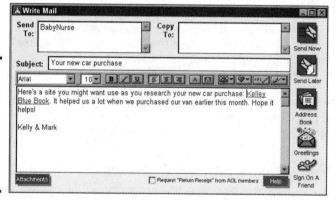

Figure 3-5:
You can add hyperlinks to Internet addresses in your e-mail messages.

To check the status of an e-mail message you send, follow these steps:

1. Click the Read button and then click the Sent Mail tab.

The Mailbox window hops into view, displaying the Sent Mail tab.

2. Click the message that you want to check to select it and then click the Status button at the bottom of the window.

A Status window appears, showing the time and date the recipient(s) read the message. If the recipient hasn't read the message yet, the Status window reads Not yet read; if the recipient deleted the message without reading it, the Status window reads Deleted.

Unsending e-mail

If you write a message that makes you think twice after sending it, try unsending it. Follow these steps to unsend an e-mail message:

1. Click Read and then click the Sent Mail tab.

The Mailbox window appears, open to the Sent Mail tab.

2. Click the message in question to select it.

3. Click the Unsend button at the bottom of the window.

A dialog box appears asking whether you really want to unsend the message.

**Book VII
Chapter 3**

Using AOL E-Mail

4. Click Yes in this dialog box.

The message is unsent, and a small dialog box pops onto the screen displaying a terse `The message has been unsent` notification.

5. Click OK.

Think fast — you can only unsend an e-mail up to the point that the recipient opens the mail to read it. (See the "Checking e-mail status" section earlier in this chapter.) After that, you're stuck buying flowers or ice cream for the recipient.

This trick works only for unread messages that you sent to other America Online members. You can't unsend an e-mail message that you send to an Internet address. (Choose your words wisely if they're heading for the Net.)

Setting your e-mail preferences

You can choose from several e-mail preferences. You can set preferences to save copies of incoming and outgoing mail automatically, use AOL style quotes in mail messages, and turn off the annoying Your Mail Has Been Sent dialog box. For information about these settings and many others, see Book VII, Chapter 1.

Addressing E-Mail by Using the Address Book

The *Address Book* remembers the e-mail addresses of your friends and associates. You can use it to create mailing lists, to track names and e-mail addresses, or to do a little of both.

With America Online 7.0, you can use your Address Book when you're online, offline, and even when you sign on to AOL on your friend's computer. Plus, you can now print your entire Address Book or information for the people you select — a huge boon for AOL members who use different computers at home and at work.

Adding an entry

To create an Address Book entry, follow these steps:

1. Choose Mail⇨Address Book.

The Address Book window opens, as shown in Figure 3-6.

2. Click either the Add Contact or Add Group button to open the appropriate window.

Add Contact creates an Address Book entry for an individual's screen name. Add Group creates a single Address Book entry for a group of screen names or Internet addresses, such as a list of family members who receive the annual Happy Holidays newsletter via e-mail.

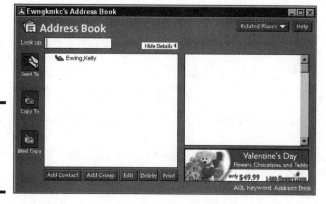

Figure 3-6:
AOL's
Address
Book
window.

3. Enter the appropriate name and address information in the Contact Details or Manage Group window.

- **In the Contact Details window:** Enter the person's first name, last name, and screen name or Internet address in the text boxes, as shown in Figure 3-7. Enter any information that you want to remember about that person using the Contact, Home, Work, Phone, and Details tabs.

Figure 3-7:
Enter the
name,
e-mail
address,
and other
vital
information
in the
Contact
Details
window.

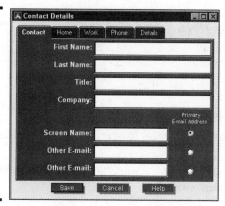

- **In the Manage Group window:** Enter a name for the group, such as Family, Friends, or Work Associates, in the Group Name text box. Then enter the screen names or Internet addresses of the group's members in the large Addresses text box.

4. **Click OK.**

   The name that you type in the First Name and Last Name text boxes or the Group Name text box appears as an entry in the Address Book.

Changing or deleting an entry

To change or remove an existing Address Book entry, follow these steps:

1. **Choose Mail➪Address Book.**

   The Address Book opens on-screen.

2. **Click the name in your Address Book that you want to change or delete.**

3. **Click the Edit button to change the entry or click the Delete button to remove it.**

   - **Edit:** Click the Edit button to change the name or e-mail address of an entry. Make any changes you want in the Contact Details dialog box, and then click Save to save the changes.

   - **Delete:** Click the Delete button to remove an entry from the Address Book. After a dialog box appears asking whether you're sure, click Yes. The entry is toast.

If the Address Book entry disappears without showing the dialog box and that situation bothers you, set your Filing Cabinet Preferences to ask you to confirm before single items are actually deleted. (See Book VII, Chapter 1, for details.)

Writing e-mail by using the Address Book

To save time in writing e-mail messages, you can copy the recipient's address directly from the Address Book. Just follow these steps:

1. **Click the Write button on the toolbar.**

   The Write Mail window appears.

2. **Click the Address Book button on the right side of the window.**

3. **After the Address Book window appears, select the name of the person or group that you want to contact and click the Send To button — or simply double-click the entry.**

That person's e-mail address appears in the Send To text box of the Write Mail window.

4. Close the Address window.

What's your Internet e-mail address?

Your Internet e-mail address is your America Online screen name. Type your AOL screen name in all-lowercase characters (the Internet ignores uppercase in mail addresses) and add **@aol.com** to the end.

Attaching a File to an E-Mail Message

Use the Attachments button in the Write Mail window to send a file along with the e-mail message itself. The file then downloads to the receiver's computer. (See the section "Receiving an Attached File in an E-Mail Message," later in this chapter.)

To attach a file to an e-mail message, follow these steps:

1. Click the Write button to open the Write Mail window.

2. Click the Attachments button at the bottom left of the window.

The Attachments window opens.

3. Click the Attach button to open the Attach dialog box (see Figure 3-8).

Figure 3-8: In this dialog box, select the file that you want to attach to your e-mail message.

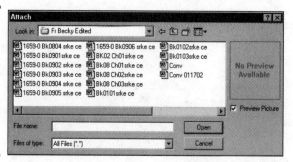

4. In the File Name text box, type the name of the file that you want to attach to your message and click the Open button, or locate the filename in the list of files and double-click the name.

The filename appears in the Attachments window.

5. **If you want to attach only the one file, click OK; if you want to attach more than one file, skip to Step 6.**

   The filename then appears beside the Attachments button in the Write Mail window.

6. **To attach a second (and any subsequent) file, repeat Steps 3, 4, and 5 until your file collection is ready to launch.**

   You can attach multiple files to an e-mail message. After you add a second file, AOL adds a comma to the filename beside Attach. You can view your attached file list by clicking the Attachments button. If you like the attachment list, click OK. If you don't like the attachment list, you can use the Attach or Detach button in the Attachments window to modify the list until it satisfies you. Click OK when you're done.

7. **Fill in the e-mail address of the recipient and a subject to describe the e-mail message; then write a note in the message box explaining the attachment and click Send Now (or Send Later).**

TIP

Sharing favorite places in an e-mail message

To tell your friends about the latest cool Web page or America Online forum, send them an e-mail with a link to the site. Just follow these steps:

1. **Type the keyword or Web site address to open a window that contains the cool site that you want to link in the message.**

2. **Click the Favorite Places icon in that window.**

   A small Favorite Place dialog box opens, telling you that you selected a Favorite Place.

3. **Click the Insert in Mail button.**

   A new Write Mail window opens with the subject line already filled in and some blue underlined text in the window. That's the link!

4. **Enter the person's screen name or Internet address and add any additional information in the Message text box.**

5. **Click Send Now.**

After the recipient opens your mail message and clicks the blue text, he goes directly to the Web site. E-mail links are great for press releases promoting a Web site or an America Online service area.

To send a friend a Favorite Places link after you've already begun writing her a message, use the Insert Favorite Place button at the top of the Message text box in the Write Mail window. (It's the third button from the right.) Click the button and your Favorite Places list appears. Highlight the favorite place that you want to send, and America Online automatically inserts it into your mail message wherever your cursor rests. Pretty cool, eh?

Using a Signature in E-Mail

You can sign your e-mail messages with flair. A signature enables you to personalize your e-mail closing without retyping lines of text each time that you write a message. Best of all, you can create several different signature files to represent the various life roles that you play: Create a different e-mail signature, for example, for your professional life, hobbies, family, and volunteer work.

In a signature file, you can include a link to your Web page or a brief description of your home business — here's where you can "advertise" your wares if you want people to know about your Web site or what you do for a living.

As does everything else that passes through the America Online portals, your signature file must follow Terms of Service guidelines. So keep it clean, or the TOS cops are sure to find you in short order. For your own protection, you don't want an e-mail signature to include a home address, phone numbers, or other identifying information that someone may use to find you.

Creating a signature file

To create an e-mail signature file, follow these steps:

1. **Choose Mail⇨Mail Signatures to open the Set Up Signatures window.**

2. **Click the Create button.**

The Create Signature window opens, as shown in Figure 3-9.

Figure 3-9:
Type the text of your signature in the Create Signature window.

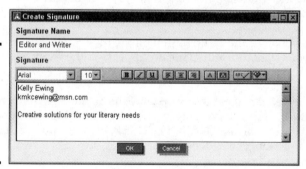

3. **In the Signature Name text box, type a name for your Signature that best describes its purpose, such as** Business, Pet Sitting, **or** Editor and Writer.

**Book VII
Chapter 3**

Using AOL E-Mail

4. **In the Signature text box, include your contact information and anything else that you want readers to know.**

5. **After you finish, click OK to establish the signature file.**

    The signature takes its place in the Signatures text box of the Set up Signatures window.

To edit a signature in the Set up Signatures window, highlight the signature and click Edit. Make your changes and then click OK.

Dropping a signature into your e-mail

After you create a signature file, the next step is to actually use the signature in an e-mail message. America Online gives you two options for using signatures. You can designate a default signature that drops into the Write Mail window every time that you create a message, or you can select a signature individually whenever you want to use one.

To designate a default signature, follow these steps:

1. **Choose Mail⇨Mail Signatures to open the Set Up Signatures window.**

2. **Click to highlight one of the signatures in your Signatures list.**

3. **Click the Default On/Off button to select that signature as your default e-mail signature.**

    A check mark appears next to that signature, showing that it's the default e-mail signature.

4. **Close the Set up Signatures window by clicking the Close button in the top-right corner.**

Whenever you click the Write button on the toolbar to open the Write Mail window, your signature automatically appears in the window's Message text box.

Turn off the default signature by opening the Set up Signatures window as we describe in Step 1 of the preceding steps, highlighting the checked signature, and clicking Default On/Off. The check mark disappears, and the signature is no longer the default.

To switch between signatures, click to highlight any signature in the list and then click the Default On/Off button. The check mark jumps to the new signature filename, and it becomes your default signature.

To select a particular signature from the list, follow these steps:

1. **Open the Write Mail window by clicking the Write button on the toolbar.**

   If you've already using a signature as your default, it appears in the Message text box of the Write Mail window.

2. **Highlight the default signature and press the Delete key to make it go away.**

3. **On the text formatting bar in the Write Mail window, click the last button, which looks like a pencil.**

   A drop-down menu appears, displaying your current signatures.

4. **Click a signature in the drop-down menu and it appears in the Write Mail window.**

5. **Type your message at the cursor, which appears in the blank line above the signature.**

6. **Enter an e-mail address and a subject and then click Send Now.**

You can use a signature to create a large heading for your e-mails. The signature doesn't always have to reside at the bottom of your messages.

Reading and Replying to E-Mail

If your account contains mail and you have a sound card with the speakers turned up, America Online notifies you with a cheery "You've Got Mail!" announcement as you sign on. You can read messages while online or use an Automatic AOL session to download unread mail that you can then read offline.

Reading e-mail online

To read new mail while you're online, follow these steps:

1. **Click the You've Got Mail link on the Welcome screen or click the Read button.**

   Your mailbox appears, as shown in Figure 3-10.

2. **Use the mouse or arrow keys to navigate to the message that you want to read.**

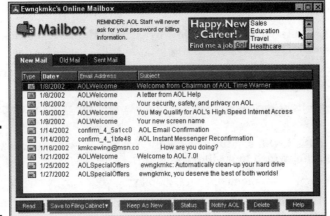

Figure 3-10:
Which
message do
you want to
read?

3. **Double-click the highlighted message or click the Read button at the bottom of the window.**

   The e-mail message opens.

Reading e-mail offline

To access your new mail so that you can read it offline, just follow these steps:

1. **Use an Automatic AOL session to download unread e-mail.**

   See the section "Automating Your AOL Sessions," later in this chapter.

2. **Choose Mail⇨Filing Cabinet and then choose Incoming/Saved Mail from the menu that appears.**

   The Incoming/Saved Mail window opens.

3. **Select the message that you want to read and click Open, or double-click the message to open it.**

Click to select the message in the Incoming/Saved Mail window and then click Delete if you no longer need the e-mail. Remember, however, that after you delete a message, it's gone for good.

Replying to an e-mail message

E-mail relationships last only if you write back. Respond to messages by following these steps:

1. **With the original e-mail message open, click the Reply button.**

   A new mail window appears with the address and subject already filled in.

To include text from the original message in your reply, right-click anywhere inside the original message box, choose Select All, and click the Reply button. A new mail window appears with the e-mail address and Subject line (with the addition of Re: at the beginning) already filled in, as well as a complete copy of the message. Erase the parts that you don't want to send back; type << and >> at the beginning and end of paragraphs that you want to keep from the original to show that those paragraphs are quoted material.

If you want to quote only a small portion of the e-mail message, highlight that sentence or paragraph and then click Reply. The Reply Mail window opens containing a copy of that portion of the message, complete with quotation marks.

2. **Type your replies and comments in the Message text box.**

3. **Click Send Now.**

Receiving an Attached File in an E-Mail Message

If you open the listing for new mail and see a message with a small disk icon underneath the message icon in the Online Mailbox window, that message has an attachment of some kind. Document files, programs, and sound files are some of the possible attachments that you can receive with e-mail.

**Book VII
Chapter 3**

To download the attached file, follow these steps:

1. **Double-click the message to open it.**

2. **Click one of the two buttons at the bottom of the message — Download Now or Download Later:**

   • **Download Now:** This option opens the Download Manager dialog box so that you can select a destination for the attachment and then click Save.

   • **Download Later:** This option places the file in the Download Manager. Whenever you're ready to download, choose Mail➪Filing Cabinet to open the File Download window. If necessary, click Select Destination to change where the file goes on your hard drive. Finally, click Download.

Using AOL E-Mail

If you use Automatic AOL to download your mail and you previously selected Automatic AOL's Download Files That Are Attached to Unread Mail check box, Automatic AOL copies the file to your hard drive during the Automatic AOL session. You still need to locate the file on your hard drive and open it, however. It's waiting for you in the destination file that the Download Manager lists.

To stay safe in these times of unmuzzled hackers on the Internet, never download any file from someone you don't know. The 7.0 version of the AOL software enables you to send multiple attachments in e-mail, but only the first attachment's name appears in the recipient's mail message. So the first attachment may be a text file, but a subsequent attachment may be an executable virus. Better to stay safe and apologize later than experience the time and trouble of recovering from a hacker's twisted joke.

Deleting an E-Mail Message

Annoyed by unwanted marketing junk mail? No problem — that's why America Online created the Delete button. (For related information, see the section "Unsending e-mail," earlier in this chapter, and the following section, "Undeleting an E-Mail Message.")

After you delete a message from your America Online mailbox, it's gone after 24 hours. Nothing can bring it back.

If you're really, really sure that you want to trash that spam or any e-mail message, follow these steps:

1. **Click the You've Got Mail icon in the Welcome screen or click Read.**

   The Online Mailbox window appears.

2. **Use the arrow keys or click the message name to select the message in the New Mail window.**

3. **Click Delete at the bottom of the Online Mailbox window.**

A similar process works for mail that you've previously read:

1. **Use the arrow keys or click the message name to select the message in the Old Mail window.**

2. **Click Delete at the bottom of the Online Mailbox window.**

After you send an e-mail message, a copy remains in your outgoing mailbox at America Online. If you don't want the copy hanging around, follow these steps to delete it:

1. **Click Read to open the Online Mailbox with the Sent Mail tab displayed.**

2. **Use the arrow keys or click the message name to select that message in the Sent Mail window.**

3. **Click Delete at the bottom of the Online Mailbox screen.**

Undeleting an E-Mail Message

On those days that your fingers move faster than your brain and you delete some impressively important e-mail message, you no longer need to panic. Take a deep breath — fix yourself another cup of java if you want — and then undelete the e-mail you mistakenly toasted.

You've Got Pictures!

AOL's You've Got Pictures feature places your newly developed photos online so that you can create online photo albums to share. You can also download individual pictures onto your hard drive to use in newsletters or print out for friends. To use You've Got Pictures, take your pictures to an authorized You've Got Pictures photo developer.

Here's how to find out which developers participate in your area:

1. **Click the You've Got Pictures link in the Welcome window or type the keyword Pictures to open the You've Got Pictures window in your browser.**

2. **Click the Learn How link.**

3. **Click the Photo Developer link.**

   The Dealer Locator dialog box opens.

4. **Enter your zip code into the Zip Code text box and then click Find Now.**

   The system offers a list of developers, along with addresses and phone numbers.

When you take the film for processing, check the AOL You've Got Pictures box on the film envelope and fill in your e-mail address (*screen name*@aol.com). That way, whenever the film's ready, you get an e-mail notification. If you hear "You've Got Pictures" as you sign on to the system, you know that your pictures are scanned and ready for viewing online. Keyword **Pictures** takes you to the You've Got Pictures area and automatically opens the New Rolls section. Using the You've Got Pictures service costs an extra $5.95 per roll at the developer.

After your pictures are online, you can take any of the following actions:

✔ Look at them by clicking the View Pictures button in the You've Got Pictures window.

✔ Give the film roll a new name. Something a little more intuitive than MYKAUF231359 may prove helpful.

✔ Create and edit your own online albums from your saved pictures. Click the My Rolls & Albums tab to start out.

✔ Share your newly created albums with friends and family. Click the My Rolls & Albums tab, select an album, and then click the Share Pictures button to begin.

To undelete an e-mail message, follow these steps:

1. **Choose Mail⇨Recently Deleted Mail.**

   The Recently Deleted Mail window opens.

2. **Highlight the wayward e-mail message by clicking it.**

3. **Click Keep As New.**

   The message takes its rightful place in your New Mail window.

Use the Read button to look at the e-mail contents if you need to know exactly which received message you want to resurrect. If you find one or two that you're sure you don't want, highlight them and click Permanently Delete. They're history.

Automating Your AOL Sessions

Automatic AOL automatically signs on to America Online and downloads your e-mail and files into your computer. You then can read the e-mail offline, which cuts down on connect time and, in turn, saves you money if you subscribe to one of America Online's measured-service options.

Setting up Automatic AOL

Before you can use Automatic AOL, you must tell the America Online software what you want to do with it. Just follow these steps:

1. **Choose Mail⇨Automatic AOL.**

   You don't need to be online to set up Automatic AOL. If you've set up your Automatic AOL before, continue on to Step 3 to click the check boxes for the various options to select or deselect them. (If you select no new options (and deselect existing ones), by the way, the Automatic AOL session still runs but actually does nothing.)

   The Automatic AOL Walk-Through window opens.

2. **Click either Expert Setup or Continue.**

   If you've never set up an Automatic AOL before, click Continue. AOL walks you through the setup, describing each Automatic AOL option. Follow the instructions on-screen and click OK after you reach the Congratulations screen. You're done! Skip the rest of these directions and go straight to the following section, "Using Automatic AOL."

3. **Click the check boxes for the tasks that you want Automatic AOL to perform.**

   You can choose among the following options:

- **Send Mail from the "Mail Waiting to Be Sent" Folder:** This option sends e-mail that you've written offline and saved to send later.

- **Get Unread Mail and Put It in "Incoming Mail" Folder:** This option downloads all new, unread e-mail to your computer.

- **Download Files That Are Attached to Unread Mail:** Select this option if you want America Online to download any files attached to e-mail messages at the same time that it downloads the e-mail messages themselves. We leave this option deselected and download all files manually if we decide that we want them. Doing so minimizes the chance of discovering too late that you downloaded a hacker file.

- **Send Postings from the "Postings Waiting to Be Sent" Folder:** This option sends any newsgroup postings you may have written to their respective newsgroups.

- **Get Unread Postings and Put in "Incoming Postings" Folder:** If you select this option, America Online grabs the new postings from any newsgroups to which you subscribe and downloads them to your computer.

- **Download Files Marked to Be Downloaded Later:** Selecting this option copies to your computer any files that you found while roaming around America Online and for which you clicked the Download Later button. You find the files in the folder you designated for downloads under Download Preferences (keyword **Preferences**).

4. **Click the Schedule Automatic AOL button to tell AOL when to download your e-mail.**

   The Schedule Automatic AOL window appears.

5. **Specify the days, times, and frequency that Automatic AOL should be run; then select the Enable Scheduler check box to activate the scheduling feature and click OK.**

6. **Click Run Automatic AOL Now to begin an Auto AOL session immediately.**

   A small dialog box appears, asking whether you want the system to sign you off after the Automatic AOL session finishes.

7. **Select the Sign Off When Finished check box if you're ready to leave America Online for a while and then click Begin.**

   If you click Begin without selecting the check box, the system downloads your e-mail and then awaits your next keyword or mouse click.

8. **Click the Automatic AOL window's Close box to save your changes.**

**Book VII
Chapter 3**

Using AOL E-Mail

If you want your computer to sign on to America Online automatically and download your e-mail, you must store the passwords for the screen name(s) on your computer. To do so, click Select Names in the Automatic AOL window. The Select Screen Names dialog box appears. Click the check boxes next to the screen name(s) that you want to use and type the password next to the corresponding screen name(s). Click OK to save your changes or Cancel if you change your mind.

If you enter your password in the Select Names section, remember to use the Schedule Automatic AOL button to select the days and times for the Automatic AOL sessions. Select the Enable Scheduler check box in the Schedule Automatic AOL dialog box or your password entry work is for nought.

Storing your password in the Automatic AOL screen doesn't provide general access to your account. No one can get to your computer and sign on to America Online under your name. The password that you include here enables your computer to download your e-mail from America Online without your physical help.

Using Automatic AOL

After you patiently set up the Automatic AOL information, you can watch Automatic AOL do its stuff. Follow these steps:

1. **Choose Mail⇨Automatic AOL.**

   The Automatic AOL dialog box pops up, as shown in Figure 3-11.

Figure 3-11: The Automatic AOL dialog box.

2. **Click Run Automatic AOL Now.**

   The Run Automatic AOL Now dialog box appears.

3. **Click Begin.**

   The Status window appears and displays the steps that AOL is performing.

Chapter 4: Sharing Web Pages and Files through AOL

In This Chapter

✔ Joining the techno-elite by creating your own Web home page

✔ Finding others' pages on AOL Hometown

✔ Finding files to download

✔ Uploading files

✔ Filling up your hard drive with files from FTP sites

At the time that the Internet quietly started back in the mid-'60s, few people guessed that it would turn into the worldwide power that it is today. What began as a small military experiment grew slowly through the '70s, matured in the '80s, and absolutely exploded in the '90s. Today, this global network of networks enables you to express yourself with your own Web site, share files, and find an incredible array of information through FTP sites. Best of all, each of these services is available through America Online.

Connecting with Friends at AOL Hometown

AOL Hometown is what America Online calls its members' Web page area. It's completely free to America Online members. You can upload your Web page to AOL Hometown for other members to see or spend an evening reading through other members' Web pages (see Figure 4-1).

Viewing other people's pages

Divided into categories, AOL Hometown features member pages that discuss entertainment, education, health, hobbies, culture, and sports. AOL Hometown even contains a Business Park category for members who want to promote their businesses through a Web page.

Keyword **Hometown** opens the AOL Hometown Welcome screen. To browse by general topic and subtopic, click the <u>Site Map</u> link at the bottom of the page. If you want to locate a specific topic or Web page, type it in the text box and then press Enter or click Search.

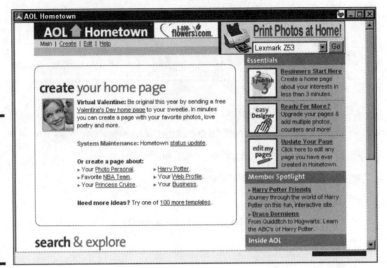

Figure 4-1:
You can
create a
Web page
or browse
members'
pages at
AOL
Hometown.

Other Internet denizens who want to visit AOL Hometown (and who don't
know your exact screen name) can see your page by using the Web address
hometown.aol.com.

Building your own home page

In Internet lingo, a *home page* is your personal spot on the World Wide Web.
A home page is a place to showcase your interests, promote your business,
or expound the virtues of your particular viewpoint. What sets the Web
apart is its worldwide reach — your words are available to anyone with a
Web browser and Internet access.

For all the Web's power and reach, building a home page doesn't take a
great deal of complex programming. In fact, putting your best foot forward
on the Web doesn't take much programming at all. The key to this simplicity
is America Online's 1-2-3 Publish (keyword **123 Publish**), an interactive tool
that handles the technical stuff for you.

To create your own Web page using America Online 1-2-3 Publish, follow
these steps:

1. **Press Ctrl+K, and then type keyword** 123 Publish **to open 1-2-3 Publish
in the browser window.**

The screen fills with a list of template suggestions. Decide what kind of
Web page you have in mind. Do you want a page that showcases your

baby's photos? Is this Web site's purpose to advertise your business? Would you like to post favorite recipes or share your delight over a television show? If ideas such as these interest you, you can find them (and more) in the item list.

2. **Click a page template's link to select it and then progress through the next screen's sections one at a time, entering a title for your Web page, selecting background colors, and including text.**

   If you want to include a photo in your page design, you can do so, too. Click the Browse button to locate the picture or graphic. AOL uploads it automatically.

3. **To see how the page is going to look after you enter all the information, click Preview My Page.**

   Your page is previewed in the browser window. If you want to change anything in your new page, you can click the Modify button while previewing it.

4. **To upload your page to AOL Hometown, the Web storage space that comes with your screen name, click Save.**

For more advanced information on Web page construction, use the keyword **Hot Dog Express**.

Get more in-depth information about America Online Web page design from *America Online For Dummies*, 7th Edition, by John Kaufeld (published by Hungry Minds, Inc.).

Finding and Downloading Files

America Online offers a marvelously extensive software library with files for Macintosh, Windows, DOS, and other operating systems and computers. Locate them in two ways:

✦ **To browse through file lists:** Use keyword **Download Center** to open the main software center screen, as shown in Figure 4-2.

✦ **To search the online libraries:** Use keyword **Download Center** and then click the Shareware button. The main Software Search window covers primarily DOS and Windows programs.

From the shareware list box on the right side of the Download Center, double-click a category that looks interesting. In the window that appears, double-click a subcategory on the left and then a library on the right. A list of available files pops onto the screen, as shown in Figure 4-3. At this point, you can look at a file's description, download it, or mark it for downloading later.

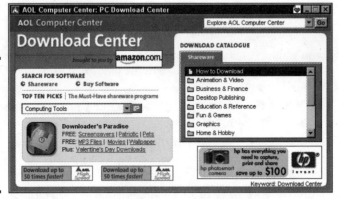

Figure 4-2: Find the software you want to download in the Download Center.

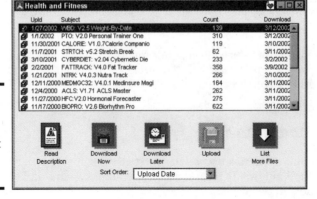

Figure 4-3: Choose the actual file from the list of available files.

- **To see a description of the file:** Double-click the file's entry in the list or click the Read Description button. A window that tells you everything you ever wanted to know about the file hops onto the screen.

- **To download the file right now:** Click Download Now. When the Download Manager window pops up, select a destination for the file (and change the filename, if you like). When you're ready to go, click Save or press Enter. The file begins to make its way to your computer.

- **To download the file later:** Click Download Later. America Online notes the filename and location in the Download Manager and presents a dialog box on-screen telling you that the file was successfully added to your download list.

If you choose Download Later, remember to start the Download Manager (choose File⇨Download Manager) to finish transferring the file to your computer. Otherwise, when you sign off, the software politely shows you a dialog box that asks whether you want to download the files you marked earlier.

Downloading files later with the Download Manager

The Download Manager tracks files that you mark with the Download Later button, and it remembers the files that you downloaded in the past. It's pretty bright — it even knows how to unpack ZIP files.

To open the Download Manager, choose File⇨Download Manager. The Download Manager window lists all files that are waiting to be downloaded. When you click Download Later while looking at a file, the Download Manager stores that file's information in this window.

Downloading files in waiting

To download the waiting files in the Download Manager, click Download. The File Transfer dialog box appears, providing an estimate of the download time, as shown in Figure 4-4. After the files are downloaded, a File Transfer Status window appears, showing the time it took for each file to download. Simply close the window.

Figure 4-4:
AOL
estimates
the time
remaining
for the file
transfer.

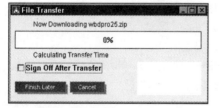

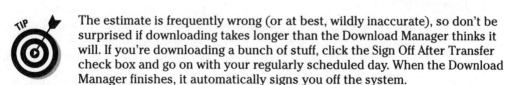

The estimate is frequently wrong (or at best, wildly inaccurate), so don't be surprised if downloading takes longer than the Download Manager thinks it will. If you're downloading a bunch of stuff, click the Sign Off After Transfer check box and go on with your regularly scheduled day. When the Download Manager finishes, it automatically signs you off the system.

Removing files from the download list

To remove a file from the Download Manager's list of waiting files, click the filename you want to remove and then click Remove Item. A dialog box appears, asking whether you're sure that you want to delete the file. Click Yes, and the entry vanishes without further argument.

Seeing which files you already downloaded

From the Download Manager, you can look at a list of files you've already downloaded. Just click Show Files Downloaded. The Files You've Downloaded window appears. By default, it shows your last 100 downloads. If you want America Online to remember more (or fewer) than 100 files, click Download Preferences on the Download Manager window and change the Retain Information About My Last xx Downloads entry.

Choosing where to store files to download

To tell the Download Manager where to store files waiting for download, click Select Destination. In the Select Path dialog box, use the folders to click your way to the right path. If you decide not to change the storage location, look for all your files in your AOL software's Download folder (see Figure 4-5).

Figure 4-5:
You can select the folder in which to store your downloaded files.

Don't worry if the word *path* is in the File Name area of the dialog box — that's acceptable, if somewhat odd, behavior.

Uploading Files

Submitting a file to America Online gives you a good feeling, like you're contributing to the community. When possible, offer something in return to the online community by uploading your favorite shareware programs or artwork.

Remember that you can only upload freeware or shareware programs, text files that you wrote, or artwork that you created. You can't upload commercial programs. (In fact, America Online will probably cancel your account if you do, because uploading commercial programs violates federal copyright law.)

To submit a file to America Online, follow these steps:

1. **Type the keyword** Upload.

2. **Double-click the Category you're interested in.**

3. **Click the Upload button, shown in Figure 4-6.**

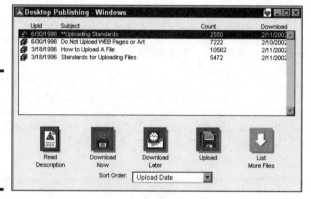

Figure 4-6:
Click the
Upload
button to
begin
uploading
your file(s).

4. **Fill out the informational entries in the next window.**

Pay particular attention to the Description sections, as shown in Figure 4-7. People who want to download your file rely on you for this information.

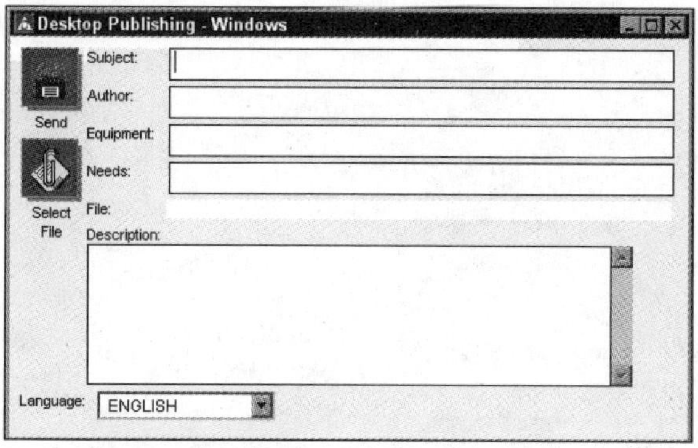

Figure 4-7:
Provide a
complete
description
for your
uploaded
file.

5. **Click Select File.**

The Attach File dialog box pops up.

6. **Find your file among the teeming multitudes in the dialog box list. To include the file in your upload, double-click its entry.**

The Upload File dialog box shows the name of the file that's destined for America Online.

ZIP Files

In the world of Windows, ZIP files rule as the undisputed leaders of file compression. Although the AOL software understands ZIP files, having your own unzipping software handy is still a good idea.

In a Windows environment, the popular choice is the Niko Mak WinZip program. To download a copy, use keyword **Download Center** and search for WINZIP. (Click the Shareware button to open the Software Search window). For DOS, use the original PKZIP program. PKZIP is available online, too — use keyword **Download Center** and then search for PKZIP.

VBRUN files (Visual Basic Runtime Modules)

Many shareware authors use the Microsoft Visual Basic system to write their programs. To execute a program written with Visual Basic, you need a special file called a runtime module on your system. Basically, a runtime module is a collection of instructions that the program uses when it runs. Think of runtime modules as crib notes for your software.

Each runtime module available on America Online corresponds to a different version of Visual Basic; the number in the filename is the version number of Visual Basic that the particular library supports.

Each library supports only its specific version of Visual Basic. The Version 4 runtime library, for example, won't do a thing for a program written to look for the Version 2 file. Because of this, you may need multiple runtime libraries — not just the most recent one — in your WINDOWS/SYSTEM subdirectory. On the other hand, if only one of your programs requires a VBRUN file, just install that particular file. (After all, there's no sense wasting hard drive space.)

The following VBRUN files are available through the Download Center:

VBRUN100.EXE	Runtime library for Visual Basic Version 1.0
VBRUN200.EXE	Runtime library for Visual Basic Version 2.0
VBRUN300.EXE	Runtime library for Visual Basic Version 3.0

For runtime modules above VBRUN300.exe, go to Download.com (at www.download.com) and search for visual basic runtime. Here you can download modules for Visual Basic versions 4.0, 5.0, and 6.0. As with all the other Visual Basic Runtime Modules, these files are free to download and use.

File Transfer Protocol (FTP)

The Internet, being the odd place that it is, uses its own special system for downloading files. *FTP,* short for *file transfer protocol,* is the Internet's file-transfer magician. FTP is also sometimes known as *Anonymous FTP,* because most of the computers that offer files through FTP don't ask you for a special password. Because the computers are open to everyone, the service is deemed anonymous.

To access the FTP area, use keyword **FTP**. The FTP window appears on-screen, as shown in Figure 4-8. From there, you can check out some general FTP information, search for FTP sites, or set up a connection to a particular site.

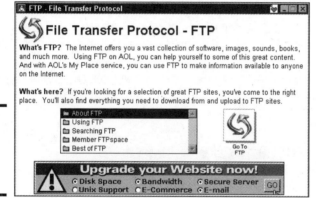

Figure 4-8:
The File
Transfer
Protocol
window.

**Book VII
Chapter 4**

**Sharing Web
Pages and Files
through AOL**

Don't download files through FTP unless you have a virus-checking program running on your computer. Carefully virus-check *absolutely every file* that you get through FTP — don't trust *anything.*

Using a particular FTP site

Getting into a specific site is easy with the America Online FTP system. Just follow these steps:

1. **Press Ctrl+K, type keyword** FTP **and click OK. From the FTP window, click Go To FTP.**

2. **In the Anonymous FTP window that appears, click Other Site.**

The Other Site dialog box appears.

3. **Type the address of the FTP site that you want and then either press Enter or click Connect.**

   The addresses for FTP sites usually start with FTP — for example, `ftp.apple.com` or `ftp.microsoft.com`. If the address you have starts with `www`, the address is for a World Wide Web site and not an FTP site.

Downloading from FTP sites

Copying a file from an FTP site isn't hard, but the process is a little more complicated than downloading a file from America Online. Follow these steps:

1. **Press Ctrl+K, type keyword FTP and click Go. From the FTP window, click Go to FTP.**

2. **In the Anonymous FTP window that appears, pick an FTP site from the list or use the address of another site:**

   • **To choose a site from the list in the Anonymous FTP window:** Scroll through the list until you find the site you want; then double-click its entry.

   • **To enter your own special address:** Click Other Site. Type the site address in the Other Site dialog box and then click Connect, as shown in Figure 4-9.

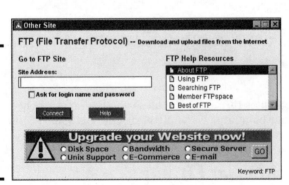

Figure 4-9: Enter a specific FTP site address in the Other Site dialog box.

Either way that you use to choose an FTP site, America Online responds after a moment, either to say that you made the connection or to report that something didn't work. If you connect to the FTP site, a list window appears showing you all the files available in the FTP computer's current directory. If the connection doesn't work, America Online suggests that you check your spelling and try again.

If the FTP window says something about *mirror access*, that's okay. That message means that you connected to a copy (or *mirror*) of the FTP site, which America Online created to give you faster access to the same information.

3. **Browse by double-clicking entries on the list.**

   Enjoy yourself — this part is fun.

4. **If an entry piques your interest, click it.**

   If the Download Now button comes to life, that entry's available for downloading. If not, the file isn't available. After you click the button, America Online briefly opens a Retrieving Data dialog box. Behind the scenes, the America Online computers are copying the file at a very high speed from wherever it resides on the Internet. After the AOL computers finish receiving the file, the Download Manager window appears on-screen, asking what you want to call the file on your computer.

5. **Type a name for the file in the Download Manager window and then press Enter.**

   The download starts immediately.

6. **After the file finishes downloading, America Online beeps and tosses up a simple report announcing that the file arrived safely.**

7. **To download more files, repeat Steps 4 through 6.**

8. **After you finish downloading files, click the Close button to close the FTP window.**

Closing the FTP window after you finish downloading is important. America Online keeps a connection to the FTP site until you close the site's window. Because many sites limit the number of people who can download files at once, other people on the Net often can't access the site until you leave by closing the FTP window.

Uploading to FTP sites

Some (but not all) FTP sites accept file uploads from Internet users. If you have software to share, consider uploading it to an FTP site.

Upload *only* files that you write yourself or shareware programs — don't even *think* about uploading a copy of your favorite commercial program or game. (We don't want you to break the copyright laws!)

**Book VII
Chapter 4**

**Sharing Web
Pages and Files
through AOL**

To upload files to an FTP site, follow these steps:

1. **Type the keyword** FTP **in the address box, and then click Go to FTP.**

   The Anonymous FTP window appears.

2. **To connect to the site that you want, click Other Site, type the site's address in the text box, and then press Enter or click Connect.**

   If the connection works, you're in; if it doesn't, check the spelling and try again. The correct name opens the FTP site's window.

3. **In the FTP site's window, click the Upload button.**

   A file name dialog box appears. If an upload button doesn't appear on-screen, you can't upload files to this FTP site. Sorry, but that's how it goes.

4. **Type the name of the file in the dialog box as you want it to appear on the FTP server.**

   You're not telling America Online where to find the file on your computer yet. Instead, the software wants to know what to call the copy you're uploading to the FTP computer.

5. **If you're uploading a plain-text file or HTML files (Web pages), click the ASCII option button; if the file is anything other than plain text or HTML, click the Binary option button.**

6. **Double-check your entries for accuracy and then click Continue.**

   The Upload File dialog box appears.

7. **Click Select File.**

   The Attach File dialog box pops up.

8. **Scroll through the dialog box until you find the name of the file that you want to send and then double-click it.**

   The file's name and path appear in the Upload File dialog box.

9. **Click Send to start the transfer.**

   A File Transfer dialog box updates you on the transfer. Finally, an annoying little dialog box appears telling you that the transfer is complete.

10. **Click OK.**

11. **To send more files, repeat Steps 3 through 10.**

12. **After you finish sending files, click the Close button to close the FTP window.**

If you want to upload files to your private Web space on AOL, press Ctrl+K, type the keyword **My FTP Space**, and then click the See My FTP Space button in the My FTP Space window. You go directly to a window by the name of members.aol.com:/screen name. After you're there, open the Private folder and begin at Step 3.

Winsock Applications and AOL

In the world of Internet software, *Winsock* is a piece of programming that helps Windows applications interact with the Internet. Thanks to America Online's built-in Winsock support, you can use almost any standard Internet program through AOL, including Telnet, Internet Relay Chat (IRC), and World Wide Web client applications.

AOL for Windows 95/98/XP supports a full 32-bit Winsock, which means that AOL for Windows 95/98/XP works with just about any Winsock-compatible program out there. For more details about using Winsock programs with AOL, plus a library of downloadable Winsock software, use the keywords **Winsock** and **Telnet**.

Chapter 5: Reading Newsgroups with AOL

In This Chapter

✔ Finding and subscribing to newsgroups

✔ Searching and browsing for particular topics

✔ Reading newsgroups online and offline

✔ Posting messages to a newsgroup

✔ Replying to a posting

*S*hortly after the Internet started, the researchers who were using it created an electronic bulletin board for online discussions. This bulletin board evolved into the Internet *newsgroups*, a collection of several thousand rollicking conversations covering computers, hard science, industrial music, and almost everything in between. America Online offers a complete collection of the world's newsgroups. (For much more on newsgroups, see Book V, Chapter 1. This chapter relates specifically to using AOL to access newsgroups.)

Accessing Newsgroups from within AOL

To get into the Newsgroups window, use keyword **Newsgroups**. (The first time you use this command, AOL may display instructions for filtering junk messages in newsgroups.) The Newsgroups window, shown in Figure 5-1, offers useful information about how newsgroups work in general, plus some specifics about using them through America Online. Take a few minutes to read through the documents there.

The Terms of Service rules, which give America Online its family orientation, don't extend to the Internet newsgroups. Free, uncensored speech is often the rule, not the exception. If frank (and sometimes downright rude) language offends your sensibilities, you may want to avoid the newsgroups. (See Book VII, Chapter 1, for information on using Parental Controls.)

Keeping up-to-date with News Profiles

Studying current events in China? Keeping an eye on your company's competition? Looking for the latest tidbits about your favorite team? Stop searching for stories the hard way — let the news come to you with a My News profile.

This personalized news service constantly scans for stories that contain terms you specify. Each profile captures up to 50 stories per day from news sources, such as Reuters World Service, PR Newswire, Business Wire, Sports Ticker, Variety, and others. Whatever your news needs are, the America Online News Profiles system delivers the latest stories straight to your e-mail box. Best of all, using My News is free.

To enroll in the My News, follow these steps:

1. **Get into the My News area with keyword My News.**

   The My News dialog box appears.

2. **To make a new profile, click Go to Step 1.**

Creating a profile is easier to do than explain, thanks to the step-by-step My News profiles system. Just follow the on-screen instructions and keep clicking the Next button — before you know it, your news profile is off and running and you'll begin receiving articles in your AOL mailbox. Updating your profile is just as easy.

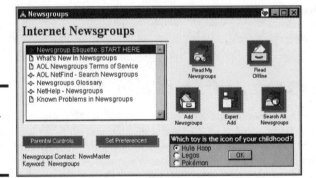

Figure 5-1:
The Newsgroups window in AOL.

Subscribing to a Newsgroup

When a friend tells you about the cool pattern she found in rec.crafts. textiles.needlework, subscribe to the newsgroup by using Expert Add and check out the place for yourself.

You need to know the exact Internet name of any group you want to subscribe to. If you aren't sure of the name, use the newsgroup search feature described in the next section, "Searching for a Particular Topic."

To subscribe to any newsgroup, follow these steps:

1. In the Newsgroups window, click Expert Add.

The Expert Add dialog box appears, as shown in Figure 5-2.

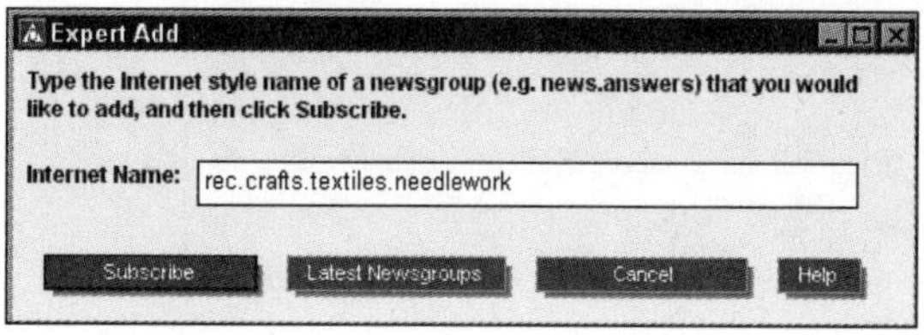

Figure 5-2:
Use the
Expert Add
dialog box
if you know
the exact
name of the
newsgroup.

Expert Add

Type the Internet style name of a newsgroup (e.g. news.answers) that you would
like to add, and then click Subscribe.

Internet Name: | rec.crafts.textiles.needlework |

| Subscribe | Latest Newsgroups | Cancel | Help |

2. Type the name of the newsgroup you want to join; then press Enter or click Subscribe.

After a moment, America Online either confirms your subscription or says `Invalid groups`.

3. Click OK to close the dialog box.

Searching for a Particular Topic

The America Online newsgroup search system covers most of the newsgroup hierarchies. It searches on the newsgroup name or parts of the name. This procedure is useful if you don't know the exact name of the newsgroup you want.

To use the newsgroup search system, follow these steps:

1. In the Newsgroups window, click Search All Newsgroups.

The Search All Newsgroups dialog box appears.

2. Type a word or two describing your interest; then press Enter.

After a moment, the search system proudly displays its results, as shown in Figure 5-3.

3. (Optional) If the system says that it can't find anything, click OK and search for a different word.

To get the best results, search for one word or part of a word (*compu* instead of *computer,* for example). Remember, you're searching newsgroup titles, which are sometimes a little arcane.

**Book VII
Chapter 5**

Reading
Newsgroups
with AOL

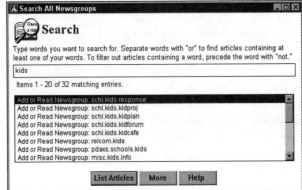

Figure 5-3:
Does
anything
interest you?

4. **Browse through the list and look for a newsgroup that interests you. Double-click a newsgroup's name to open the Add or Read Newsgroup window.**

   This window lets you view a description of the newsgroup and read the newsgroup's postings or subscribe to the newsgroup, as detailed in the following list:

   • **To subscribe to a newsgroup:** Click the <u>Subscribe to Newsgroup</u> link. A window opens with a list of unread postings. Double-click any posting title to open it.

   • **To read a newsgroup's postings without subscribing:** Click the <u>List Articles in Newsgroup</u> link. A list of the newsgroup's active articles appears.

5. **Close any open newsgroup windows and the Add or Read Newsgroup window when you finish.**

Browsing through the Lists

Sometimes, you're just curious about what's out there. When those moments hit, browse through the newsgroup lists. With more than 13,000 newsgroups out there, you'd better bring your patience along for the trip.

To browse through the newsgroup lists, follow these steps:

1. **In the Newsgroups window, click Add Newsgroups.**

   A list of newsgroup hierarchies appears, as shown in Figure 5-4. (See Book V, Chapter 1, for a list of the most popular newsgroup hierarchies.)

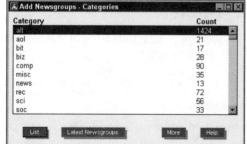

Figure 5-4:
Double-click
a hierarchy
that inter-
ests you.

2. **Double-click a hierarchy that looks interesting.**

   A list of newsgroups pops into view.

3. **Scroll through the list and look for something that interests you; then do one of the following:**

   - **See a listing of the newsgroup's articles.** Double-click the news-group's name; its window then appears, listing active postings.

   - **Subscribe to a newsgroup.** Click the newsgroup name and then click Subscribe. If all goes well, America Online announces that you're subscribed. Click OK to make the dialog box go away.

   After you subscribe to a newsgroup, a Group Preferences window opens (see Figure 5-5). This window affects only the newsgroup you just sub-scribed to.

**Book VII
Chapter 5**

**Reading
Newsgroups
with AOL**

Figure 5-5:
The Group
Preferences
window.

4. **Click the settings you want and then click Save.**

Reading Newsgroups Online

After subscribing to a newsgroup, take time to read the messages. To read the message online, follow these steps:

1. **Use keyword** Newsgroups **to get to the Newsgroups window.**

2. **Click Read My Newsgroups.**

   You see your personalized list of newsgroups. AOL starts you out with a handful of groups (including news.announce.newusers, news.answers, and news.groups.reviews) and some AOL help groups.

3. **Double-click the newsgroup that you want to read.**

   A list of unread newsgroup messages opens on-screen.

4. **Scroll through the list until you find a message that looks interesting, and then double-click the message to read it.**

5. **When you finish with the message, close its window.**

   Do likewise when you finish with the newsgroup.

In the Newsgroups window, click the Set Preferences button and then click the Filtering tab on the window that appears. You can choose to filter out (skip viewing) classes of messages based on size, excessive cross-posting (repeated off-topic posting), specific text in the subject, or postings by a specific author.

Reading Newsgroups Offline

Newsgroups are fun and interesting, but they're also time-consuming. Keep your phone line free by reading the newsgroups offline. Reading the newsgroups offline is a two-step process. First, you configure the America Online software to read the newsgroups you want. Then you actually download the newsgroup messages and read and reply to them offline.

To set up the software to read newsgroups offline, follow these steps:

1. **Subscribe to the newsgroups that you want to read offline.**

If the newsgroup is extremely active, you may want to clear the posts by clicking the Read My Newsgroups button, highlighting the newsgroup in question, and clicking the Mark Read button. Then when you download the newsgroup postings to your hard drive, you don't need to wade through 3,000 unread postings.

2. **In the Newsgroups window, click Read Offline.**

   The Choose Newsgroups window pops onto the screen.

3. To read a newsgroup offline, double-click its entry in the Subscribed Newsgroups list.

After a moment, the newsgroup hops to the Newsgroups to Read Offline list. Repeat this step for all the newsgroups that you want to read offline.

If you double-click the wrong newsgroup or want to stop reading a newsgroup offline, double-click its entry in the Newsgroups to Read Offline list. The newsgroup returns to the regular Subscribed Newsgroups list.

4. When you finish, click OK.

America Online returns you to the Newsgroups window.

5. To finish configuring America Online to retrieve your newsgroup messages for offline reading and replying, choose Mail➪Automatic AOL. Click the check boxes beside these folders:

- Get Unread Postings and Put in "Incoming Postings" Folder

- Send Postings from the "Postings Waiting to Be Sent" Folder

6. Close the window when you finish.

It's a quick and easy process to read newsgroups offline. Just follow these steps:

1. Download newsgroup messages to your computer. Choose Mail➪ Automatic AOL to start an Automatic AOL session, just as you do to download your mail.

A small Automatic AOL Status dialog box appears and gives you play-by-play commentary as the Newsgroup messages come down the phone line into the Filing Cabinet. (See Book VII, Chapter 3, to find out more about Automatic AOL.)

Stop by every now and then to check the Automatic AOL process. If America Online decides that your newsgroups contain too many postings, it shuts down your Automatic AOL session with a terse message: `Too many articles — download remaining articles in another Auto AOL (FlashSession)`. If that happens, begin another Automatic AOL session right away; the system happily downloads more postings to your computer.

2. To read and reply to the messages, choose Mail➪Filing Cabinet.

3. Scroll through the Filing Cabinet to find the Newsgroups folder.

New messages are in the Incoming/Saved Postings folder and are organized by subject line. Replies and new messages you write offline live in the Postings Waiting to Be Sent folder.

4. Double-click a message to read it.

**Book VII
Chapter 5**

**Reading
Newsgroups
with AOL**

Posting a New Message to a Newsgroup

A newsgroup audience is just waiting to hear what you have to say. Share your thoughts by posting a message. Before posting to a newsgroup, however, take time to read several days' worth of postings. Listen to what the members discuss and how they do it. When you do speak up, make your posting appropriate for the newsgroup, both in topic and in tone.

To post your message, follow these steps:

1. **In the Newsgroups window, click Read My Newsgroups.**

   If you're doing this offline, open the Filing Cabinet instead and go directly to Step 3.

2. **In the Read My Newsgroups window, double-click the name of the newsgroup to which you want to post a message.**

3. **Click the New Message button.**

   The Post New Message window appears.

4. **Type your message, give it a Subject, and then click Send.**

   After you finish writing messages, use Automatic AOL to post them. (See Book VII, Chapter 3, for more information on Automatic AOL.)

Replying to a Newsgroup Posting

Newsgroups live for discussion. When something in a newsgroup piques your interest (or ire), add your opinion by posting a reply.

To reply to a posting, follow these steps:

1. **View the message to which you're replying.**

2. **Decide what kind of reply you want to send; then click the Reply button at the bottom of the window.**

   The Post Responses window opens, showing the message in the Original Message Text box.

3. **Check the Post to Newsgroup option if everyone out there would find your words interesting; do this only if your reply is part of an ongoing discussion. Check the Send Via E-Mail option if you have a specific question or if most of the newsgroup would yawn at the topic.**

4. **Type your reply and click Send.**

These same steps work when you're reading your newsgroups offline — but remember to run Automatic AOL to send the reply when you finish reading. (See "Reading Newsgroups Offline," earlier in this chapter.)

Remembering a Newsgroup with Favorite Places

If a particular newsgroup tweaks your fancy, store it in the Favorite Places list so that you can leap into it quickly.

To store a newsgroup in Favorite Places, follow these steps:

1. **With the newsgroup window open, click the heart-on-a-page icon in the window's upper-right corner.**

2. **Click Add to Favorites to add the newsgroup to your Favorite Places.**

To access the newsgroup through Favorite Places, click the My Favorites button on the toolbar; then double-click the newsgroup's entry in the Favorite Places window. The Newsgroups window then appears. (See Book VII, Chapter 2, for more information about Favorite Places.)

Unsubscribing from a Newsgroup

When it's time to say good-bye to a newsgroup, don't make it a long, drawn-out farewell. To unsubscribe to a newsgroup, follow these steps:

1. **Use keyword** Newsgroups **to open the Newsgroups window.**

2. **Click Read My Newsgroups.**

The Read My Newsgroups window appears.

3. **Click the newsgroup that you want to remove from the list.**

4. **Click Remove.**

A dialog box confirms that you no longer subscribe to that newsgroup.

5. **Click OK to make the dialog box go away; then close the other newsgroup windows.**

(For information on subscribing to newsgroups, see "Subscribing to a Newsgroup," earlier in this chapter.)

Chapter 6: Meeting and Chatting with Friends Online

In This Chapter

✔ Chatting interactively for hours on end

✔ Calling for help when chat room conversations get out of hand

✔ Tracking friends on the system

✔ Using the Member Directory and Member Profiles

✔ Using your Buddy List

✔ Carrying on a private conversation with instant messages

✔ Swapping notes on a discussion board

T he heart of America Online beats with interactive discussion and chatter. Wherever people congregate to discuss issues, lifestyles, or interests, cyberspace flutters with activity. Join the fray! This chapter tells you how to locate online friends and engage in live talk in the chat rooms.

And what would an online service be without discussion boards? Sharpen your cyberpencil and share your views on life, politics, hobbies — whatever makes your heart flutter. This chapter also tells you how to find and join a discussion on the message boards.

Chatting on AOL

Chat rooms are the live-interaction areas of America Online. Most of the online forums use chat rooms for interest-specific chats and presentations; the People Connection consists entirely of chat rooms. People Connection chat rooms are divided into categories, which are further split into public rooms created by America Online and member rooms created by AOL members.

Private chat rooms and event arenas are other options for America Online interaction. Anyone can create a private chat room to meet with friends. Large arenas, such as the Rotunda and the Coliseum, are reserved for scheduled presentations with guest speakers.

General chat room do's and don'ts

As with any place that hosts a gathering of people, chat rooms have their own protocol for what is and isn't proper. Sometimes etiquette differs among chat rooms, and the formality of a presentation alters etiquette as well.

The following are all-around etiquette guidelines for chat rooms:

✦ **DON'T SHOUT.** Typing in all caps is considered shouting and is generally frowned upon.

✦ **Refrain from vulgarity.** Not only is this a general rule of AOL etiquette, but it's also part of the Terms of Service (TOS). Swearing in a chat room can cause trouble.

✦ **Create a Member Profile for your screen name.** Profiles function as introductions in the online world, and other members like to see who they're talking to. (See "Using the Member Directory," later in this chapter.)

✦ **Stick to the topic at hand.** If you visit a cooking chat room and begin a long, involved discussion about industrial rock music, other members may request that you return to the topic or leave.

✦ **Feel free to question what people say in a chat room** (after all, conflict is the basis of many good discussions), but you can't question their right to say it. The only exception to this is when someone violates the Terms of Service by swearing or being generally obnoxious.

Connecting with people

Communicate with the world through People Connection — the doorway to interactive chats on America Online. To reach the People Connection screen, click the People & Chat button at the bottom of the Welcome screen.

This action takes you to the opening window of the People Connection screen. From there, use the buttons to navigate to the chat room of your choice. Choose from Find a Chat (which gives you a choice of chats by category), and Chat Now (which drops you right into a general chat room).

For general help about life in the People Connection, click the Help button in the upper-right corner of the chat room screen. If someone's being obnoxious, click the Notify AOL button in the lower-right corner of the chat window.

Finding a chat room

You can find a chat room in one of several ways:

✦ Click the People & Chat button in the Welcome screen to open the People Connection window; then click Find a Chat, and click AOL Chat

Schedule. The AOL Chat Schedule window lists system-wide chats for the week. Some of the chats occur in various online areas; others are part of the regular People Connection roster.

✦ Choose People➪Find a Chat from the toolbar. Select a chat category that looks interesting. When you double-click a category, its chat rooms appear in the item list box to the right of the category list. Click one of the chat rooms in the list box to highlight it, and then click Go Chat. You land in the chat room.

✦ Go through AOL Live (keyword **AOL Live**) to see what's coming up. Click the Coming Attractions button or browse through the Live Events list box to view the upcoming presentations. Click an item that looks interesting to find out more about it. If you miss a chat, browse through Live Today to download the transcript. Click the Transcripts button on the AOL Live window to reach the AOL Live Transcripts window. It's the next best thing to attending!

If none of the public rooms in the Find a Chat window (get there by choosing People➪Find a Chat) turn you on, click the Created by AOL Members tab in the Find a Chat window to change the item lists. Now, only rooms created by members appear in the lists. Double-click a category to see its rooms. Highlight a room name, click the Go Chat button, and America Online sends you to that room.

Expressing yourself in a chat room

How do you convey emotion and facial expressions in an all-text medium? The Internet pioneers had that same problem — and thus began the character-based symbols known as emoticons or smileys. If you've seen characters in a chat room like :), which stands for a smile, or {{}}, which means virtual hugs, but never really understood what these characters meant, you can find a list of popular emoticons in Book II, Chapter 1.

Along the same lines, you can't hang out for long in the chat rooms without seeing shorthand like AFK or LOL scroll across the screen. You're not watching an apoplectic typist; rather, these letters are abbreviations for commonly used terms. Away From Keyboard and Laughing Out Loud define only two of the abbreviations developed by busy typists. Because they appeared in e-mail first, you can find more of them listed in Book II, Chapter 1.

Chat room fonts and formatting

Add flash to your chat room conversations with the chat-room formatting bar. Perched above the text-entry field, the buttons on this bar let you change fonts (say, using Old English text to participate in a medieval role-playing game). Use the buttons next to the text field to change text color or add formatting, such as bold, italics, or underline, to your text.

Playing sounds in a chat room

Noise livens life, so why not use it to add spark to a chat room? In a chat room, type **{S *soundname***. Replace *soundname* with the name of the sound. (By the way, you must use a capital S in the command; otherwise it doesn't work. Capitalization doesn't matter in the sound name.) Standard America Online sounds include *Welcome, Drop, IM, Gotmail,* and *Goodbye.*

To play any sound in your America Online folder or Windows directory, type the name of the sound file itself. For example, to play a sound called `poink.wav`, type the command **{S poink**.

Playing too many sounds in a chat room gets annoying very fast, so use sounds sparingly.

Chats run by AOL Protocol

Many scheduled presentations use America Online Protocol, which adds a layer of complexity to the chat room but generally keeps things running smoothly. These chats often feature guest presenters, but they're scheduled in a regular service area chat room rather than in one of the large arenas. When participating in a chat that uses protocol, follow these general guidelines:

✦ Type and send **?** (a question mark) to ask a question, but wait until the room host recognizes you before you send the question itself.

✦ Type and send **!** (an exclamation point) to comment; then wait until you're recognized to type the comment itself.

✦ Wait until called upon to ask a question or voice a comment. The room host calls upon members by typing **GA** (for Go Ahead) and your screen name.

Creating a Member Chat Room

You can create a member chat room to discuss a favorite interest — live.

To create a member chat room, follow these steps:

1. **Choose People⇨Start Your Own Chat.**

The Start Your Own Chat dialog box appears, awaiting your instructions.

2. **Click the Member Chat button.**

The Create a Member Room window jumps to the screen.

3. **Select a category for your chat room; then type in a name for the new room and click Go Chat.**

   You land in your newly created chat room. (Now if someone else would just show up!)

Creating a Private Chat Room

To talk privately with someone (or a group of someones), create a private chat room.

To create a private chat room, follow these steps:

1. **Choose People▷Start Your Own Chat.**

2. **Click the Private Chat button.**

   The Private Chat dialog box appears, as shown in Figure 6-1.

Figure 6-1:
Invite your
AOL friends
to your own
private chat
room.

Book VII
Chapter 6

Meeting and
Chatting with
Friends Online

3. **Enter a name for your new private room, and click Go Chat.**

   You zoom off to the new private domain.

When you create a private chat room, keep the following points in mind:

✦ Your chat room name must be unique — the more unique, the better. Don't be surprised if, every now and then, someone drops into your private room because they accidentally thought up the same name as you did.

✦ Anyone who wants to join you must know the room's name and the correct spelling. Otherwise, they create another private room and sit there all alone.

Want to meet new people? Create a private chat room called "hello" or "chat" and see who shows up! You might be amazed at how little time you spend sitting in an empty private chat room.

Going to a Friend's Chat Room

Friends hide in the most unlikely places, but joining them is easy if they're hanging out in a chat room. If the friend is part of a Buddy List Group (see "Creating a Buddy List Group," later in this chapter), you can find her by following these steps:

1. **Choose People⇨Buddy List or use keyword** Buddy.

The Buddy Lists window opens.

2. **Click the member's name in your Buddy Lists window.**

3. **Click the Buddy Info button at the bottom of the window.**

America Online looks for your friend and gives you a report in Info dialog box. You can choose to send e-mail or an instant message, add to the Address Book, view a profile, view a Web page, or locate a buddy. If the member is online, clicking Locate Buddy opens the Locate dialog box and gives the name of the chat room, as shown in Figure 6-2.

Figure 6-2:
You can jump directly to the chat room your friend is visiting.

4. **Click Go to leap directly into the chat room.**

If your friend's screen name is mysteriously missing from your Buddy List Groups, find her online this way:

1. **Choose People⇨Locate Member Online.**

You see the Locate Member Online dialog box.

2. **Type the member's screen name in the text field and press Enter or click OK.**

   If your friend is visiting a chat room, the dialog box tells you where she's hiding.

3. **Click Go to join your friend in the chat room.**

The Locate feature may reveal that your friend is in a private room. In that case, send an instant message to find out the name of the room. Of course, the person may respond that she's in a private room and you can't come . . . so there! But if she's a true friend, she gives you the name of the private room. After you know the room name, joining her there is easy.

To join your friend in a private chat room, follow these steps:

1. **Choose People⇨Start Your Own Chat.**

2. **Click the Private Chat button.**

   The Private Chat dialog box appears.

3. **Enter the name of the private chat room in the Private Chat dialog box, and click Go Chat to join the private fun.**

Ignoring Someone in a Chat Room

When someone in a chat room gets too obnoxious, ignore him. (It's the best form of revenge.) After you ignore the person, none of his text appears in your Chat window.

To ignore a person in a chat room, follow these steps:

1. **Double-click the obnoxious person's screen name in the People Here list.**

   The People Here list is the list of names on the right side of the chat room window.

2. **When the dialog box pops up, check the Ignore Member box.**

3. **Close the dialog box.**

Repeat these steps to stop ignoring someone (assuming that he repented his crime).

Reporting Problems in a Chat Room

Occasionally, in a chat room, you run into someone who just won't play by the rules. The person may use foul language, fill up the screen by continually sending irrelevant messages (such as "I exist!"), or just be downright obnoxious.

Before doing anything else, ask the person to stop. If the person persists, follow these steps:

1. **Highlight the offending text and choose Edit⇨Copy (or press Ctrl+C) to copy it.**

2. **Click the Notify AOL button at the bottom-right corner of the chat room screen (the second button in the right column).**

   The Notify AOL window opens, as shown in Figure 6-3.

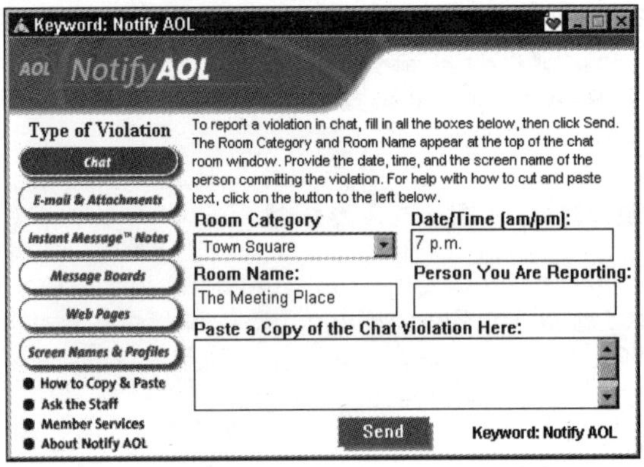

Figure 6-3:
You can notify AOL about problems encountered in a chat room.

3. **Choose the name of the person to report.**

4. **Click in the large box called Paste a Copy of the Chat Violation Here, which you can find in the lower-right of the Notify AOL window.**

5. **Choose Edit⇨Paste (or press Ctrl+V) to paste the text in the box.**

6. **Click the Send button at the bottom of the window.**

   The report goes to the AOL Community Action Team. The team reviews the report and decides on an appropriate action.

If, for some reason, the Notify AOL button seems to be on holiday (such as when you are in a private chat room), use keyword **Notify AOL** and then click the Chat button.

Using Chat Logs to record an ongoing chat

Following everything that's going on in a chat room is tough, particularly if a constant stream of instant messages or other interruptions is distracting you. To combat this problem, America Online includes a recording feature called *Chat Logs*. Chat Logs store every word uttered in the current chat room. They're great for taking minutes at online club meetings, recording a special online presentation, or just tracking who said what.

To create a chat log, follow these steps:

1. **Head into the chat room and choose My Files⇨Log Manager.**

   The Logging dialog box appears.

2. **Click Open Log in the Chat Log portion of the window.**

   The Open Log dialog box appears, displaying the name of the chat room as the filename.

3. **Press Enter or click Save.**

   The log is on and ready to record.

4. **To close the log when you finish, choose My Files⇨Log Manager; then click Close Log.**

   You can't view the log file until you close it.

Chat logs are plain text files, so any word processor or text editor can open them.

Book VII
Chapter 6

Meeting and
Chatting with
Friends Online

Locating People on America Online

Looking for someone? Try using the Member Directory to search for the person's name or screen name. The Member Directory lists AOL members who have created Member Profiles. If the person created a profile, then the member's information is indexed in the Member Directory. If the person doesn't have a profile entry, you can't find the name by searching the directory (in fact, you probably can't find it at all). You can also create your own profile so that other AOL members can find out about you.

Searching the Member Directory

You can search the Member Directory to find people who share your interests. To find the Member Directory window, do one of the following:

✦ Choose People⇨Locate Member Online.

✦ Click the Member Directory button in any chat room window.

✦ Use keyword **Member Directory**.

If you're looking for specific answers to individual fields in the Member Profiles (such as single men who use Macintosh computers and have chosen "To be or not to be" as a personal quote), choose the Advanced Search tab and fill in the appropriate fields. If you're just out for a quick search, the aptly named Quick Search tab should suit you fine.

To perform a Quick Search of the Member Directory, follow these steps:

1. **Choose People⇨Member Directory.**

2. **Type whatever you're looking for (screen name, hobby, age, or whatever) in the Search Entire Profile for the Following Words text box (see Figure 6-4).**

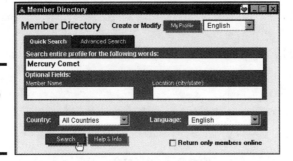

Figure 6-4: Specify the search criteria here.

3. **If you know the name of the person you're looking for, or if you're looking for someone who lives in a certain city or state, fill in the optional Member Name and Location fields.**

4. **Select a country from the Country drop-down list box if you want to find a member from a particular country that America Online serves. Otherwise, leave the selection set to All Countries.**

5. **Click Search.**

The search engine returns only a maximum of 100 results. If a topic matches 18,000 entries in the database, the search directory still returns only 100. So narrow your topic as much as you can before you start your search.

If you're looking for someone with a common name, include an interest, occupation, or place of residence to narrow the search.

Viewing Member Profiles

Profiles identify America Online members. The profile is also your listing in the Member Directory. When you meet people in a chat room and want to know a little more about them, take a peek at their profiles. Profiles tell you as much or as little about a member as that person wants you to know. Some profiles are very specific, listing first and last names, occupations, and hobbies. Others are downright silly. (But that's what makes life fun.)

To view another AOL member's profile, follow these steps:

1. **Choose People➪Get AOL Member Profile or press Ctrl+G.**

The Get a Member's Profile dialog box opens.

2. **Enter the screen name of the member into the text box, and then click OK or press Enter.**

3. **If the member has a profile, the Member Profile window opens (see Figure 6-5).**

If no profile exists, a dialog box appears that states that no profile is available for a user by that name.

Figure 6-5: Get to know another AOL member by viewing his or her profile.

Book VII Chapter 6

Meeting and Chatting with Friends Online

TIP

To locate the member online, use the Locate button at the bottom of the Member Profile window. To send an e-mail, click the E-Mail button. The Write Mail window leaps to the screen with the member's screen name already entered into the Send To text field.

If you happen to be in a chat room when the profile urge strikes, double-click any screen name in the member list to the right of the chat room window. A small Screen Name dialog box appears. Click the Get Info button, and the profile appears if it's available.

Creating your Member Profile

Your Member Profile tells the world who you are, what you think, and why you exist on the planet. If you want everyone on America Online to know something about you, put the information into your profile. You use the same steps to both create and change your Member Profile.

To create (or update) your Member Profile, follow these steps:

1. **Press Ctrl+K, type the keyword** Profile, **and press Enter.**

The Member Directory window opens.

2. **Click the My Profile button.**

The Edit Your Online Profile window appears, but the window is unreadable due to the warning dialog box that jumps to the screen directly on top of the Profile window. The warning dialog box begins by telling you that all America Online members can see your AOL Member Profile. Then it suggests that no member include personal information in any profile — all good stuff to know.

3. **Click OK after you read through the helpful dialog box and proceed with your regularly scheduled Member Profile. If you never want to see the warning again, check Please Do Not Show Me This Again and then click OK.**

4. **Enter your information into the spaces in the profile window (see Figure 6-6).**

Include as little or as much information as you like; some members include only their screen names and general geographic location, while others complete each line and even include a personal quote.

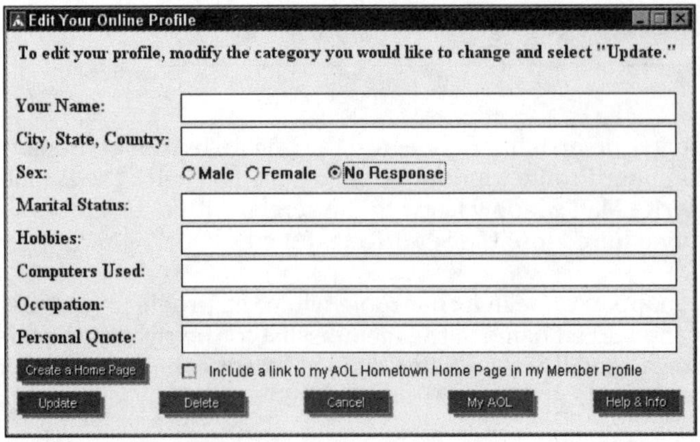

Figure 6-6:
Remember:
Anyone on
AOL can
see the
information
in your
profile.

Edit Your Online Profile

To edit your profile, modify the category you would like to change and select "Update."

Your Name:

City, State, Country:

Sex: ○ Male ○ Female ● No Response

Marital Status:

Hobbies:

Computers Used:

Occupation:

Personal Quote:

Create a Home Page ☐ Include a link to my AOL Hometown Home Page in my Member Profile

Update   Delete   Cancel   My AOL   Help & Info

5. **Click Update to store your changes or click Cancel to forget the changes.**

   Within a few minutes (sometimes longer), the new profile proudly takes its place in the Member Directory.

If you want to include more information than the profile allows, try creating your own Web page. Clicking the Create a Home Page button in the Edit Your Online Profile window takes you to AOL Hometown, where you can upload your current Web page, if you have one, or design a new one. You can also get there with the keyword **Hometown**.

America Online gives you the capability to customize your profile. *America Online For Dummies*, 7th Edition, by John Kaufeld (published by Hungry Minds, Inc.) contains a whole chapter on cool profile tricks.

Using Your Buddy List

Use the Buddy List, shown in Figure 6-7, to find your friends as they sign on to America Online (keyword **Buddy**). This list window appears when you sign on to the service, and you can set it to notify you when certain people sign on. You can use the Buddy List to send your buddies instant messages or start chats. You can also set your preferences to keep certain screen names from locating you with their Buddy Lists.

Book VII
Chapter 6

Meeting and Chatting with Friends Online

Figure 6-7:
You can create multiple Buddy List Groups.

By default, your Buddy List appears on-screen when you sign on to America Online. If your Buddy List doesn't appear for some reason, use keyword **Buddy** or choose People⇨Buddy List to make it appear.

Adding a buddy to your Buddy List

Before you can start using your Buddy List, you need to add buddies to it. Here's how:

1. **Click the Setup button in your Buddy List.**

2. **In the area on the left, highlight the group that you want to add the buddy to.**

   By default, you have three groups: Buddies, Family, and Co-Workers. If you want to create your own, see the section, "Creating a Buddy List Group." You can also rename the default groups with the Rename button.

3. **Click Add Buddy.**

   A little Add New Buddy window opens.

4. **Type your buddy's name in the text box and click Save.**

Creating a Buddy List Group

You can create your own group for your role-playing friends, your knitting club, or whatever you like. To create a Buddy List Group, follow these steps:

1. **Click the Setup button.**

   The Buddy List Setup window opens.

2. **Click the Add Group button.**

3. **Type a catchall name for this Buddy List Group, such as Puzzle Club or Pet Monkey Support Group, and then click Save.**

   You now start adding buddies to your new group.

Renaming buddies and groups

Sometimes, your Buddy List needs a little tweaking to stay current. To rename buddies or groups in your Buddy List:

1. **Click the Setup button.**

   The Buddy List Setup dialog box appears.

2. **Highlight the group or buddy that you want to rename and then click the Rename button.**

   A Rename window appears.

3. **Type the new name for your buddy or group in the text box and click Save.**

Deleting buddies and groups

If you and a buddy part ways or your rock group disbands, you'll probably want to remove the buddy or group from your list. To do so:

1. **Click the Setup button.**

2. **Highlight the group or buddy that you want to remove.**

3. **Click the Remove button.**

A dialog box appears and asks whether you're sure you want to delete the group.

4. **Click OK.**

Instant Messages

Communicate privately and individually with online friends through *instant messages*. These little windows appear on the top-left side of your screen. Instant messages enable you to drop someone a quick question or comment if she's online (or talk privately with another member while sharing a public chat room).

Sending an instant message

To start an instant message (IM) session, double-click the person's name on a chat room list and click Send Instant Message. You also can click the IM icon on the toolbar, choose People⇨Send Instant Message, or press Ctrl+I), and then type the member's screen name. If someone in your Buddy List is online, you can simply highlight his name and click Send IM.

Use the buttons in the Instant Message window to make your IMs look like professional documents. Located at the top of the message text box, these eight buttons do almost the same tasks as the e-mail formatting buttons. To use a button to format an IM, click the button before typing text or highlight text after typing and then click the desired button.

To send a friend the name of a really neat place you found on America Online, open the area you want to tell your friend about. Then click the Favorite Places icon and click Insert in Instant Message. An Instant Message window opens with a blue underlined title inserted. That's your link!

Receiving an instant message

Sometimes, an instant message appears on your computer screen, especially if you're cruising the chat rooms or several people have you in their Buddy Lists.

To respond to an instant message, follow these steps:

1. **When you receive an instant message, a small window pops up in the upper-left corner of the screen. The sender's screen name and message appear in the top window.**

2. **Type your response in the lower window, using the format buttons to spice up the text.**

3. **Click the Send button.**

   Your response jumps to the top text box of the Instant Message window so that the original sender can read it.

4. **Continue the conversation by typing in the lower window, clicking Send, and then reading the response in the upper window.**

If you're tired of the constant barrage of instant messages that clutter your screen, take a breather by blocking the little suckers:

✦ To block instant messages, send an instant message to the screen name $IM_OFF. The text part of the message doesn't matter.

✦ To turn instant messages back on, send an instant message to $IM_ON. The message text can be anything.

Reporting problems in an instant message

Offensive instant message senders take two forms: password scammers who want your account information or credit card number, and folks who are just plain offensive. Sometimes, if you ask politely, the members sending you offensive messages will either stop and become polite or go away and leave you alone.

To report a violation, click the Notify AOL button or use the keyword **Notify AOL** and then click the Instant Message Notes button.

Discussion Boards

Discussion boards resemble electronic bulletin boards. You wander in, read the messages that other folks have posted, and perhaps add a few messages of your own. The process is like a chat in slow motion. The online symbol for a discussion board is often an index card with a little red tack through it. Click anything that has this icon to go to the discussion boards for that area. (Sometimes, a Messages button marks the boards.) Look for discussion boards on every America Online channel.

Reading a discussion board message

To find out what others think about a topic, read the messages posted in a discussion board.

To read a discussion board message, follow these steps:

1. **Open the forum and look for the discussion board icon.**

   You might see a square icon that looks like a note fastened with a pin, or you might find a button cleverly labeled "Messages" or "Boards."

2. **Double-click the icon or click the button to open the messages window.**

3. **Highlight a topic in the Topics list and click List All.**

   Simply double-clicking the topic works, too.

4. **Highlight a Subject and click Read Post (or double-click the subject).**

   A message window opens and shows the first message.

5. **To read all the postings under that subject, click Next Post when you want to move forward. To jump to the next subject, click the Subject button at the right side of the window.**

   When any arrow turns gray, you've reached the end of the messages in that direction.

After you visit a discussion board for the first time, on your next visit you can click List Unread, rather than List All, to see the new topics and pick up where you left off.

Checking for new discussion board messages

Flipping through the boards and looking for new messages defines the word *tedious*. Make your life easier by using the Find By drop-down list at the bottom of the discussion board window.

To check for new discussion board messages, follow these steps:

1. **Use the Topics windows to locate the forum of your choice (see Steps 1 through 3 in the preceding section.**

2. **Click the online area's messages icon to enter the discussion board.**

   The discussion board window hops onto the screen, showing you a list of subject folders.

Book VII Chapter 6

Meeting and Chatting with Friends Online

3. **Highlight a folder, and click the Find By drop-down list; then select Date to open the Find Since dialog box.**

   In the middle of the dialog box, you see three option buttons, as shown in Figure 6-8.

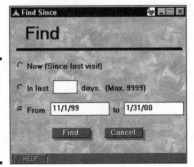

Figure 6-8:
Specify the
criteria that
you want to
use for the
search.

4. **Click the option button next to your choice, fill in any requested information, and then click Find.**

   If you select the second or third option, type in the number of days you want to search or the date range.

Posting a reply to a discussion board

Lively discussion requires two-way conversation. On the America Online discussion boards, posting a reply to someone's comment enables you to add your opinions to the topic at hand. You can either reply publicly to the board itself, or you can reply privately via e-mail.

Replying to the board

When you reply to the board itself, your input is public. Anyone can browse the boards and see what you've written.

To reply to the discussion boards, follow these steps:

1. **Find a message that you want to discuss, and click Reply.**

   A Reply window opens, with the subject line already entered. In most cases, leave the subject line as it appears so that others can follow the discussion.

2. **Enter your response in the Reply Window box. Use the formatting buttons along the top edge of the text box to jazz up your post.**

3. **To include some or all of the previous poster's message in your reply, use the Original Message Text box and highlight the words, sentences, or phrases that you want to include. Then click the Quote button (see Figure 6-9).**

   The highlighted text jumps into the Reply window, complete with a message board quote mark.

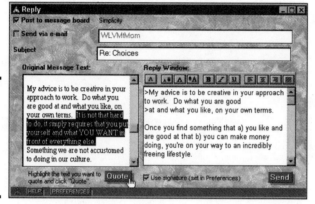

Figure 6-9:
You can quote text from the original message in your reply.

4. **Type either your name or your America Online screen name at the bottom of the message, or check Use Signature at the bottom of the message box.**

5. **Check the Send Via E-Mail box to send your post to the author of the original message, check the Post to Message Board box to add your thoughts to the message thread, or check both boxes.**

6. **Click the Send button.**

Click the Preferences button at the bottom of any of the colorful message board windows to set your Message Board Preferences. These preferences let you sort messages, show messages posted within so many days, or add a special signature to your message board posts.

Replying via e-mail

Replying to a discussion post via e-mail enables you to voice your opinions privately to the original poster. These messages never reach the discussion boards. Instead, they go directly to the America Online member's mailbox. To post a reply, follow these steps:

1. **Click Reply to open the Post a Reply message box.**

2. **In the Original Message Text box, highlight any material that you want to include from the previous post. Then click the Quote button.**

3. Write your response in the Reply Window text box.

4. Type your name.

5. Check the Send Via E-Mail box.

6. Uncheck the Post to Message Board box.

7. Click Send.

You can also use the Write Mail window to send your reply, if you like. See Book VII, Chapter 3, for more on creating and sending e-mail.

Index

Book VIII

Internet Activities

The 5th Wave   By Rich Tennant

"For 30 years, I've put a hat and coat on to make sales calls, and I'm not changing now just because I'm doing it on the Web from my living room."

Contents at a Glance

Chapter 1: Shopping Online

In This Chapter

✔ Observing the rules for buying online

✔ Searching for a deal on the Internet

✔ Using bots to compare-shop for items

✔ Buying items at online auctions

✔ Sampling the many things you can buy on the Internet

The Internet has become, among other things, a giant shopping mall. Retailers are rushing to offer their goods online. The U.S. Commerce Department predicts that people will buy 300 billion dollars' worth of merchandise on the Internet in the coming decade. Although shopping malls won't go the way of the dinosaur, many people do prefer shopping online to shopping at the mall. Who wants to deal with crowded parking lots and long lines? Some predict that people will buy basic goods, such as groceries and drugstore items online, and that trucks delivering these online bargains will soon fill streets and highways everywhere.

This chapter is dedicated to the idea that, if you want it, you can buy it online. It explains the pitfalls of buying online, how to go about a search of the Internet for the items you want, and how to employ a *bot* — an electronic robot — in searches. You discover how and where to participate in online auctions. This chapter also includes the names of scores of Web sites where you can do your shopping.

Ten Rules for Buying Items Online

Somewhere, somebody is trying to figure out a way to make odors travel over the Internet. Somebody else is working on technology that permits you to reach into your computer monitor and touch an item that you want to buy. Until these mad scientists complete their work — and they aren't likely to complete it soon — buying items online holds the same risks as buying items from a catalog. You can't smell or touch the item. Practically speaking, you can't tell what you've purchased until it arrives on your doorstep.

How safe is online shopping?

Naturally, people have concerns about shopping online. Sending a credit card number across the Internet can be disconcerting. Is the number going to end up on a computer somewhere for anyone to see and steal?

You don't need to worry. Buying items with a credit card *is* safe. Online merchants have gone to great lengths to make sure that credit card information is kept private:

✔ Sensitive information is scrambled and encrypted on merchants' Web servers so that outsiders can't read it.

✔ Encryption technology is used to establish the identity of the buyer so that no one can pose as someone else.

If you're not sure whether a company has secured its site, just look in the bottom right corner of your screen. Secured sites contain a lock, while nonsecured sites do not.

What's more, as an online buyer, the same federal laws that protect mail orders and telephone orders also protect you. You have the right to return an item if it's broken or not what you thought you ordered.

Items such as perfume, clothing, and jewelry are hard to judge online. Maybe the most important rule for shopping online also happens to be the most important rule for shopping: Let the buyer beware. Other than that, here are ten rules for buying items online. Disregard these rules, and you do so at your peril:

✦ **Always pay by credit card.** That way, if the deal goes sour, you can challenge the purchase by calling your credit card issuer and canceling it.

✦ **Know what the shipping and handling charges are.** Some companies that sell items at a discount make up the lost revenue by charging exorbitant fees for shipping and handling.

✦ **Don't do business with a company that doesn't have a refund and return policy.** The terms of the policy should be stated somewhere on the Web site. What happens if you're unhappy with an item you purchased? Can you return it? How soon must you return it? Who pays for returning the item if returning it is an expensive proposition?

✦ **Take note of what the seller offers in the way of customer service.** Will the seller pay for repairs if any are needed? For high-tech products, does the seller offer technical and setup assistance? In their rush to get on the Internet, more than a few businesses have forgotten that "the customer always comes first."

✦ **Ask yourself how difficult the item is to assemble, if it needs assembling.** Not everyone can interpret the complicated directions that come with items you have to put together yourself. Not everyone can wield a screwdriver. Because online purchases are delivered by mail, they need assembling more often than other purchases. If you're not good at assembling things, make sure that the items you buy are already assembled.

✦ **Don't do business with a company that does not provide its street address on its Web site.** A post office box won't do. Any company that doesn't have a genuine address is suspect.

✦ **Keep a well-documented paper trail of your dealings with the seller.** After you have filled out the order form, print it. When the seller sends you a confirmation notice by e-mail, print that, too. Keeping a paper trail is a hassle, but if you lose your customer order number or aren't sure when the package arrives whether everything you ordered is inside it, you will be glad you kept the papers. For that matter, print the Web page that describes the item. That way, you can be sure that you purchased what you thought you were purchasing.

✦ **Know the company's privacy policy.** Does the company intend to sell your name? Can you request that your name and personal information be kept private? Online privacy, we believe, will be a big issue in the years to come. As a matter of principle, we don't do business online with any company that doesn't post its privacy policy on its Web site.

✦ **Inspect your purchase as soon as it arrives.** Is this what you ordered? Some online retailers, especially during the holiday season, are so hurried that they fill orders incorrectly.

✦ **Trust your instincts.** If you're uncomfortable purchasing an item over the Internet, don't do it. If "supplies are running out," you're being pressured to buy an item, or you feel uneasy about it, don't buy. Make a cup of tea or putter in the garden instead.

The American Bar Association maintains a Web site called SafeShopping.org (www.safeshopping.org) that explains, from a legal point of view, everything you need to know about online shopping, including what your rights are as an online customer.

Going Shopping Online

Things cost less on the Internet than they do in shops. This is because you, as the buyer, have many more choices, so you can find the best bargain. And although it's true that you have to pay shipping and handling charges for the goods you buy, you don't have to pay sales tax.

These pages explain how to find goods on the Internet. Finding places to shop online is easy. Think of your favorite store, and you're halfway there. You can also hire a robot to find items for you. You can even look in one of the Internet's "everything stores."

Going to the Web site of your favorite merchant

Your favorite store likely has a Web site. Try paying it a visit before you poke around the Internet for an item that you want. Perhaps you can get it cheaply from the store you know and love.

To find a store's Web site, start by making an educated guess as to its Web site address. In the Address or Location text box (or whatever the box where you type the URL is called in your browser), type `www.companyname.com` (where *companyname* is the name of the store), press the Enter key, and see what happens.

If nothing happens, you have to resort to a search engine to find the store. To find out how to conduct a search by using Internet Explorer, refer to Book III, Chapter 2; if you want to do a search with Netscape, see Book IV, Chapter 1.

Letting a bot do your shopping

A *bot* is a software robot whose job is to scour the Internet for something or other — digital cameras, cocktail dresses, or sports memorabilia, for example. After the bot has done its job, it returns home with a list that shows which online merchants sell the item and the price they charge for it.

Bots are great for comparison shopping on the Internet. Instead of going from Web site to Web site in search of an item, you can make the bot do the work. And you can be sure to find the best price. The disadvantage of bots, however, is that they usually take several minutes to do their work. Moreover, you have to know the exact name, make, and model of the item you're looking for.

These bots are worth a try when you know exactly what you want, and you want to buy it on the Internet:

✦ **EvenBetter.com:** This bot specializes in books, music, videos, and DVDs. Address: `www.stepware.com/evenbetter`

✦ **MySimon:** MySimon is on speaking terms with more than 2,000 online merchants. The merchants are organized by category, as shown in Figure 1-1. Click a category, enter a keyword, and compare prices from different online merchants. Address: `www.mysimon.com`

✦ **Search.com:** This is a "search of all searches" Web site. Begin a search starting here, and CNET Search.com makes use of more than 800 search engines to find what you are looking for. Address: `www.search.com`

When you search with a bot, try to list a price range as part of the search. That way, you search for bargains instead of just searching for items.

Figure 1-1:
Scouring
the Internet
with the
MySimon
bot.

Pay a visit to BotSpot.com (`www.botspot.com`) to learn more about bots or to test-drive bots not mentioned in this book.

Searching at an "everything store"

An "everything store" is a site on the Internet that sells, or tries to sell, just about everything. Personally, we don't care for everything stores. With all that clutter, finding an item can be difficult. And we have discovered that getting lost in the bureaucracy when you have a question or concern about a purchase is easy at an everything store. Still, the stores offer good prices for their wares; maybe you'll have better luck than we have. Check 'em out:

✦ **Amazon.com:** The mother of all everything stores, Amazon started as a bookseller but has expanded and now sells music, videos, DVDs, electronics, software, and toys. Visitors to the site, which is shown in Figure 1-2, can review and read reviews of the products. Address: `www.amazon.com`

✦ **Buy.com:** This self-styled Internet superstore sells computers, software, music, books, electronics, and golf stuff. Click the Clearance tab to look for bargains. Address: `www.buy.com`

✦ **iQVC.com:** This all-purpose site is a sort of cybershopping channel. It features apparel, home furnishings, jewelry, health and beauty products, collectibles, and toys. Address: `www.qvc.com`

**Book VIII
Chapter 1**

Shopping Online

Figure 1-2:
Amazon.
com is
perhaps
the most
well-known
online
merchant.

A stroll through the cyberbazaar

A chapter about shopping online isn't complete without some tips about
where to shop. Following are Web sites that have won acclaim for offering
exceptional goods. In this cyberbazaar are beauty products, books, clothing,
computers and computer software, electronics, flowers, food and beverages,
furniture, gardening supplies, houses, music, and toys.

Beauty products

✦ **Beauty.com:** Natural hair care, makeup, and skin care accessories.
   Address: www.beauty.com

✦ **BeautyAndSoul.com:** Health and beauty products for people of African
   descent. Address: www.beautyandsoul.com

✦ **Sephora.com:** More hair care, makeup, and skin care stuff. Address:
   www.sephora.com

Books

✦ **Barnes and Noble:** Searching for books by author or category is easy in
   this Web site, which offers an enormous number of books. Address:
   www.bn.com

✦ **Bibliofind:** Starting here, you can search for used and rare books and periodicals offered by thousands of booksellers. Address: `www.bibliofind.com`

✦ **Jessica's Biscuit:** The place to go to for cookbooks. Address: `www.jessicas.com`

✦ **Powell's Books:** Offers out-of-print and rare books, as well as new books. Address: `www.powells.com`

Clothing

✦ **Beau Ties Ltd.:** In their words, "We exist to meet the bow-tie-needs of the world's bow tie wearer." Address: `www.beautiesltd.com`

✦ **Brooks Brothers:** Ivy League clothes at Ivy League prices. Address: `www.brooksbrothers.com`

✦ **Delia's:** G.I. hula board shorts, asha skirts, and other items for teenage girls. Address: `www.delias.com`

✦ **Underneath.com:** Underwear, socks, and brassieres for all occasions. Address: `www.underneath.com`

✦ **Village Hat Shop:** Whether you wear hats or not, check out the variety at this site. Address: `www.villagehatshop.com`

Computers and computer software

✦ **Chumbo.com:** Specializes in inexpensive software. Address: `www.chumbo.com`

✦ **Egghead:** Offers electronics and hardware, as well as software. Address: `www.egghead.com`

✦ **NECX Direct:** Click the <u>Shop by Product</u> hyperlink to start your search. Address: `www.necxdirect.com`

✦ **Outpost.com:** Computers, software, peripherals, and cameras are offered here. Address: `www.outpost.com`

Electronics

✦ **800.com:** Includes a forum where customers rate cameras, TVs, and other products. Address: `www.800.com`

✦ **Hifi.com:** Easy-to-search site that includes buyer's advice. Address: `www.hifi.com`

**Book VIII
Chapter 1**

Shopping Online

Flowers

+ **1-800-Flowers.com:** Flowers with a "seven-day freshness" guarantee. Address: www.1800flowers.com

+ **Flowerbud.com:** Delivers flowers the next day anywhere in the United States. Address: www.flowerbud.com

+ **FTD.com:** The Internet version of the established FTD flower-delivery service. Address: www.ftd.com

Food and beverages

+ **GreatFood.com:** Order a gift basket from this site, which offers a huge selection of gourmet food. Address: www.greatfood.com

+ **Penzeys Spices:** For the gourmet cook, offers 250 spices, herbs, and seasoning blends. Address: www.penzeys.com

+ **Send.com:** Scotch, champagne, wine, fine foods, cigars — a classy saloon they got here. Address: www.send.com

+ **Wine.com:** An enormous selection of wine is found at this easy-to-search Web site. Address: www.wine.com

+ **Zingermans.com:** An online deli, with no waiting in line. Address: www.zingermans.com

Furniture

+ **FurnitureFind.com:** Search by room for articles of furniture. Address: www.furniturefind.com

+ **Shaker Furniture:** Elegant, expertly crafted furniture from time-tested Shaker designs. Address: www.shakerworkshops.com

Gardening supplies

+ **Landscape USA:** Offers gardening tips and gardening products. Address: www.landscapeusa.com

+ **Territorial Seed Co.:** Besides being a supplier of seeds and gardening products, you can get advice here. Address: www.territorial-seed.com

Houses

+ **HomeStore.com:** Search the 1.3 million homes in the National Association of Realtors database. Address: www.homestore.com

+ **MSN HomeAdvisor:** Search by city or zip code from a database of 750,000 homes nationwide. Address: www.homeadvisor.com

✦ **Owners.com:** The "For Sale by Owner" Web site. Avoid 6 percent sales commissions. Address: `www.owners.com`

Music

✦ **CDNOW:** A great selection of CDs at an easy-to-search Web site. Address: `www.cdnow.com`

✦ **Thursday's Golden Goodies:** The good old vinyl record is not dead! You can still get them here. Address: `www.thursdays.com`

✦ **Tower Records:** Enormous selection of CDs and DVDs at low prices. Address: `www.towerrecords.com`

Toys

✦ **Catch the Wind:** Offers exotic kites, windsocks, and other items that dance in the sky. Address: `www.catchthewind.com`

✦ **Copernicus Toys & Gifts:** Educational toys for bright kids and kids whose parents think they're bright. Address: `www.copernicustoys.com`

✦ **Mobileation:** Offers wagons, go-carts, and other items that kids can ride. Address: `www.mobileation.com`

Buying at an Online Auction

If you're the kind who stops the car at every garage sale you come to, you'll like online auctions. The success of eBay (`www.ebay.com`), the most famous auction house, has inspired others. Some four dozen online auction houses offer everything under the sun — flea-market items, antiques, electronics, clothing, collectibles, art, and toys. And, these being auction houses, you get to name the price — as long as someone doesn't outbid you.

Online auction houses fall in two categories:

✦ **Person-to-person houses:** Person-to-person auction houses bring buyers and sellers together. A seller posts his or her wares at the auction house's Web site. Each item appears on a Web page. Buyers can go to the Web page, read about the item, and often view a picture of it. In return for posting sellers' Web pages, the auction house takes a percentage of each sale. The seller decides the method of payment and is responsible for delivering the goods.

✦ **Merchant houses:** Merchant houses deal in manufacturers' overstock items. They own the items they auction. Buyers beware: Sometimes the items at merchant houses are outdated or have been cast off by manufacturers.

Most online auctions last a week or more, with the bidding (if any bids are made) getting more frenzied as the deadline draws near. If you have the time to look around, you can find great deals at online auctions.

Online auctions: Ten rules of engagement

Here are ten rules of engagement for participating in an online auction:

✦ **Avoid impulse bidding.** Yes, the beanbag chair is being offered at a good price, but do you really need a beanbag chair?

✦ **Browse by category, not by entering keywords, to look for items.** A keyword search, especially at a place like eBay, usually turns up more items than a mortal can look through in a lifetime. At person-to-person auction houses, which resemble a vast flea market, browsing is the way to go. If you're looking for something specific, look to a merchant auction house or a retailer.

✦ **Investigate the price.** Just because an item is being auctioned online doesn't mean that it's a good buy. An excellent place to investigate prices is www.consumerworld.org/pages/shopping.htm.

✦ **Investigate the item as much as you can online.** Besides reading the description thoroughly, telephone or e-mail the seller. Most sellers gladly answer questions about their wares.

✦ **Investigate the seller.** The National Consumer League's Internet Fraud Watch reports that online sellers were responsible for 78 percent of online-scam complaints in 2000. At person-to-person auction houses, you can go to a Web page where other buyers have described their dealings with the seller. Visit the page and read the seller's modus operandi. While you're at it, make sure that you know the seller's policies. How does he or she accept a payment? Can the item be put in escrow?

✦ **See about returning items.** Some sellers allow items to be returned within a certain time period.

✦ **Find out whether the auction house offers insurance for items that were not received.** For example, eBay pays $200 less a $25 deductible for items that were paid for but not delivered.

✦ **Find out whether the auction house offers escrow services.** Being able to put a payment in escrow gives the buyer an element of security. Until the buyer approves the item, the escrow service holds the payment. The payment is returned to the buyer if the item proves unsatisfactory.

✦ **Read the help screens before you take the plunge.** No one likes reading help screens, but knowing how an auction house conducts auctions is essential.

✦ **Observe the ten rules of buying online** (see "Ten Rules for Buying Items Online," earlier in this chapter).

TIP

If someone else outbids you in an online auction, don't despair. Try e-mailing the seller and asking whether he or she has a second copy of the item that you can bid on. Many sellers operate small businesses through online auction houses. These sellers often have more than one copy of an item.

Online auction houses

Dozens of online auction houses operate online. These are the established houses with the best reputations:

✦ **Amazon.com:** A person-to-person auction house, Amazon.com came late to the online auction business. The site doesn't offer as many items as eBay, but the screens are easy to manage and navigate. (Click the <u>Auctions</u> hyperlink.) Address: `www.amazon.com`

✦ **eBay:** eBay is the granddaddy of online auction houses (see Figure 1-3). eBay, a person-to-person auction house, is the merchandise equivalent of Noah's Ark. Just about anything that you can imagine is up for bid — new and used items, antiques, electronics, flea-market stuff, you name it. Browsing goods and bidding is easy. And eBay offers free insurance and an escrow service. Address: `www.ebay.com`

✦ **Yahoo! Auctions:** Yahoo! runs a person-to-person auction house at this site. Like all things Yahoo!, the site is easy to navigate, and the help directions are clear and straightforward. Antiques, collectibles, clothing, computers, garden tools, and toys are auctioned. Address: `auctions.yahoo.com`

Figure 1-3: If you're the kind who stops the car at every garage sale you see, you'll like eBay.

Book VIII Chapter 1

Shopping Online

People who desperately seek a certain item can search for it at several auction houses at once. Go to CNET Search.com (`www.search.com`) and look under Shopping. Then enter the name of the item you are seeking and click the Search button. The results will show items being auctioned at Amazon.com and other auction houses.

Ten Unusual Places to Shop Online

"Variety," Shakespeare wrote, "is the spice of life." Following are ten spicy Web sites that sell unusual goods. Come to think of it, some of the goods sold here aren't as unusual as they are weird:

- ✦ **Antler Works of Arkansas:** Yes, that table, that chair, and that lamp are made from antlers! The proprietors of this site make antler furniture to order. And you can even supply the antlers yourself, if you happen to be fond of a set or two. Address: `www.antlerworks.com`

- ✦ **Archie McPhee:** From this site (see Figure 1-4), you can buy the Texas lunchbox, the luche libre nodder, the catcher's mitt chair, and, of course, the classic rubber chicken, among other items. What is all this stuff exactly? You have to see for yourself. It's indescribable. Address: `www.mcphee.com`

- ✦ **Art.com:** Art.com offers thousands of interesting paintings, photographs, travel posters, billboards, advertisements, and the like. You can find many thumbnail pictures that you can click to enlarge. And weren't these guys lucky to get there first and nab the name Art.com? Address: `www.art.com`

- ✦ **The Electric Gallery:** Take a stroll through the Electric Gallery, which offers examples of naïve and insider art by painters the world over. We consider this site a shining example of what commercialism on the Internet can be — a chance to make goods from far-flung places available to everyone. Address: `www.electricgallery.com`

- ✦ **eZiba.com:** eZiba.com offers a neat collection of crafts from around the world. You can browse the catalogue or click a map of the world to look at handicrafts from different regions. Address: `www.eziba.com`

- ✦ **Just Balls:** This Web site has balls — leather balls, basketballs, baseballs, you name it. Only balls are sold here. Be sure to check out the Ball Encyclopedia, which gives the official circumference, diameter, and air pressure of every kind of ball, including takraw balls. Address: `www.justballs.com`

✦ **PetJewelry.com:** Based in Beverly Hills (where else?), PetJewelry.com presents designer pet collars and blankets for designer dogs and designer cats. You've gotta see this site to believe it. Address: `www.petjewelry.com`

✦ **The Sharper Image:** The Sharper Image is the home of the Ionic Breeze Quadra (it clears and circulates air in total silence), the Ultrasonic Wave Cleaner (it "supercleans" glasses and jewelry), and the exclusive Light and Sound Soother (it calms the auditory and visual senses). Go here to find something new for the man or woman who has everything — except what's offered on this Web site. Address: `www.sharperimage.com`

✦ **Spy Guys:** To the tune of "Theme from Mission Impossible," this site offers electronic devices for spying, including night vision scopes, wire-tapping devices, and miniaturized microphones and tape recorders. Very creepy. Check it out and shiver. Address: `www.spyguys.com`

✦ **Vintage Vixen:** Vintage Vixen is the Web site for vintage clothing buffs. Evening gowns, cocktail dresses, and nightware and lingerie — among other items — from the 1870s to the 1970s are sold here. Each item has been photographed so that you can see precisely what you will wear to your next party. Address: `www.vintagevixen.com`

Figure 1-4:
Archie McPhee: Gifts for the person who has everything except a rubber chicken.

Chapter 2: Travel Planning Online

In This Chapter

✔ **Planning your next vacation**

✔ **Getting directions from the Internet**

✔ **Looking for cheap flights and buying cheap tickets online**

✔ **Booking a room on the Internet**

✔ **Getting ready for a trip abroad**

✔ **Eccentric Web sites for eccentric travelers**

Most people, however tentatively, are planning their next vacation. You need something to look forward to. About 3 p.m., when the afternoon starts to wane, lunch is a distant memory, and two or three hours of work are still due at the office, most people dream of being on vacation: backpacking in the Sierra Nevada, partying at Mardi Gras in New Orleans, cruising up the Amazon in a steamer, or basking in the sun on a beach in Bali.

This chapter is dedicated to those people who want to make their next vacation the best ever. We describe how to research a destination — how the Internet can help you find out where to stay and what to do while you're away. You find out how to obtain inexpensive airfares, hotel rooms, and rental cars. This chapter presents Internet resources for traveling abroad and offers a few eccentric Web sites for people stricken with wanderlust.

Researching a Destination

Taping a map to the wall and throwing darts at the map to decide where to go next is one way of travel planning. Mathematicians, however, have determined that the amount of pleasure you derive from a vacation is directly proportional to the amount of time you spend planning it.

Read on to find out how the Internet can help you plan itineraries, locate attractions on the map, and get directions for driving from here to there. You also discover how to get up-to-date information about the weather and road conditions where you want to travel.

Deciding where to go and what to see

The hardest decision to make when you are planning a travel itinerary is deciding where to go and what to see when you get there. The following

Web sites can help you match your desires and interests with attractions and destinations:

✦ **Arthur Frommer's Budget Travel Online:** This site is the Internet companion to the famous *Frommer's Travel Guides*. Besides travel advice, you can look for hotel accommodations, nightlife, shopping, and dining opportunities in cities the world over. Address: `www.frommers.com`

✦ **Citysearch.com:** This site currently offers comprehensive guides to 40 U.S. cities and 33 cities abroad. The guides are up to date, with detailed information about local restaurants, nightspots, clubs, and shopping. Address: `www.citysearch.com`

✦ **Excite Travel Destinations:** This site is part of the Excite search engine and is an excellent place to research itineraries, book hotel rooms, and investigate attractions. What's more, a search starting here plugs you into three other travel-planning Internet services: City Search, Digital City, and Preview Travel (all of which are described in this chapter). Address: `www.excite.com` and then click Travel.

✦ **Fodor's Travel Online:** Starting here, you can create a miniguide to a city you want to visit. Choose a city, declare what kind of information you want — hotel accommodations, dining, and so on — and you get suggestions about where to stay, eat, and visit. Although you won't stray too far off the beaten path, you will get solid information about the city of your choice. Click the Destinations hyperlink. Address: `www.fodors.com`

✦ **Online City Guide:** From this site, you can pinpoint a city in the United States, find a list of hyperlinks with information about the city, and click a link to help plan your vacation. The links are to private Web sites and sometimes are not the greatest, but try your luck. Address: `www.olcg.com`

✦ **Yahoo! Travel Pages:** Starting from this page at Yahoo!, you can begin investigating any number of travel subjects, including eco-tourism, train travel, and hitchhiking. Address: `dir.yahoo.com/Recreation/Travel`

Finding out how to get there

The Web sites listed here are meant to keep you from getting lost. These Web sites present online maps and online mapping tools to help you go precisely where you want to go. Still, before you look at the Web sites, consider the advantages of getting lost. Being lost quickens the senses. It makes you acutely aware of your surroundings. It makes you feel alive. Someday, a genius is going to put up a Web site with instructions that help people get lost.

Meanwhile, visit these Web sites when you are planning your vacation and you want to know where an attraction is and how to get there from your hotel or the airport:

✦ **How far is it?:** As the crow flies, how far is Athens, Georgia, from Athens, Greece? The answer: 5,628 miles (or 9,058 kilometers). This friendly Web site for crows and travel planners calculates distances in no time at all. Address: `www.indo.com/distance`

✦ **MapBlast!:** This is the best map site on the Internet. Displaying a map is pretty simple, and the tools for zooming in, zooming out, and printing are easy to understand and use. After you register, you can enter two addresses (see Figure 2-1) and generate a map that shows how to get from one address to another. Address: `www.mapblast.com`

✦ **MapQuest:** Click <u>Maps</u>➪<u>City</u>➪<u>Driving Directions</u> to get instructions for going from one place to another. Address: `www.mapquest.com`

✦ **Maps On Us:** This is another map and directions site, but what makes this special is the opportunity to get directions that avoid major highways. Choose Avoid Major Highways from the Route Type menu to find, theoretically at least, the most picturesque route between two places, or choose Favor Major Highways to find the fastest route. Address: `www.mapsonus.com`

✦ **Rand McNally Travel Site:** In the text box, type an address and a city. A map will show you the location of the address you entered. You can click to zoom in and examine the map more closely. By entering two addresses, you can get directions for going from place to place. Address: `www.randmcnally.com`

✦ **The Subway Navigator:** For 100 cities around the world, 15 of them in the United States, plan a subway or light train route from one station to the next. Address: `www.subwaynavigator.com`.

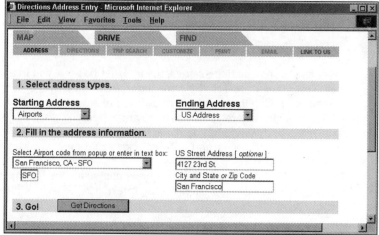

Figure 2-1: Getting driving directions at MapBlast!

Weather and road conditions

Ants and mosquitoes can ruin a good picnic, but that's nothing compared to what a vigorous storm can do to a weekend at the beach. Before you leave, check out these Web sites to see whether the roads are passable and what kind of weather you will encounter:

✦ **AccuTraffic:** From here, you can get the latest report about road conditions on American highways. Simply click <u>Traffic</u>, click a state, and then click <u>Weather-Related Road Conditions</u>. Weather reports are also available from this site. Address: `www.accutraffic.com`

✦ **USA Today Online Weather Almanac:** For travel planning, this site offers monthly climate data for cities the world over. Go here to find out what the average monthly high and low temperatures, rainfall, and snowfall are in a vacation spot that you are eyeing. Address: `www.usatoday.com/weather/walm0.htm`

✦ **The Weather Channel:** While you're deciding whether to pack a sweater or umbrella, pay a visit to the Weather Channel. By entering a city or zip code, you can find out what meteorologists think the weather will be for the coming week at your destination. Do you remember what Mark Twain said about the weather? He said, "Everybody talks about the meteorology, but nobody does anything about it." Address: `www.weather.com`

On the subject of road conditions, The Speedtrap Registry (`www.speedtrap.com`) describes speed traps — places where you are likely to get snagged for speeding — in the 50 states and in some European countries as well. Say the makers of the site, "This page in no way encourages speeding and recommends you always follow the posted speed limit. You are responsible for your own actions."

Online Travel Services

As far as purchasing tickets goes, the Internet has put you in the driver's seat. Now you can search the same databases that travel agents search. Instead of looking into prices at one airline or rental car service at a time, you can declare where you want to go and when you want to go there, and make everybody come to you. Your search of the Internet can turn up flights, rental cars, hotel rooms, and railway tickets that meet your travel needs.

Read on to find out how to look for inexpensive airline tickets, hotel rooms, rental cars, and railway tickets on the Internet.

Visiting an all-purpose travel site

These travel sites attempt to be all things to all people. You can book a hotel room, buy an airline ticket, or reserve a car from these sites. The advantage of looking here is that these sites are user-friendly. We suggest looking here first and then looking further afield in sites that specialize in airline tickets, hotel reservations, and rental car reservations. (Those sites are described later in this chapter.) Compare prices and services and pick the one you like best.

✦ **Expedia.com:** From here, you can buy airline tickets, reserve hotel rooms, and reserve rental cars. So-called wizards make it easy to search for good rates. Address: `www.expedia.com`

✦ **Travelocity.com:** Besides the usual travel-planning stuff, this is the place to go if your flight dates are flexible and you don't need to search for a ticket on a specific date or time. You'll get a list of low airfares on different days. Choose a day to travel instead of choosing a ticket. Enter your information in Find Me the Best Round Trip Search. Address: `www.travelocity.com`

✦ **Trip.com:** This is another comprehensive site where you can buy an airline ticket, book a hotel room, or rent a car, as shown in Figure 2-2. Check out the FlightTracker feature, which you can use to find out whether flights in the air are on time or are running late (choose FlightTracker at the bottom right corner.). Address: `www.trip.com`

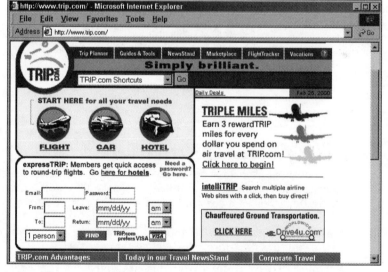

Figure 2-2: Look for a cheap flight, a good room, and a trusty rental car at Trip.com.

Book VIII Chapter 2

Travel Planning Online

Buying airline tickets

When you shop online, the old rule for finding an inexpensive airline ticket still applies: Buy the ticket early. Not that you can't snap up a bargain ticket at the last minute, but to do so, you have to conduct a vigorous search of the Internet. Here are places to look for inexpensive airline tickets:

✦ **1travel.com:** The "Low Price & Great Advice" site specializes in airline tickets (see Figure 2-3). This no-nonsense Web site is great because you can start searching for airline tickets without registering (or divulging your address, phone number, and e-mail address). Address: `www.1travel.com`

✦ **Cheap Tickets:** This site specializes in bargain tickets, and we've heard many good things said about it. Unfortunately, it isn't a user-friendly site, and registering is a long-winded procedure. Address: `www.cheaptickets.com`

Figure 2-3: At 1travel. com, you can start searching for airline tickets without registering first.

Booking a hotel or motel room

The all-purpose Web sites described earlier in this chapter are the best places to book chain hotels. But if you're looking for something special — a romantic retreat or a cozy hideaway — look to these sites:

✦ **BedandBreakfast.com:** If impersonal hotel chains turn you off, this is the site to visit. Address: `www.bedandbreakfast.com`

✦ **Fodor's Travel Online:** From this site, you can locate accommodations that suit your taste, although the site does favor chain hotels, such as Hilton and Holiday Inn. Click the <u>Destinations</u> hyperlink, choose your destination, click the Where to Stay check box, click the Continue button, and describe the kind of hotel or motel you want — its location, price range, and facilities. Address: `www.fodors.com`

✦ **HomeExchange.com:** At this site, you can look into exchanging vacation time at your home with the home of someone in a destination that you want to visit. Address: `www.homeexchange.com`

✦ **InnSite:** This is a guide to inns and bed and breakfasts in the United States and abroad. This site is slow, perhaps because it indexes 50,000 pages of inn directories, but the wait is worthwhile. Address: `www.innsite.com`

✦ **Vacation Direct:** Owners list their vacation homes and condos at this site, where you can find descriptions of the vacation rentals and instructions for contacting the owners. Address: `www.vacationdirect.com`

Traveling by rail

Traveling by rail offers the pleasures of traveling by car without the hassles. You can get up and stretch your legs. Instead of fast-food restaurants and highway clutter, the picturesque and the seedy roll past the window. Railroads cut through mountain passes and fly above wild rivers. The planet never looks as beautiful as it does from a railroad car.

Here are some Internet resources for traveling by rail:

✦ **Amtrak:** This, of course, is the United States passenger railway service. From this site, you can plan a trip by railroad and purchase tickets. Address: `www.amtrak.com`

✦ **European Rail Travel:** This site offers planning tips and advice for traveling by rail in Europe. You can get information about the famous Eurail Pass, as well as schedules of all European trains. Address: `www.eurorailways.com`

✦ **Yahoo! Resources for Hopping Freight Trains:** Hopping freight trains, as practitioners say, is the last great red-blooded American adventure. For itinerant laborers, it's the chief means of getting from job to job (and is, therefore, tolerated in some farming states). Hopping freights is also dangerous and illegal. This Web page at Yahoo! offers resources for people who are interested in this extremely alternative means of travel. Address: `dir.yahoo.com/Recreation/Travel/Train_ Travel/Train_Hopping`

Resources for Traveling Abroad

Many people like to travel abroad. When you go to the expense and trouble of traveling, you may want to land in a place where things look different and no one speaks English. That way, you really feel like you've traveled somewhere!

Book VIII Chapter 2

Travel Planning Online

Here are some Internet resources for world travelers:

✦ **Centers for Disease Control — Traveler's Health:** This invaluable Web site offers advice for staying healthy during your vacation. It explains which vaccinations you need and presents health information about specific regions. Address: `www.cdc.gov/travel`

✦ **Crazy Dog Travel Guide:** This site offers tips, advice, and numerous hyperlinks to help budget travelers all over the world plan their adventures. Address: `www.crazydogtravel.com`

✦ **Foreign Languages for Travelers:** How do you say, "Excuse me" in Swedish? You say, "Ursakta," as this Web site so ably points out. What makes this site cool and useful is its sound capabilities. When you click a foreign-language phrase, the Windows Media Player comes on-screen, and you can actually hear the phrase (as long as your computer is capable of playing sound). Address: `www.travlang.com/languages`

✦ **Lonely Planet Online:** From this superb Web site, you can research different destinations, get travel tips from others, or post a travel question that is bound to get an answer from Lonely Planet's legion of adventurers. Click the <u>Search</u> hyperlink to research a destination abroad or in the United States. Click <u>The Thorn Tree</u> hyperlink to see what others say about a destination or post your own question about it. Address: `www.lonelyplanet.com`

✦ **Time Out:** This site focuses on nightlife and entertainment in a couple dozen European cities (and a few American and Asian cities as well). Address: `www.timeout.com`

✦ **The Universal Currency Converter:** One United States dollar will fetch how many Malaysian ringgits? The answer: 3.799 (as of this writing, anyway). Go to this easy-to-use Web site to see what happens when one currency is converted into another. Address: `www.xe.net/ucc`

✦ **U.S. Customs Service — Traveler Information:** This helpful Web site explains such matters as how to import a car and why you were taxed for what you thought was a duty-free purchase. Address: `www.customs.ustreas.gov/travel/travel.htm`

✦ **U.S. State Department — Travel Warnings and Consular Information Sheets:** Here, you can find the visa and entry requirements that Americans must fulfill to travel to every country in the world. You can also find safety statistics, descriptions of medical facilities, and embassy addresses. Address: `travel.state.gov/travel_warnings.html`

Ten Eccentric Sites for Eccentric Travelers

Finally, here are ten eccentric sites for eccentric travelers. One of the drawbacks of getting travel information from the Internet is that corporate hotel chains that want to sell you something are the source of much of the information you find. The following sites are devoted strictly to travel, its spontaneous joys, and its occasional apprehensions.

✦ **Backpacker's Café:** Starting here, you can find out where to locate an Internet café — a café where you can, for a fee, surf the Internet or collect your e-mail while you are on the road. Address: `www.backpackerscafe.com`

✦ **Bureau of Atomic Tourism:** This site is dedicated to the promotion of tourist locations worldwide that have witnessed atomic explosions or display exhibits about the development of atomic devices. It's hard to tell how far the creators of this site have thrust their tongues into their cheeks. At any rate, you can see many photos of nuclear devastation and, yes, detailed tour schedules and visitor information are available, too. Address: `www.oz.net/~chrisp/atomic.html`

✦ **Dead Presidents:** Manus Hand, surely one of the most eccentric people on the Internet, has made it his hobby to take photographs of himself at the graves of the presidents of the United States. Writes Mr. Hand, "If you're into dead presidents (and gosh, who isn't?), you came to the right place. By simply clicking your mouse button, you can see pictures of me, Manus Hand, visiting the final resting places of every one of them (save three — I'm still working on it!)." This site is living testimony that any excuse will do when it comes to traveling. Address: `www.starship.python.net/crew/manus/Presidents`

✦ **Fielding's Danger Finder:** Traveling to dangerous places can be exciting. Traveling vicariously to dangerous places can be exciting as well, as this site demonstrates. Here, you can read tales of dangerous locations and get advice for traveling to dangerous places if you feel like taking the plunge. Address: `www.fieldingtravel.com/df`

✦ **Local Times Around the World:** You're going to Uzbekistan, and you want to arrive fit and refreshed. To do that, however, you have to put yourself on Uzbekistan time three or four days before departure. What time is it in Uzbekistan? You can find out at this Web site. Address: `www.hilink.com.au/times`

✦ **National Caves Association:** This site is dedicated to spelunkers and their friends who enjoy exploring caves and caverns. Click the <u>Caves & Caverns Directory</u> link to go to the United States map. From there, you can click a state to look into its caves, caverns, and spelunking opportunities. Address: `www.cavern.com`

✦ **The Opinionated Traveler:** Say the makers of this site, "This is the uncompromising, opinionated, picky, and at times humorous site for the inside scoop on travel around the globe. Unlike other travel sites, we are not selling tickets, hotel rooms, or destinations. It's just the truth, the whole truth, and nothing but truth in travel." Address: `www.opinionatedtraveler.com`

Book VIII
Chapter 2

Travel Planning Online

+ **Roadside America:** This is unquestionably one of the best sites on the World Wide Web. Where to begin? How about the Electronic Map? Click this link to go to a page with links to weird roadside attractions in 50 states (New Jersey, with the Uniroyal Giantess and Palace of Depression, seems to have more than its share). Check out the pet cemetery or the Travel Brain Trauma Center or the Miraculous Virgin Mary Stump. Figure 2-4 shows this site. Address: www.roadsideamerica.com

+ **Tommy's List of Live Cams:** Perhaps you'd like to see what a destination looks like, right at this very moment, before you consider going there. From this site, you can do that. Tommy's List of Live Cams offers links to hundreds, if not thousands, of "cams" — live camera views that are updated every half hour or so. If nothing else, peering through a cam is the best way to find out what the weather really is somewhere else. Address: chili.rt66.com/ozone/cam.htm

+ **The Walking Connection:** Walking, if you have the time and you are in good company, is the best way to travel. This site is devoted to walking tourism. It offers a message board for walkers, news of upcoming walks, and plenty of advice about good shoes. Address: www.walkingconnection.com

Figure 2-4:
Go to Roadside America to find out where the roadside attractions are.

Chapter 3: Investing Online

In This Chapter

✔ **Finding investment strategies on the Internet**

✔ **Researching companies in which you want to invest**

✔ **Reading the latest news about companies and industries**

✔ **Investigating a mutual fund or stock on the Internet**

✔ **Trading stocks with an online broker**

✔ **Banking online**

*I*n the old days, only the wizards of Wall Street had enough information at their fingertips to evaluate stocks and other investments. A tickertape told them the value of each stock. Expensive newspapers, magazines, and newsletters told them about trends, investments worth buying, and investments worth shunning.

Today, anyone with a PC can plug into the Internet and find all kinds of information about investing. Finding out the current value of a stock has become as easy as typing its ticker symbol in a text box. All across the Internet are Web sites that offer investment advice and information. If you're careful and know where to look, you can get your hands on the same information that experts use to play the market. You can read company prospectuses, financial newsletters, and magazines. You can visit a Web site tailor-made to provide a certain kind of information to investors. And the best part is that most of this stuff is free for the taking.

This chapter looks into how the Internet can help you start investing and become a better investor. It demonstrates how to research a company, points the way to financial news services on the Internet, and spells out how to research stocks and mutual funds. You find out what trading stocks online entails and how online banking works. Finally, this chapter presents ten online investing resources that you shouldn't miss.

Before you make a single investment, decide what your financial goals are. Figure out how much you can risk and consider diversifying your investments. Investing in many different areas can help to minimize your risks.

This chapter describes a bunch of Web sites where you can plan investment strategies and learn about investing. You may also want to take a look at *Investing For Dummies*, 2nd Edition, by Eric Tyson, or *Investing Online For Dummies*, 3rd Edition, by Kathleen Sindell (both published by Hungry Minds, Inc.). Investing is a serious undertaking, and you need to go into it with your eyes wide open.

Getting Help with Investment Basics

Looking before you leap is always the best policy, so before you take the leap and start investing, go on the Internet and discover what investing is all about. Many brokers and banks are eager for you to start investing. For that reason, the Internet is filled with tutorials, online classes, and courses that you can take to learn the ropes.

Can't decide how much of your savings to devote to investments? Don't know what a market index is? Check out these Web sites, which offer online tutorials in investing:

+ **The Investment FAQ:** Search for investor information by category, or conduct a keyword search. This site, which is shown in Figure 3-1, also offers tours for beginning investors (click the <u>For Beginners</u> hyperlink). Address: `invest-faq.com`

+ **MoneyCentral:** This Microsoft Web site offers general information about planning an investment strategy, as well as late-breaking financial news. Address: `www.moneycentral.com`

+ **Motley Fool:** Take online courses in investing styles, how markets work, and evaluating investments, among other subjects. (Click the <u>Fool's School</u> link at the bottom of the home page; then read through The 13 Steps to Investing.) Address: `www.fool.com`

+ **Vanguard Group:** Attend classes at "Vanguard University" and learn the basics of investing and retirement planning. (Click the <u>Education, Planning & Advice</u> link.) Address: `www.vanguard.com`

Figure 3-1:
Just the
FAQs,
ma'am:
Searching
for answers
at The
Investment
FAQ.

Playing the investment game

Investing isn't a game, of course, but you can make a game of it. These Web sites offer investment games to sharpen your strategies and skills. Here, you can play the game for a few months before graduating to the real thing:

✔ **EduStock:** Read the tutorial and then test your skill by buying and selling stocks at up-to-date prices. Players start with 100,000 fantasy dollars that they can use to build a portfolio. You can practice researching stocks and securities from the Web site. Address: `library.thinkquest.org/3088`

✔ **Fantasy Stock Market:** Start with the requisite $100,000 in play money and try to best the other players in building a healthy portfolio. Players are ranked, and a new game starts each month. You can also research stocks from this Web site. Address: `www.fantasystockmarket.com`

✔ **Investment Challenge:** "The most realistic stock market simulation for students," boast the makers of this site. Here, you start with $100,000 in your fictional account. Different games are designed for middle school, high school, and college students. Address: `www.ichallenge.net`

**Book VIII
Chapter 3**

Investing Online

Researching a Company Online

Before you invest in a company, you owe it to yourself to research it. Has the company undergone a financial setback? Has management experienced a shakeup? What were the company's profits or losses in the last quarter?

To research a company, start by finding the company's Web site on the Internet. You can do that, first, by making an educated guess as to the company's Web site address. Type **www.companyname.com** (where *companyname* is the name of the company) in the Address box of your browser, press the Enter key, and hope for the best.

Failing that, a visit to Companies Online (www.companiesonline.com) usually does the job. The Companies Online Web site (see Figure 3-2) offers a search mechanism for finding companies' Web sites.

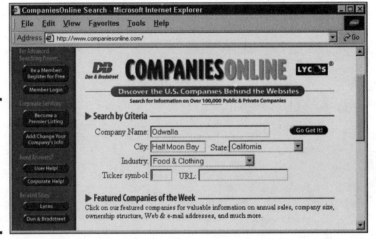

Figure 3-2: Use Companies Online to locate a company's Web site on the Internet.

Obviously, a company puts its best foot forward on its Web site. After you've read the wonderful things that the company has to say about itself, look for more objective information. You can do that by visiting one of these Web sites:

✦ **OneSource CorpTech:** The focus here is high-tech companies. The site offers company profiles, links to news articles about companies, and stock charts. The site is good at listing the names of company executives. Give one a call and see what happens. Address: www.corptech.com

✦ **Hoover's Online:** This site provides profiles, revenue reports, balance sheets, and charts on 12 million small to mid-sized businesses and 9,000 non-U.S. public companies. (Click the <u>Companies & Industries</u> hyperlink.) Address: `www.hoovers.com`

✦ **Public Register's Annual Report Service:** This site presents free annual reports from over 3,600 companies. Mind you, the companies themselves provide these reports, so give them a shrewd reading. Address: `www.prars.com`

✦ **U.S. Securities and Exchange Commission:** Publicly traded companies are required to file financial data with the Securities and Exchange Commission (SEC). From the SEC Web site, you can download details about a company's operations, including financial statements, executive pay, and other information. (Click the <u>Search for Company Filings</u> hyperlink.) Address: `www.sec.gov`

✦ **Wall Street Research Net:** This site offers a special Research section for researching companies. This is an excellent all-purpose site with many resources for investors. Address: `www.wsrn.com`

The next step, after you have done your initial research on a company, is to look for news sources. Perhaps the company has startled the world with an innovation or embarrassed itself with a glorious flop. Start at the company's Web site, where you can usually find a handful of press releases that describe the company's latest activities. Then look to these sources for more objective news:

✦ **Company News On-Call:** Search by company name in the PR Newswire database for articles published in the past year. Beware, however, because only news about large companies is available here. Address: `www.prnewswire.com/cnoc.html`

✦ **Company Sleuth:** The makers of this site "scour the Internet for free, legal, inside information on companies you select." And they will forward the information to you by e-mail, if you desire. Address: `www.companysleuth.com`

In addition to visiting the Web sites listed here, try running a conventional Internet search for information about a company. You may find news articles and opinions about the company that way. Book III, Chapter 2, explains how to conduct a Web search in Internet Explorer; refer to Book IV, Chapter 1, if you're using Netscape.

Reading the Financial News

Savvy investors stay on top of late-breaking financial news. And keeping abreast of changes in the economy and the political climate isn't a bad idea either. A smart investor gets there first, before the fools rush in.

Book VIII
Chapter 3

Investing Online

The Internet offers a daunting number of newspapers, magazines, newsletters, and news organizations that are devoted to financial news and opinions. Visit a few Web sites. Soon you'll find a favorite site that focuses on news that matters to the kind of investing you want to do.

Major news services

First, a few mammoth corporate Web sites. Most of these sites — such as ABCNews.com and MSNBC.com — are sponsored by news services that predate the Internet. You won't find eccentric opinions here, but the news stories are trustworthy and the financial advice is as solid (if as plain) as granite:

✦ **ABCNews.com:** This site presents news about financial markets, commentary by experts, and a special section about mutual funds. This is an all-purpose news source. You can also get daily news and science and technology news. (Click the MoneyScope hyperlink.) Address: `www.abcnews.com`

✦ **Bloomberg.com:** Here, you can find advice for money management, news about financial markets, and columns. Address: `www.Bloomberg.com`

✦ **CBS MarketWatch:** This all-purpose site (see Figure 3-3) does more than offer financial news. You can get market data, stock quotes, company portfolios, advice for managing your personal finances, and performance charts. Address: `cbs.marketwatch.com`

Figure 3-3: Whether you want to read the news or investigate a stock, CBS MarketWatch is a good place to start.

✦ **Dow Jones:** More business news and articles about the economy are available at this site. Address: `www.dowjones.com`

✦ **MSNBC:** Click the <u>Business</u> link to go to a Web page with business news, stock market news, and news about e-commerce. Address: `www.msnbc.com`

✦ **TheStreet.com:** This site offers financial news but, better yet, it includes a nice selection of columnists. This is the place to go when you want to gather others' financial opinions. Address: `www.thestreet.com`

Financial newspapers and magazines

Perhaps financial newspapers and magazines are more to your taste. The online editions of these popular newspapers and magazines are not as comprehensive as the ones you can buy at the newsstand, but they can still be valuable:

✦ **Business Week Online:** This site offers news from the financial world, as well as technology and small-business news. Click <u>Search & Browse</u>. The past issues are organized by year, and you can browse six month's worth of issues at a time for each year. Just click the link for the six-month block that interests you. Address: `www.businessweek.com`

✦ **The Economist:** *The Economist*, an English financial magazine, is simply the best magazine of its kind in the world. Its cosmopolitan outlook puts to shame some of the narrow-minded, homegrown magazines on the news rack. Read the current issue of this magazine for its world view of economics and business. Address: `www.economist.com`

✦ **FT.com:** The online version of the *Financial Times* offers market data, news, and analysis. You can also find late-breaking news developments in capsule format. Address: `www.ft.com`

✦ **Kiplinger Online:** More than a magazine, the online edition of *Kiplinger's Personal Finance Magazine* offers shopping services, advice for buying insurance, and other valuable stuff. Of course, you also get business and market news. Address: `www.kiplinger.com`

✦ **CNNMoney:** The online edition of CNN*Money* magazine provides many news articles and expert opinions. You can also get stock quotes and company profiles here. Address: `www.money.com`

✦ **New York Times:** The venerable newspaper is online! And because New York is a company town whose center is Wall Street, this isn't a bad place to grab the latest stock market news. Address: `www.nytimes.com`

✦ **Wall Street Journal:** The online edition of the famous newspaper also presents news summaries and insider information about American businesses. You can also get company reports and stock quotes. Address: `www.wsj.com`

Online newsletters

The Internet has made it possible for every Tom, Dick, and Harry to post a Web page and call it an investor newsletter. Far be it from us to decide which newsletters are worthy. Instead, you be the judge. Go to the Newsletter Access Web site (`www.newsletteraccess.com`) and search for a newsletter that whets your appetite (click the <u>Search</u> hyperlink). To conduct the search, enter a keyword or browse the different categories.

Researching Mutual Funds and Stocks on the Internet

Mutual funds and stocks are the two most popular kinds of investments. Not coincidentally, you can find numerous Web sites devoted to stocks and mutual funds on the Internet. From these sites, you can check the latest price of a stock or mutual fund. You can also dig deeper to investigate or screen funds and stocks. In the following pages, we unscrew the inscrutable. We show you where to go on the Internet to research mutual funds and stocks.

To find out anything about a security on the Internet, you usually have to know its ticker symbol. A *ticker symbol* is an abbreviated company name that is used for tracking the performance of stocks, mutual funds, and bonds. You can usually find these symbols on the statements that you receive from brokers. If you don't know a security's ticker symbol, go to PCQuote (`www.pcquote.com`) and use the search engine there to find it (look for the <u>Symbol Lookup</u> hyperlink).

No terminology is harder to understand than investment terminology. Do you know what a price/earnings (P/E) ratio is? A short sell? A put? A shot-put? When an investment term leaves you stumped, go to the glossary on the Yahoo! Finance Web site at `finance.yahoo.com` (look under Education, and click the <u>Glossary</u> hyperlink). The Yahoo! glossary is thorough, well-written, and easy to search.

Researching a mutual fund on the Internet

Mutual funds are the favorite of investors who want to reap the benefits of investing without doing the legwork. A *mutual fund* is a company that buys stocks, bonds, precious metals, and other securities. Investors buy shares in the fund. If the fund managers know their stuff, the securities that the mutual fund owns increase in value — and shares in the fund increase in value as well. Owning shares in a mutual fund is like owning shares of stock in a company. The difference is that a share of a mutual fund represents ownership in many different companies, as well as bonds and other securities.

Many people don't have the time, the expertise, or the inclination to research investment opportunities. For those people, mutual funds are ideal. You can rely on the fund managers' investing know-how. You can buy shares in a mutual fund without speaking to a broker. By definition, a mutual fund is diversified because it owns shares of many different securities, so you don't have to worry about diversification when you invest in a mutual fund.

Before you start dabbling in mutual funds, you need to know how fees are levied, about the different kinds of funds, and about the risks. After you know that, you can start looking for a fund that meets your needs. Here are some Web sites where you can acquire the basics of mutual fund investing:

✦ **Brill's Mutual Funds Interactive:** This is the all-purpose Web site for mutual fund investing. Here, you can read about mutual fund investing or search for funds by name and read about them. Address: www.fundsinteractive.com

✦ **Mutual Fund Investor's Center:** This excellent Web site offers articles about mutual fund investing and ranks mutual funds in various ways. You can also search for mutual funds by using different criteria. Address: www.mfea.com

✦ **Mutual Funds Online:** This site offers advice about choosing, buying, and selling mutual funds. Address: www.mfmag.com

At last count, investors could choose from among 10,000 mutual funds. After you know what you want in a mutual fund, check out these Web sites, where you can search for a mutual fund that fits your investment strategy:

✦ **MoneyCentral Investor:** Enter keywords that describe what you want in a mutual fund. This site, shown in Figure 3-4, also offers charts and performance analyses. Address: moneycentral.msn.com/investor/home.asp

✦ **Morningstar.com:** The granddaddy of mutual fund analysis, this site offers reports on 7,000 mutual funds. You can get fund profiles, performance reports, financial statements, and news articles. (Click the <u>Funds</u> hyperlink.) Address: www.morningstar.com

✦ **SmartMoney.com:** This site offers a sophisticated search engine for pinpointing mutual funds. (Click the <u>Funds</u> hyperlink and then the <u>Fund Finder</u> hyperlink.) Address: www.smartmoney.com

✦ **Standard & Poor's Micropal:** This Web site is an excellent place to start researching a fund. Select the type of fund that you are looking for and then describe the fund by entering keywords in text boxes. (Click the <u>Fund Information Research</u> hyperlink to get started). Address: www.micropal.com

Book VIII
Chapter 3

Investing Online

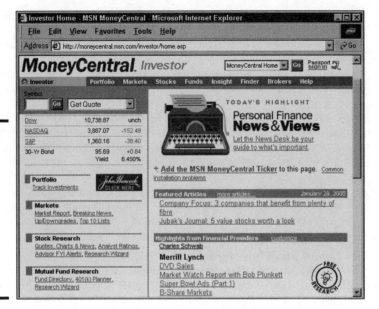

Figure 3-4:
Starting
from the
Money-
Central
Investor
site, you
can locate
a mutual
fund that
fits the bill.

Researching stocks on the Internet

The stock market, it has been said, is 85 percent psychology and 15 percent economics. And that's only half the problem. The other half has to do with its hard-to-understand terminology and the numerous confusing ways to buy and sell stock.

One thing is certain: Stocks, historically, are the best investment in terms of how much they grow in value. Since 1950, the value of the average stock has grown 13 percent a year. Money managers are nearly unanimous in saying that investing in stocks and holding onto them for long periods of time is the surest way to increase the value of a portfolio. Since 1987, when the stock market underwent a massive correction and lost a quarter of its value, the markets have performed like champions. At the end of 1987, the Dow Jones Industrial Average stood at barely 1,000. Currently, the Dow is hovering at 10,000.

If you decide to forsake mutual funds and jump into the stock market on your own, more power to you. This book cannot possibly delve into everything you need to know to invest in the stock market, but we can point the way to a few Web sites that can help you on the road to riches.

Socially conscious investing

Investing is a bit like casting a vote. When you invest in a company, you endorse its products, its business practices, and its labor practices. For better or worse, your investment helps shape the world in which we live.

On the idea that most people object to child labor, unsafe working conditions, pollution, and unhealthy products, a number of mutual fund managers have taken the lead and established socially conscious mutual funds. These funds do not buy into companies that practice what the managers think is bad business behavior.

To find out more about socially conscious investing and perhaps buy shares of a socially conscious mutual fund, check out the Co-op America Web site (www.coopamerica.org) and the Social Investment Forum (www.socialinvest.org). By the way, studies show that socially conscious mutual funds perform on average as well as other mutual funds.

To get general-purpose information about stocks and stock markets, read stock tips, and discover stock-picking strategies, try these sites, which are good starting places:

✦ **DailyStocks.com:** This site provides links to market indexes, news sources, earnings figures, and newsletters. Address: www.dailystocks.com

✦ **Wall Street Research Net:** This site offers links to many financial resources, including brokerage sites and government data. Address: www.wsrn.com

When you want to hunker down and examine specific stocks, go to one of these sites (and be sure to read "Researching a Company Online" earlier in this chapter as well):

✦ **Briefing.com:** Get stock quotes, reports, and historical charts. Address: www.briefing.com

✦ **MoneyCentral Investor:** Look under Stock Research and click a hyper-link to find a stock quote, a chart, and analyst ratings. You can also screen stocks from this Web site. Address: investor.msn.com

✦ **PCQuote.com:** As shown in Figure 3-5, you can enter a ticker symbol and get stock quotes and charts. This site also presents market news, a stock pick of the week, and news articles about the markets. Address: www.pcquote.com

**Book VIII
Chapter 3**

Investing Online

✦ **Yahoo! Finance:** Enter a ticker symbol, and you can get a price chart, news articles about a stock, charts that track its performance, and links to the company's SEC filings. Address: `quote.yahoo.com`

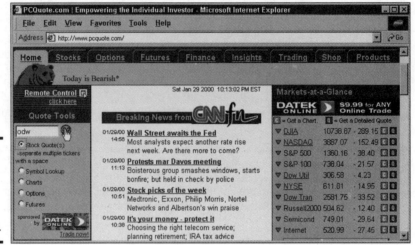

Figure 3-5:
Research-
ing a stock
from
PCQuote.
com is easy.

Suppose that you want to target a stock but you don't know what it is yet. In other words, you believe that the future is bright for a certain industry and you want to buy shares in companies in that industry. Or you want to buy a certain kind of stock — stock in a foreign corporation, a small cap stock, or a blue-chip stock. Searching for stocks this way is called *screening*. From these Web sites, you can screen stocks and find the one you are looking for:

✦ **Market Guide's NetScreen:** This site offers two-stock screening data-bases, one with which you can search using 20 variables and one using 75 variables. (Click the Screening Tools hyperlink.) Address: `www.marketguide.com`

✦ **Quicken.com:** This stock screener is easy to use, and its help instruc-tions are genuinely helpful. (Click the Investing hyperlink, click the Stocks tab, and then click the Stock Screener hyperlink.) Address: `www.quicken.com`

✦ **Silicon Investor:** This screener is easy to understand and fill out. (Look under Research and click the Stock Screener hyperlink.) Address: `www.siliconinvestor.com`

Tracking the value of your portfolio

Many Web sites and most online brokers offer you a means of tracking your portfolio online. The problem, however, with tracking portfolios online is that investments are only a part of your financial picture. Savings are another part. The income you keep in checking accounts is another. You have to consider taxes and your outstanding debts and mortgages, too. The portfolio-tracking programs that Web sites and online brokers provide are not comprehensive and can't give you a true picture of your overall financial condition.

If you really want to track the investments in your portfolio, track them with Microsoft Money or Quicken. Both software packages make it easy to track investments. You can download security prices right into the Microsoft Money or Quicken window and thereby keep your investments up to date. And when you want to see how your investments fit into your financial picture, you can generate a report or chart that tells you right away.

The following figure shows the Your Portfolio window in Microsoft Money. A glance at this window clearly shows how investments are performing. And these numbers are completely up to date.

Your portfolio

Portfolio	Accounts	Markets	Stocks	Funds	Insight	Finder	Brokers			
News	FYI	Symbol	Name		Last Price	Change	Total Quantity	Market Value		Gain
⊟ Joint Investments										
		MCD	McDonalds		44 ¾	13/16 ↑	55.000	2,461.25		495.80
		OAKMX	Oakmark Fund		41.090	0.000	125.000	5,136.25		-343.05
		TOY	Toys R Us		18 1/16	-¼ ↓	70.000	1,264.38		-587.87
		DIS	Walt Disney Company		27 9/16	-¼ ↓	40.000	1,102.50		-469.85
		WOGSX	White Oak Growth Stock		50.610	-0.460 ↓	110.000	5,567.10		1,504.80
			Cash --- US Dollar					68.35		
			Total Account Value					**15,599.83**		**599.83**
⊟ Charlie's 401(K)										
		FBALX	Fidelity Balanced		17.810	0.000	1,613.427	28,735.13		4,375.22
		FCNTX	Fidelity Contrafund		60.980	0.000	1,534.170	93,553.68		25,868.88
		FGRIX	Fidelity Growth & Income		49.010	0.000	2,053.439	100,639.05		18,313.48
		FMAGX	Fidelity Magellan		125.400	0.000	1,030.754	129,256.61		25,825.39
			Contributions --- US Dollar							
			Total Account Value					**352,184.47**		**74,382.97**
⊟ Amy's Keogh										
		FIIIX	Invesco Industrial Fund		16.120	0.000	454.116	7,320.35		1,369.28
		MBTCX	Merrill Lynch Technology B		6.090	0.000	423.056	2,576.41		38.65
		OAKMX	Oakmark Fund		41.090	0.000	150.957	6,202.82		1,161.07
		SGROX	Strong Growth Fund		26.010	0.000	239.557	6,230.87		561.45
			Contributions --- US Dollar							
			Total Account Value					**22,330.45**		**3,130.45**
			Grand Total					**390,114.75**		**78,113.25**
Change: $17.19 (0%)			Market Value: $390,114.75				YTD Return: +6.99%			

Trading Stocks Online

Not too long ago, if you had mentioned the words online trader or online broker, you would have been met with a blank stare. But now, more than 250 companies offer online brokerage services, and 10 million people trade online.

First, the Internet made it possible for anyone to research investments. Now the Internet has made it possible to trade stocks from home or from a desk in an office. The following sections explain how to find the best online broker for you and where to look for an online broker on the Internet. You also find out how to avoid the pitfalls of online trading.

Finding the right online broker

As you shop for an online broker, get the answers to these questions. And while you're at it, go to the Web sites in Table 3-1 to investigate online brokers.

✦ **What is the cost?** Commissions — the cost of making a trade — range from $5 to $30, but the commission isn't the only cost to consider. Sometimes, you have to pay a setup fee, fees for buying on margin, fees for large trades, fees for placing limit orders, and administrative fees for sending out stock certificates. No matter what the cost, however, trading online is cheaper than trading with a conventional broker. If you are a hypertrader, someone who trades daily or weekly, a low commission is the way to go. But if you don't trade particularly often, consider paying a high commission so that you can take advantage of the services that brokers who charge high commissions usually offer.

✦ **How many services do you want?** Some brokers, besides assisting in trades, offer banking services. Some brokers give their customers investment-tracking software. Some allow you to buy and sell mutual funds, as well as stocks.

✦ **Do you feel comfortable at the broker's Web site?** If the forms for buying or selling stocks are hard to manage, or if research tools take forever to load, try another broker. These days, an online broker that is worth anything offers demos and tours on its Web site. Take the tour and try out the demonstration screens to see whether you feel comfortable at the Web site where you will do your trading.

✦ **Can you get in touch with the broker when its Web site is down?** Some companies offer toll-free numbers that you can call to complete a trade when the Web site is down. Some companies also offer an alternate Web site you can use.

✦ **What kind of technical support can you get?** Ideally, someone should be available at all hours to answer the telephone and help you fix a software problem.

✦ **How well does the broker handle bookkeeping?** Transaction records should be easy to read and understand. Portfolios should be updated minute by minute, not day by day. Examine the account pages in the demo to see whether they are easy to read.

✦ **How good is the broker at putting trades through?** Trades are not made instantaneously. In effect, trading online is simply e-mailing a broker instead of calling him or her. Not all trades are made successfully. Go to the Keynote Web site at www.keynote.com (and click Performance Trademarks⇨Broker Trading Index) to see a comparison of the speed and transaction success rate of different online brokers.

Table 3-1	Web Sites Where You Can Investigate Online Brokers	
Site	*Address*	*How It Ranks Brokers*
Gomez.com	gomezadvisors.com	By cost, customer confidence, ease of use, and other criteria. This site also describes brokers that are suitable for different kinds of investors. (Click Consumers⇨Brokers/Full-Service.)
Investor Guide	investorguide.com	By rank according to *Barron's, Money, Kiplinger's Personal Finance Magazine,* and other financial magazines. From here, you can click a magazine name and read an article about a broker. (Click the Stocks tab and then click Broker Rankings under Stock Trading.)
Keynote	keynote.com	By speed and transaction success rate. (Click Performance Benchmarks under Metrics and then click Broker Trading Index.)
Discount Stock	www.sonic.net	By cost and service.

The Investor Protection Trust (www.investorprotection.org) maintains a Web site where you can investigate brokers (online or otherwise) to see how trustworthy they are.

Avoiding the pitfalls of trading online

Trading online is exciting. Because a broker isn't standing in your way telling you what to buy and sell, trading online gives you the impression that you are, at last, the master of your financial destiny.

Studies show, however, that online traders do not profit as well as people who trade with brokers. Online traders, when they start out, trade twice as often as traditional traders, and when the novelty of online trading has worn off, they continue to trade 30 percent more often than others. This type of trading runs counter to the old stock market adage, "Slow and steady wins the race" — in other words, hang onto your stocks a long time to make the biggest profits.

**Book VIII
Chapter 3**

Investing Online

As an online trader, you need to exercise self-control. Apart from that, here are some concrete steps that you can take to check your worst impulses:

✦ **Devise a strategy for playing the stock market and stick to it.** Before you buy or sell a stock, ask yourself whether the trade fits in your strategy or whether you are merely chasing after a profit.

✦ **Set aside a certain amount of money for online trading.** If the money in the account runs low or the account is empty, stop trading online.

✦ **Slow down!** You are trading with your money on the Internet. Online trading is not a video game.

Online Banking

The era of online banking is upon us. Many people rely on home computers to do most of their banking. Obviously, you can't make cash withdrawals from your floppy disk slot as you can from an ATM machine (although that would be very nice!). But bank statements can be delivered over the Internet instead of the mail, and you can look up a bank account balance online. You can also pay bills online without writing checks by hand, sealing them in an envelope, and dropping them in the mailbox.

The fastest way to tell whether your bank offers online services is to call the bank or visit its Web site. At the bank's Web site, look for demonstration screens that show how the services work. If you decide to sign up, the bank sends you a PIN (personal identification number) and instructions for online banking. As a security measure, you must submit the PIN whenever you access your bank records online.

The following sections offer a brief description of online banking. You also get a glimpse of the most sophisticated and, maybe the best way, to bank online — with Microsoft Money or Quicken. For more detailed information on online banking, check out the book *Banking Online For Dummies,* by Paul A. Murphy (Hungry Minds, Inc.).

A look at online banking services

Large banks usually offer their customers these online services:

✦ **Account balances:** Go to a Web page and see how much money is in your bank accounts.

✦ **Bank statements:** Go to a Web page and see your bank statement, like the one shown in Figure 3-6. The statement lists deposits, withdrawals, and transfers that have cleared the bank.

✦ **Paying bills:** On a form, describe the bill that you want to pay — list the payee, the payee's address, and other identifying information — and instruct your bank to pay the bill. The bank sends the money, sometimes by printing a check and mailing it, and sometimes by transferring the money directly from your account to the payee's account. The money is deducted from your account when the payment is made. A $5 monthly fee is usually charged for this service.

✦ **Transferring money:** Go to a Web page where you give instructions for transferring money between accounts. You can only transfer money between the accounts you have at the same bank.

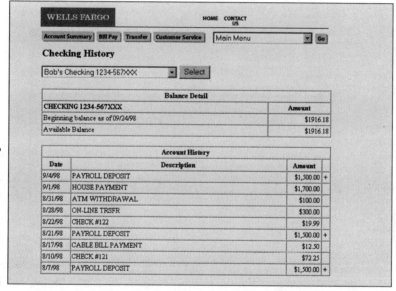

Figure 3-6:
With online banking, you can read your bank statement whenever you want.

Banking online with Microsoft Money or Quicken

The other way to bank online is a bit more sophisticated — but also more rewarding. People who own Microsoft Money or Quicken can use those programs to bank online or pay bills online. Again, you must sign up with your bank to do so.

The chief advantage of banking online with a computer program is that you can download transaction records from the bank to your computer, as shown in Figure 3-7. After the records are in hand, you can review them and enter them in your account registers. (Users of Money and Quicken will recognize the term "account register," the windows in Money and Quicken where you track activity in a bank account.) Banking online saves you the administrative headache of entering transaction records yourself. And you can compare your records to the bank's to make sure that the bank's records are accurate.

Click an account name . . .   . . . to view the records
                                            you downloaded from the bank

Figure 3-7:
Reviewing
bank
transactions
in Microsoft
Money 2000.

Microsoft Money is a great tool for banking online. Between its online banking and online portfolio-tracking services, Microsoft Money is invaluable.

Check out these Web sites to learn more about Money or Quicken:

✦ **Microsoft Money:** Recently, Microsoft was offering a free 60-day trial version of the Deluxe edition of Money. The Deluxe edition of the program costs $64.95; the Standard edition, $34.95. Address: www.microsoft.com/money

✦ **Quicken:** Intuit, the maker of Quicken, offers two home versions (along with a couple versions for businesses) of its program as well. The Deluxe edition is $59.95. Address: www.intuit.com/quicken

Ten Online Investment Resources You Shouldn't Miss

Nobody can claim to know the ten best online investment resources because there are so many of them. These are the ten, however, that we have found most useful or interesting during our journeys on the Internet.

✦ **CBS MarketWatch:** Of all the corporate Web sites that offer financial news and views, CBS MarketWatch (cbs.marketwatch.com) is the easiest to navigate. The articles are insightful and well written. You can do any number of things from this Web site — get stock quotes, get performance charts, and investigate entire industries.

✦ **The Economist:** That you can get the current issue of *The Economist* online for free is almost too good to be true (www.economist.com). The magazine, which is based in England and takes a cosmopolitan outlook, covers Asia, Africa, and Latin America like no other financial magazine. If you invest in foreign markets, or if you are interested in the emerging global economy, you owe it to yourself to check out this online version of the famous magazine.

✦ **Fund Alarm:** How refreshing — a noncommercial Web site for investors. At Fund Alarm (www.fundalarm.com), you can get information about mutual funds and stocks, as well as tutorials in investing. You will also find a lively discussion board where you can post a question or find out what others have to say about their investing activity.

✦ **MoneyCentral Investor:** MoneyCentral Investor (moneycentral.msn.com) is a Microsoft-sponsored Web site, so it's not as if you can find eccentric opinions or brilliant flashes of intuitive insight here. Still, this is the place to go if you want straightforward advice for investing, saving, choosing insurance policies, or planning ahead for retirement or a child's college education. Investing is only one part of building a strong financial future. You need to look into the other areas as well, and this site is a good place to do that.

✦ **Motley Fool:** The people at the Motley Fool (www.fool.com) believe that the so-called investment wizards are not as smart as they think, and that amateurs, by exercising old-fashioned common sense, can beat the pros. The Motley Fool Web site offers all kinds of investment strategies, explanations of financial terms and financial markets, and tips. And it does so in a lighthearted, amusing way.

✦ **National Association of Investors Corporation (NAIC):** The National Association of Investors Corporation (NAIC) is the place to go if you want to find out about or join an investment club. Members of an investment club each contribute a certain amount of money. Then the club invests the money and, if the investments turn a profit, the members share the proceeds.

**Book VIII
Chapter 3**

Investing Online

At the NAIC Web site (www.better-investing.org), you can get advice for starting an investment club, find out how clubs do their research, and share information with other club members. Of course, you can also join the NAIC from this Web site.

✦ **Newsletter Access:** Newsletter Access (www.newsletteraccess.com) is the place to start if you are looking for financial newsletters — or newsletters of any kind, for that matter. Click a topic and go to a list of newsletter names, each of which is a hyperlink that you can click to get the URL of the newsletter. You can also search the newsletter list by keyword. This Web site is fascinating, if only because it demonstrates how many topics are available for investigation on the Internet.

✦ **StockSelector.com:** Picking a stock is no easy chore, but StockSelector.com (www.stockselector.com) has taken some of the sting out of the ordeal. This site offers financial news and market briefs, as well as the means to look up stock quotes and view analysis charts. Better than that, however, is the stock-screening software, which is the easiest to use on the Internet. To use it, click <u>Screen</u> and follow the instructions.

✦ **Wall Street Research Net:** Wall Street Research Net (www.wsrn.com) is like one of those giant department stores that offer a little bit of everything. From here, you can research stocks, mutual funds, and bonds. You can search for a broker. You can read the latest market news and sample commentary from one or two experts. There is even a cartoon called "Street Humor" that pokes fun at investors.

✦ **Yahoo! Finance:** Anything on the Internet with *Yahoo!* attached to its name is bound to be good, and the Yahoo! Finance Web site (finance.yahoo.com) proves yet again that the people at Yahoo! know how to index and present information in such a way that you can find it quickly. Here, you can find links to market news, reference material, financial advice, and tax advice. We suggest making this site your investing home page.

Chapter 4: Genealogy Online

In This Chapter

✔ **Doing the background research before you go online**

✔ **Searching from a comprehensive Web site**

✔ **Looking for census records on the Internet**

✔ **Investigating a surname and records from a locality**

✔ **Obtaining vital records about an ancestor**

✔ **Using ten good genealogy Web sites on the Internet**

The Internet has given genealogists a powerful boost. What used to require a trip to a Vital Records office can be done in minutes on the Internet. Genealogists, who used to practice their hobby in obscurity, have discovered one another. All across the Internet are sites where genealogists post their findings for others to see. A brisk trade in genealogical data goes on all day long. And a number of people have discovered long-lost relatives in the course of their genealogical research.

That's the good news. The bad news is that much of the genealogical data is in list form. Much of it is still on microfiche. You can't, for example, download your great-grandma's birth certificate from a site on the Internet. But you can find census data on an ancestor. You can find census indexes, property records, and immigrant records. You can quickly find out where data is kept and write to obtain the data. And your chances of finding another genealogist who is working the same vein as you get better by the day. We are, it appears, entering a golden age of genealogy.

This chapter explains a handful of ways to research your ancestors on the Internet. You find out how to search census records, scour the Internet to find information about a surname, look up someone's military records, and peer into the ghastly sounding Social Security Death Index to locate your ancestors. This chapter also looks into researching ancestors who lived in a particular place and obtaining vital records. Before you start researching your ancestors, however, you have to do a little background work.

Doing the Detective Work

Before reaching into the misty past to connect with your ancestors, you need to make like a detective. Would Sam Spade (as played by Humphrey

Bogart) search for the Maltese Falcon on the Internet without knowing what bird he was searching for? Of course not. The same goes for genealogical research. Before you jump in, take stock of what you already know, gather all the material records you can, interview your relatives, and devise a plan for storing all the data.

You probably already know the names and birthplaces of the previous one or two generations of your family. Start by writing down what you know about them. Why write it down? Because, like a detective, you can start putting the clues together after you have written them down. Write down your ancestors' names, birthdays, and places of residence. Write down their occupations and the names of clubs, groups, and institutions to which they belonged. Every scrap of evidence you have about an ancestor might be an important clue.

Next, assemble the material records about your family. Land titles, letters, diaries, certificates of birth and death, court records, family Bibles, and newspaper articles are examples of material records. These records can be invaluable. A birth certificate, for example, reveals not only when an ancestor was born, but also in which county his or her parents lived at the time of the birth. Some birth certificates list the parents' occupations. Ask around for copies of material records that pertain to your family. Maybe you'll get lucky and stumble upon a packrat who has saved old newspaper articles, baptismal certificates, and the like.

On the subject of asking around, interview your relatives. They will be delighted to tell you about the past. Here are some good questions to ask them:

✦ When and where were you born?

✦ When and where were you married?

✦ Where did you go to school, and what clubs or institutions were you affiliated with?

✦ From which country or countries did our ancestors come?

✦ Can you tell me anything about other relatives? When and where were they born? Where did they go to school? What clubs or institutions were they affiliated with?

✦ Were you in the military? Do you know of anyone in the family who was in the military? To which units did you or other family members belong?

✦ Do you have any material records — birth certificates, photos, family letters — that I can borrow and copy?

Bring along a tape recorder and photographs when you interview relatives in person. Photographs tend to jog peoples' memories.

Organizing Your Genealogical Data

One task remains after you've determined what you know, assembled the material records, and interviewed your relatives: Think of a way to organize your genealogical data. Dropping scraps of paper in a desk drawer won't do the trick. Look at it this way: For each generation you research, the number of parents doubles. A search that goes back four generations requires tracking 30 different people. Go back five generations, and you are tracking 62 ancestors.

Some people make do with 3-x-5-inch index cards and manila folders. Others create a database and work from there. Here are a handful of Web sites where you can get advice for tracking your ancestors:

✦ **Genealogy Software Springboard:** Software manufacturers have jumped in to fill the need with computer programs, such as Family Tree Maker and Family Origins. These ancestor-tracking programs make organizing genealogical data easier. At this Web site, users of the software rate the different software programs. Address: www.gensoftsb.com

✦ **Heritage Quest — A Beginner's Guide:** Come here to find out the basic steps of undertaking a genealogical investigation. Address: www.heritagequest.com/genealogy/help

✦ **Numbering Systems in Genealogy:** Genealogy is a science, and genealogists make use of advanced numbering systems to track their ancestors. This Web page describes the different systems — the Sosa-Stradonitz, the de Villiers/Pama, the Henry system, and others. Visit this site if you get engulfed in genealogy and want to know how the experts do it. Address: www.saintclair.org/numbers

✦ **Organizing Your Family History:** Lynn Searcy, the noted genealogist, presents thorough instructions for tracking your family history at this site. Address: www.micronet.net/users/~searcy/Resource.htm

The following Web sites are excellent sources for beginners who are seeking advice before they undertake a genealogical expedition:

✦ **Ancestry.com:** Click the <u>Learn</u> hyperlink at this Web site for a basic introduction to genealogy. The site offers free Family Tree software from Ancestry. Address: www.ancestry.com

✦ **Genealogy Instruction for Beginners, Teenagers, and Kids:** This site offers advice for, well, you get the idea. Address: home.earthlink.net/~howardorjeff/instruct.htm

✦ **National Archives and Records Administration (NARA):** The NARA presents an introduction to genealogy on this Web page. Address: www.nara.gov/genealogy/begin.html

**Book VIII
Chapter 4**

Genealogy Online

✦ **National Genealogical Society:** Click the <u>Getting Started</u> hyperlink on the home page of the National Genealogical Society for an introduction to genealogy (see Figure 4-1). The Getting Started page offers suggestions for beginners, an introduction to genealogy, and a FAQ sheet. Address: `www.ngsgenealogy.org`

Figure 4-1: The National Genealogical Society is a good place to start your adventures in genealogy.

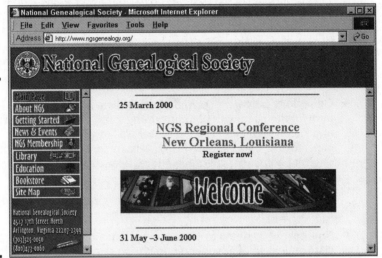

All-Purpose Searching Sites

Maybe the best way to get acquainted with all the different sites on the Internet that pertain to genealogy is to visit one or two all-purpose genealogy Web sites, click a few hyperlinks, and see where the adventure takes you. Genealogists come in all stripes and colors. Your expedition will take you to online government offices, online graveyards, and everything in between:

✦ **Cyndi's List:** You can't go wrong at Cyndi's List. This Web site lists hundreds, if not thousands, of links to genealogy Web sites. Bookmark this site. Its A-to-Z index is invaluable. Address: `www.cyndislist.com`

✦ **The Genealogy Home Page:** Click the hyperlinks at this user-friendly Web site to sample the different resources on the Internet. The authors of this site have divided genealogy into a dozen or so clearly defined categories to get you started. Address: `www.genealogyhomepage.com`

✦ **Genealogy Resources on the Internet:** You'll find a vast, eccentric A-to-Z index of genealogy Web sites here. This is another place to find out just how many types of genealogy Web sites there are. (In the address, notice that a hyphen, not a period, appears after www.) Address: `www-personal.umich.edu/~cgaunt/gen_web.html`

Searching the Census Records

Article 1, Section 2, Clause 3 of the United States Constitution tells the Congress to carry out a census "every subsequent Term of ten Years, in such Manner as they shall by Law direct." And that is certainly good news for genealogists. Starting with the first census in 1790, the United States Government has collected census records and maintained them at the offices of the National Archives and Records Administration (NARA). By law, census records can be made public only after 72 years have passed, so records from the 1930 census and before are available to the public.

Not that all of them are available online, though. And they're not available from a central location. One way to look up census records is to go to an all-purpose Web site (see the previous section in this chapter), find a link that takes you to the state where your ancestor lived, and see whether you can find a census database to search.

Sounding out the Soundex system

Occasionally, when you submit surname searches in genealogy databases, you are given the opportunity to submit a name under the *Soundex system*. The Soundex system is an attempt to account for surnames that sound the same or sound alike but are spelled differently. For example, instead of conducting four different searches for Christian, Christianson, Christiansen, and Christiani, you can conduct one search with the Soundex code C623.

Here is how the Soundex code works:

- ✔ Each name, no matter how long it is, comprises exactly four alphanumeric characters, with one letter and three numbers.

- ✔ The first letter of the name is the first letter of the code.

- ✔ Each consonant in the name (vowels are excluded) is assigned a number using the

Soundex key: 1 = b, f, p, v; 2 = c, g, j, k, q, s, x, z; 3 = d, t; 4 = l; 5 = m, n; 6 = r. The following letters are disregarded and thus not assigned a number: a, e, h, i, o, u, y, w.

- ✔ Zeroes are used if the end of the name is reached prior to three digits.

Confused? Fortunately, a handful of Web sites have come to the rescue and can convert a name to a Soundex code in the wink of an eye. Soundex codes really are a more efficient way of searching databases. To convert a name to its Soundex code, visit one of these Web sites:

- ✔ Soundex Converter: www.ourancestry.com/soundex.html

- ✔ The Soundex Machine: www.nara.gov/genealogy/soundex/soundex.html

TIP

If you're willing to pay to look in the census records, Ancestry.com (www.ancestry.com) is the place to go. For $29.95, you can search the census records for three months. (Other, more expensive plans are available as well.) According to Ancestry.com, the company's databases contain 1.3 billion names. Besides census records, you can look in church records, military records, immigration and naturalization records, and land records.

Figure 4-2 shows the results of a search at Ancestry.com. This is an *index entry*. It refers to a *census record*, a form that was filled in by the census taker in 1880. To obtain a microfilm copy of a complete census record, which offers more information than is found in the index, you can write to the National Archives and Records Administration (NARA) in Washington or one of NARA's 12 regional offices. (Go to this Web site to get the address of an NARA office: www.nara.gov/nara/gotonara.html#CA.) If you write NARA, be sure to include the year, county, state, township, database, and ID number in the index entry in your letter so that the clerk can look up the microfilmed census record.

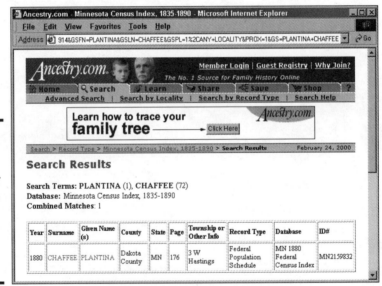

Figure 4-2: If a census record for an ancestor is available, the record appears in an index entry like this one.

Searching for a Surname

You probably aren't the only person conducting a genealogical investigation of a surname. Others are also looking for Chaffees, Goughs, or whatever surname you happen to be looking for. Wouldn't it be great if you could connect with someone who is doing the same research as you?

Following the history of a surname

The Hamrick Software Surname Distribution Web site is fascinating. From the Web site, you can discover — in the 1850, 1880, and 1920 census, or 1990's phone books — how common a surname was. Here, for example, the results of the 1920 census show that McPhee was a common name in the Dakotas, Washington, and Michigan, but not very common elsewhere in the United States.

Go to the Hamrick Software Surname Distribution Web site to trace the path of a surname across the United States from 1850 Census, 1880 Census, 1920 Census, and 1990's phone books. Enter a surname in the text box, choose a census year, and click the Display button. Address: `www.hamrick.com/names/ index.html`

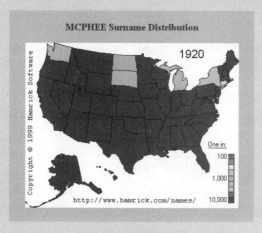

From these Web sites, you can look into a surname and perhaps swap data with another lonely soul who is looking down the same path you are. You can also list your e-mail address or Web page at these sites to make your research available to other genealogists.

✦ **Family Tree Maker.com:** Enter a first and last name in the text box, click the Go button, and see what happens. From this site, you can access 470 million names in census, Social Security, marriage, and death records. You can also get in touch with others on the message board. Address: `www.familytreemaker.com`

✦ **Genealogy.com:** As Figure 4-3 shows, you can search in more than one place from this Web site. Besides the Internet, you can search the Genealogy Library at Genealogy.com (for a fee), message boards, Family Home Pages, and commercial CDs (for a fee). Enter a surname, and click the Search button. Address: `www.genealogy.com/ifftop.html`

✦ **GeneaNet:** GeneaNet is a bold attempt to index all the genealogy databases in the world. You know the routine — enter a surname in the text box, and click the Search button. If the name you entered can be found, you see a list of resources, including an e-mail address you can click to write for information. Address: `www.geneanet.com`

✦ **GenSource — I Found It:** From this Web site, you can look up Web pages devoted to a surname. Enter a surname in the text box, and click the Go button. Address: `www.gensource.com/ifoundit/index.htm`

✦ **Rootsweb Surname List:** Enter a surname, click the Submit button, and get a list of other genealogists who are researching the name you entered. The list shows others' e-mail addresses, and, in some cases, their Web pages. From here, you can send e-mail messages to other researchers. (Click the Search the RSL Database hyperlink.) Address: `rsl.rootsweb.com/#search`

✦ **SurnameWeb's Genealogy Search Engine:** From this site, you can search for variants of a name as part of the search. Address: `www.surnameweb.org/search/Search.cgi`

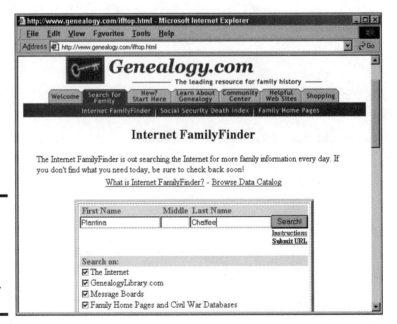

Figure 4-3:
Search several places at once with Genealogy.com.

To find out more about conducting genealogical research online, check out *Genealogy Online For Dummies*, 3rd Edition, by Matthew L. Helm and April Leigh Helm (published by Hungry Minds, Inc.). For help with using the Family Tree Maker software, see *Family Tree Maker For Dummies*, also by Matthew and April Helm (published by Hungry Minds, Inc.).

Are you interested in the old-world origins of a surname? In that case, you might pay a visit to an outfit called The Guild of One-Name Studies (`www.one-name.org`). Each member of the Guild is assigned a surname. The member's job is to identify the origins of the surname and track its distribution over the centuries. From the Web site, you can look up a surname, get the name and address of the person to whom it has been assigned, and e-mail or write the person to learn more about the name.

Book V, Chapter 1 describes newsgroups, how to find them, and how to post queries to a newsgroup. Here are a handful of newsgroups that pertain to surnames:

```
soc.genealogy.surnames.britain
soc.genealogy.surnames.canada
soc.genealogy.surnames.german
soc.genealogy.surnames.global
soc.genealogy.surnames.ireland
soc.genealogy.surnames.misc
soc.genealogy.surnames.usa
```

Obtaining Vital Information from the Social Security Death Index

The Social Security Death Index, also known as the Death Master File (how do you like these macabre names?), contains the names of people for whom a lump-sum Social Security benefit was paid at the time of death. Usually, a surviving family member, lawyer, or mortician requests the payment. Over 67 million names are in the index, and, more importantly, you can find out a lot by looking in the index. You can find out when an ancestor was born, when he or she died, and where he or she died. Then, for $7, you can write the Social Security Administration to obtain a copy of your ancestor's Social Security application. The application includes this vital information:

✦ Place of birth

✦ Mailing address at the time the application was filed

✦ Father's full name

✦ Mother's full name, including her maiden name

✦ The name and address of the person's employer

To search the Social Security Death Index and obtain an ancestor's Social Security application, follow these steps:

1. **Open your browser and go to the following address:**

   www.ancestry.com/search/rectype/vital/ssdi/main.htm

   Or, if typing long addresses isn't your cup of tea, go to www.ancestry. com, click the Search⇨Record Type⇨Birth, Marriage, & Death Records⇨ Social Security Death Index.

2. **Fill in the form as best you can (see Figure 4-4).**

   The more information you can enter on the form, the better. Common names, such as Smith and Martinez, can generate many thousands of database entries, so the more information you enter on the form, the less time you spend sorting through names in the database.

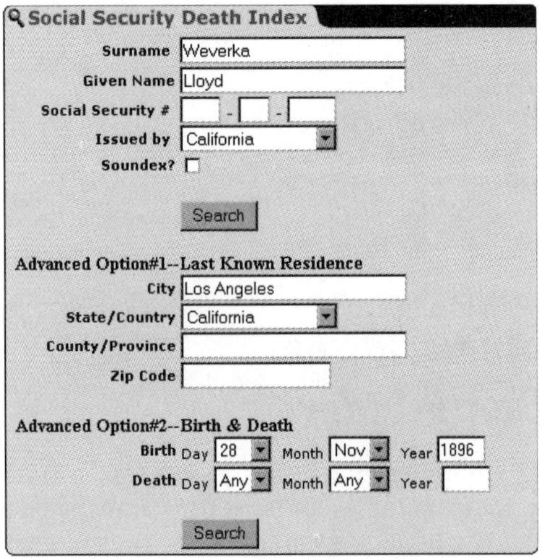

Figure 4-4:
Searching
for an
ancestor in
the Social
Security
Death Index.

3. **Click the Search button.**

   If the name can be found, it appears in the search record.

4. **Click the Request Information hyperlink to see about writing a letter to the Social Security Administration to obtain a copy of your ancestor's Social Security application.**

   Notice the Click Here to Generate a Letter hyperlink. If you click the link, you get a written copy of a letter that you can print and send. Don't forget to write your address on the letter and enclose the $7.

Obtaining Data from Localities

At some point, the search for your ancestors might take you to a state, country, city, or other locality. Now you're getting somewhere. You have pin-pointed where an ancestor lived. Your next step is to look for resources on the Internet that are specific to different locales. Try starting from these sites:

✦ **Ancestry.com — State Resources:** Choose a state to visit a Web page with genealogical resources in the state. Address: `www.ancestry.com/search/locality/main.htm`

✦ **Genealogy.com — Genealogy Toolbox:** When a map of the United States appears, click the state you want more information about. Address: `www.genealogy.com/00000174.html`

✦ **North American Genealogy Resources:** A comprehensive list of genealogical resources in each state and in Canada is found at this Web site. Address: `www.genealogyhomepage.com/northamerican.html`

✦ **USGenWeb Project:** This is the place to go if you happen to know the county where your ancestor was born, lived, or died. Click a state name, and you come to a list of counties in the state. From there, click a county name to view the online genealogy resources in the county. Address: `www.usgenweb.org/statelinks-table.html`

Don't be discouraged if none of these Web sites turns up anything. The Internet is full of genealogical societies, city directories, cemetery listings, and other places where long-gone ancestors' names may have been recorded. Refer to Book III, Chapter 2 (Internet Explorer), or Book IV, Chapter 1 (Netscape), for information on how to conduct an Internet search. Try running a search using your ancestor's name, a place name, and the word *genealogy* as the keywords. Maybe something will turn up.

Writing to Obtain Vital Records

In the United States and its territories, certificates of births, marriages, deaths, and divorces are kept on file in the Vital Statistics office of every city or county where the event occurred. Some states also maintain offices where the records are kept. As long as you know where and when an ances-tor was born, was married, died, or was divorced, you can write to the Vital Statistics office to obtain a copy of a certificate.

Go to these Web sites to find out where to write to obtain vital records:

✦ **Family History SourceGuide:** This site lists offices by state where you can obtain records. Address: `www.familysearch.org`

**Book VIII
Chapter 4**

Genealogy Online

✦ **Vital Records Information — United States:** Click the State hyperlink to see a list of states and U.S. territories. Then click a state name to find out how to obtain vital records there. Address: vitalrec.com

Getting Records of Military Service

As the descendant of someone who served his or her country, you have every right to be proud of your ancestor. And you also have a golden opportunity to look up his or her military records. For the most part, the military has been good at keeping records. Where the military didn't keep records very well, amateur genealogists have stepped in. You can find many places on the Internet where Revolutionary War and Civil War buffs maintain Web sites that list veterans of those wars.

Here are a couple places to look up ancestors who served in the military:

✦ **Cyndi's List — Military Resources Worldwide:** Cyndi Howells has done her usual excellent job of maintaining links to genealogical resources, in this case to military resources. Go here to start an expedition for military records the world over. Address: www.cyndislist.com/milres.htm

✦ **National Archive and Records Administration:** Scroll down the page and look under Military Records. You can find several fascinating databases that you can search. Address: www.nara.gov/genealogy/genindex.html

---

Locating a city or county in the United States

At some point in your quest to find an ancestor, you will be asked for a city or county name and be completely befuddled. You may know, for example, that an ancestor was born in Duluth, Minnesota, but to continue a search, you may have to know the name of the county where Duluth is located.

In times like these, go to the gazetteer at the United States Geological Survey (USGS) and look up a place name. Follow these steps:

1. **Type the following address in your browser and press Enter:**

   mapping.usgs.gov/www/gnis/

You land in the USGS Mapping Information page.

2. **Scroll down the page, look under Query the GNIS Online Data Bases, and click the United States and Territories hyperlink.**

   You see a form for describing the item you are looking for.

3. **Fill in the form and click the Send Query button.**

   Your search results appear on a new page.

Ten Great Genealogy Web Sites

Unquestionably, the Internet has been very good for genealogy. All you have to do is glance at a genealogy Web site on the Internet to realize that there are thousands upon thousands of such sites, because the sites are linked together. Here are ten sites that we have found especially useful or interesting in our genealogical travels.

✦ **Ancestry.com:** Ancestry.com is the granddaddy of genealogy Web sites. Starting here, you can conduct many different kinds of searches, although you have to pay a fee for some of them. Address: `www.ancestry.com`

✦ **Christine's Genealogy Web Site:** Prior to 1870, marriages between slaves weren't officially recognized or recorded, so researching African-American ancestors can be difficult. Fortunately, Christine's Genealogy Web site picks up some of the slack. From here, you can find many resources for researching African-American genealogy. The links to historical records are excellent. Address: `www.ccharity.com`

✦ **Cyndi's List:** Cyndi Howells, a passionate genealogist with years of experience, maintains this Web site. Here, you can find numerous genealogical resources in an A-to-Z index and hyperlinks to other genealogy sites. This place is a sort of crossroads on the Internet for genealogists. You can spend hours here and never waste a minute. Address: `www.cyndislist.com`

✦ **Family Tree Maker:** From this free Web site, you can search any number of databases: census records, Social Security records, marriage records, and death records. We're very fond of the message board. One of us found a long-lost cousin here who happened to be researching the very same people that he was. Address: `www.familytreemaker.com`

✦ **The Genealogy Home Page:** If you are getting your feet wet, this may be a good place to start. From here, you can find out how to undertake a genealogical investigation and look into many different genealogical resources. The Genealogy Home Page is the most user-friendly genealogy site on the Internet. Address: `www.genealogyhomepage.com`

✦ **Genealogy Page — National Archive and Records Administration (NARA):** Besides being a guide to all the genealogical resources of the federal government (and they are many!), this Web site gives advice for doing genealogical research and offers hyperlinks to other Web sites that can be useful to genealogists. Address: `www.nara.gov/genealogy/genindex.html`

✦ **Guild of One-Name Studies:** Shakespeare asked, "What's in a name?" At this site, you can find the answer to a similar question, "What's in a surname?" From this Web site, you can research the origins of a name by contacting a member of the Guild of One-Name Studies. He or she will tell you where the name originated, what it meant, and how far it has traveled from its place of origin. Address: `www.one-name.org/register.shtml`

✦ **Rand Genealogy Club:** At this Web site, employees of the Rand Corporation share genealogy links and tips for researching your ancestors. Have the Rand employees been searching the Internet at work? It appears so. A very nice selection of genealogy links can be found at this Web site. Address: `www.rand.org/personal/Genea`

✦ **USGenWeb — State Pages:** USGenWeb has done a fine job of organizing genealogical sites by state. Starting here, you can click the name of a state and go directly to genealogical resources that pertain to the state whose name you clicked. Address: `www.usgenweb.org/statelinks-table.html`

✦ **WorldGenWeb Project:** At some point, a genealogical expedition has to cross the ocean and look for data in Asia, Europe, Africa, South America, or Australia. When that happens, look into the WorldGenWeb Project, which offers hyperlinks to resources abroad. Address: `www.worldgenweb.org`

Index

Book IX

Internet Directory

The 5th Wave — By Rich Tennant

"Honey — remember that pool party last summer where you showed everyone how to do the limbo in just a sombrero and a dish towel? Well, look at what the MSN Daily Video Download is."

Contents at a Glance

Chapter 1

Internet and Computer Help

Directories and Search Engines

The Web is many things, but the one thing it's not is organized. Although you can easily click your way around by following hyperlinks, you may not be able to easily find exactly what you're looking for. Finding specific information is where *Web directories* come in handy. Web directories are like maps of the cyberlandscape, organized into topics that help you narrow down your browsing.

Search engines also enable you to find what you're looking for on the Web, but they differ from directories in that you perform searches by using keywords. *Keywords* are like hints that you give the search engine to help it find what you need. A keyword search string, as they're called, can be as simple as *movies* or as complex as *old movies humphrey bogart.* The real purpose of search engines is to save you hours of browsing — which is not to say that browsing isn't fun. But when you want to find something fast, use your favorite search engine.

Many Web sites, such as Lycos and Yahoo!, offer both directories and search engines on the same site — enabling you to choose your desired search method for the task at hand.

Tip: The Cheat Sheet for this book (the convenient tear-out reference card just

inside the front cover) provides a handy listing of the most popular directories and search engines described here.

AltaVista

www.altavista.com

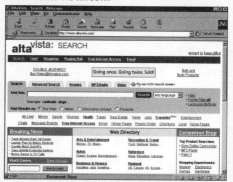

Sophisticated Internet searching: AltaVista remains one of the premier search engines, with some unique features for advanced keyword searching. The site also has a nifty feature that lets you refine searches by selecting and eliminating certain words and concepts from your current search results displayed at the top of each resulting page, narrowing the field of relevant links. AltaVista is a good search engine for exploring advanced options, all of which are explained by clicking the Help link on any keyword entry page.

Dogpile

www.dogpile.com

Simultaneous multiengine searching: A multiengine search service, Dogpile (where *did* they come up with that name?)

automatically scours the indexes of Yahoo!, Excite, Lycos, Infoseek, AltaVista, and several other databases, with your keywords. You can select whether to search the Web, newswires only, Usenet, or two of the three in a certain order if you use the Custom Search features, and you can set a time limit (up to a minute in ten-second increments) by which Dogpile must deliver the results. Dogpile does a good job, even if it doesn't provide enough ways to narrow down the results.

Excite

www.excite.com

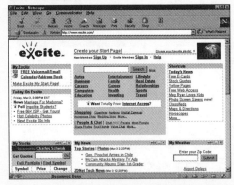

Good selection of sites and reviews: Excite presents its directory information as a mix of site links and magazine-style flow. Excite's search engine is devoted to finding *information,* regardless of what you need. It provides many services that help you find your particular needle in the Internet haystack — Yellow Pages, maps, a People Finder, and Email Lookup. Excite enables you to enter keywords and phrases without worrying about the computer taking you too literally or messing with search operators.

EZ-Find

info.theriver.com/TheRiver/ezfind.htm

Several search engines on one page: EZ-Find serves as a consolidator of search engines,

giving you access to several services on one page. Head over to the EZ-Find URL and check out the buttons beneath the keyword entry form — each button sends your keyword search request to a different major search engine. Below the buttons are drop-down menus that enable you to determine how you want your keywords interpreted, using basic functions that all the search engines understand.

GO.com

go.com

Popular Internet directory and search engine: Like other Web directories, GO.com provides links that take you to locations for finding people, e-mail addresses, maps, chat sites, and other Internet attractions. GO.com lets you define topics, news, companies, and newsgroups as channels within which your keywords search. Use the White Pages to find names, addresses, and e-mail addresses.

Google

www.google.com

More than a directory of Usenet newsgroups: Anyone who has ever scoured a gigantic master list of the thousands of individual newsgroups trying to find a particular one can see how valuable this site could be. Google expanded its archives when it purchased Deja News in 2001. To access its online directory, simply click the Directory tab.

HotBot

www.hotbot.com

State-of-the-cool Net searching: HotBot takes its name from the software robots that automatically scour the Web for new sites. (All search engines use some kind of software *bot,* sometimes called a *spider* or *worm.*) HotBot is a search service developed by HotWired, the online version of *Wired* magazine. Try the fast, accurate, comprehensive search engine hiding beneath the Day-Glo home page. You may need to experiment to get the hang of all the options, but it's worth enduring a learning curve to find information more quickly. HotBot is state-of-the-art searching.

Lycos

www.lycos.com

Magazine-style Web directory and basic searching: The Lycos directory has the appearance of a Web magazine divided into 17 main topics. Each topic also lists subtopics on the home page, so you can click Lodging under Travel and go directly to that page, for example. Searching in Lycos gets you just about anything on the entire Internet that meets your criteria. Use the Advanced Search to get more targeted results. You won't mistake the advanced options for the sophistication of AltaVista or HotBot, but Lycos gives you a little more control over your search results.

My Starting Point

www.stpt.com

Small, compact Net directory: My Starting Point takes a graphical approach to Web navigation. Although My Starting Point doesn't have the complexity of Yahoo!, Lycos, or the other monsters, you may prefer the coziness of the site as well as the wealth of links here. The directory

selections contain nothing unusual, and no descriptions or reviews clutter the tastefully laid-out pages. You won't give up your job to roam this site, but it is — as the title suggests — a starting point.

WebCrawler

www.webcrawler.com

Veteran search engine with new directory: WebCrawler is one of the oldest of all search engines, and if the search box on the home page isn't enough, you can also find links below the box that can help you locate information on a number of other topics. You get a compact list of result links, unaccompanied by descriptions or reviews. Click the Help link for an extensive list of topics on how to use the WebCrawler system.

Yahoo!

www.yahoo.com

The granddaddy of Internet directories: Yahoo! is probably the best known of all online maps and one of the most-visited Web sites. The directory is a testimonial to the huge complexity of the Web. Yahoo! attempts to link to every site on the Web. The directory probably doesn't quite accomplish that noble goal, but it comes as close as anyone could want. Yahoo! is the directory to use when you don't want to miss a single site. The Yahoo! search engine links you to sites that relate to your keywords as well as to different parts of its own directory.

Other Sites to Check Out

www.achoo.com
Directory of healthcare sites

www.looksmart.com
Internet directory with a uniquely useful design

www.yahooligans.com
Kid-safe Internet directory

Downloads

Downloading is usually reserved for sites that specialize in offering programs and files. A few of the sites maintain enormous inventories of available files, like software supermarkets. Other sites fill more specific niches, such as games or screen savers. But all these selections provide a good interface for browsing and initiating downloads.

Beyond.com

www.beyond.com

Buy software online: Beyond.com (formerly BuyDirect.com) is a download site devoted to commercial software and some hardware sold through the Internet. The programs sold through Beyond.com include everyday desktop applications as well as Internet assistance programs, such as browsers, chat client software, server utilities (such as MPEG-encoding programs), Java programming tools, and other development and communications tools. Using the Beyond.com site is a lot quicker than going to the store, and the selection of Internet-related titles is better.

Download.com

www.download.com

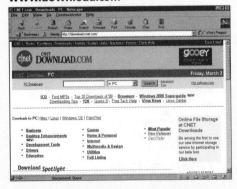

Huge selection of shareware: Download.com is a major portion of the CNET Web site and one of the most important download pipelines on the Web. The huge site is organized into categories of software — Business, Games, Home & Personal, Internet, Utilities, and so on. The site amounts to a multilevel directory of software, listing the actual programs on the third level. Or you can use the handy search engine if you know what you're looking for. Download.com contains both shareware and commercial programs in its archives.

Dr. Download

www.drdownload.com/home.htm

Essential downloads for Internet beginners: Dr. Download writes all its text — introductions and reviews — in the doctor's highly personable, informal voice, which makes browsing fun. More than just a good read, Dr. Download cuts through the shareware jungle by selecting and offering only handpicked programs, saving you tons of time downloading worthless software. Dr. Download is a good starting point for the shareware beginner.

Macdownload.com

www.zdnet.com/mac/download.html

Vast software selection for Macs: Macdownload.com groups its offerings in eight categories, listed on the bottom of the home page. Everything from publishing to games to software for the Newton is included. New software is also noted.

PC Magazine Downloads

www.zdnet.com/downloads

High-quality free downloads from the magazine: PC Magazine Downloads offers downloads of past PC Tech sections of the magazine, plus the actual software benchmark tools that the magazine uses to compile its renowned equipment reviews. The programs are freeware, not shareware, and uniformly excellent, making them the best and most famous bargains on the Net (with the exception, perhaps, of free Web browsers). The average surfer will find the <u>Internet</u> link, which takes you to a selection of handy Internet programs, to be of great value.

Other Sites to Check Out

www.davecentral.com
Handpicked shareware and freeware

itprodownloads.com
Games and other shareware downloads

www.jumbo.com
Shareware supermarket

www.tucows.com
Large selection of browser add-ons and plug-ins

Technology Publications

Web publications covering high-tech subjects are a mix of print magazines gone virtual and *e-zines*, which began on the Internet and serve only a logged-on readership. As in other fields, the online editions of computer magazines may or may not include all the content of the printed edition but almost certainly contain special articles or interactive features specific to the Web. Subscription costs are rare. When money does come into play, the fees usually apply to only a special portion of the site and not to the whole thing.

Byte

www.byte.com
Online magazine about hardware and computer technology: Byte Magazine's editorial emphasis is on the broad topic of information management, and it carries articles on server technology, Web site management, intranets, data warehousing, and other high-tech esoterica related to supervising the flow of data. The glossary comes in handy as you're trudging through a dense archive of over 6,000 articles.

Computer Shopper

www.zdnet.com/computershopper
How and where to buy computer stuff: You've seen the huge, bricklike printed magazine in stores. Computer Shopper is a pretty dry read, but the magazine isn't about entertainment; it's about shopping for and buying computers and peripherals. The Web site carries on the tradition but without all the mail-order ads of the printed book.

HotWired

www.hotwired.com

Ultra-hip online magazine for the wired generation: HotWired has an independent and creative editorial staff. Famous departments include Webmonkey, which offers you assistance in developing your own site; Animation Express, which offers the latest in Web animation; and the RGB Gallery, with some interactive multimedia art. The site is fully searchable using the handy drop-down menus on the home page.

Macworld/MacWeek

macworld.zdnet.com

Information feast for Mac lovers: A joint product of IDG and Ziff-Davis (two heavy-weights in the technology information business), the site includes elements of *Macworld* magazine and *MacWeek*. Just go to the section you want information on and read to your heart's content.

PC Magazine Online

www.zdnet.com/pcmag

Computer reviews and columns from the printed magazine: The biweekly magazine for hard-core PC users puts out the best hardware tests in the industry, includes a great range of software reviews, and has renowned columnists. *PC Magazine* is the kind of must-have publication that thousands of people subscribe to year after year and read from cover to cover the day it arrives. The Web site archives the PC Labs hardware reviews and includes much of the printed material, enhanced by snazzy Java applets and continually updated site recommendations.

WorldVillage

www.worldvillage.com

Award-winning, informative community: A uniquely designed e-zine, WorldVillage serves up software reviews; directories of downloadables, game reviews, and tips; and interactive community features. It's a magazine; it's a news source; it's an online community. The site's home page clearly breaks out the key sections. WorldVillage is fun but never loses sight of its mission to be informative and useful.

Other Sites to Check Out

www.boardwatch.com
Coverage of online services and the Internet

www.zdnet.com/equip
The digital-age lifestyle

Chapter 2
News and Information

Entrepreneurship

More people look for ways to have only one boss — themselves. The following sites not only help you look for ways to accomplish the American dream, but also help you sustain and prosper in that goal.

Business@Home

www.gohome.com

Making a life while making a living: That's the motto of this site targeted toward individuals who operate a business from their homes. You find resources to maintain and improve your home business through feature articles that cover topics, such as marketing, taxes, family management, telecommunications, and the law. All told, this is a great support site for those already involved in a home-based business.

Entrepreneurs' Help Page

www.tannedfeet.com

Advice in layman's terms: When you can't afford to hire a lawyer for consultation or have a CPA set up the books, this site can get you on the right track. Neatly organized into categories like Business, Finance, and Legal, the pages let you find your way around this site with ease. In all, a plentiful site with easy-to-digest information.

Small Business Administration

www.sba.gov

A helping hand from Uncle Sam: The Small Business Administration and its programs may be a financial boon to your business startup. With programs ranging from loans to learning, the SBA site outlines everything for you. Even if you're not going to take out a loan through the SBA, this site is still probably the best starting point as you take steps toward becoming your own boss.

Other Sites to Check Out

www.betheboss.com
Franchise opportunities for sale

guru.com
Create your profile and find work

Financial News

Money is a huge topic on and off the Internet. Because the Web includes so many financial news sites, we're forced to omit some good locations. The following sites provide a wealth of useful information, however. (For a much more complete list, check out *Internet Directory For Dummies*, 3rd Edition, by Brad Hill, published by Hungry Minds, Inc.)

ABCNEWS.com: Business

abcnews.go.com/sections/business

Compact updates of essential business news: This site's great layout makes finding information easy. The site covers stories on a variety of topics, such as mutual funds, financial planning, and retirement.

Bloomberg News

www.bloomberg.com

Profound depth of international financial coverage: Bloomberg News excels at providing a concise briefing on the day's top business news. To get the briefs beyond the headlines, click <u>News</u>; then, for more, click <u>Top Financial News</u>, <u>Top World News</u>, or whatever your particular interest is. A lot of other information is presented in the Bloomberg site, so keep poking around.

Business Wire

www.businesswire.com

Bulletins from the business world: Business Wire is a resource that you can quickly become dependent on for hourly headline updates on corporate culture, stocks, and general finance.

Office.com

www.individual.com

Customizable directory of business news: Office.com NewsPage is a can't-do-without site for many people who get their business news on the Net. This site offers a directory-style database of headlines divided into topics relating primarily to business and technology. You can customize the topics presented to you by specifying your job and industry.

USA Today Money

www.usatoday.com/money/mfront.htm

Tons of information and bright colors: Information reigns supreme at the Web translation of the financial section of *USA Today,* starting with the familiar, colorful banner at the top of the page and continuing through the data-rich stories, graphs, and tables. The site displays quickly and is an excellent bookmark for getting crucial information fast.

The Wall Street Journal Interactive Edition

http://interactive.wsj.com

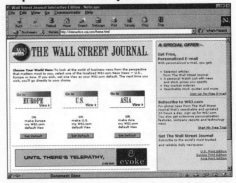

A variety of free and subscription business news: This section wouldn't be complete without a reference to the Web site of the famous institution of financial publishing: *The Wall Street Journal* (WSJ). The Web site contains a goodly amount of information for investors interested in Europe, Asia, and the Americas. The WSJ was one of the first publishers to attempt a Web site that charges for admission (you pay by the month or annually).

Yahoo! Finance

quote.yahoo.com

Broad range of financial and investment information: This site was previously known as Yahoo! Quotes — the name was changed to reflect the broadening content of this excellent site. Most people who manage investments online use Yahoo! Finance dozens of times every day. The blazing speed mixes well with the wealth of features and links.

Other Sites to Check Out

www.barrons.com
Professional analysis and commentary

www.businessweek.com
Online edition of famous financial weekly

money.cnn.com
Interesting articles from the editors of CNN and *Money* magazine

www.fortune.com
Online version of a great magazine

www.mutual-funds.com/mfmag/
Highly useful evaluator of mutual funds

Financial Services

Every site in this section provides a tangible service online, not just a placard for an offline company that provides a service. Fortunately, the fields of investment, business, and personal finance are among the quickest growing on the Web. Here is a directory of the finest financial services that the Internet has to offer. You can find tremendous value in the sites that follow. (Some sites may charge for certain features.)

Tip: Refer to Book VIII, Chapter 3, for online investment tips and strategies, as well as a top-ten list of investment resources that you shouldn't miss.

Ameritrade

www.ameritrade.com
Cheap rates for basic trades: Ameritrade touts one of the lowest equity market trade prices around: $8 over the Internet for an unlimited number of shares. The price goes up if you want to trade over the phone or talk to a broker, of course. The minimum to open an account is $2,000. Busy traders should look into Ameritrade if saving money on commissions is a priority.

eSignal

www.esignal.com
Lots of quote and charting services: This site is bursting with information and services. From delayed quotes to tips on trading, you can find what you need.

E-Trade

www.etrade.com
Pioneer of online brokerages: One of the first — and certainly the most famous — online brokerages, E-Trade provides a wide range of brokering services for trading financial stocks and options. A true discount broker, E-Trade charges a flat fee (currently $14.95 for an online trade of NYSE-listed stocks) for the purchase or sale of an unlimited number of a company's shares, and option commissions are competitive. The amount needed to start a cash account ($1,000) is among the lowest on the Internet.

Merrill Lynch

www.merrill-lynch.com
Comprehensive financial information: Merrill Lynch, the rock-solid, time-honored Wall Street investment firm, is embracing the Internet in a big way. And the company is doing a great job of it. The Individual Investors link takes you to a financial advisor.

The Motley Fool

www.fool.com
Informal presentation of serious investment advice: The Motley Fool is set up as a Web site advice center. You can get stock quotes at the site, but its real purpose is to educate beginning investors in a certain approach to selecting stock purchases. The Fool motif running through every page keeps things fun, but the advice is serious and worthwhile.

NASDAQ

www.nasdaq.com
Online site of the major stock exchange: Colorful charts show you how the NASDAQ Composite and Dow Jones Industrial Average are performing that

day. One of the slickest quote engines on the Net retrieves prices for up to ten publicly traded companies, whether they're on the NASDAQ board or the New York or American exchanges, *and* mutual funds.

Lycos Finance

finance.lycos.com

A cornucopia of stock information: You can find press releases, market information, free real-time quotes, and more at this site. For a fee, you can subscribe to an unlimited number of charts and quotes, as well as technical analysis.

Schwab

www.schwab.com

Online trading from the famous brokerage house: Schwab is considered rather on the expensive side by Net standards, charging $29.95 per trade, with an additional per-share charge above 1,000 shares. However, large volume traders may be eligible to trade online at this site for only $14.95 per trade. The Schwab Web site is widely known to be rock-solid, rarely suffering technical difficulties.

Waterhouse Securities, Inc.

www.waterhouse.com

Deep discounts and many extra services: If page attractiveness counts for anything on a financial service site, then Waterhouse Securities gets points for a nice design. The company charges a flat-rate commission of $12 when you do up to 18 trades per calendar quarter, as well as lower fees when you do more trades. Waterhouse points proudly to its number-one ranking in a study of online brokers conducted by *Smart Money* magazine. The kudos are well earned.

Other Sites to Check Out

www.accutrade.com
Deep-discount stock and option trading

www.datek.com
Lowest commissions for online stock trading

www.quicken.com
Budget and tax planning

www.scottrade.com
Very low commissions and free research

www.123jump.com/letters/letters.htm
Unique research features for free

Magazines

This section lists general-interest magazines and newsmagazines. In almost all cases when a printed magazine exists, the site makes some kind of pitch to get you to subscribe to the printed version. The following sites are the best online editions of general and news magazines that you can find on the virtual newsstand. Most of the sites are free, although you never can tell when an online magazine is going to start charging for some of its content.

Reader's Digest World

www.readersdigest.com

Brief literature, research journalism, and humor: If you think of *Reader's Digest* as a somewhat stodgy, if venerable, recycler of literature and inspiring all-American stories first published elsewhere, visit the online site for a jolt of disillusionment. Reader's Digest World is one hip, technically advanced, glowing point of cyberspace. Multimedia games and invitations to forum discussions keep the site highly interactive.

TIME

www.time.com

Broad news coverage: TIME has created a substantial, informative, interactive source of news. The site posts stories in a complete version with small pictures that don't gum up your bandwidth.

U.S. News & World Report Online

www.usnews.com

Great use of the Internet by the staid weekly: If you visit this site, the presentation of the stories will impress you. Stories contain a liberal number of hyperlinks to locations providing background or related news.

Other Sites to Check Out

www.almanac.com
Essential trivia and folk wisdom

www.lifemag.com/Life
Gallery of photographs and past features

Newspapers

Many printed newspapers have turned to the Internet to supplement the service that they provide to readers. In some cases, the paper's content is duplicated exactly on the Web; in other cases, the content is enhanced through back-story archiving, the addition of multimedia features, color pictures, and some interactive jazz, such as automatic clipping services, e-mail delivery, or immediate-response classified ads.

This section is a directory to the finest, most extravagant newspaper creations on the Web. All the listings review big-city or national newspapers, although the Net includes hundreds of fine local publications.

The Boston Globe Online

www.boston.com/globe

Plenty of updates: The Boston Globe site is so stuffed with great features that you must explore it yourself to get the whole picture. In addition to feature stories, you can find a photo gallery of the week's best pics. The entire *Boston Globe Magazine* section, classifieds, a crossword puzzle, and comics are some of the attractions of one of the top online newspapers around.

Chicago Tribune

www.chicagotribune.com

Nice design with a Windy City slant to the news: The Chicago Tribune Web site values brevity and attempts to save visitors time by condensing its content. The concept works but seemingly at the expense of comprehensiveness. The publication emphasizes Chicago-area news and sports, of course, but it also carries major-league national reporting.

The Christian Science Monitor

www.csmonitor.com

Great international news with a dollop of inspiration: One of the most renowned and respected newspapers in the world, *The Christian Science Monitor* goes beyond its spiritual underpinnings by delivering concise, accessible, comprehensive, and intelligent reporting of international news.

Los Angeles Times

www.latimes.com

Tremendous example of what an online newspaper can be: This site is massive. However, the front page does a great job of clarifying your options by providing categories on the left side of the page for choosing sections, plus a keyword search form at the top. Archiving is valued at the *Los Angeles Times,* and you can pore through back articles, movie reviews, and so on.

The New York Times

www.nytimes.com

The gray lady dances on the Net: The New *York Times* Web site conveys the basic visual impression of the famous *Times* layout, without the graphic load that would slow down the pages. If you want a more streamlined route, click the Text Version link (found halfway down the menu on the left) for a simple, text-based table of contents. The site's design is effective, but the main emphasis is its world-class reporting content.

USA Today

www.usatoday.com

Oooh, fast with bright colors: USA Today on the Web is a sprawling, info-rich, picturesque, bustling, oft-updated site that divides its info neatly into five main sections: News, Money, Sports, Life, and Weather. As with the newspaper, the online version of *USA Today* is bright, colorful, and simple, and it delivers the essentials quickly, without ever drawing outside the lines.

Other Sites to Check Out

www.iht.com
International site worth digging into

www.washingtonpost.com
Great Internet features and renowned reporting

Phone Books and E-Mail Directories

The following are the major people-finding and business-finding Web directories. Just as phone books aren't 100 percent accurate on the day they're published, online phone books sometimes have old information. Still, the listings here are the best the Web has to offer, and the price is right. In addition to white and yellow pages, you'll discover e-mail pages that enable you to look up a person's e-mail address.

Search-It-All

www.search-it-all.com/peoplefinder.asp

The Ultimate Reference Tool: Combining the power and data of many search engines across the Internet, Search-It-All is one of the better reverse search engines. All you have to do is provide a phone number, e-mail address, or street address, and Search-It-All combs through data on the Web to return as much information as possible based on your input.

SuperPages

superpages.com

Interactive yellow pages: As interactive yellow page directories go, SuperPages is currently state of the art. That doesn't mean it's perfect, but it's useful. In SuperPages, you can enter the category of business or the name of a specific business, plus the city and state.

Yahoo! People Search

people.yahoo.com

Find old friends in cyberspace: Yahoo! has acquired the former Four11 site. You'll see that this site has aspirations of being a one-stop search center for e-mail addresses, postal addresses, and business locations, but it's mostly known for locating old friends. It's a pretty great resource, and it gets better all the time as more people join.

InfoSpace

www.infospace.com/info.zip

Yellow pages with memory: InfoSpace can find a business, search for addresses, get directions, get maps, and find a person. The map feature is nice because it can be enlarged or panned in eight directions.

Other Sites to Check Out

www.switchboard.com
Find people and then send them a postcard

www.teldir.com
Telephone directories organized by continent

www.whowhere.lycos.com
Track people down

www.worldpages.com
Gigantic, international phone book

Technology News

The field of technology news covers computers; software; the Internet and online services; and all the commentary, speculation, and general ranting that accompanies news about such a volatile industry. Some of the sites that we list in this section represent the best that the Web has to offer in terms of page design, content quality, and interactive features.

CNET

www.news.com

Massive technology news site with plenty of audio: CNET is a Web legend in its own time. Almost like a small online service in its ambitious scope, CNET boasts more than 1 million members. The tremendous wealth of RealAudio content in the site makes CNET resemble nothing short of an online radio station devoted to technology reporting. The old saying applies: If you visit just one technology news site, make it CNET.

IDG.Net

www.idg.net

Impressive array of international technology news: The site of International Data Group brings together information from the more than 400 worldwide newspapers, magazines, and Web sites with which the company is affiliated.

USA Today Tech Report

**www.usatoday.com/life/cyber/tech/
ct000.htm**

Technology articles from the daily newspaper: Efficiency is the name of the game at this site. Although *USA Today* produces the site, the Tech Report is a Web production separate from the printed newspaper's content. You get the day's top technology headlines, updated every few hours, or as stories evolve. This site trims the fat and delivers the goods without any waste.

ZDNet News

www.zdnet.com/zdnn

Respected technology publishing organization: ZDNet News is a top high-tech news source on the Web. When you arrive on Page One, you get a rapid-fire burst of news, which is constantly updated throughout the day. The Breaking News headline column links you to stories as they develop and is designed to be a cutting-edge, breaking-news feature. This packed site provides a lot of substance to browse through.

Other Sites to Check Out

www.cnn.com/TECH/index.html
Science and high-tech news

www.newslinx.com
International news about the Web

www.wired.com/news
High-tech news with an attitude

Television and Radio News

Live news on the Net is a small, but growing, area. As technology inches closer to a *broadband* environment — where most people access the Internet with cable or wireless systems through which Web pages load much more quickly than through modems — you'll see more television and radio stations incorporating Webcasts into their operations. In this section, we review the pioneers of Webcasting.

ABCNEWS.com

www.abcnews.go.com

Check the icons for audio and video: The ABC News site gives visitors a tip as to whether sound and pictures accompany a story. Check the headline and short summary of a story and then note the icons at the end. A small speaker denotes an audio report, and a frame of film points to a video. Clicking the interactive icon, which looks like dual arrows forming a rectangle, links you to another Web page that contains multimedia clips and a possible interactive display window that you can click for different points of the story.

Fox News

www.foxnews.com

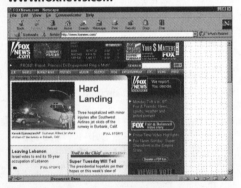

Ambitious, glitzy, multimedia site: The Fox News site enlivens typical news sections with news tickers across the top of the home page, a generous supply of audio and video clips, and a live simulcast of the Fox News Channel. This is one cutting-edge news site.

MSNBC

www.msnbc.com

The cable channel's online residence: MSNBC, the hybrid news and entertainment organization, which Microsoft and NBC created, puts out a jazzy Web tribute to the multimedia possibilities of delivering news over the Internet. The Web site is closely linked with the cable station of the same name and carries some shows through browser plug-ins. (You need Windows Media Player to make the most of this site.)

Weather

Besides providing data about weather conditions in certain locations, the best weather sites also furnish forecasts for the following day and sometimes for several days in advance. What you're really looking for is a site that enables you to type in a location (the more specific the better) and get a regional forecast as well as current conditions. The following sites do the best job blending conditions, forecasts, and other weather information.

AccuWeather

www.accuweather.com

AccuThis, AccuThat, AccuNice: Get your local five-day forecast just by typing your zip code on the front page of this Web site. You can get hour-by-hour forecasts for up to ten days and access to the most current local radars. Satellite and radar images, weather maps, and conditions and forecasts are available.

USA Today Weather

www.usatoday.com/weather/wfront.htm

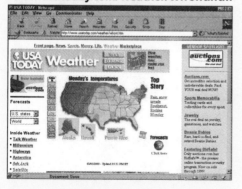

That famous U.S. weather map: This Web site features the trademark *USA Today* color-coded national temperature map, surrounded by lots of information about weather. You can read about hurricanes, tornadoes, thunderstorms, and other upsetting weather developments. Of course, you can just get forecasts, too. The USA Today Weather five-day outlooks tend to be simpler to follow than those provided by The Weather Channel Web site.

The Weather Channel

www.weather.com/twc/homepage.twcg

More than just forecasts: The Weather Channel treats meteorological events as if they're fascinating plot lines, like a running soap opera of wind, rain, sleet, and sunshine. The Weather Channel Web site is similarly ambitious, providing an "online magazine" about weather. Headlines and top stories fit under the Breaking Weather category, and a summary of current conditions for major cities scrolls across the screen. You can also get a local forecast.

Other Sites to Check Out

www.fema.gov/fema/trop.htm
Warnings of emerging storms

www.intellicast.com
Comprehensive site for world travelers

www.nws.noaa.gov
Weather disaster warnings

www.stormtrack.org
Go get that tornado!

Wire Services and Daily Updates

Current events proliferate on the Web. Presenting daily news is a task well suited to the Internet, where it doesn't cost much to update facts frequently. All the sites in this section update the news at least daily and sometimes even more frequently.

ABCNEWS.com

www.abcnews.go.com

Solid news and fancy Web tricks: This site has more headlines than the front page of a typical newspaper, and you can click the arrows to get the full details of the story and even some background info. By registering for immediate local news, you can link to your local ABC affiliate. ABCNEWS.com is full of little tricks and interactive snacks such as radio news through RealAudio. If you need your news fast, we suggest that you avoid the audio and video links on the site.

CNN Interactive

www.cnn.com

An online news juggernaut: The cable TV news giant provides one of the most-visited sites for daily news. The home page is a marvel of clear efficiency, linking to every portion of the gigantic site without appearing overbearing. The Local page offers a national map; clicking any region takes you to news pages provided by CNN regional affiliates.

Other Sites to Check Out

www.drudgereport.com
Controversial commentary, plus a directory

www.infojunkie.com
Up-to-the-second headlines

www.defenselink.mil/news/ releases.html
Defense department press releases

www.whitehouse.gov/news/briefings
White House Press briefings

Chapter 3
Research and Education

Education Services

Education is such a wide-ranging field that you *need* a computer just to keep track of all the possibilities, whether you're looking for information on admissions, financial aid, teaching, tests, or careers. Here, we present a collection of sites representing the multifaceted topic of education, from high school college-prep tests to financial aid, from teaching resources to scholarly Web links.

College Board Online

www.collegeboard.org

Help in taking tests: For those facing crucial tests along the educational path, this site is a nonintimidating way to see how the College Board operates and to find out about its test dates. The site covers SAT testing as well.

Educational Finance Group

www.schoolfunds.com

How to get government education loans: The Educational Finance Group site has the real scoop on U.S. government education loans. The site lays out all the facts concerning requirements, applications, disbursements, and paybacks. It tells you when to apply and even gets you preapproved online if you care to fill in a reasonably short form. The site could hardly be clearer or more encouraging about financing higher education.

FinAid

www.finaid.org

How to borrow money for education: The Financial Aid Information Page offers a clearinghouse of information for college students who need tuition help. FinAid contains an astounding wealth of information, including glossaries; FAQs (frequently asked questions); special topics for international and disabled students; links to financial aid Web pages, books, videotapes, and consultants; and much more.

Kaplan Educational Center

www1.kaplan.com

Helps students face and take scholastic tests: Kaplan is one of the finest educational service sites on the Net. The site answers students' questions with deep resources, lots of reassurance, and helpful information that just doesn't quit. When it comes to the SAT, PSAT, GRE, GMAT, and other examinations, Kaplan archives past tests, analyzes strategies, and discusses the relative importance of high or low scores in certain departments.

Petersons.com

www.petersons.com

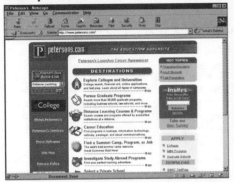

Online college and career guides:
Peterson's, the famous college guide company, enables you to access its database of information related to all kinds of education: from kindergarten to graduate schools to distance learning. Families who need information on colleges should add this site to their bookmark list.

Other Sites to Check Out

www.collegenet.com
Search for colleges using various criteria

www.ets.org
Online site of Educational Testing Service

www.gsh.org
Educational technology for teachers

www.scholarstuff.com
Directory of education sites

Environment

Earth-friendly and animal-savior organizations and publications comprise this section. The sites tend to be modestly designed and quick to navigate.

The Earth Times

earthtimes.org

Online edition of the magazine: The Earth Times is a printed magazine covering environmental issues and offering an online edition. Global in scope, *The Earth Times* reports on sustainable development in Africa, Asia, the Americas, and Europe. *The Earth Times* is upbeat (when possible) and helpful in its suggestions and admonitions.

EnviroLink

www.envirolink.org

Online environmental community: Founded as a simple newsletter in 1991 by a first-year student at Carnegie Mellon University, EnviroLink has grown into one of the most impressive environmental information clearinghouses on the Web. The front page meets three criteria that seem to befuddle others: It's classy looking, informative and useful, and easy to understand.

Greenpeace International

www.greenpeace.org

Information about the organization: Greenpeace is an environmental action group that specializes in innovative, non-violent confrontation to expose environmental problems and force solutions. Greenpeace's ideals include the protection of biodiversity, the prevention of pollution, the elimination of nuclear threat, and the promotion of peace.

Sierra Club

www.sierraclub.org

Information about the organization: For environmental news, you'd do well to add the

Sierra Club URL to your bookmark list. The news articles at this site are replicated from three publications: *SC Action* (daily political and environmental update newsletter), *Sierra* (the Sierra Club magazine), and *The Planet* (an activist resource).

Genealogy

Looking for your ancestral roots with such a new-fangled search tool may seem rather odd, but genealogy is one of the hottest topics on the Web. Literally thousands of commercial and reference pages exist to help you in your search for ancestors. The following sites are just a sampling of the many Web resources available for genealogists. If you want to dig deeper into your background, an excellent resource is *Genealogy Online For Dummies,* 3rd Edition, by Matthew L. Helm and April Leigh Helm (Hungry Minds, Inc.).

Tip: See Book VIII, Chapter 4, for an entire chapter of helpful information on how to search the Web for data on your ancestors.

Family Tree Maker

www.familytreemaker.com

Software and valuable sites: Family Tree Maker is a software product marketed by Broderbund (one of many genealogy software packages available), and you won't be surprised by how many pages at this site tout the software's advantages. You can buy the software here, but you can also explore a wealth of resources for free just by visiting Family Tree Maker.

GeneaNet: Genealogical Database Network

www.geneanet.org

Search online for surnames: The goal of GeneaNet is to use the Internet's capabilities to build a database indexing all the world's genealogical resources. The resources that GeneaNet focuses on are families studied by genealogists, genealogical publications, manuscripts from libraries and archives, and other official sources, such as church registers and deeds.

Other Sites to Check Out

www.ancestry.com
Build your family tree online

www.gendex.com/gendex
Index of genealogical databases

www.genhomepage.com
Links to genealogy sites

Health

Most people rely on the established medical community to diagnose and treat illness. Generally, mainstream medicine is geared toward healing ailing conditions instead of maintaining healthy conditions, but preventive medicine is gaining ground. In addition to institutional sites, this section includes some health-news sites that cover primarily mainstream issues.

American Cancer Society

www.cancer.org

Information on the ACS and on cancer: The American Cancer Society (ACS) has a broadly utilitarian site that provides information, hope, and resources for anyone who is touched by cancer. This site is full of information, but it may not tell you absolutely everything you want to know. If you don't find an answer about a specific cancer on this site, look for a more specialized site or try doing some research offline.

CNN Health

http://cnn.com/HEALTH/index.html

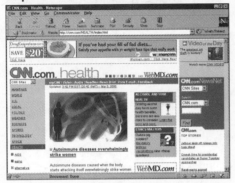

Links to CNN health-news stories: If you seek the broadest possible approach to medical and health news, you can't do better than CNN Health, which delivers objective journalism on every aspect of health and sickness. The main portion of the site is strictly a news source that dishes up stories as they break, regardless of the subject.

Mayo Clinic

www.mayohealth.org

Health news and resources: One of the foremost medical clinics in the world has done a fine job of creating a Web site that delivers both general health news and resources on specific conditions. As such, Mayo Clinic is one of the best health sites on the Net.

Other Sites to Check Out

www.goaskalice.columbia.edu
Database of questions and answers

www.healthcentral.com
Alternative/holistic health resources

www.menshealth.com/index.html
Online edition of *Men's Health* magazine

www.womens-health.com
A friendly, interactive place for women to discuss health

History

History is not the most ragingly popular topic on the Web. Most people, besides history hobbyists, probably don't want to be reminded of their school days, during which history was the most lifeless class in the world. However, some history sites are absolutely among the best things on the Web — beautifully produced, educational, and even fun to browse.

History Net

www.TheHistoryNet.com

A browser's paradise: Probably the best all-around history site on the Web, History Net displays a front page that immediately makes clear that the site contains too much information to absorb in any one sitting. The site is updated weekly, with new features coming online for each update. The site is a hobby page, more suitable for browsing than for serious research.

Library of Congress

marvel.loc.gov

Historical research: This site is an astonishing resource. You can access a raft of research services from (no surprise) the Using the Library section. You can access all the major sections and spin-off sites from the home page, making this site one of the most intelligently organized Web sites.

National Archives and Records Administration

www.nara.gov

Government documents: National Archives and Records Administration (NARA) is the government agency that stores and ensures the accessibility of essential national records. The NARA site is a great historical trip — especially if you spin off to the Online Exhibit Hall.

Smithsonian Institution

www.si.edu

History of the Smithsonian and the United States: The Smithsonian Institution site includes a list menu of links that bring the vast Smithsonian-related resources to your computer. For example, you can check out the Smithsonian's fabulous *Air and Space* magazine from the site or learn about the Mpala Research Centre in Kenya. The rich site is a delightful place to spend a few hours exploring the past.

Other Sites to Check Out

www.historychannel.com
The History Channel's site

www.museum-london.org.uk
Ancient to modern London history

Homework Sites

The classroom extends onto the Internet in the form of homework sites that help kids with research issues or actually provide answers. Question-and-answer sites are the most popular form of Web-based homework helpers. Some of the following sites provide bare facts, however; others are primarily link sites that point to other research stations on the Net.

Ask Dr. Math

mathforum.org/dr.math/dr-math.html

Math help for students ages 5 to 18: Dr. Math is a landmark homework-helper site on the Web, furnishing problem-solving assistance for kids between the ages of 5 and 18. (A new section of the site answers questions at the college level and beyond.) Anybody can send a question to Dr. Math, and the authoritative and trustworthy answers are added to the archive.

B. J. Pinchbeck's Homework Helper

school.discovery.com/homeworkhelp/ bjpinchbeck/index.html

Subject resources: Bruce Pinchbeck (B. J., or Beege) is a 12-year-old who, with his father, scoured the Internet for good homework sites. This site is formal, professional, and comprehensive. The directory link lists organized by B. J. and his dad are awesome.

Britannica Online

www.eb.com

Online version of the Encyclopedia Britannica: The famous *Encyclopedia Britannica* reproduces all its content in an online format at this site. Britannica Online is one of the few learning Web sites that charges a monthly subscription rate, but it also offers a free trial period. If your children get hooked during the free trial (or if you do), you may have to fork over the subscription fee to feed the learning habit.

BigChalk

www.bigchalk.com/cgi-bin/WebObjects/ WOPortal.woa/db/Home.html

To help narrow the searching, you can find links on the home page to sections specifically targeted toward elementary, middle, and high school students, as well as teachers and librarians.

World Factbook

www.odci.gov/cia/publications/factbook/index.html

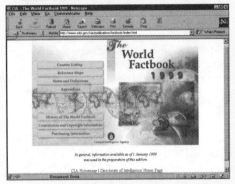

Basic information on all countries: This site is for pure, no-frills research on the basic data of any country in the world. The Central Intelligence Agency produces World Factbook, so you can be sure that it's pretty accurate. Aside from the home page, the World Factbook doesn't waste time with unnecessary graphics or commentary, so it's a quick and complete data resource to use when you're working on reports.

Other Sites to Check Out

encarta.msn.com
State-of-the-Net virtual schoolhouse

www.knowledgeadventure.com/features/kids/
Kids encyclopedia

scssi.scetv.org/mims/ssrch2.htm
Math and science resources

www.startribune.com/stonline/html/special/homework
Message boards for students

Housing Services

You can find lots of housing resources on the Web. Here are some good sites.

Homestore.com

www.homestore.com

More than just links: More than just a links directory, Homestore.com also has some truly unique programs that make a visit worthwhile. The Lifestyle Optimizer under Tools & Calculators, for example, helps match you to a community by asking your opinions on things such as town size and crime rate, comparing those answers to town demographics, and then producing a list of "ideal" communities for you to consider. The Salary Calculator compares the cost of living in hundreds of cities. Yes, this information is available on other Web sites, but Homestore.com pulls it all together in one convenient, unique package.

REALTOR.COM

www.realtor.com

Professional agents' organization: One of the simplest ways to buy a home is to get a Realtor, tell him or her what you want, and then wait for him or her to search for homes that match your wish list. Guess what? This site, from the National Association of Realtors, does the very same thing. You simply click Find a Home, click the maps to identify where you want to search, and then narrow your search by giving additional information.

Other Sites to Check Out

homescout.iown.com
Lets the Web do your searching

www.owners.com
Homes for sale by owner

Job Searching

Classified ads on the Internet are getting seriously useful. Recently, classified sites have created international databases divided into local categories, accessible with the help of drop-down menus and other navigational aids. At least, that's how the best sites work. Check out the sites assembled here for a glimpse of how good online classifieds can be.

Tip: If you want to do a little more in-depth research on job searching online, try *Job Searching Online For Dummies,* 2nd Edition, by Pam Dixon (published by Hungry Minds, Inc.). The book is a great resource for everything involved in using online information to get the job you want, not just finding sites.

America's Job Bank

www.ajb.dni.us

Job listings by category and state: Using a sophisticated and sometimes complex keyword search and sort system, America's Job Bank helps you navigate a massive database of job listings. All the available choices get a bit complicated, but the important point is that America's Job Bank has a ton of listings. And it's free.

Best Jobs in the USA

www.bestjobsusa.com

Job listings with detailed descriptions: One of the strong points of this site is its description of jobs, which goes way beyond a mere listing. Some jobs have several paragraphs of descriptive text outlining requirements, company atmosphere, and benefits. The initial result of your

search is a simple list of links. Click any one of them to see the job description.

CareerPath.com

www.careerpath.com

Classifieds from newspapers around the United States: Take your pick! Search for jobs from the newspaper or from the Web. As for the newspaper listings, this incredible service takes a unique approach to posting job openings: It doesn't. That is to say, it doesn't create its own classifieds section. Instead, it borrows the classified databases of newspapers, which you can search in multiple ways.

Monster.com

monster.com

A wealth of resources for the job seeker: This site provides much more than job listings. In addition to searching for jobs by category, you can use the Resume Builder to create an effective resume and obtain career advice in the Career Center. Be sure to check out My Monster, which enables you to create and store up to five résumés, track online applications, create Search Agents that help you find the job you want, and receive news articles customized to your interests.

Other Sites to Check Out

www.netjobs.com
Employment guide for Canada and America

www.overseasjobs.com
International job openings and links

Parenting

Unsure parents — and what parent doesn't have moments of uncertainty? — have many virtual resources to rely on. Some of these sites are essentially support groups;

others provide more practical content in the way of children's activities, games to teach your kids, and parental techniques.

All About Kids Online

www.aak.com

Communal site about kids: Taking advantage of Internet interactivity features, this site provides a sense of community through the Forum, a series of parenting discussions in message-board format. An excellent list of links to local resources is available in the Directories section under Resources. Each monthly issue carries a surprisingly large number of useful articles, making All About Kids Online a seemingly bottomless resource.

Parents.com

www.parents.com

Based on *Parents* magazine, this site offers tips for parents of kids of all ages, from birth to age 12. You can find a wide range of topics, including how to get your baby to sleep and how to deal with a 5 year old who refuses to dress himself. You can also find interactive online polls.

Parent Soup

www.parentsoup.com

Many parents' favorite Web site: Parent Soup is a major Web spot for parents. The site is a cross between an electronic magazine and a community center, featuring deep informational resources and a busy schedule of interactive attractions. Viewer participation is encouraged at every turn, starting on the home page with a daily Parent Poll. Most impressive is the daily rundown of chat topics.

Other Sites to Check Out

www.ala.org/parentspage/greatsites
Internet guide and list of family-oriented sites

www.parentsplace.com/index.html
Parenting message boards and chat

www.workingmother.com
Information geared to professional moms

Politics and Government

Two basic kinds of political pages are on the Web: sites that explain politics and sites that serve some government function. We cover both kinds in this section. General political sites are close in content to general news sites because much of today's mainstream news is political in nature. Still, the specialized political news sites go deeper into the political stories and are more satisfying for people who follow politics closely.

CNN Interactive AllPolitics

cnn.com/ALLPOLITICS/

Daily political news: For a totally political brain hit, you can do no better than the CNN Interactive AllPolitics site. Formatted like an electronic newspaper, the site provides daily updates of headlines and in-depth stories that should sate anybody's appetite for government and candidacy news.

Electronic Policy Network

epn.org

Public policy resources: The Electronic Policy Network is a sprawling site that encompasses several other spin-off sites. You may want to bookmark the home page, from which you can launch your way to the many individual sections, or you may want to browse those sections and bookmark individual portions. With too much content to describe adequately in a short review (a search engine helps make sense of everything), the Electronic Policy Network is a meaty site and definitely worth a visit.

Public Affairs Web

www.publicaffairsweb.com

Comprehensive political information: Public Affairs Web has high aspirations: It wants to be the only Web site that you need for all questions of public policy, pending legislation, candidacy, and elections. The site is a treasure house of information, and it apparently will only get better, with its promise to provide more frequent updates in the near future.

Other Sites to Check Out

www.democrats.org/index.html
Democratic politics

www.fbi.gov
Information about the FBI

www.gpo.ucop.edu
Directory of government databases

www.mrsmith.com
E-mail addresses of members of Congress

www.odci.gov
Information about the CIA

www.rnc.org
Republican politics

www.senate.gov
Information on the Senate

thomas.loc.gov
Database of legislative action

www.whitehouse.gov/news/briefings
White House press information

Reference

Online dictionaries and encyclopedias have one great value: They enable you to search interactively by typing keywords (at least, some of them have this feature).

Random access is the big advantage of computers, and it certainly comes into play at reference sites.

Merriam-Webster Online

www.m-w.com

Online version of the dictionary and the-saurus: The Merriam-Webster Dictionary and Thesaurus comprise what is now called Merriam-Webster Online. Using the site is simple: You type a word, and a new page tells you what the word means or gives you synonyms. One nice feature is that the definition/synonym pages are cross-linked.

PC Webopedia

www.pcwebopedia.com

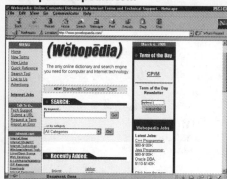

Encyclopedia of computer and Internet information: This excellent reference site is an encyclopedia of computer and Internet information, with an interface that looks like a dictionary. PC Webopedia's database is good, but its cross-referencing of that database is extraordinary, which simply means that you're likely to get much more than you came for.

Roget's Thesaurus

www.thesaurus.com

Online version of the thesaurus: The online version of Roget's Thesaurus is a brilliant accomplishment. Simply select Thesaurus from the Search: drop-down list, then type your word into the For text box, and click OK. Your results appear on a new page in as many categories as will fit there. You also can search the Dictionary or Web pages for the typed word.

U.S. Gazetteer

www.census.gov/cgi-bin/gazetteer

Maps of the United States: The operation of this site is simple. You type a U.S. zip code or geographical name, and the site spits the formal name of the place and a few basic facts (population and longitude and latitude) back at you. The page also enables you to look up more statistical information in table form, but the map is more fun because you can manipulate it. Zoom in or out interactively, add features such as highway markings and various topographical labels, or subtract features. Are you having fun yet?

Other Sites to Check Out

www.bartleby.com
Provides links to online reference books

www.dictionaries.travlang.com
Translations of foreign words

www.facstaff.bucknell.edu/rbeard/ diction.html
Directory of dictionaries

Science

Science makes the transition from the physical world to cyberspace beautifully; in fact, science is a big topic on the Net. Astronomy sites in particular have proliferated like uninhibited rabbits over the past couple of years. Also, broadly scientific sites and organizational Web sites, such as NASA's, keep viewers up-to-date on current projects and missions.

American Museum of Natural History

www.amnh.org

Virtual museum: At first glance, the American Museum of Natural History site appears to be nothing more than a brief advertisement for the physical museum in New York City, with little or no informative value of its own. In fact, it just takes a little digging, and before you know it, following one link after another, you're on an interesting knowledge expedition.

Hubble Space Telescope Public Pictures

oposite.stsci.edu/pubinfo/Pictures.html

Deep-space photographs: This site, which has a repository of images from the Hubble Space Telescope, looks good on any monitor, but if you have a 17-inch computer screen or are using a WebTV system, the fabulous space shots will really knock your socks off.

Human Anatomy Online

www.innerbody.com/htm/body.html

Virtual anatomy: This site is worthwhile only if you view it in a fully Java-enabled browser, such as a recent version of Navigator or Explorer. Start by choosing a body section or system from a group of small images. Clicking one image expands it to a large image, interactively loaded with hot spots that change to labels when you move the mouse pointer over them.

NASA

www.nasa.gov

Information about the space agency: The NASA site, far from being a bureaucratic placard (like some government agencies' Internet sites), is a vibrant, informative, wide-ranging Web science location that is download heaven if you're interested in multimedia science files. The Multimedia

Gallery is an almost unbelievable repository of pictures, audio clips, and movies available for viewing online (with the correct browser plug-ins) or for downloading.

PlanetScapes

planetscapes.com

Travel guide to the solar system: You won't find a more phenomenal resource for facts, figures, and views of the solar system. PlanetScapes is an exhaustive compendium of data about planets, comets, asteroids, and the sun, yet it manages to avoid stuffiness or tedium.

Other Sites to Check Out

www.discovery.com
The Discovery Channel

**www.perspective.com/nature/
index.html**
A directory of all species

www.thetech.org/hyper
Virtual science museum

Chapter 4
Sports and Leisure

Hobbies

The Web started out as a hobby. It was invented as a research project, and college students first adopted it for recreational purposes. Although the Web quickly became a commercial venue, it makes sense that you can find plenty of stuff about hobbies online, too.

Apogee Photo Magazine

www.apogeephoto.com

Articles on all aspects of photography: Apogee Photo Magazine is an online photography magazine that cuts Netizens a good deal with excellent, free features. A message board and chat room enable you to ask questions and meet other shutterbugs, and a link to an online bookstore is available.

Collect.com

www.collect.com/buysell/dealers/ NewSearch.asp

Directory of collectibles retailers: Collect.com doesn't allow you to transact online purchases, although you can browse a heck of a lot of retail Web sites. That's really this site's strong point: It's a fine directory of online and offline retailers of collectible merchandise.

Home, Garden, and Kitchen

The home, garden, and kitchen are surprisingly well represented on the Internet. As this section demonstrates, some spectacular sites on those subjects exist.

Epicurious Food

food.epicurious.com

Information for gourmets: "For People Who Eat," it says. That doesn't leave out many folks. And this site deserves a wide audience, replete as it is with information about the love of food, not to mention two magazines — *Bon Appétit* and *Gourmet* — that spin off from the home page.

The Growing Edge

www.growingedge.com

Gardening techniques: A bimonthly magazine of gardening techniques, *The Growing Edge* provides superb coverage of indoor gardening, which is its main claim to fame.

Internet Chef

www.ichef.com

Worshipful articles on food: The Internet Chef site expresses its reverence for food through monthly articles, columns, a spotlighted recipe every week, and an astounding archive of recipes.

National Gardening Association

www.garden.org

Former "Gardens for All" online: The National Gardening Association (NGA) has a number of education-oriented programs, so it shouldn't be a surprise that the group is cultivating a following on the Web. The deepest resource on the site is the online version of *National Gardening* magazine, which offers a sampling of the magazine's news and features.

This Old House

www.pbs.org/wgbh/thisoldhouse

Home-restoration information from the PBS series and magazine: The well-known TV show and magazine, featuring methodically explained restorations of beautiful old houses, makes a medium splash on the Web.

Other Sites to Check Out

www.hometime.com
Home-improvement plans

www.kitchen-bath.com
Kitchen and bath improvement

livinghome.com
Informative community for homeowners

www.wconline.com
Walls and ceilings directory

Pets

Pets are a recreational passion for a lot of people. At these sites, you may find grooming hints, answers to pet-care questions, training techniques, and interactive community features for talking with other pet lovers.

Animal Network

www.animalnetwork.com

Links to Web pet sites: Animal Network is the hub of a vast array of pet sites on the Web. Each link goes to an online magazine, trotting out information about breeds, pet care, and pet products. You may want to bookmark Animal Network and use it as a hub to find the pages that really interest you.

mypetstop.com

www.mypetstop.com

Information for users all over the world: This multilingual Web site supplies information about all kinds of pets, including dogs, cats, birds, and horses. You can find out how to solve biting and digging problems, as well as how to sweeten your furry friend's breath. You also find links to animal shelters, vets, and missing pets, to name just a few.

Other Sites to Check Out

www.canines.com
Dog-training information

www.fanciers.com
How to care for cats

Shopping

Polls indicate that many people still feel unsafe about shopping on the Internet. Granted, there are risks. Using a credit card in any medium carries risks, and each individual must tread through the rocky shoals of contemporary digital life as he or she sees fit. This section is comprised of several categories containing popular items for which people shop online.

Tip: For more helpful hints and suggestions on shopping online, including how to purchase items at online auctions, refer to Book VIII, Chapter 1.

Automobiles

Autobytel

www.autobytel.com

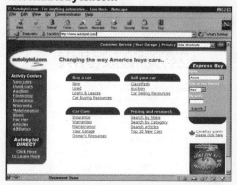

State-of-the-art auto site: The Express Buy area on the right dominates Autobytel's home page. This site is for people "who know what they want" and are ready to buy. And if you're one of those people, few sites are simpler than Autobytel.

Edmund's

www.edmunds.com

Online version of new and used car price guide: Edmund's produces a book that's sort of a Bible of numbers to U.S. car buyers ready to battle car dealers over the bottom line. Using the guide, you can look up what the dealer paid for a particular car (or at least what the experts at Edmund's estimate is the real amount the dealer paid) and negotiate a better deal.

Microsoft CarPoint

carpoint.msn.com

Let Bill Gates help sell you a car, too: CarPoint has one of the flashiest online car showrooms around, with top-notch design and features. You can scout out information on new or used cars, submit specs to get a quote from an affiliated U.S. or Canadian dealer, browse the used car classifieds, and generally do just about anything you'd hope to at an online auto site.

Trader Online

www.traderonline.com

From sedans to earthmovers: The printed versions of Trader publications are basically classified ads, and Trader Online simply builds on that concept. And does it ever. At the home page, you can select ads for cars, pickups, motorcycles, RVs, big trucks, and heavy equipment.

Flowers and Gifts

Gift shopping was the original Internet commercial application, and it's still going strong. Flowers and gifts seem inextricably intertwined — flower shops have gifts, and gift shops have flowers.

FTD

www.ftd.com

Online network of florists: The largest delivery system for flowers, FTD presents a Web site that makes your choices clear and coherent. FTD is more than just an agent for flowers — it's a network of florists. As such, it offers you two choices: shopping from the FTD catalog or shopping from an FTD florist's store selection. The Web site offers both alternatives.

Hallmark

www.hallmark.com

Electronic greetings for e-mail friends: Hallmark, the greeting card and gift chain, provides a site that contains surprisingly hip features. The e-mail reminder service is a helpful feature, as are the other customization services — like your own personal calendar, address book, and profile.

Other Sites to Check Out

www.800flowers.com
Fast, efficient gift shopping

www.americangreetings.com
Personalized greeting cards

Miscellaneous Internet Shopping

The following are worthy shopping sites that don't fall into any other categories. They represent types of virtual buying that may increase in the near future, such as groceries and event tickets.

NetGrocer

www.netgrocer.com

Packaged groceries delivered to your door: Online grocery shopping has been tried with some success on local levels, but NetGrocer is the first attempt to provide Web-based grocery ordering and delivery on a nationwide scale. By using FedEx for next-day delivery, it's a feasible idea.

Priceline.com

www.priceline.com

Smorgasbord of items at a low price: Imagine going to one Web site where you can purchase airline tickets for a vacation, book your hotel room, buy a new car, or make changes on the financing of your home. Priceline.com offers these services and usually at a good price.

Ticketmaster Online

www.ticketmaster.com

Buy tickets to events: It's a good match, and an obvious one: concert and event tickets over the Internet. Merge a big-ticket database with the computer's ability to search by keyword, and happy concertgoers should be the result. Many of the listings include directions to the venue.

Music and Books

We group book shopping and music shopping together, because books and music tend to be sold together in large offline stores like Barnes & Noble. Book and music shopping on the Internet get a lot of publicity, mostly surrounding just a few huge retailers that have set up shop on the Web.

Tip: Be sure to get the RealAudio plug-in before shopping for music.

Amazon.com

www.amazon.com

Vast online bookstore with music section: Amazon.com is a legendary Web shopping location, having caught the Internet wave early and creating one of the few successful virtual retail businesses. Arguably the world's largest bookstore, Amazon.com makes it easy to track down just about any book, video, or CD you can think of, order it with a credit card, and receive it within days. Substantial price discounts are applied to every title.

BarnesandNoble.com

bn.com

Online store of the giant book retailer: While Amazon.com may be the largest bookstore on the Web, Barnes & Noble is the largest offline, physical bookstore. The Barnes & Noble site looks like an online magazine, with featured items on the front page and links at the top.

CDNOW

www.cdnow.com

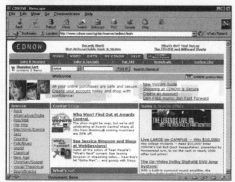

Popular online music CD store: One of the most popular shopping sites on the Web, CDNOW makes the most of streaming audio by enabling you to listen to selected excerpts of many CDs before buying them. This site offers a terrific searching service that you can use to track down a recording by song title, artist, album name, record label, or soundtrack.

Sports

Sports are huge on the Net. The Web is particularly suited to following sports, mainly because it can provide scores with up-to-the-minute currency. Furthermore, sports statistics translate well to any computer medium.

CBS SportsLine

www.sportsline.com

CBS sports information: Many good sports sites are available, and CBS SportsLine is one of the best. Making great use of Web technology, the site is a multimedia playground in the delivery of sports news, opinion columns, radio programs, and scores.

ESPN.com

espn.go.com

Sports news from the cable network: ESPN.com is one of the great Web sports sites and probably the most famous. The complete sports service includes terrific photos, updated scores (some scoreboard pages update and reload automatically every minute), feature articles, contests, viewer participation, columns, and live audio.

GreatOutdoors.com

www.altrec.com/go_index.html

Camping and hiking with plenty of multimedia: GreatOutdoors.com is a fantastic Web publication that covers a wide range of outdoor sports — climbing, cycling, diving, fly fishing, hiking/camping, mountain biking, paddling, sailing, skiing, snowboarding, surfing, and windsurfing.

majorleaguebaseball.com

www.majorleaguebaseball.com

Official Major League Baseball site: This site is the official Web presence of Major League Baseball (MLB). MLB is an attractive magazine-style site, complete with news, standings, scores — the whole shebang.

NBA.com

www.nba.com

The official league site: The National Basketball Association scores a three-pointer with its fast-driving, fancy-dribbling Web site. Covering basic news and inside reports, NBA.com puts special emphasis on fan interactivity.

NFL.COM

www.nfl.com

Official NFL site: The official site of the National Football League does a good job of getting fans involved in the site and getting sports professionals involved. A chat area holds special live events occasionally, and transcripts of past events are available.

SportsWeb

www.sportsweb.com

Global perspective on the games: SportsWeb is a good place to find out about what's being played around the world. This multilingual Reuters service offers a newspaper-style format, with the main stories headlined down the front page.

Other Sites to Check Out

www.nascar.com
Stock car racing's online home

www.nhl.com
Hockey's hometown on the Web

www.pga.com
Golf: from tee to shining tee

www.usta.com/index.html
U.S. tennis updates

Travel

This section gives you a tour of the best travel sites available on the Web. These sites perform a service by providing information about destinations, as well as enabling you to book your own travel arrangements.

Tip: Refer to Book VIII, Chapter 2, for help on using the Internet to plan your next vacation. If you want even more information, check out *Travel Planning Online For Dummies,* 2nd Edition, by Noah Vadnai and Julian Smith (published by Hungry Minds, Inc.).

Arthur Frommer's Budget Travel Online

www.frommers.com

Feature-packed travel guide with frank and witty advice: The Frommer's travel site is written in a somewhat bold style and occasionally is controversial. Frommer certainly doesn't hold back his criticism in his travel reviews at times, but the main event of this site's soapbox is the daily online travel newsletter.

Fodor's Travel Online

www.fodors.com

Trip planning and destination reviews: You can often tell right away when a Web site is going to make your life easier by its clarity of presentation. Fodor's Travel Online is such a site. Here's a tip: Forget the surrounding links and go straight to creating your own miniguide. Your Personal Trip Planner lets you select a destination from a fairly extensive list.

Maps On Us

www.mapsonus.com

Interactive maps: One of the niftiest and most fun interactive travel pages on the Web, Maps On Us provides U.S. maps (duh) and much more. On the home page, get started quickly by clicking the Maps button and then typing a street address. In less than a minute, another page displays a street map of the neighborhood.

Microsoft Expedia

expedia.msn.com

Extraordinary travel resource: Expedia, one of the largest and most important travel destinations on the Web, is a combination of magazine, community, travel agent, and resource guide from Microsoft. Offering the feel of a travel encyclopedia, the site is a pleasure to look at.

TheTrip.com

www.thetrip.com

One of the best online travel-booking sites: TheTrip.com made a splash when it first appeared on the Web, partly because of what was, at the time, an astonishing new feature: the ability to track information on flights in progress. Although the site is avowedly for business travelers, it's just as useful and simple to use for anyone, even infrequent flyers.

Travelocity

www.travelocity.com

Full-service online travel agent: Travelocity is a combination destination guide and travel agent with nifty features. You can use the Find/Book A Flight airline reservation feature on the front page, and the other sections enable you to reserve a rental car, book a hotel room, or sign up for a cruise. You can check the arrival or departure time of a current flight and even arrange to have flight information changes sent to your e-mail address.

USA Today: Travel

**www.usatoday.com/life/travel/
ltfront.htm**

Travel news from the information-rich daily newspaper: USA Today takes a newsy approach to its online travel publication. General travel news stories dominate the front page, with a featured destination just below and a Travel Tips section in the lower-right corner. Specific tips sections are provided for business and leisure travel, befitting the different audiences.

Other Sites to Check Out

www.amtrak.com
Train schedules and reservations

travel.lycos.com/Destinations
Information on world cities

www.travelsource.com
Links to theme travel packages

www.travlang.com/languages
Online multilanguage phrase book

www.weekendguide.com
Tips for weekend trips

www.xe.com/ucc/
Count your cash in foreign
denominations

Chapter 5
Arts and Entertainment

Cultural Arts

This section is devoted to the refined side of entertainment, including classical music, art, ballet, and photography — high culture, in other words. In a sense, just about everything that happens in the world is a cultural event when you think of culture as a sociological phenomenon. But that approach would make the topic too big for effective cataloging, so this section gathers just some of the best artistic sites and online publications.

American Ballet Theatre

www.abt.org

Web site of New York City ballet company: The American Ballet Theatre rises above the purgatory of self-promotion with a site that goes way beyond its congratulatory review quotes and membership links. Although the American Ballet Theatre's headquarters are in New York City, the site has more than enough information here to warrant visits from out-of-towners.

ArtNet

www.artnet.com

Samples of art exhibitions around the world: ArtNet promises to be the most comprehensive art site on the Web. That claim may be true — it's certainly one of the most professional. Incorporating an online magazine and a list of online exhibitions, the site displays lots of art on your screen.

CultureFinder

www.culturefinder.com

Find cultural events in different cities: CultureFinder locates performances and other art events by date, city, or performing arts organization. You can also sign up for a free newsletter.

National Gallery of Art

www.nga.gov/collection/collect.htm

Extraordinarily fine online museum: The National Gallery of Art Web site sponsors a fun, attractive, and easy-to-use site. You can enjoy one of the finest art collections in the world with the help of a completely searchable and attractive interface, at no charge whatsoever, from the comfort of home.

Other Sites to Check Out

wwar.com
Comprehensive directory of arts on the Net

www.oir.ucf.edu/wm
Galleries of many artists

Entertainment

This section covers the entertainment supersites that provide news and gossip about movies, TV, and music. It also serves as a directory to entertainment publications on the Web. Because entertainment is such a huge Web topic, this section skims over the top, collecting the cream of the crop. You'll see pics of your favorites stars, catch up on the latest gossip, meet people (if you want), and get up to speed on showbiz news.

E! Online

www.eonline.com

Cool entertainment megasite: One of the major, ever-so-cool, must-see watering holes for entertainment news on the Web, E! Online dazzles visitors with flying text, plenty of photos, late-breaking gossip, enough TV and movie reviews to glut a cocktail party, and online games.

USA Today Life

www.usatoday.com/life/lfront.htm

Online version of the newspaper's entertainment section: As a transposition of the national newspaper's daily Life section, the USA Today Life Web site offers reviews of current movies, TV shows, and music albums and then archives them in a vast library that's easy to navigate.

Other Sites to Check Out

www.ew.com
Online version of Entertainment Weekly

www.tvguide.com
Online version of TV Guide

Literature

Compared to the high-tech image of cyber-space, books seem almost like antique anachronisms — dusty remnants of a previous era. But the truth is, the book industry in general is thriving, more titles than ever are being published, and books are a fairly big topic of interest on the Net. These trends don't seem to reflect any danger that a computer monitor is on the verge of replacing the comforting, familiar bound book. How cozy is it to curl up in your favorite chair with your computer, scrolling through a book?

This section surveys Web sites that give general information about books and the book industry, provides book reviews, and even tells about a few literary e-zines.

BookPage Online

www.bookpage.com

Readers contribute book reviews: BookPage is a book-review publication (printed and virtual) that wants to help you select books and learn more about their authors. In each monthly edition, the site usually offers more than 50 reviews, plus an archived backlog of previous reviews.

BookWire

www.bookwire.com

Publishing information plus a Web directory: BookWire is a one-stop resource to other literary sites on the Web, as well as general information about the publishing industry. This site is no multimedia playground, but it's full of useful book info.

Publishers Weekly

www.publishersweekly.com

Online version of an industry Bible: Publishers Weekly, the printed magazine, is a sort of Bible for writers and publishers alike. It reports on trends, statistics, and industry news in the publishing business. The Web site carries much of the printed content, and in the case of the famous bestseller lists, the site posts them three days before they appear in the magazine.

Other Sites to Check Out

www.bookmagazine.com
Online version of Book magazine

www.scifi.com/sfw/
Sci-fi e-zine

Movies

Internet movie databases have become plentiful as of late. Most are easy to use and include movie news, reviews, and articles. This section introduces you to the best movie databases that are currently available on the Web.

Hollywood.com

www.hollywood.com
Movie information, especially soundtracks: Hollywood.com's MovieTunes section (accessed via the Soundtracks link on the main page) is a database of soundtrack selections, accessed by browsing or searching. Hollywood.com mixes database services with a slick design — one of the best movie database sites.

The Internet Movie Database

www.imdb.com
Everything you want to know about every movie: The Internet Movie Database (IMDb, as it's affectionately called by devotees) occupies a place of honor on most movie fans' bookmark lists. The site grabs attention for its flexible search engine and its wonderful cross-referencing of all kinds of movie information. You can locate a movie or actor by title or keyword.

MovieFone

www.moviefone.com
Local movie schedules: MovieFone is the premier Web site for finding what's playing down the street, no matter where you live in the United States. It works by asking for your zip code and then remembering it every time you visit.

Other Sites to Check Out

www.boxoff.com
Reviews and feature articles

www.moviefinder.com
Find movies that correspond to your tastes

Music

Music lovers take note: The Web is now a very musical cyberspace. Music was a popular topic on the Net even before audio files were so easy to listen to, and now that RealAudio and other streaming formats are so simple to use, music is playing through logged-on computers everywhere.

Billboard Online

www.billboard.com
Music industry newspaper: Billboard is a trade newspaper for the music industry, and Billboard Online replicates most of the press releases and trade reports that you find in the printed edition. The renowned *Billboard* charts — setting the standard of success for albums and singles in many genres of music — appear on the site in their entirety.

MTV Online

www.mtv.com
The music channel online: MTV uses just the right amount of multimedia technology

to deliver a blend of news, program guides, enhancements to the television content, and live events.

Pollstar

www.pollstar.com/

Who's playing when and where: Many entertainment sites cover concert tours as part of the news fare they dish up. Pollstar's agenda is to provide the most comprehensive music tour information on the Web, and nothing else. Pollstar is a site for anyone who likes attending live music events.

VH1

www.vh1.com

Modest online version of the cable channel: The best site for VH1 fans is the Inside VH1 page, which features the channel's artist of the month, events, and interviews, with video clips for most.

Other Sites to Check Out

www.columbia.edu/~hauben/music/ web-music.html
Massive lists of music links

www.festivals.com
Information on music festivals

www.sonicnet.com
Live concert simulcasts on the Web

Television

You hear a lot of talk about TV on the Internet, the Internet on TV, and the general convergence of computers and televisions. That total convergence is still a long way away, so in the meantime, you can turn to the Web to help you more fully enjoy TV. This section deals with Web sites about popular shows, TV network sites, and online schedule guides.

ABC.com

abc.go.com

The network's Web site: Watching television may be a passive activity, but ABC.com begs visitors to get involved. The Message Boards section offers you the chance to post comments, complaints, praise, and whatever else is on your mind about virtually any show on the ABC schedule. If you'd prefer just to know more about the shows, you can use the Shows link on the home page or work your way through the front-page links.

Eye on the Net — CBS

www.cbs.com

Bland but comprehensive: Major network sites tend to be fairly bland, and CBS does nothing to violate that grand tradition, although the site has improved.

Fox.com

www.fox.com

Good content from the network's online site: Fox.com conveys the impression that the Fox television network has created a fantasy domain that provides endless fascination and delight. Although that characterization may be stretching the truth, the Web site certainly goes beyond the call of duty in providing service to Netizens.

HBO

www.hbo.com

Generous displays of HBO content: You can tell immediately, upon entering the HBO site, that it's feature-packed and fun. But you have no idea how generous the premium cable network is with sharing its content for free on the Net. However, be aware that some adult content may be added in the future. Parents should supervise children's visits to this site.

NBC

www.nbc.com

Lots of information, nice style: NBC has enjoyed good fortune in the network ratings wars, and many people turn to the official sites of such hit shows as *Frasier, ER,* and *Friends* to get updates, cast biographies, and previews. The NBC Web presentation is more useful than most network sites.

Other Sites to Check Out

www.audiencesunlimited.com
Free tickets to television show tapings

www.tvshow.com/tv/
Global TV listings

www.tvguide.com
The online home of TV Guide

www.ultimatetv.com
Schedules, articles, and polls

Theater

The sites in this section cover all aspects of theater, including musicals and plays. You can find reviews, historical information, listings, and much more.

Aisle Say

www.aislesay.com

Online theater magazine: Aisle Say is an online theater magazine that stakes its claim to fame on good writing and a solid database of reviews. The enduring value of the site lies at the bottom of the home page, where you find a list of review databases divided into cities.

Playbill On-Line

www.playbill.com

International theater news: Playbill On-Line provides a full range of international theater news, Tony award updates and recaps, listings of shows, audio clips and other multimedia goodies, a way to buy tickets online, and feature articles about the stars and future productions on and off Broadway. Playbill is a valuable resource for aspiring actors, singers, and technicians, thanks to the industry job postings.

Theatre Central

**www.playbill.com/cgi-bin/
plb/central?cmd=start**

Theater information for audiences and professionals: Acquired by Playbill On-line, Theatre Central is a locus of theater news, links, listings, industry jobs, and features. Theatre Central is unique in providing interactive industry listings into which aspiring and established theater pros can enter their own classified information.

Other Sites to Check Out

www.aact.org
Community theatre information

www.londontheatre.co.uk
Guide to the West End (London) and beyond

www.nycopera.com
The New York City Opera

www.tdf.org
Offers discount theatre tickets

Chapter 6
Fun and Free Stuff

As problematic as multimedia still is on the Web, it's fun to play with and even harder to avoid, as more site designers consider it an indispensable design feature. This section gathers a few of the most interesting, fun, impressive, and cutting-edge Web locations featuring audio and video.

Alternative Entertainment Network

www.aentv.com

Entertainment and documentary programming: The focus of AEN is not on live programming, but all kinds of entertainment features and clips are available on demand. From previously censored clips of *The Smothers Brothers Comedy Hour* to Abbott and Costello performing "Who's on First?" on television, from a library of stand-up performances at the Improv to "Leonardo DiCaprio: In His Own Words," the Alternative Entertainment Network tosses up a smorgasbord of Internet shows.

InterneTV

www.internetv.com

Internet television in its infancy: The Internet's first dedicated television station, InterneTV resembles television only by a stretch of imagination. InterneTV is struggling for programming content. But at least the "station" is in operation, and you can watch it grow and develop. Links are provided for all the plug-ins that you need.

LiveConcerts.com

www.liveconcerts.com

Live Netcasts of rock concerts: This gorgeous site has a noble cause: to bring live music to the Internet through RealAudio. LiveConcerts.com hooks up with KCRW in Santa Monica, California, to provide some radio simulcasts on the Net, but the main focus is concert Netcasts of popular rock acts. Upcoming events are searchable, and every concert is archived.

Other Sites to Check Out

www.annonline.com
Online talk show

www.dccomics.com/radio/index.html
Original 1940s *Superman* radio broadcasts

Comics and Humor

This section lists sites whose content deals with comic books, comic strips, and literary humor. Like all other topics, but perhaps more glaringly, some Web humor is decidedly mediocre. But that mediocrity just makes the good sites seem all the better.

Comics.com

www.comics.com

Strips from United Media: ComicZone presents information about the serious and funny funnies brought to you by United Media. All your Sunday favorites are here, including *Dilbert, Robotman, Eek & Meek, Herman*, and *Nancy*. The site also enables you to meet the mind and pen behind the funnies by featuring many of the artists.

The Corporation

www.thecorporation.com

Corporate-culture satire: This humor site is everyone's over-the-top nightmare of corporate arrogance. Playing it deadpan all the way, The Corporation has page upon page of tongue-in-cheek memos, statements, and press releases concerning its affairs, labor relations, and policies.

Marvel Online

www.marvel.com

Online site for the comic book company: Marvel Comics is the home to some of the world's most famous comic characters (Spiderman, Captain America, and the X-Men, to name a few) and arguably the world's best-known comic character

creator (a man named Stan Lee). They're all well represented on Marvel Online, which doesn't display the comic books online — unless you want to sign up for The Marvel Zone, which broadcasts original "cybercomics" in streaming audio and video for free.

UComics

www.ucomics.com/comics

Archives of UPS strips: United Press Syndicate (UPS), a distributor of many favorite comic strips, is generous in its online offerings. This site archives about a month of UPS strips, starting about two weeks after they appear in newspapers. *Doonesbury* is here. *Foxtrot, Stone Soup, Cathy, Crankshaft, Garfield, Tank McNamara, Ziggy* — all here.

Family Sites

The number of family sites that saturate the Web is really surprising, considering that parents — especially young parents — generally don't have a great deal of time to cruise the Internet. But facts are facts, and family issues are well represented on the Web.

Education Place

www.eduplace.com

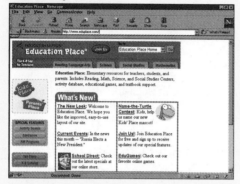

Ideas and products for kids and parents: Education Place is a solid value for kids and parents, separately or together. Information on famous authors (which you can find under Author Spotlight on the Reading/Language Arts page) links to other sites that are dedicated to those authors.

Family Internet

www.familyinternet.com

Links to family resources: Family Internet is a lush, gloriously designed site aimed at older kids and their parents. For the family computer, this would make an excellent home page because it is full of news headlines, health information, travel tips, and entertainment events.

Family.com

www.family.go.com

A family site from Disney: A production of the Walt Disney Company, Family.com is like a daily electronic magazine featuring articles about travel, kids' issues, parenting subjects, activities, educational info, recipes, message boards, and chat rooms.

Other Sites to Check Out

www.drtoy.com
Guide to children's products

www.familyfriendlysites.com/ FamilyFriendly/default.asp
A directory of approved sites for families

Games

Internet games are some of the best family sites on the Web. Not every site in this section is perfect for young kids because some sites require mature skills. None, however, have inappropriate or violent content. Most of these sites are for solo players, but a few enable you to hook up with real-time opponents.

Chess.net

www.chess.net

Virtual chess: Chess.net is the premier interactive chess-partnering site on the Web. Providing its own software (if needed), the total package enables you to log into the Chess.net server, find a playing partner, and view the game in progress on your monitor.

MSN Gaming Zone

www.zone.msn.com/default.asp

Microsoft's entry into gaming: After you sign in (for free), you can enter a game's room and begin playing and chatting. The offerings are diverse but generally family friendly, including Microsoft's own *Age of Empires,* bridge, *Jedi Knight: Dark Forces II,* and spades. Internet Gaming Zone also stages tournaments and ranks players.

The Station

www.station.sony.com

No Vanna, no Alex, but lots of fun: This Sony Web site includes — not surprisingly — online versions of *Jeopardy!* and *Wheel of Fortune.* You have a choice to play alone or with two other live contestants.

Other Sites to Check Out

www.80s.com/Trivia
Electronic games from the 1980s

www.dujour.com/riddle
Riddles posted daily

www.prizes.com
Contests, lotteries, and big prizes

www.trivialpursuit.com
Online edition of the board game

www.webcontests.com
Reviews of gaming sites

Kids' Sites

Kids love the Internet, lots of kids are around, and lots of kid-oriented sites abound, too. In finding your own Web locations for children, remember the Yahooligans! directory, listed in the "Directories and Search Engines" section of Book IX, Chapter 1 of this minibook. This directory is a kid-safe universe of Web links, divided by topic, and is one of the best resources on the Net for young folks. Look them up at: www.yahooligans.com.

Coloring.com

coloring.com

Online coloring book: Coloring.com has been online since 1994 and is going strong with a fun, simple site for young kids. Offering a selection of bold, clear line drawings with color palettes on the pages, the site invites kids to select a color, click a portion of the picture, and see a fresh display with that portion colored in. Kids can print their creations, too.

Educational Web Adventures

www.eduweb.com/adventure.html

Great learning games: The folks behind Educational Web Adventures have teaching experience that ranges from kindergartners to adults, so it should be little surprise that they've produced a great Web site that should appeal to all ages. Parents, ignore this site at your own risk.

FunBrain.com

www.funbrain.com

Math and spelling made fun: FunBrain.com offers games that reinforce basic educational skills, but in a fun way, by making games out of math, spelling, money, and so on.

Girl Tech

www.girltech.com/index.html

Resources for girls: More than a virtual club, Girl Tech is a haven and a point of empowerment for girls around the world who feel under-represented on the Internet. Hailed by CNN, *Ms.* magazine, and the national director of the YWCA, Girl Tech provides lots of features and lots of interactivity.

Kids Domain

www.kidsdomain.com

Gentle site for kids and parents: The dancing teddy bear on this home page serves notice that this is a bright, cheery, non-threatening site. Kids Domain has five main areas (Kids, Download, Grownups, Reviews, and KDUK) that offer online games, activities, downloads, links, reviews, and advice.

Mister Rogers' Neighborhood

www.pbs.org/rogers

Online companion to the TV series: Mister Rogers has a home in cyberspace, and it's located at this Web site. Designed to correlate with the themes of the television program, the site offers kids a range of activities and fun and includes an extensive reading list on topics that the show covers.

Seussville Games

www.randomhouse.com/seussville/games

Online companion to the Dr. Seuss books: Random House, publisher of the Dr. Seuss books, created this Web site filled with games for kids, most of which involve the Dr. Seuss characters.

Starchild

starchild.gsfc.nasa.gov

Astronomy information: Starchild is a learning center for young astronomers. One of the site's best features is its division of information into two levels. Level one is for young kids; it keeps explanations simple and brief. Level two goes a little deeper, assuming more knowledge of science and language.

Wacky Web Tales

www.eduplace.com/tales

Create hilarious, nonsensical stories: Parents who remember the side-splitting *Mad Libs* books from their young years have the gist of Wacky Web Tales, except that a single person can play the Web version. Stories that contain crucial blank spots are provided. The idea is to fill in the blanks before ever seeing the story and then read it back with outrageously irrelevant nouns, verbs, and adjectives sprinkled through it.

ZuZu

www.zuzu.org

Online magazine partly written by Web visitors: Often visited and frequently updated, ZuZu is an online magazine for kids, featuring artwork, stories, poetry, creative writing, jokes, interviews, and profiles of kids.

Other Sites to Check Out

Kids' Space

www.ks-connection.org
Filled with visitor-submitted material from around the globe.

kids.msfc.nasa.gov
NASA-sponsored space site

www.yakscorner.com
Fun and attractive magazine for kids

Meeting Places

People actually meet other people in cyberspace, as the news programs sometimes remind us with occasional horror stories of seduction and invaded privacy. But considering the millions of meetings that occur every day, the Net is a relatively safe place, especially if you take these basic precautions:

Don't give personal information to someone you meet online. Guard your postal address and phone number, and even your e-mail address.

Don't believe that you know somebody well through online chatting. The Internet is a one-dimensional environment.

Don't get addicted to virtual contact. Keep the online world in its place.

With those precautions in mind, you can now trip gaily into the world of online chatting and message boards. Chat rooms are fun, although far less sophisticated than message boards, with less substantial content.

CoolChat

www.coolchat.com

Chatting and free Web sites for members: CoolChat is a complete, planned Internet chatting community. You get a free Web site, too, as well as an internal e-mail system. Membership is free, and the registration process is fairly harmless; several demographic questions are optional.

GeoCities

geocities.yahoo.com/home

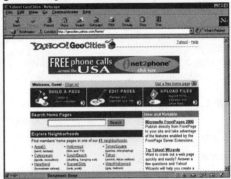

Virtual community complete with neighborhoods: GeoCities, by Yahoo!, is a significant virtual community. GeoCities offers its members free Web-site space and free e-mail. If you're interested in an online community and in having your own Web page, check out GeoCities first.

Talk City

www.talkcity.com

Chatting for adults and teens: Talk City is one of the big chat emporiums on the Web. You don't need special software in Talk City, but your browser must be Java-capable. This area isn't a secure, safe area for kids, however, and as is true of other chat domains, only adults should be present.

Other Sites to Check Out

www.chathouse.com
Wide selection of chat rooms

communicate.excite.com/index.html
Generic virtual community

www.yack.com
Directory of live chatting events

Index

W

Y

Z

Book X

Appendix

The 5th Wave   By Rich Tennant

INTERNET ACCESS
.50¢ - Min.

Contents at a Glance

Appendix: Glossary

ActiveX: A Microsoft object technology that enables you to embed intelligent objects in Web documents to create interactive pages.

ADSL: Asymmetric Digital Subscriber Line. A technology that lets you transmit data over phone lines faster — as much as 8 million bps — in one direction than in the other. Also just *DSL*.

AltaVista: An excellent Web search engine, at www.altavista.com.

America Online (AOL): A value-added online service that provides many services in addition to Internet access, including access to chat groups.

anchor: In an HTML document, you use the <A> tag to create a hyperlink.

applet: A program written in Java and embedded in an HTML document. An applet runs automatically whenever someone views the Web page that contains the applet.

archive: A single file containing a group of files that have been compressed together for efficient storage. You have to use an unzipping program, such as PKUNZIP, StuffIt, or WinZip, to get the original files back out.

attachment: A computer file electronically stapled to an e-mail message and sent along with it.

attribute: In HTML, a code that's included within an HTML tag to provide specific information for the tag, such as the name of an image file to be inserted or the URL of a Web page referred to in a hyperlink.

AU: A format for sound files that's popular on Unix systems. AU stands for Audio.

AVI: Audio Video Interleaved. The Microsoft standard for video files that can be viewed in Windows.

baud: The number of electronic state changes per second that a modem sends down a phone line.

Bcc: Blind carbon copy. Bcc addressees get a copy of your e-mail without other recipients knowing about it.

BinHex: A file-encoding system popular among Macintosh users.

bits per second (bps): A measure of how fast your modem can transmit or receive information between your computer and a remote computer.

bookmark: The Netscape Navigator term for a Web site that a user has cataloged for easy retrieval. Similar to the Internet Explorer term *favorites.*

browser: A program that you use to access and view the Web. The two most popular browsers are Microsoft Internet Explorer and Netscape Navigator.

cache: An area of a computer's hard drive used to store data recently downloaded from the Internet so that the data can be redisplayed quickly.

Cc: Carbon copy, or courtesy copy. Cc addressees get a copy of your e-mail, and other recipients are listed in the message header.

channel: In Internet Relay Chat (IRC), a group of people chatting together. America Online and CompuServe call channels *rooms.* Value-added providers use *channel* to refer to a major interest area that you can get to easily, like a TV channel.

chat: To talk live to other network users from any and all parts of the world. To chat on the Internet, you use IRC. America Online and CompuServe have similar services.

client: A program that runs on an Internet user's computer rather than on a server computer.

clip art: A collection of graphic images from which you can pick and choose images to use in your Web pages.

cookie: A small text file, sent to your hard drive by a Web site that you have visited, that contains information to remind the site about you the next time you visit it.

dial-up networking: The Internet communications program that comes with Windows 95/98/XP and enables you to connect to another computer or the Internet via a modem.

digest: A compilation of the messages that have been posted to a mailing list during a certain period, usually a few days.

DNS: Domain Name System. The way that Internet domain names are located and translated into IP (Internet Protocol) addresses. The DNS enables us to use almost intelligible names for Web sites, such as `www.microsoft.com`, rather than incomprehensible IP addresses such as `283.939.12.74`.

domain name: The address of an Internet site, such as `www.dummies.com`.

download: To copy a file from one computer to another, such as from a computer somewhere on the Internet to your computer at home.

DSL: Digital Subscriber Line. See *ADSL.*

e-mail: Electronic mail. An Internet service that enables you to send and receive messages to and from other users.

emoticon: A combination of special characters that portray emotions, such as :-) or :-(. Also called a *smiley*.

FAQ: Frequently Asked Questions. A file containing answers to the most commonly asked questions about a particular program or topic. Internet users appreciate FAQ files posted at a Web site.

favorite: The Internet Explorer term for a Web site that a user has cataloged for easy retrieval. Equivalent to the Navigator term *bookmarks*.

File Transfer Protocol (FTP): A system that enables the transfer of files over the Internet.

form: A Web page that gathers information from an Internet user and sends the information back to the server for processing.

frame: An area of a Web browser's window that displays a separate Web page.

FTP: See *File Transfer Protocol*.

FTP server: A computer on the Internet that stores files for transmission by FTP.

GIF: Graphics Interchange Format. The preferred format for low- and medium-quality images on the Web. For photographic-quality images, use JPEG instead.

header: The beginning of an e-mail message containing To and From addresses, the subject, the date, and other information that's important to the programs that handle your mail.

help page: Provides information about how to use a Web site.

hierarchy: The category to which a newsgroup belongs. The major hierarchies are `comp`, `humanities`, `misc`, `news`, `rec`, `sci`, `soc`, and `talk`, although hundreds more exist.

hit counter: A Web page element that displays a count of how many times the page has been visited. Also called a *use counter*.

home page: The main page of a Web site, the one normally displayed first when a user visits the site. The home page contains links to all the major areas in the site.

host: A computer that operates as a Web server.

hotspot: A region of an image map that acts as a hyperlink.

HTML: HyperText Markup Language. The language used to write pages for the Web. This language lets the text include codes that define fonts, layout, embedded graphics, and hypertext links.

HTML editor: A program that enables you to create and edit documents that contain HTML tags.

HTTP: HyperText Transfer Protocol. The protocol used to transmit HTML documents (that is, Web pages) over the Internet.

HTTPS: A variant of HTTP that encrypts messages for security.

hyperlink: A bit of text or a graphic in a Web page that a user can click to go to another Web page.

hypertext: A system in which documents are linked to one another by text links. When the user clicks a text link, the document referred to by the link is displayed.

ICQ: Pronounced *I Seek You*. A Web-based chat service.

image file: A file that contains a graphic image, such as an icon, a scanned photograph, or a clip-art picture.

image map: An image displayed on a Web page, in which one or more regions of the image serve as links to other pages.

Internet: A vast worldwide collection of networked computers — the largest computer network in the world.

Internet Explorer: The Microsoft program for browsing the Internet. The latest and greatest version is Internet Explorer 6, although plenty of people still use Internet Explorer 5.

Internet Service Provider: Also known as an *ISP*. A company that provides access to the Internet.

intranet: A private version of the Internet that lets people within an organization exchange data by using popular Internet tools, such as browsers.

IP: Internet Protocol. The rules that computers use to send data over the Internet.

IRC: Internet Relay Chat. A system that enables Internet folks to talk to each other in real time (rather than after a delay, as with e-mail messages).

ISDN: Integrated Services Digital Network. A faster, digital phone service that operates at speeds of as much as 128 kilobits per second.

ISP: See *Internet Service Provider*.

Java: An object-oriented programming language created by Sun Microsystems and designed to be used on the Web. Use Java to add sound, animation, and interactivity to Web pages.

JavaScript: A scripting language from Netscape that enables you to embed programs directly in HTML documents. JavaScript is used with Netscape Navigator, but Internet Explorer has its own version, called JScript.

JPEG: Joint Photographic Experts Group. A popular format for picture files. JPEG uses a compression technique that greatly reduces a graphic's file size, but also results in some loss of resolution.

Kbps: A measure of a modem's speed in thousands of bits per second. A common modem speed is 28.8 Kbps.

key: A block of information used to unlock a unique pattern of encryption.

link: See *hyperlink*.

LISTSERV: A family of programs that automatically manages mailing lists by distributing messages posted to the list and adding and deleting members, thus, sparing the list owner the tedium of having to do these tasks manually.

lurk: To read a newsgroup, mailing list, or chat group without posting any messages.

MacBinary: A file-encoding system that's popular among Macintosh users.

mail server: A computer on the Internet that provides mail services.

mailbot: A program that automatically sends or answers e-mail.

mailing list: A special kind of e-mail address that remails all incoming mail to a list of subscribers to the mailing list. Each mailing list has a specific topic, so you subscribe to the ones that interest you.

marquee: A Web page element in which text automatically scrolls across the screen.

MIDI: Musical Instrument Digital Interface. A file containing musical instructions that the synthesizer on a computer's sound card can play.

MIME: Multipurpose Internet Mail Extension. A format used to send pictures, word processing files, and other nontext information through e-mail.

mirror: A Web server that provides copies of the same files that another server provides.

modem: A gizmo that lets your computer talk on the phone or cable TV. Short for *mo*dulator–*dem*odulator.

moderator: The person who looks at the messages posted to a moderated mailing list or newsgroup before releasing them to the public.

MPEG: Moving Pictures Experts Group. A type of video file found on the Net. Files in this format end in MPG.

MP3: MPEG level 3. An adaptation of MPEG used to send music files over the Net.

navigation bar: An element on a Web page that enables the user to go to other pages at the Web site, such as the home page or the next or previous page in a sequence of pages.

net: A network, or (when capitalized) the Internet. When these letters appear as the last part of a host name, they indicate that the host computer is run by a networking organization, often an ISP.

Netscape: The maker of the popular Web browser Navigator that comes in Windows, Mac, and Unix formats. Now owned by AOL.

Netscape 6.2: A suite of Internet products from Netscape that includes Navigator and other programs, such as Messenger, Composer, Conference, and Calendar.

Netscape Navigator: The Netscape Web browser. Navigator is currently the most popular Web browser, but Internet Explorer is catching up. Navigator is available by itself or as the main component of Netscape Communicator.

network: Computers that are connected and often share peripherals, such as printers. Computers in close physical proximity to one another are generally joined by cables and are connected by a *local-area network (LAN)*; those not in close physical proximity are joined by high-speed, long-distance communications or satellites and are connected by a *wide-area network (WAN)*.

news server: A computer on the Net that receives newsgroups and holds them so that you can read them.

newsgroup: A topic area in the news system.

newsreader: A program that lets you read and respond to the messages in newsgroups.

object: Web page elements that you can manipulate with scripts written in JavaScript or VBScript.

online service: A computer network containing information that's available only to subscribers. Popular online services include America Online (AOL) and The Microsoft Network (MSN).

page: A document on the Web. Each page can contain text, graphics files, sound files, video clips — you name it.

PGP: Pretty Good Privacy. A program that lets you encrypt and sign your e-mail. For more information, visit web.mit.edu/network/pgp.html.

PKZIP: A file-compression program that creates a ZIP file containing compressed versions of one or more files. To restore these files to their former size, you use PKUNZIP, ZipMagic, or WinZip.

plug-in: A computer program that you add to your browser to help it handle a special type of file.

PNG: Portable Network Graphics. An image file format that was developed as a successor to the GIF format.

POP: Post Office Protocol. A system by which a mail server on the Internet lets you pick up your e-mail and download it to your PC or Mac. Also called *POP3*.

PPP: Point-to-Point Protocol. A scheme for connecting your computer to the Internet over a phone line. Most dial-up Internet accounts use PPP.

protocol: A set of conventions that govern communications between computers in a network.

public-key cryptography: A method for sending secret messages whereby you get two keys: a public key you give out freely so that people can send you coded messages and a second, private key that decodes them.

QuickTime: A video format popularized by Apple for its Macintosh computers. QuickTime is now available for Windows, too.

RealAudio: A popular streaming-audio file format that lets you listen to programs over the Net. You can get a player plug-in at www.real.com.

RSAC: Recreational Software Advisory Council. The organization that developed and oversees the use of Internet ratings.

script: A type of program that you can embed in an HTML document. Scripts are written in languages such as JavaScript, VBScript, and AppleScript.

search service: A Web site, such as Yahoo!, Lycos, or AltaVista, that enables you to search for pages on the Web.

secure server: A Web server that uses encryption to prevent others from reading messages to or from your browser, such as ordering information.

server: A computer that provides services to other computers on the Internet or on a local area network. Types of Internet servers include news servers, mail servers, FTP servers, DNS servers, Proxy servers, and Web servers.

Shockwave: A standard for viewing interactive multimedia on the Web. For a copy of the Shockwave plug-in for your browser, visit `www.macromedia.com/shockwave`.

site map: A page that provides an overview of a Web site's structure.

smiley: See *emoticon*.

SMTP: Simple Mail Transfer Protocol. The method by which Internet mail is delivered from one computer to another.

SND: A popular format for sound files on Macintosh computers.

spam: The act of sending e-mail to thousands of uninterested recipients or of posting inappropriate messages to uninterested newsgroups or mailing lists.

streaming audio: A system for sending sound files over the Net that starts playing the sound before the sound file finishes downloading. This system enables you to listen with minimal delay. RealAudio is the most popular.

surf: To browse the World Wide Web, looking for interesting stuff.

tag: In HTML, a special code that is written between < and > symbols to provide formatting information for a document.

TCP/IP: Transmission Control Protocol/Internet Protocol. The way networks communicate with each other on the Internet.

Telnet: A program that lets you log in to other computers on the Net.

template: A predefined Web page that can be used as a starting point when you create Web pages.

text editor: A program that enables you to edit text files and dabble with HTML codes directly. The most popular text editors are Notepad and WordPad.

thread: An article posted to a newsgroup, together with all the follow-up articles, the follow-ups to follow-ups, and so on.

Uniform Resource Locator: URL. The address of any resource available on the Internet, used when browsing the Internet. The URL of Hungry Minds, for example, is `www.hungryminds.com`.

Unix: An operating system originally developed by Bell Labs and widely used for Internet servers.

upload: To copy a file from one computer to another — for example, from your computer to the Internet.

URL: See *Uniform Resource Locator.*

uuencode/uudecode: Programs that enable you to send binary files as e-mail.

VBScript: A version of Visual Basic that enables you to create scripts that can be embedded in HTML documents.

WAV: A popular format for sound files (WAV files) found on the Internet.

Web: See *World Wide Web.*

Web browser: A program that can find pages on the Web and display them on your home computer. Internet Explorer and Netscape Navigator are the two most popular Web browsers.

Web page: An HTML document available for display on the Web. The document may contain links to other documents located on the same server or on other Web servers.

Web page editor: A program that enables you to create and edit Web pages, usually in WYSIWYG fashion.

Web Publishing Wizard: A program that comes with Internet Explorer that enables you to easily post HTML documents that you've created to a Web server.

Web server: A server computer that stores HTML documents so that people can access the documents on the Web.

Web site: A collection of related Web pages that users access from a common home page.

Winsock: Short for Windows Sockets. A standard way for Windows programs to work with TCP/IP. You use it if you directly connect your Windows PC to the Internet, with either a permanent connection or a modem by using PPP.

WinZip: A file-compression program that runs under Windows. It reads and creates a ZIP file that contains compressed versions of one or more files.

World Wide Web: Also referred to as the *Web*. The Web is the most popular part of the Internet. The Web is based on *links*, which enable Web surfers to travel quickly from one Web server to another. The Web allows pages with fancy graphics and multimedia elements to be constructed.

WYSIWYG: What You See Is What You Get. In word-processing programs, the idea that what you see onscreen will closely resemble the printed text.

Yahoo!: A popular Internet search service in which you can catalog your Web site. See www.yahoo.com.

ZIP file: An archive that has been compressed by using PKZIP, WinZip, ZipMagic, or a similar program.

Index

1

Notes

Notes

Notes

Notes

Notes